Re/Thinking Chickens:

The Discourse around Chicken Farming in British Newspapers and Campaigners' Magazines, 1982–2016

by

Elena Lazutkaite

Series in Communication

VERNON PRESS

www.vernonpress.com

In the Americas:
Vernon Press
1000 N West Street,
Suite 1200, Wilmington,
Delaware 19801
United States

In the rest of the world:
Vernon Press
C/Sancti Espiritu 17,
Malaga, 29006
Spain

Series in Communication

Library of Congress Control Number: 2020942360

ISBN: 978-1-64889-012-3

Cover design by Leon De Backer.

Appendices A-E are provided online at https://vernonpress.com/book/1075 .

Acknowledgements

This book is an edited version of my PhD thesis “Re/Thinking Chickens: The Discourse around Chicken Farming in British Newspapers and Campaigners' Magazines, 1982–2016”, which I wrote at the School of Cultures, Languages and Area Studies at the University of Nottingham. It would not be possible without the Cultural & Scientific Perceptions of Human-Chicken Interaction project funded by the Arts and Humanities Research Council. I am extremely grateful to my PhD supervisors Judith Still and Christopher King for their invaluable support. Their guidance and patience have been indispensable in the pursuit of this project. I also thank an anonymous reviewer for helpful comments on this manuscript. Phil Brooke and Compassion in World Farming, and Ben Martin, Mark White and Animal Aid are kindly acknowledged for their permissions to use their archives and reproduce texts and images from CIWF and AA publications. My warmest thanks to Greta Lazutkaite for her brilliant proof-reading skills and suggestions on early drafts of this manuscript. I owe to Alby Roseveare for his insightful comments and genuine interest in the topic. I extend heartfelt thanks to my parents Andrius and Liudmila Lazutkos for support. The creative birthing process was more strenuous that I could have expected and completing this book was not easy. Therefore, I also express my deepest gratitude to my partner Leon De Backer. His fortifying love and encouragement during the process brought great comfort.

Dedicated to my grandfather Prof. Stanislovas Lazutka.

Table of contents

List of figures

List of tables

List of acronyms and abbreviations

AA	Animal Aid
AF	Absolute frequency
A-IC	Animal-Industrial Complex
BPC	British Poultry Council
BSE	Bovine spongiform encephalopathy
CAS	Critical Animal Studies
CDA	Critical Discourse Analysis
CIWF	Compassion in World Farming
CL	Corpus Linguistics
div	Division by zero is disallowed
EFSA	European Food Safety Authority
FAO	Food and Agriculture Organization of the United Nations
FAWC	Farm Animal Welfare Committee (former Farm Animal Welfare Council)
FMD	Foot and mouth disease
LL	Log-likelihood
NF	Normalised frequency
NFU	National Farmers' Union
PDA	Positive Discourse Analysis
PETA	People for the Ethical Treatment of Animals
RSPCA	Royal Society for the Prevention of Cruelty to Animals
UN	United Nations
WHO	World Health Organisation

Preface

Judith Still

University of Nottingham

Chickens are, as Elena Lazutkaite[1] shows, the animal of the Anthropocene par excellence. This is not only because of the size of their population today. Chickens are everywhere and nowhere—they are hiding in plain sight. There are more chickens in the world than any other bird. More than 60 billion chickens are reared annually as a source of meat and eggs. In the United States alone, more than 9 billion chickens are slaughtered each year for meat, and more than 300 million chickens are reared for egg production.[2] Chickens raised for meat are then the first animal species suggested as a marker of the Anthropocene Epoch: "broiler chickens, now unable to survive without human intervention, have a combined mass exceeding that of all other birds on Earth; this novel morphotype symbolizes the unprecedented human reconfiguration of the Earth's biosphere."[3] But they are confined, hidden—in the United States they do not exist in Federal law; how often do you see, let alone touch, a (living) chicken, as opposed to 'chicken' disguised in some obscure form or other? Nicholas Royle suggests indeed, with his aptly-named 'Hides' in his 2017 novel *An English Guide to Birdwatching*, that 'ornithomorphic' linguistic play tends to be simultaneously revealing and concealing:

> Closely linked to that world of crime [the disavowal of vicious cruelty to chickens], is the outrage of naming. People say *chicken* in the singular when they are actually talking about *chickens* in the plural. Mixing their metaphors in a vague toilet

---

[1] Elena completed her PhD thesis, on which this book is based, at the University of Nottingham in 2020. I had the pleasure of co-supervising her work in the Centre for Critical Theory with colleagues in Archaeology, first Naomi Sykes (who was leading a large AHRC chicken project) and then, following Naomi's move to Exeter, with Christopher King.

[2] The Food and Agriculture Organisation notes that worldwide 68.8 billion chickens were slaughtered for meat in 2018; in the USA, 9 billion chickens were slaughtered for meat and 391 million hens were reared for eggs in 2018. Thanks to Elena Lazutkaite for up to date information.

[3] Carys E. Bennett and Richard Thomas, Mark Williams, Jan Zalasiewicz, Matt Edgeworth, Holly Miller, Ben Coles, Alison Foster, Emily J. Burton and Upenyu Marume (2018), 'The broiler chicken as a signal of a human reconfigured biosphere', *Royal Society Open Science* 12 December 2018 https://doi.org/10.1098/rsos.180325, p.1. Thanks to Christopher King for recommending this article to me.

> panic, they try to flush out—meaning flush away—their knowledge of what they are doing by resorting to an abstract plural, a strictly fictional turn of phrase, as part of an elaborate strategy to gloss over the reality of what they are doing. In this seemingly small but telling detail they behave precisely in the manner of *headless chickens.*[4]

Lazutkaite's book is a fascinating case study providing ample empirical evidence to support her analysis of the representation of farmed chickens in four British newspapers and two animal campaigning magazines. Her work shows how chickens are 'screened'—shown as objects produced and consumed while disguised as subjects with emotional or mental lives as well as physical existences. It is unusual in that it brings together a corpus linguistics methodology which allows a large number of texts to be examined, preventing any accusation of cherry-picking quotations, and ensuring breadth, with discourse analysis that enables a more in-depth and forensic approach to the assumptions underlying news items as well as opinion pieces. Lazutkaite shows that in news items farmed chickens are typically objectified, viewed from a human-centred perspective. They are the raw material producing profit or loss for farmers, whether the worst factory farmers or the best organic farmers, or they are the source of protein for consumers, whether unhealthy 'cheap' food for the masses condemned by the likes of Jamie Oliver or delicious (expensive) dishes promoted by the likes of Hugh Fearnley-Whittingstall. They are also figured as a reservoir of disease transmissible to humans when food scares (salmonella) or other threats (bird flu) emerge, necessitating the slaughter of many chickens—a holocaust presented as worrying because it reduces the profits of farmers. If chicken suffering is ever evoked, then it is typically treated as a necessary by-product of the human right to eat flesh; at best, lesser suffering (enriched cages) is weighed favourably as more humane against greater suffering (battery cages). Yet 'high welfare' chicken farming, as Lazutkaite shows, is something of a misnomer if we take welfare in its more usual sense.[5] In opinion pieces, the ethics of meat-eating are occasionally raised,

---

[4] Nicholas Royle, *An English Guide to Birdwatching* (Brighton: Myriad Editions, 2017), p. 270. Royle cites some of the notorious practices of today's 'chicken production' such as 'beak trimming' to avoid cannibalism – a violent mutilation causing lasting pain - typically described as if a mere haircut pp. 271-3.

[5] See Tom Regan, *Defending Animal Rights* (Urbana and Chicago: University of Illinois Press, 2001), chapter 5 'What we learn from Alice'. Regan has no confidence in what animal industries say about their business, arguing that the meaning of e.g. 'humane treatment' is whatever they want it to mean like Humpty Dumpty (p. 78). Regan emphasises that words (such as 'high welfare') have meanings (p. 79), and so industry representatives are lying whether they know they are or not – this is the 'Disconnect Dictum' – what they do does not match what they say. For my discussion of Regan and Singer as representative of animal rights philosophers (who have largely had a positive influence, but tend to 'over-egg' the rationality of their arguments) see, Judith Still, 'Thoughts From France on the Animal-Human

notably in *The Guardian,* which sometimes allows space for animal rights philosophers such as Peter Singer. Yet even the *Guardian* discussions often raise environmental or socio-political issues which relate to industrial farming without specifically addressing the question of chickens as sentient beings to whom humans might have responsibilities. The lack of attention to intersectionality is shown to be lamentable across all the publications that Lazutkaite analyses. I should note that this may have changed a little with the advent of Covid-19. A recent comment piece in *The Guardian* by Jonathan Safran Foer and Aaron S. Gross is entitled: "To Prevent the Next Pandemic We Must Take on Factory Farming."[6] They argue that "commercial poultry operations appear to be the Silicon Valley of viral development" (p. 1). This sentiment, I would argue, has been bleeding (if only a little) into news items discussing the link between viruses and "the most powerful industrial complex in the world – the factory farm" (p. 2) as well as the trade in wild animals.[7]

Nevertheless, the well-intentioned debate about the production of "genetically uniform, immune-compromised and regularly drugged animals" (*Ibid.* p. 1) does not necessarily approach the horrors from the perspective of the animals themselves. A very recent 'long read' (again outside Lazutkaite's time period) reveals the shocking conditions for women working in a chicken plant in Arkansas.[8] These women (many Latina) are forced to accept very low pay and horrifying conditions which on a daily basis mean, for example, wearing adult diapers so that they can manage without toilet breaks. Health and safety standards are appalling, resulting both in extreme industrial accidents and quotidian danger. When the company stopped feeding human antibiotics to chickens in 2017, and instead started spraying antimicrobials on the chicken carcases, the workers (and there are 250,000 poultry workers in the USA) were exposed to levels of peracetic acid that cause serious health risks. Amongst other issues, these workers are even more vulnerable to Covid-19. The article concludes with the words of one of the worker-activists: "For the future of the country, we must think deeply about the meaning of these workers in our daily lives and stand up for their human rights and dignity – because they've always been essential, and if they don't survive, we won't survive" (p. 8). This is indeed a scandalous situation, and I hope no reader would wish to undermine the position of food-processing workers (struggling to physically

---

Borderline: Derrida and Animal Rights Philosophers' in *French Thought and Literary Theory in the UK* ed. I. Goh (Routledge, 2019), pp. 49-65.

6 *Guardian Journal* 21/4/20, pp. 1-2.

7 See the editorial comment 'The Virus is a Warning that Britain's Food System Must Change', *The Guardian* 18/4/20 which cites 'chlorinated chicken and the American mega-farms that it symbolises. Antibiotics, steroid hormones and pesticides' – and does mention animal welfare considerations *en passsant.*

8 Mya Frazier, 'Women On the Front Line', *The Guardian* 17.4.20, *Journal* pp. 5-8.

distance in the workplace) now starting to die from Covid-19. However, as Lazutkaite's own recent article suggests, coronavirus itself should not be considered in isolation from human-animal relations.[9] More broadly, nowhere in this very lengthy *Guardian* article does anyone question whether it is indeed *essential* to eat meat—and whether humans could *survive* without killing other animals. If we were instead to make the assumption that our diet could in fact be plant-based, then we could turn to the *ethics* of meat-eating in general.

Lazutkaite argues (with animal rights activists) that since chickens are sentient beings, they should be treated as subjects rather than objects—and thus killing and eating them or their products (notably eggs) is unethical. This is a view which, to her regret, emerges only exceptionally in her corpus in the occasional *Guardian* opinion piece, and, more often, in the campaigning magazine *Outrage* (published by the animal rights organisation Animal Aid). The other campaigning magazine that she analyses, *Farm Animal Voice*, is produced by the animal welfare organisation Compassion in World Farming, which is cited by Singer as instrumental in the first generation of the modern animal movement that began in the 1960s in the UK.[10] Nevertheless, founded by a dairy farmer, this organisation and its publication is in favour of reform of farming rather than a vegan revolution in the way we humans eat.

In a recent essay, Henry Buller summarises and develops some of the strong arguments for the intersubjective bond between farm animals and stockpeople "grounded in the situated practice (and therefore moral significance) of interpersonal relations rather than in the more abstract ethical categorisations that are always so problematic when it comes to non-human animals."[11] He cites Gordon Gatward's argument that a basic component of the *care* of animals is "the ability of the individual stock keeper to form a close and even affectionate working relationship with their animals" (Buller, *Farming*, p. 207).[12] I think that it is interesting to reflect on the possibility of "interspecies, inter-individual negotiation between the achievement of different goods and benefits" (*Ibid.*), familiar to many who live lives entangled with the lives of their companion

[9] Elena Lazutkaite, 'How did we get here? Covid-19, climate crisis and the sixth mass extinction', Lithuanian Radio and Television 7 April 2020 https://www.lrt.lt/en/news-in-english/19/1160498/how-did-we-get-here-covid-19-climate-crisis-and-the-sixth-mass-extinction-opinion.

[10] See Singer, 'Introduction' in *In Defense of Animals: The Second Wave* ed. Peter Singer (Oxford: Blackwell, 2006) , pp. 1-10.

[11] See Henry Buller, 'Farming' in *The Edinburgh Companion to Animal Studies*, ed. Lynn Turner, Undine Sellbach and Ron Broglio (Edinburgh: Edinburgh University Press, 2018), pp. 198-214, p. 206.

[12] Gatward, *Livestock Ethics* (Devon: Chalcombe Publications, 2001).

animals.[13] However, I would note that chicken are included in the argument only when Buller discusses what used to be oxymoronic, but is now simply fact, "factory farming" where: "Individual animal lives become metricated moments in pre-determined productive cycles, animal bodies are materiality-in-the-making driven by feed-weight ratios in an industry where technology and biology, machine and animal, medicines and matter are increasingly intertwined" (Buller, p. 202). When he turns to something more like a pastoral idyll of companionability, the examples tend to focus on large mammals such as cows, sheep and pigs. This need not be the case—Lazutkaite references the phenomenon of backyard chicken keeping (often the source for the few stories she finds which allow individual chickens some agency and personality) which is gradually on the rise—but she makes the case that chickens are particularly (and unfairly) ridiculed as 'bird-brained' (dim and comical) in the national discourse represented in the media.

In fact, chickens as companions to farmers and their families have a long history, although an even longer history tells of them as exotic prizes.[14] I shall give an example from eighteenth-century America, the end (for white folk anyway) of the colonial period, and look briefly at the emblematic figure of "the American farmer." How did he relate to his chickens? The sympathetic Farmer James, a fraternal and decent settler in Pennsylvania, writes that every time he sees an egg on his table he regrets that "but for my gluttony," the hen will never live and never lead her chicks.[15] He continues:

> It might have been a gentle useful hen leading her chickens with a care and vigilance which speaks shame to many women. A cock, perhaps, arrayed with the most majestic plumes, tender to its mate, bold, courageous, endowed with an astonishing instinct, with thoughts, with memory, and every distinguishing characteristic of the reason of man! (p. 28)

These reflections do not prevent him from eating the eggs—nor, we readers presume, the flesh. And yet—he lives with chickens whom he sees as fellow creatures, perhaps even *semblables.* In his final Letter XII, "Distresses of a Frontier-Man" (pp. 187-217), he returns to the chicken, alongside iconic wild

---

[13] See notably Donna J. Haraway, *The Companion Species Manifesto. Dogs, People, and Significant Otherness* (Chicago: Prickly Paradigm Press, 2003), and the even more controversial Vicki Hearne, *Adam's Task: Calling Animals by Name* (New York: Alfred A. Knopf, 1986). I discuss some of these questions, particularly that of love between human and other animals in my *Derrida and Other Animals: The Boundaries of the Human* (Edinburgh: Edinburgh University Press, 2015).

[14] See Naomi Sykes, *Beastly Questions: Animal Answers to Archaeological Issues* (London: Bloomsbury, 2014).

[15] J. Hector St. John de Crèvecoeur, *Letters from an American Farmer,* edited by Susan Manning (Oxford: OUP, Oxford World's Classics, 1997 [1782]), p. 28.

animals, as a perhaps surprising potential *model* for behaviour in an extreme situation of war: "The fox flies or deceives the hounds that pursue him; the bear, when overtaken, boldly resists and attacks them; the hen, the very timid hen, fights for the preservation of her chicken, nor does she decline to attack, and to meet on the wing, even the swift kite" (p. 196). My final example comes from the third volume of his French *Lettres,* so much more than a translation of his *Letters.*[16] It is the sixth of a series of 49 anecdotes entitled '*D'un coq et d'une poule*' [Of a cock and a hen]. Amidst the horrors of the War of Independence, and the terrible English depredations, the author's mother lost everything except one chicken (*Lettres,* III, p. 107). A friend had saved one cockerel in his cellar (p. 108). Together they founded a new dynasty of chickens. This could of course be an accurate anecdote, but whether it is or not, it shows the indomitable American spirit at the moment when the United States is born. The chickens are the symbol of new life—we might recall that in some ways, the ancient philosophical paradox of the chicken and the egg suggests eternity or infinity in the way that antecedence cannot be established. However, they emblematize life not only in themselves—they live on and reproduce (hence survival even after death)—but they also, through their eggs and flesh, their deaths, give sustenance and thus life to the starving colonists.

Why chickens again? I would argue that they are the extreme example of the Fall, if such it be, from sacrifice to holocaust in human-animal relations.[17] These beautiful feathered friends have such a very long history of cohabitation with human beings across most of the globe, often not as natives but as exotic and precious imports. Even today in Britain, shameful home to Bernard Matthews and his like, backyard chickens, once the resource of the less well-off, have risen again as the beloved pets of the liberal bourgeoisie. Chickens were not first domesticated as a source of protein (flesh and eggs), or certainly not merely for food. Archaeologists have found complete chicken remains alongside human remains in ancient graves, as if prized goods if not companions. They played a key

---

16 *Lettres d'un cultivateur américain* (Paris: Cuchet, 1784-7) 3 vols.

17 In *The Animal That Therefore I Am,* trans. David Wills (New York: Fordham University Press, 2008), Derrida discusses the huge shift in our relation with animals since the end of the eighteenth century, a period which is widely regarded as the location of the third revolution in relations between humans and animals. This agricultural revolution involves scientific breeding, the forerunner of industrialization of food production. Derrida points out that exploitation, training, hunting, experimentation and so on did not begin in the Enlightenment but are as old as man and 'what he calls his world, his knowledge, his history, and his technology' (*The Animal That Therefore I Am,* p. 25). Yet in the last two centuries there has been a 'bouleversement' thanks to the conjoined development of 'savoirs' and 'techniques' – with genetic experimentation and the manipulation of the genome, industrialization of food production (*The Animal That Therefore I Am,* p. 25), and the advent of mass species extinction.

role in religious rituals, and their feathers were valued. Of course, they are also bred to fight—both a particularly spectacular cruelty (unlike the hidden violence of the industrial cage) and, like bullfighting, a practice which involves cherishing and veneration—cockfighting continues even in Europe today. As protein they have shifted from the apex of the weekly communion around a table. Chickens had a particular nourishing role in the French imaginary of food; Henri IV is believed to have declared around 1600 that he would ensure that no one in his kingdom was so poor that he could not afford "a chicken in his pot." Now globally industrially—we have "chicken"…

Holding chickens close, as Crevecoeur did, does not rule out killing or consumption, but the monstrous scale of the dirty secret of industrial farming is something relatively recent. Domestication has led to scientific breeding. Human bodies and minds have developed in—perhaps—the survival of the fittest. Other domestic animals have sometimes been bred for the brief survival of the weakest—whether fancied dogs who cannot breathe or chickens who cannot walk. Not only are they bred to die, but bred with lethal characteristics. There is an imaginary residue in language, writing, or pictures in children's books, marketized in figures of happy chickens on egg boxes (to sell eggs produced under lamentable circumstances) but, as Lazutkaite demonstrates, quotidian discourse in the press generally encourages the instrumentalization and objectification of broilers and layers. We all (arguably even vegans) kill to live on some level; all life involves sacrifice. However, the unanswered question, posed by Jacques Derrida, remains: to what extent can we nevertheless "eat well," live doing less rather than more harm to other beings? Our definition of other beings is still a fluid one—some include only (some?) human beings, others would include trees or rivers.[18] But if we were to take chickens as a case study, granted how many chickens we humans have brought into the world, and reflected on how we could live with chickens more equitably, both species "eating well," that thought experiment would require a significant displacement from the narrow mindset revealed in Lazutkaite's meticulous dissection of print journalism.

---

[18] One recent and unusual attempt to imagine chickens raised on an industrial egg farm as (tortured) minds as well as matter is Deb Olin Unferth's *Barn 8* (Minneapolis: Grey Wolf Press, 2020). A different and highly controversial art piece that stages fowl sacrifice is Adel Abdessemed's video of living cockerels whom he has set on fire; see Stéphanie Boulard, '*Printemps* Hélène Cixous – Adel Abdessemed' in *Ententes – A partir d'Hélène Cixous*, ed. Stéphanie Boulard and Catherine Witt (Paris: Presses Sorbonne Nouvelle, 2018). This was hard to swallow for me personally, however contradictory that response, granted the quotidian horror of chicken lives and deaths in which we are perhaps all to some degree complicit if only by turning a blind eye never mind enjoying eggs.

1.
Introduction

This book adds to the literature on discursive representations of the "other". It is informed by a social constructionist approach to meaning-making and belongs to an emerging field of discourse analysis of communication around farmed animals. More specifically, I analyse discourses around chicken farming in British newspapers and campaigners' flagship magazines published between 1982 and 2016. In total, the study corpus comprises 1754 texts published in broadsheets *The Guardian* and *The Daily Telegraph*, tabloids the *Daily Mirror* and the *Daily Mail* (including their Sunday editions *Sunday Mirror* and *Mail on Sunday*) and magazines *Agscene* and *Farm Animal Voice* produced by the animal welfare organisation Compassion in World Farming (CIWF) and *Outrage* and *The Uncounted Dead: Farming's Unofficial Victims* published by the animal rights organisation Animal Aid (AA).

My choice of analysing newspapers against other forms of media is explained by their watchdog, gatekeeper and agenda-setting role with the general public, political elites and other forms of media. By choosing their topics, lexis, and sources to cite, newspapers produce identities and shape public discourses, and this applies to most topics including chicken farming. Moreover, since "lay" people may have little or no knowledge nor direct experience of chicken farming, newspapers are important sites of meaning creation.[1] Ironically, the Cultural & Scientific Perceptions of Human-Chicken Interaction project, which I was part of as a PhD student, received some negative feedback in the British newspapers; this backlash and the evident perception of chickens as an illegitimate or unworthy object of study sparked my interest in contemporary framings of chicken farming in British newspapers. *The Daily Express* reflected the view of chickens as comical, trivial, and culturally unimportant "food" animals and was predominantly concerned with the fact that the project was assigned £1.9 million to study human-chicken relationships. It was suggested the project was a waste of tax-payers' money: "Robert Oxley of the Tax-Payers' Alliance called the chicken study 'ridiculous', adding 'the amount doled out certainly isn't chicken feed'" (Dawar, 2013). The *Daily Mail* went further with

---

[1] My public engagement activities within the Cultural & Scientific Perceptions of Human-Chicken Interaction project showed that "lay" people were lacking knowledge about industry practices such as debeaking or the slaughter age of chickens farmed for meat.

the headline "A birdbrained idea? Outrage as academics are handed £2m to study how humans interact with chickens" (Salkeld, 2013).

Moreover, when I first started this project in 2014, I was surprised at the lack of guidelines for writing about nonhuman animals in the newspapers' style books. *The Guardian* (2014) guidelines for journalists had little on nonhuman animals except that they suggested to use the pronoun "it" unless the gender is known. *The Daily Telegraph* (2014) guidelines mentioned nonhuman animals only to deny their personhood in grammar. Acknowledging animal gender is seemingly unprofessional; animals "are neuter even if we are well aware of their gender. Anthropomorphism has no place in balanced news reporting" (*The Daily Telegraph*, 2018). No style guides were found for the *Daily Mail* and *Daily Mirror*, and the tabloids did not respond to my request for information.

In search of inspiration, I then turned to campaigners. In their "Master Brand Toolkit", the animal welfare charity CIWF provided guidelines for photos and meticulously described the colours and fonts the charity uses (CIWF, 2015a). Yet the toolkit did not provide any guidelines for writing about farmed animals. Personal communication with the ambassador Joyce D'Silva (November, 2014) confirmed that campaigners had a set of rules for visual communication, but did not have instructions for language or a preferred vocabulary. The animal rights advocacy group AA did not respond to my request for a comment on their linguistic style. This shortage of progressive style guides indicated that insufficient attention is paid to linguistic representations of nonhuman animals even by animal welfare and animal rights activists.

The richness of the debate on animal welfare versus animal rights is beyond the scope of this book. In this study, "animal welfare views" are broadly understood as diverse perspectives concerned with reducing the suffering of animals used by humans. The term "animal rights perspectives" is used not as a single philosophical position, but as a catch-all description of views that nonhuman animals are not resources for human use. The selection of the two animal advocacy organisations is deliberate — to engage with different and perhaps at times opposing views on chicken farming. While CIWF seeks welfare reform, AA seeks abolition; both campaign and lobby governments in order to (re)shape the contemporary cultural politics of chicken farming. In doing so, the organisations continuously reach for public support and media attention; newspapers, on the other hand, can (dis)empower animal advocates, who have less access to resources to participate in public debates. For example, my initial research revealed that in *The Guardian* commentary on horse racing, AA is called "the extremist animal rights group" and their director Andrew Tyler is labelled as an extremist too, "There is little point denying that Tyler is a committed, tireless and effective campaigner. Extremists often are" (*The Guardian*, 22/9/2014 [G33]). AA is blamed for not giving "intensive chicken farms and the industrialised rearing of livestock the same amount of attention" as horse racing (*The Guardian*, 22/9/2014 [G33]). As we shall see, this is an exception for *The Guardian* corpus, but the rhetoric that "there are other and more important things to worry about" reappears in *The Daily Telegraph* texts that find an "alibi" to shift the attention from one issue to another.

1.1 Author's perspective and vocabulary

The conceptual framework of my study, namely Critical Discourse Analysis (CDA), requires making the researcher's position and values as explicit and transparent as possible without being apologetic (van Leeuwen, 2006). Therefore, I shall briefly outline my socio-political stance. I trained as an animal welfare scientist and conservationist. In this book, however, I found my "intellectual home" in Critical Animal Studies (CAS), which are rooted in critical theory as well as animal liberation and holistic understandings of intersectionality and oppressions (Best, 2009).[2] CAS calls for an engaged critical praxis and argues for "the collapsing of academic/activism boundaries" and "for political stances that provide a much-needed deconstruction of the binary opposition between human and nonhuman animals" (Almiron et al., 2018). In the spirit of CAS, my aspiration is not only to add to the existing body of knowledge, but to help campaigners, researchers, journalists and other interested parties to embrace the intrinsic value of nonhuman animals in their language and ultimately bring about genuine change. I hope my findings could serve as a basis for action to change the "real-life" situation of chickens farmed for their flesh and eggs. For to de-normalise the routine violence against chickens, it is crucial to debate the cultural politics of animal farming and the question of the moral standing of farmed animals beyond academia.

A reflection on my own vocabulary within this book is necessary. I try to avoid the terminology that objectifies chickens and presents them merely as a protein resource. Yet some problematic language remains; the term "animal" itself is highly contentious. To eschew the human-animal binary, I employ terms such as "nonhuman animals" and "other animals". Due to space limitations, however, I also interchangeably use the term "animal" to mean "nonhuman animal", when the meaning is unequivocally defined in context, e.g. when referring to animal welfare or farmed animals. The definition of "farmed animals" is narrowed to

---

[2]Animal oppression in my study is understood as the economic, physical, and psychological exploitation of nonhuman animals resulting from the social system of control maintained by humans.

nonhuman animals exploited for food, wool, skin, or work. I choose the term "farmed animals" over "farm animals" to highlight that being used for agricultural purposes is not something inherent to nonhuman animals but is done against their interests. In addition, killing is typically lexicalised differently for humans and farmed animals. The former are "murdered" or "killed", whereas the latter are "destroyed", "culled", "harvested", "disposed of" or "slaughtered". I choose the verbs "kill" and "slaughter" (unless quoting) to avoid euphemising. "Slaughter" is, however, only shocking for humans and some other animals of a higher social status (e.g. dogs), while an accepted term for chickens.

The term "poultry", which does not specify between varieties of birds raised on farms, is avoided, as is the industry term "broiler" for a chicken farmed for meat. The term "broiler" originates in the USA in connection to a type of grilling, i.e. "broiling" (Horowitz, 2006, p. 105). The animal activist Joan Dunayer (1995) argues that a term developed after a method of cooking is derogatory. The terms "meat chickens" and "laying hens" are also problematic. They are instrumental and define chickens solely in regard to human use. I replace these with "chickens raised/farmed for meat/their flesh" and "hens raised/farmed for eggs". It is difficult, however, to entirely avoid instrumental terms for the reasons of clarity and comprehensibility, since the reader should be able to distinguish between chickens farmed under different living conditions.

To highlight the problematics of other difficult terms and emphasise their ideological implications I use scare quotes. For example, scare quotes are used for "ethical" in situations where it may be argued that "ethical" consumption of products derived from nonhuman animals is impossible due to the implications for the animals. I use double quotation marks with the term "higher welfare", which I suggest is loaded. Depending on the point of view, if "conventional", i.e. industry-standard, intensive systems are considered *low welfare,* then the improved systems could be at best *satisfactory* or *acceptable* welfare. The term "higher welfare" exploits the comparative adjective to embody positivity. Additionally, the terms "humane" or "inhumane" are placed in scare quotes as they impose the human claim of morality, flatter humans and further perpetuate the human-animal dualism. Using an adjective derived from our own species name to define what is kind implies that being kind and compassionate is something inherent and restricted to humans, whereas nonhuman animals supposedly cannot possess these qualities. Equally, "inhumane" implies that being cruel is somehow "not human". My preferred term for "inhumane" is "cruel". Some other terms such as "efficient" in the context of intensive chicken farming, "sustainable" in the context of a farming system, which excludes chicken welfare as a factor for sustainability, and "enriched" for colony cages, are also placed in quotes due to their loaded nature. The term "welfare" is used without quotation marks, although it could be perceived as a euphemism; it is vague and can be used to frame practices that are essentially causing suffering to farmed animals in a reassuring and positive way.

When lacking alternative substitutes, I have slipped into using widely accepted yet less sensitive terms. In my defence, I must note that the aim of the study is not to impose "verbal hygiene". My struggle to avoid speciesist language altogether when writing this book demonstrates the extent to which meat culture is ingrained and the area is under-researched. Here I refer to meat culture as defined by the cultural studies scholar Annie Potts (2016). Potts (2016) notes that the "history of creating contemporary 21st-century 'meat culture' is an industrial history that blends agricultural science and technologisation with mass production, vertical integration production systems with globalised economies, and the hyper-stimulation of consumer demand" (p. 1). Meat culture "maintains the invisible belief system that meat is normal, natural, necessary and nice" (Potts, 2016, p. 20).

1.2 Research questions and the structure of this book

The "status" of chickens, the descendants of the red junglefowl of the Asian jungle, has been subject to much change. Chickens may have been initially domesticated for other reasons than food such as for cockfighting (Sykes, 2012). They have been associated with deities, divinity, the afterlife, and both bravery and cowardice (Sykes, 2012). In ancient Greece, the cockerel symbolised warfare and (homo) sexuality (Shelton, 2007, pp. 102–106). In the Roman world, chickens were linked with the cult of Mithras and the Roman deity Mercury, whose portrayal often included cockerels (Crummy, 2007). The strongest cultural meaning of chickens in Roman Britain may be that of abundance, prosperity, and wealth (Feider, 2017). A variety of cultural chicken-related activities such as cockfighting still exist today. Chickens retain some symbolic meaning; the mother hen is a widely accepted symbol of nurturance and the egg is a symbol of rebirth or resurrection in pagan and Christian traditions. Chickens are still used in rituals and as objects of art (Neto et al., 2011; Stinckens et al., 2015). They become story characters and companions. Nonetheless, chickens' current role is overwhelming as a source of cheap protein. As the archaeogeneticist Greger Larson pinpoints, the contemporary human-chicken relationship is "a radical departure from the way that humans have interacted with animals over the last 15,000 years" (Gorman, 2016). The ecolinguist Arran Stibbe (2012a) laments that "animals are disappearing, vanishing, and dying out — not just in the physical sense of becoming extinct, but in the sense of being erased from our consciousness" (p. 1). Regardless of the striking expansion of their numbers, chickens are an excellent exemplar of animals who are stripped of their individuality and disappear as subjects, becoming "identical units" in the production line. Globally ubiquitous chickens largely remain at a remove from urban populations, both physically and metaphorically. Chicken meat and egg meals, eaten quickly, conveniently, and frequently, could be the only contact with chickens, and it is likely to be regarded as contact with food rather than with an animal.

This book uses broadsheets *The Guardian* and *The Daily Telegraph*, tabloids the *Daily Mirror* and the *Daily Mail* (including their Sunday editions *Sunday Mirror* and *Mail on Sunday*) and magazines *Agscene* and *Farm Animal Voice* produced by CIWF and *Outrage* and *The Uncounted Dead: Farming's Unofficial Victims* produced by AA as the points of entry to investigate discursive framings of chicken farming in the UK between 1982 and 2016. The overarching research questions are:

1. How does each source problematise/normalise chicken farming? How and to what extent do framings and representations reinforce chicken exploitation? How and to what extent do framings and representations challenge it?
2. What is language revealing or hiding about chicken farming? What is the relation between the framings and the circumstances of actual living chickens? How is chicken agency constructed?
3. (How) have discourses surrounding chicken farming changed since 1982? Have discourses challenging intensive chicken farming become more pronounced or been lost or diluted?
4. What are the main differences and similarities between the newspapers (broadsheets vs tabloids, left-leaning vs right-leaning)? Between the campaigners' magazines (welfare vs rights)? Between the newspapers and campaigners' magazines? And what does this tell us?

This book proceeds to address these questions over six chapters, supported by seven appendices. Chapter 1 has introduced the scope of research, aims and questions. In the following section, it argues that this is an extraordinary historical moment to be studying the relationship between humans and chickens, once exotic, but now most abundant and exploited birds worldwide. Chicken farming is positioned not as a singular problem of animal welfare, but as a complex global issue where human and nonhuman entities are inextricably entangled with one another. The chapter considers the historical emergence of intensive chicken farming and provides an overview of chicken welfare issues, with special reference to associated legislation, market trends, public health risks and environmental impact. Major events over the course of 34 years are signposted, which should prove helpful when analysing the data from the newspapers and campaigners' corpora.

The theoretical strand starts with Chapter 2. I briefly introduce the moral arguments with regards to the treatment of nonhuman animals and review the relevant literature on discursive nonhuman animal representation. My study is situated in the context of previous research pertaining similar topics and the shortcomings of previous research are addressed. Chapter 3 continues the theoretical strand. It focusses on the data sources and research methods and outlines the analytical framework. In Chapter 4, I analyse the data from the newspapers. The chapter is divided into four sections examining *The Guardian*, the *Daily Mirror* (and *Sunday Mirror*), *The Daily Telegraph*, and the *Daily Mail* (and *Mail on Sunday*). Chapter 5 concerns the campaigning organisations CIWF and AA. I analyse the data from the campaigners' magazines comparing the animal welfare and animal rights approaches. I complete this book with Chapter 6 that weaves in the findings and expands on the discussions in Chapters 4 and 5. The implications, limitations and directions for future research are explored, and final thoughts and conclusions are drawn.

Supplementary material is provided in Appendices A–G. Appendices A-E are provided online at https://vernonpress.com/book/1075. Appendix A provides exploratory keyword analyses for *The Guardian* corpus. Appendices B, C and D provide exploratory keyword analyses for the corpora of the *Daily Mirror* (and *Sunday Mirror*), *The Daily Telegraph* and the *Daily Mail* (and *Mail on Sunday*), respectively. Appendix E provides exploratory keyword analyses for the CIWF and AA corpora. Appendix F lists all newspaper texts and Appendix G lists all texts from the campaigners' corpora cited in this book.

1.3 Chicken farming between 1982 and 2016

1.3.1 Planet of the chickens

The exact starting point of this study, the 1st of January 1982, was chosen due to practicality; the earlier issues of *Outrage* produced by AA and *Agscene* produced by CIWF were unavailable or incomplete and the newspaper articles were not available in digital format. Apart from this practicality, the period between 1982 and 2016 has been chosen for it spans a striking growth in the chicken industry, socio-economic changes, and thought-provoking events such as the avian influenza epidemic. With most of the world's religions having no taboos against eating chicken flesh or eggs, chickens have become ever more dominant in intensive farming and the global food system. Eggs are a staple food found in almost every big or small food store. Food outlets serving cheap chicken meals are more prevalent than ever and could be prime examples of successful and globalised businesses. To illustrate, one of the world's largest fast-food restaurant chains, Kentucky Fried Chicken (KFC) has around 900 outlets in the UK (BBC, 2018). In 2017, British consumers spent an estimated £2.2 billion in chicken restaurants such as KFC (Mintel, 2018).

Until the industrialisation of chicken farming in the 20th century, the economic value and nutritional contribution of chicken flesh and eggs to human diet was relatively minor. The scarcity of food in the post-war period pushed towards the intensification of chicken farming and a clear division between the chicken meat and egg industries.[3] The industries have been growing rapidly ever since and there has been an explosion in the number of chickens farmed globally. Figure 1.1 shows that over the period of 34 years global egg production has tripled in tonnes, from 27.5 million tonnes in 1982 to nearly 79 million tonnes in 2016. Although these numbers are already striking, they do not account for individual hens. Statistics on *individual* animals can be difficult to obtain as *food* production is typically described in scientific units of measurement such as kilograms, tonnes, or calories that aggregate if not erase individual animals.

With regards to the UK production of eggs, I must note that the growth is not linear. Government policies and marketing techniques led to booming egg production in the 1960s and the 1970s, but it started to decline in the 1980s. Figure 1.2 shows the drop after the *Salmonella* scare in 1988 and subsequent fluctuations due to various social, economic and political reasons, such as health concerns and avian influenza. Nevertheless, in 2016, around 722,000 tonnes of eggs were produced in the UK (FAOSTAT, 2018). The retail value of the egg market is reported as growing, from £582m in 2006 to £910m in 2016 (British Egg Information Service, 2018c). Further investigation into Defra (2016) statistics reveals that the British egg industry involves a staggering number of hens; the total for commercial "breeding and laying hens" in the UK agricultural holdings on the 1st of June 2016 was approximately 50.8 million birds. [4]

---

[3] Of note, the key transition from a small flock that ranged in the backyard into a large-scale intensive farm of single purpose birds started in the 20th century USA. Anti-regulatory, pro-business attitude of the American government led to a vertically integrated system where the ownership of chickens was kept with the integrators, whereas farmers were contractors (Godley & Williams, 2007). Rapid expansion and development of large integrator companies in the 1950s resulted in a price drop for chicken meat which led to more integration, automation, and the growth of corporations (Godley & Williams, 2007).

[4] Fluctuations in numbers are possible due to the "point in time" time nature of the survey.

Figure 1.1 Global production of eggs, 1982–2016

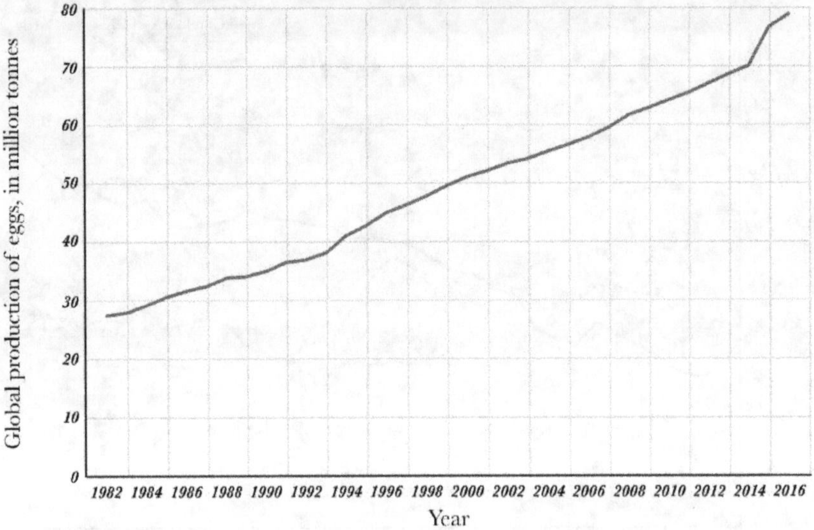

Data compiled from the UN Food and Agriculture Organization, FAOSTAT, at faostat.fao.org, accessed December 2018.

Figure 1.2 UK production of eggs, 1982–2016

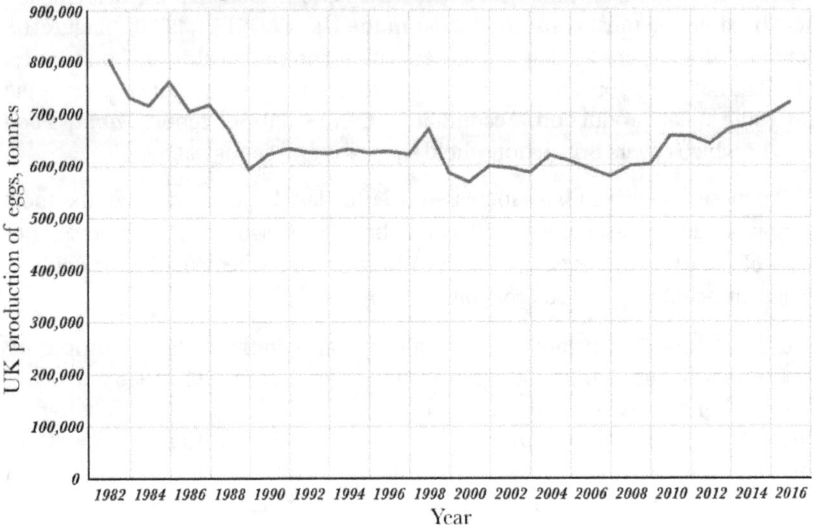

Data compiled from the UN Food and Agriculture Organization, FAOSTAT, at faostat.fao.org, accessed December 2018.

Figure 1.3 UK production of meat ("chicken", "pig" and "cattle"), 1982–2016

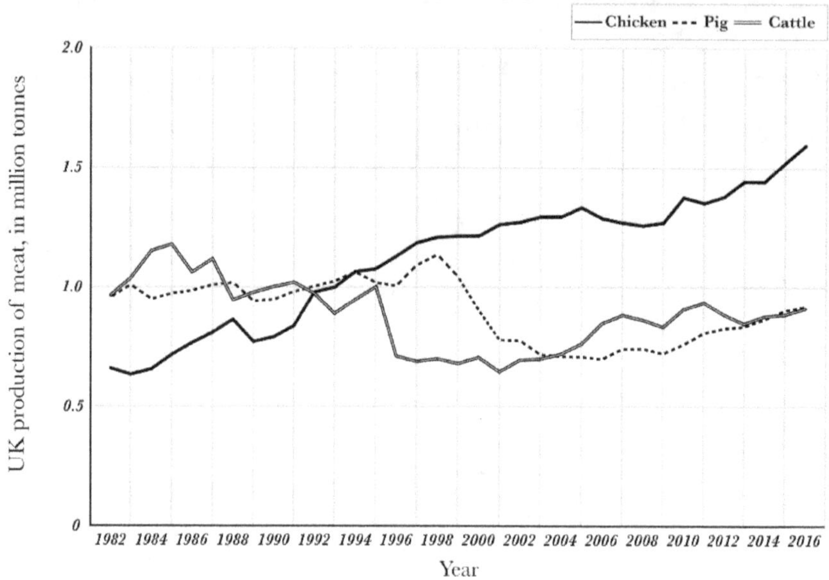

Data compiled from the UN Food and Agriculture Organization, FAOSTAT, at faostat.fao.org, accessed December 2018.

Statistics are even more striking for chicken meat production. In the 1980s, chicken meat became the most consumed meat in the UK (FAOSTAT, 2018).[5] Figure 1.3 compares the UK production of chicken, cattle and pig meat in million tonnes, showing that since 1994, the national production of chicken meat surpassed pig and cattle meat production. According to Defra's (2018b) report *Family Food 2016/17*, which covers British household shopping and eating habits:

> Purchases of chicken have increased over the last 10 years and were the most popular unprocessed meat product purchased by weight at 193g per person per week in 2016/17. This was followed by beef which has remained fairly stable in recent years at around 100g per person per week.

Figures 1.4 and 1.5 translate the units of weight into individual lives comparing the number of cattle, pigs and chickens killed for their flesh in 1986 and 2016. The number of pigs and cattle killed for meat has declined in the UK, whereas the number of chickens has more than doubled in 30 years. In 2016, more than one billion chickens were slaughtered for meat (Figure 1.5). Figure 1.6 compares the global production of chicken, cattle, and pig meat in million tonnes between 1982 and 2016. The most growth is identified in chicken meat production; in 2016, chicken meat production was nearly 107 million tonnes,

---

[5] Consider the imports of chicken meat as well.

which is close to pig meat production of nearly 119 million tonnes. Given chickens are small animals, when calculated individually, the world total for 2016 skyrocketed to 65 billion chickens killed for their flesh, in comparison to 1.5 billion pigs and 294 million cows (FAOSTAT, 2018).

Figure 1.4 Cattle, pigs and chickens slaughtered for meat in the UK in 1986

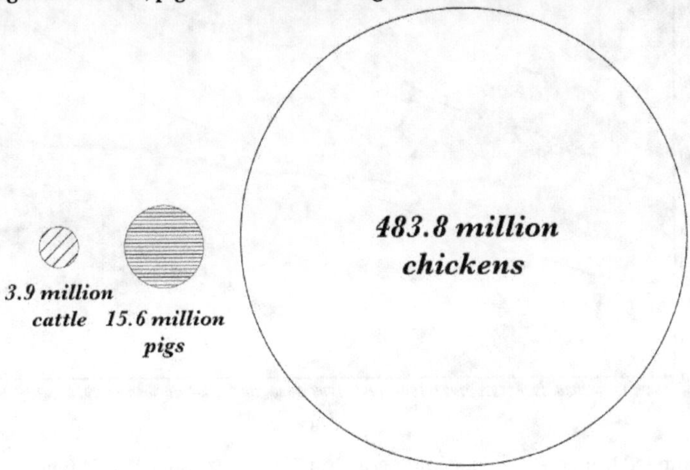

Data compiled from the UN Food and Agriculture Organization, FAOSTAT, at faostat.fao.org, accessed December 2018.

Figure 1.5 Cattle, pigs and chickens slaughtered for meat in the UK in 2016

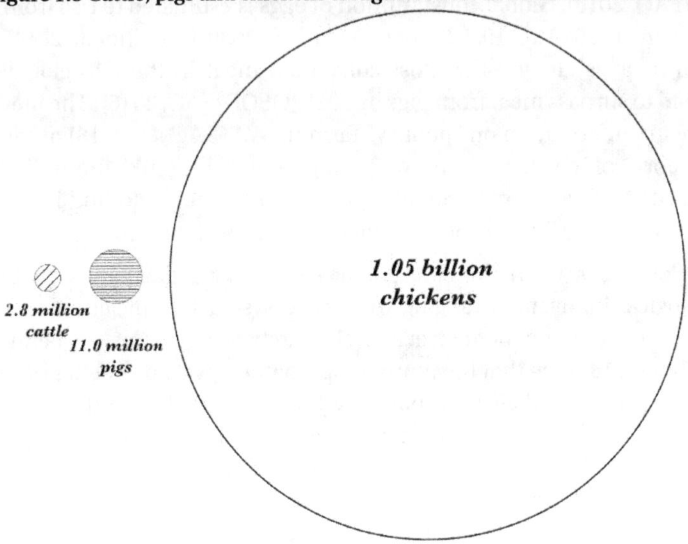

Data compiled from the UN Food and Agriculture Organization, FAOSTAT, at faostat.fao.org, accessed December 2018.

Figure 1.6 Global production of meat ("chicken", "pig" and "cattle"), 1982–2016

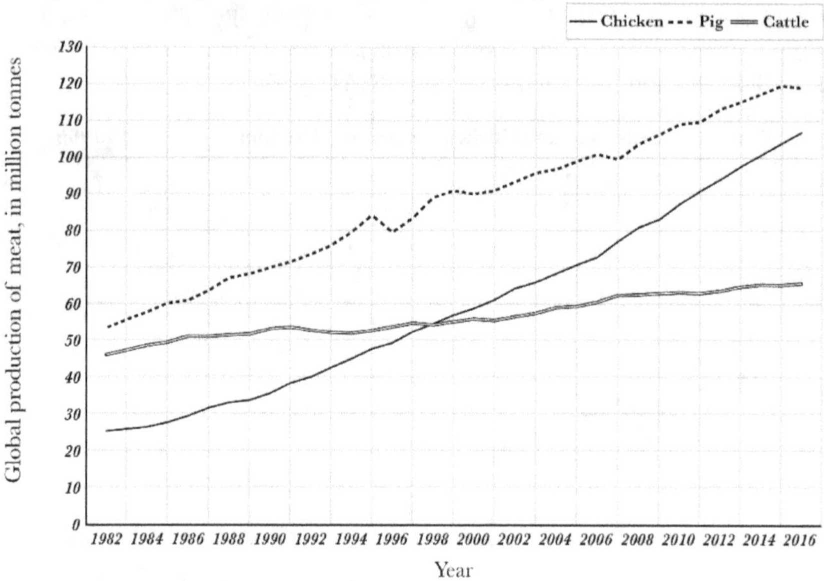

Data compiled from the UN Food and Agriculture Organization, FAOSTAT, at faostat.fao.org, accessed December 2018.

The global consumption of chicken meat and eggs is only expected to rise, making the subject of this book more important than ever before (FAO, 2011; OECD/FAO, 2016). Global consumption of eggs is estimated to rise from 9.3 kg per person in 2010 to 10.3 kg per person in 2030 (Windhorst, 2014).While chicken meat is already the most consumed meat in the UK, globally it is projected to surpass meat from pigs by 2025 (OECD/FAO, 2016). The media site for industry information on "poultry" farming WATTAgNet (2018) predicts the prominence of chicken flesh by stating that "chicken's future is bright compared to other animal proteins", a claim that one could find ironic if the suffering of billions of chickens was taken into consideration.

The global growth in the chicken meat and egg industries is enabled by technological innovation, ranging from cage systems, artificial incubation to genetic breed selection (Bennett et al., 2018). Archaeologists Carys E. Bennett and colleagues (2018) note that the morphology, pathology, and genetics of modern chickens farmed for their flesh have markedly departed from their ancestors. Changes in breeding, diet and management forced upon chickens have resulted in "at least a doubling in body size from the late medieval period to the present" and "an up to fivefold increase in body mass since the mid-twentieth century" (Bennett et al., 2018, p. 1). Consequently, chickens farmed for meat are the first animal species ever suggested to be a marker of the putative Anthropocene Epoch: "broiler chickens, now unable to survive without human intervention, have a combined mass exceeding that of all other birds on Earth; this novel morphotype symbolises the unprecedented human reconfiguration of the Earth's biosphere" (Bennett et al., 2018, p. 1).[6] I shall also note that the bodies of hens commercially farmed for eggs have too undergone significant pressure in favour of egg yields; they can "lay over 300 eggs per year, while indigenous hens often lay only 40–60" (Sørensen, in FAO, 2010).

The work of Bennett and colleagues has been covered in a BBC article titled "'Planet of the chickens': How the bird took over the world" (Briggs, 2018). Ironically, unlike the reference to the movie *The Planet of the Apes* suggests, chickens are not taking over the world in the sense of exercising their agency or assuming control over their lives. *The New York Times* article "It Could Be the Age of the Chicken, Geologically" similarly highlights that chickens are emblematic of the global consumerist society, our planet and our times and that the current era will be remembered for chicken leftovers as "the signature fossil of the modern epoch" (Gorman, 2018). With 23 billion chickens at any one time (3 chickens per person; the chicken population being higher than that of any other birds), the planet of the chickens is arguably the planet of their exploitation, while the signature of the current age is their suffering (FAOSTAT, 2018).[7]

1.3.2 Welfare, legislation and the market

While novel technologies and practices have made chicken flesh and eggs a staple in many people's diets, it was not achieved without ongoing alterations to birds' bodies and an impact on their welfare. Discoveries of the stimulating effects of lighting, antibiotics and vitamin D supplements made chickens the first farmed animals to be raised in complete captivity (Ogle, 2013, p. 105). Today, the production of chicken meat and eggs are some of the most intensive forms of animal farming; according to animal behaviourists Marian S. Dawkins and Roger Layton (2012), "chickens raise some of the most serious animal welfare issues in the whole of animal agriculture" (p. 147). Considering the scope of issues in chicken farming, the following review is a very limited attempt to address chicken welfare.[8]

In commercial farming, chickens are reduced to the biological functions of gaining weight, laying eggs and reproduction. Male and female chickens farmed for meat can reach slaughter weight in 30 days and hens farmed for eggs can be slaughtered at 72 weeks when their egg-laying ability starts to decline,

---

[6] Anthropocene is defined in a variety of ways by different scholars; Bennett and colleagues refer to Anthropocene as a new geologic time characterised human-induced planetary change (Bennett et al, 2018).

[7] The estimate provided is for 2017.

[8] The issues arising in processes such as catching, transportation and slaughtering are covered in de Jong et al. (2012) and Elson (2015).

whereas a healthy chicken could live for up to 10 years (Knowles et al., 2008; RSPCA, 2014). A common method of slaughter for chickens involves electrical water-bath stunning. However, research indicates that the method may not produce immediate stun and is not effective on all birds (Shields and Raj, 2010). Chickens may miss the stunner altogether and be still conscious with severe pain when their throats are cut. They might enter the scalding tank still alive and in conscious condition (Shields and Raj, 2010).

Chickens farmed for meat have been selectively bred to have a tremendous appetite and continuously put on weight; since the 1950s, their growth rate has increased four times from approximately 25 g per day to 100 g per day (Knowles et al., 2008). During their short life, chickens suffer from skeletal and muscle disorders, skin problems, heart disease, respiratory and mucous membrane problems (EFSA, 2010; de Jong et al., 2012). Obesity leads to lameness, which is one of the major welfare issues (Knowles et al., 2008). Paradoxically, another welfare issue is feed deprivation of birds if they are used for breeding. The word "fasting", which implies that chickens voluntarily starve, may be used to refer to feed deprivation. Since obesity negatively affects reproduction rates, the feed of chickens selected for reproduction is restricted to approximately one-quarter to one-third of the unrestricted ration, which causes chronic hunger for most of their lives (de Jong et al., 2002; Dawkins & Layton, 2012).

Chickens farmed for meat are typically not kept in cages, but in large sheds where a crowded environment is one of the major factors impacting on their welfare (EFSA, 2010; de Jong et al., 2012). The floor space that a bird has is called "stocking density". The term foregrounds that chickens are not considered as individual beings; "stocking density" is calculated as weight of chickens per square meter of usable area. Defra guidelines "Chickens for Meat and Breeding (England): Code of Recommendations for the Welfare of Livestock" advise the maximum "stocking density" for chickens to be 34 kg/m^2 (Defra, 2013). As chickens put on weight, they are left with little space to move; one should imagine 17 chickens weighing 2 kg sharing 1 m^2 of space. Strikingly, in 2014 it was reported that around 90% of chickens were farmed under the Red Tractor Assurance scheme in even poorer conditions than those recommended by Defra (de Castella, 2014). Despite the positive-sounding name, the Red Tractor Assurance is not an animal welfare scheme. It allows chickens to be crowded at a density of 38 kg/m^2 which is not illegal according to the EU regulations set in 2007 (Red Tractor Assurance, 2014). The density of 38 kg/m^2 equates to 19 chickens weighing 2 kg sharing 1 m^2, which is less than the size of an A4 sheet of paper per bird (RSPCA, 2006).

One of the major welfare issues for hens farmed for eggs is a behavioural restriction in cage systems (CIWF, 2014b). Since January 1st 2012, battery cages were banned in the EU and replaced by the so-called "enriched" cages. The overly optimistic description implies improved welfare conditions. However, "enriched" cages provide "750 cm^2 per hen — of which only 600 cm^2 has to be usable" ("usable" defines space that is of sufficient height for hens to stand upright) (RSPCA, 2005, p. 8). Compared with battery cages, the "enriched" cages provide a hen with only 50 cm^2 more usable space, which is less than the size of one beer mat (RSPCA, 2005). In 2013, a year after the ban on battery cages, 52% of hens were kept in "enriched" cages, 43% were free-range, 3% were barn-raised and 2% were under organic free-range production systems (Defra, 2014). In addition, the killing of male chicks is an issue of egg production across all systems. Male chicks cannot be used for egg production and are unsuitable for meat production due to insufficient breast muscle. The males are killed after hatching; the standard methods of killing are gassing, suffocation and "maceration" (grinding or shredding, also called by the industry as "instantaneous mechanical destruction" (Gurung et al., 2018).

Injurious pecking is another major welfare issue for hens. It is an abnormal behaviour when a hen pecks at the feathers of other hens.[9] Injurious pecking can occur in all production systems (free-range and cage); it is widespread and may result in severe feather pecking and removal, vent pecking and cannibalism. Among commercially farmed hens injurious pecking may be a primary cause of death (Weitzenbürger et al., 2005). While only some individuals initiate feather pecking, the behaviour can spread via social learning (Cloutier et al., 2002). Studies have suggested that injurious pecking may be avoided by selecting for behavioural traits or improving living conditions (Hester & Shea-Moore, 2003; Lay et al., 2011). Nonetheless, a common industry "fix" to injurious pecking is debeaking. Debeaking, also called "beak trimming" (which I propose is misleading as it implies the procedure is minor and resembles grooming), is a practice in which around one-third to a half of the beak is amputated to prevent injurious pecking (Freire et al., 2008). Debeaking is performed without anaesthesia using a hot-blade or an infra-red method. Common practice in commercial hatcheries is to carry out the procedure when chicks are one day old. The partial removal of beak causes hens acute pain due to sensitive tissue damage and, arguably, chronic pain due to the formation of neuromas in the enervated beak stump (Hester & Shea-Moore, 2003). Furthermore, debeaking may interfere with normal drinking, feeding and preening behaviours (Duncan et al., 1989). In Norway, Finland, and Sweden, debeaking is completely phased out. In the UK, debeaking of hens was banned in 2002, but this is yet to be enforced; the infrared method is allowed (See Table 1.1).

In response to intensification, the period between 1982 and 2016 has seen increasing regulation, the growth of "green" and animal welfare movements

---

[9] Here I refer to the definition of abnormal behaviour as behaviour which is different in pattern, frequency, and/or context from what is exhibited by conspecifics of species in their natural habitat (Fraser & Broom, 1990). Injurious pecking is distinctive from aggressive pecking, which is often aimed at the head, although aggressive pecking may include elements of feather pecking (Defra, 2005).

and the emerging niche market of alternatives. Legislative changes in the EU have targeted chicken farming, which was previously virtually unregulated.[10] Table 1.1 and Table 1.2 summarise the regulation imposed on the egg industry and the chicken meat industry in the EU in the past few decades. Since 2004, labelling of farming methods is mandatory for eggs (Table 1.1). The requirements for the labelling of chicken meat published in 2010 did not make it compulsory to state the farming method (Table 1.2). However, if a producer wishes to voluntarily disclose it, they must adhere to certain rules and terms.

Table 1.1 Regulation for hens farmed for eggs

Regulatory framework and key practices	Year
Council Directive 98/58/EC provides that farmed animals must be fed at intervals appropriate to their physiological needs, which consequently prohibits forced moulting	1999
Council Directive 1999/74/EC of 19 July 1999 set down minimum standards for the protection of hens	1999
Debeaking is banned in the UK. Not enforced at the time of writing 29/8/2018	2002
Mandatory labelling of farming methods for eggs	2004
Banning barren battery cages	2012

Source: Stevenson (2012)

Table 1.2 Regulation for chickens farmed for meat

Regulatory framework and key practices	Year
Council directive 2007/43/EC set minimum standards for chickens	2007
Requirements are set for labelling standards of farming type	2010

Source: Stevenson (2012)

[10] For comparative purposes, I shall note the situation in the USA. Despite numerous attempts to include birds under the Humane Slaughter Act, the act is interpreted as not covering chickens or turkeys. Moreover, a number of states exempt chickens from their cruelty laws. The power of the animal agriculture industry is evidenced not only by the traditional lobbying means resulting in the lack of regulation, but also by less traditional methods, such as the so-called ag-gag laws that prohibit taking undercover videos or photographs in farms. These laws silence whistle-blowers by penalising them. In addition to ag-gag laws, the Animal Enterprise Terrorism Act pushed by industry groups targets animal activists. The act has been criticised for its vagueness and intent to classify forms of protests as terrorism (Best, 2007).

While from an animal advocate's point of view, the legislative changes can be questioned for their benefits to chickens, they encouraged new production systems above the legal minimum standards. High-calibre campaigns promoting the consumption of *better* chicken products were launched with the help of organisations such as CIWF and the Royal Society for the Prevention of Cruelty to Animals (RSPCA), as well as British celebrity chefs Jamie Oliver and Hugh Fearnley-Whittingstall (Bell & Hollows, 2011). In 2008, Oliver and Fearnley-Whittingstall started a joint campaign with CIWF against intensive chicken farming called "Chicken Out!". Oliver demonstrated how chickens are slaughtered on the Channel 4 programme "Jamie's Fowl Dinners". Fearnley-Whittingstall built his own chicken farm and launched a documentary series "Hugh's Chicken Run" to raise consumer awareness of intensive chicken farming (Bell & Hollows, 2011). "Hugh's Chicken Run" aired on Channel 4 creating controversy and raising a discussion about farming methods. The celebrity chef also campaigned against Tesco, urging Britain's largest supermarket chain to improve the welfare of chickens farmed for meat. The ideological stance of Oliver and Fearnley-Whittingstall could be summarised as strongly condemning intensive chicken farming and strongly defending the consumption of chicken products from "higher welfare" farms.

Here, a clarification with regards to the terms "high welfare" and "higher welfare" is required. The terms are synonymous, with "higher welfare" being more popular. "Higher welfare" is used as an umbrella term for organic, free-range, and indoor farming above the legal requirements. It is associated with farmed animal welfare schemes developed by the RSPCA, the Soil Association and other institutions and retailers. For example, in 1994, the RSPCA developed its animal welfare standards for indoor and outdoor farms and launched the Freedom Food label (*The Guardian*, 10/7/1994 [G7]). In 2015, the scheme changed its name to RSPCA Assured (RSPCA Assured, 2015). The Soil Association certifies organic production ensuring free-range access, environmental enrichment, and organic diet for chickens (Soil Association, 2016). The role of retailers in shaping farmed animal welfare is also of significance in the UK. Retailers saw added value and a business opportunity in farmed animal welfare (Roe & Murdoch, 2006; Lazutkaite, 2014). During the past few decades, a growing tendency has been observed for UK retailers to develop their own farmed animal welfare schemes that go beyond the legal minimum and expand their range of "higher welfare" products (Kjaernes et al., 2007, p. 38; Lazutkaite, 2014).

1.3.3 Chicken and human health

While public health threats deserve a separate book, I shall briefly discuss a few prominent cases of chicken and human health problems as examples of global human-chicken entanglement. In 1988, the junior Health Minister Edwina

Currie infamously announced that the majority of British eggs were infected with *Salmonella*, sparking outrage from the industry (Doig, 1989). Although technically Currie was incorrect, the industry indeed had a *Salmonella* problem, which it was reluctant to admit (Cogan & Humphrey, 2003). Currie was forced to resign, but in the 1990s, a mass vaccination programme against *Salmonella* was initiated (Doig, 1989; Cogan & Humphrey, 2003). The epidemiologic investigation of a 12-year period from 2000 to 2011 concluded that the number of *Salmonella* outbreaks in the UK has markedly declined, but they still occur at regular intervals (Harker et al., 2014).[11]

Campylobacter is another group of bacteria that impact on chicken health and cause food poisoning for humans (Humphrey et al., 2014). Chickens living in a poor environment under stress are more susceptible to *Campylobacter* infections (Humphrey, 2006). In the UK, *Campylobacter* is one of the most common causes of food poisoning. Between February 2014 and February 2015 approximately 4,000 samples of fresh whole chilled chickens and packaging were collected from British supermarkets to test for *Campylobacter*, only 27% of the samples tested negative for the presence of the bacteria (Food Standards Agency, 2015). In 2016, *Campylobacter* was responsible for 58,987 cases of human infections in the UK (European Centre for Disease Prevention and Control, 2018, p. 2).

Since the highly pathogenic avian influenza (also called bird flu) virus emerged in China in 1996, researchers are assessing the risk of a pandemic human disease if the virus mutates and becomes transmissible from human to human by air (Centers for Disease and Prevention, 2014). In February 2006, the virus was detected in migratory birds in the UK. Above all, avian influenza is a serious animal welfare issue, not only because chickens get ill, but also because the outbreaks lead to mass killings of healthy as well as sick birds. Between 2004 and 2007, the disease, its management and prevention by slaughtering resulted in the deaths of 250 million birds (FAO, 2014).

Antibiotic resistance is another issue increasingly associated with animal farming, including chicken farming (Diarrassouba et al., 2007). A study published in *Frontiers in Veterinary Science* reviews data on 12 chicken pathogens:

> Poultry flocks are often raised under intensive conditions using large amounts of antimicrobials to prevent and to treat disease, as well as for growth promotion. Antimicrobial resistant poultry pathogens may result in treatment failure, leading to economic losses, but also be a source of resistant bacteria/genes (including zoonotic bacteria) that may represent a risk to human health. (Nhung et al., 2017, p. 1)

---

[11] The study looked not only at eggs but also other food sources of *Salmonella* poisoning.

On the 7th November 2017, a press release by the World Health Organisation (WHO, 2017) on new guidelines for the use of antimicrobials recommended that:

> farmers and the food industry stop using antibiotics routinely to promote growth and prevent disease in healthy animals. The new WHO recommendations aim to help preserve the effectiveness of antibiotics that are important for human medicine by reducing their unnecessary use in animals. In some countries, approximately 80% of total consumption of medically important antibiotics is in the animal sector, largely for growth promotion in healthy animals.

Nonetheless, the Director of the Department of Food Safety and Zoonoses at WHO, Dr Kazuaki Miyagishima, states that "The volume of antibiotics used in nonhuman animals is continuing to increase worldwide, driven by a growing demand for foods of animal origin, often produced through intensive animal husbandry" (WHO, 2017).

1.3.4 Environment

The material entanglement between chickens and humans manifests itself through the vast environmental impact of the chicken meat and egg industries. Chicken manure has been long known as an effective organic fertiliser (Perkins et al., 1964). However, since the chicken industry concentrated and intensified, disposal of manure has become problematic. Pollution of groundwater, surface water and soil are major problems associated with chicken manure management (Gerber et al., 2007). Since chicken manure contains considerable amounts of nutrients such as nitrogen and phosphorus, improper application of manure as a fertiliser can result in the eutrophication of receiving waters. In addition, manure may be contaminated with hormones, antibiotics, pathogenic microorganisms, and heavy metals, which can enter the water (Steinfeld et al., 2006). Pathogenic microorganisms make it a high risk to the environment (U.S. Environmental Protection Agency, 2005). Other environmental effects of the chicken industry include the destruction of ecosystems and the loss of biodiversity, which is linked to the growing production of feed crops.[12]

Despite the issues highlighted, continuously rising concerns over climate change favour the chicken meat and egg industries due to their overall lower impact on climate change compared with cow and pig farming (De Vries & de Boer, 2010). Therefore, in a world facing a climate crisis, overpopulation and resource scarcity, intensive chicken farming can be presented as a relatively "sustainable" option if animal welfare is not considered. For example, the BBC article "Can eating meat be eco-friendly?" suggests that:

---

[12] For more information on the environmental impact of the chicken industry see Gerber et al. (2007) and for the UK specifically Leinonen and Kyriazakis (2016).

> if you are worried about your carbon footprint you are much better off eating chicken than beef. And, perhaps uncomfortably for some, the most eco-friendly chickens (in terms of carbon emissions) may not be organic or free-range, but those that are raised intensively in energy efficient indoor farms. (Mosley, 2014)

The suggestion to replace "beef" with chicken flesh relies on the underlying assumption that one wants to continue eating large quantities of meat rather than reducing the consumption or choosing a plant-based diet. Similarly, the online news source for the food industry Food Navigator frames chicken meat as "an electric car — it is a better alternative, yet still very similar to what we are accustomed to" (Niamhn, 2015). Coming at the cost of billions of lives of sentient beings, such an "alternative" makes chickens even more thought-provoking subjects of inquiry.

2.
Theoretical background: discursive representation of animals

In this chapter, I shall briefly review the works on nonhuman animal representation that I have consulted for this project. The selection of works is rather eclectic, and the review is not limited to one species as resources on chickens are scarce. I will first introduce two notable moral philosophers Peter Singer and Tom Regan, who have significantly advanced current debates on the treatment of nonhuman animals. While Singer's arguments are far from universally accepted, his influence cannot be ignored; Singer and his ideas will also appear in *The Guardian* opinion pieces. In addition, I shall refer to relevant feminist works that analyse the intersections between sexism and animal oppression and deconstruct gendered discourses around animal farming. I then focus on the research that includes significant contributions to language and/or makes use of linguistic analysis. Of note, although many studies that can be (loosely) situated within human-animal studies (HAS) and CAS deploy the polysemous term "discourse", few analyse a large corpus of texts rather than a few selected texts and even fewer deploy CL tools (Cook & Sealey, 2018). In search of useful parallels, I discuss a few publications that analyse the discursive representations of nonhuman animals produced by the farming industry, news media and campaigners. The chapter ends with considerations of the knowledge gaps and addresses the shortcomings of the studies.

2.1 Species discrimination

> The exploitation of other animals and the justification of their mistreatment not only closely resemble human oppression but are inextricably tied to it. (Nibert, 2002, p. 3)

Singer and Regan have argued for the moral value and rights of nonhuman animals stressing sentience over reason as the moral divide (Singer, 1975; Regan, 2003). According to Singer's utilitarian perspective, human and nonhuman animal interests should be given equal consideration, but animals are not attributed absolute rights of freedom from suffering; in extreme cases, their suffering may be justified by "higher" ends. Regan (1983) concurs with Singer that animals are conscious and have interests such as not to suffer. He, however, adopts a deontological rights position where nonhuman and human animals are morally equal "subjects of a life" (Regan, 1983, p. 243).

Singer's book *Animal Liberation* (1975) played a key role in the modern animal rights movement and popularised the terminology of "speciesism", "oppression" and "liberation" with regards to the human-animal relationship. The term "speciesism", first coined by Richard Ryder in 1970, was promoted by Singer as discrimination based upon species membership analogous to racism and sexism. Although Singer (1975) has claimed rationality and dismissed sentimentality, French and Critical Theory scholar Judith Still (2019) highlights that Singer's version of the moral philosophy of utilitarianism is not produced independently of emotions; the argument from marginal cases illustrates Singer's appeal to emotion. Furthermore, the most notable criticism of Singer's and Regan's account of speciesism is that they "seem to avoid the opposition between man and animal that has been the classic position of philosophy for so many centuries" (Still, 2019, p. 56). Still (2019) highlights the importance of "continental philosophy", pointing out the "lack of encounter between Jacques Derrida's influential thinking on animals... and animal rights philosophers writing in English" (p. 49). In contrast to the English-language philosophers, Derrida has questioned "the fixing of the animal-human borderline by the philosophical tradition" and interrogated the "differences between animals, between humans, and between those designated as one or the other" (Still, 2019, p. 54).

Still (2015) also probes dualist ontology noting that "the thinker who perceives a gulf between humanity and animality often then also uses animal tropes to dehumanise other men and women" (p. 29). Similarly, the CAS scholar Richard Twine (2010) examines animalisation discourses highlighting that:

> categories of "nature" and animality have contributed a power of disgust to intra-human constructions of hierarchy and separation. Images of dirt, pollution and animality are a mainstay of racial and ethnic conflict... Projects of dehumanization have found great use for the "animal". (p. 399)

Some examples of dehumanizing animal metaphors used for the purpose of conflict and massacre of human groups are found in the Rwandan genocide and the Second World War; the Rwandan Hutus called Tutsis "cockroaches" (Bell-Fialkoff, 1996) and the American military and mass media referred to Japanese as "reptiles", "insects", "rats", "cockroaches", "vermin", and "baboons" (Steuter & Wills, 2008, p. 45). At this point, I must note the animalisation of Jewish people during the Holocaust as well as the problematic comparison of the Holocaust and the treatment of animals set out by a number of philosophers, writers and activists, including Derrida and the animal rights organisation People for the Ethical Treatment of Animals (PETA). Still (2015) notes that "Derrida is one of those who dares to make a comparison between the Holocaust and human behaviour towards animals, particularly in the context of the industrialisation of food production" (p. 26). Derrida refers to the Nobel Prize for literature winner Isaac Bashevis Singer, whose fictional "character Herman Gombiner, whose entire family have been killed by the Nazis and whose most affectionate and ethical relationship is with a mouse, muses that for animals all men are Nazis and life is an eternal Treblinka" (Still, 2015, p. 26). PETA, on the other hand, has used powerful Holocaust imagery in controversial campaigns on farmed animal transportation and slaughter (DeMello, 2012). Ingrid Newkirk, the president of PETA, has marshalled the Holocaust into the service of animal liberation declaring that "Six million Jews died in concentration camps, but six billion broiler chickens will die this year in slaughterhouses" (DeMello, 2012, p. 269).

As pointed out by the Jewish feminist and animal rights activist Roberta Kalechofsky (2003), the analogy can be critiqued for there are innumerable differences, e.g. the relationship between farmed animals and humans is different to the relationship between the Nazi state and Jewish people; animals are not hated nor discriminated against on grounds of religion. Nevertheless, the number of differences does not "erase the prominent similarities which give point to the comparison in the first place" (Sztybel, 2006, p. 126). Twine (2010) argues that if one responds to such comparisons with disgust, "one risks complicity with the very disgust mechanism practiced against Jewish people and partly facilitated by their animalization during Nazism. Disgust in both cases is parasitic on the assumption of human/animal hierarchy." Similarly, in her seminal book *The Dreaded Comparison: Human and Animal Slavery*, the animal rights activist Marjorie Spiegel (1988) draws parallels between the oppression of enslaved Africans and exploitation of nonhuman animals. Spiegel (1988) argues that enslaved humans and nonhuman animals are restrained, abused, separated from their kin, branded, translocated, and sold in auctions, and that both oppressions involve objectification and systemic exploitation.

A number of feminist scholars, such as Carol J. Adams (1990), Lynda Birke (1995), Karen Davis (1995), Joan Dunayer (1995), Susanne Kappeler (1995), Marti Kheel (1995) and Erika Cudworth (2008) have set out the link between speciesism and sexism arguing that one form of oppression parallels and reinforces another. In her book *The Sexual Politics of Meat: A Feminist-Vegetarian Critical Theory*, Adams (1990) analyses the social construction of women and nonhuman animals and suggests that both groups are positioned as objects rather than subjects in the patriarchal world. In the image-based volume *The Pornography of Meat*, Adams (2003) interrogates the ways the obsession with and objectification of female bodies in media, advertising and pornography correlates with the objectification of farmed animals as merely meat. Adams' (2003) analysis of pictures, including billboards, advertisement,

T-shirts, and menus, demonstrates that women are animalised in sexual exploitation, whereas female animals are feminised in discourses around farming and consumption. The use of the animal to dehumanise women impacts on the treatment of animals in a vicious circle.

With regards to chickens, Adams (2003) problematises the gendered advertisements of chicken products that state "Great Legs, Nice Breasts," "Fresh Young Chicken, extra lean – 7% body fat" or depict a chicken lifting her miniskirt to expose her delicious feminine legs. The boundary between women and chickens is further blurred by food outlets such as "Hooters Restaurants" where "Hooter's Girls" serve chicken wings while dressed in T-shirts saying "More than a mouthful" (Adams, 2003, p. 101). Such representations, according to Adams (2003), reveal how our culture is structured and who we believe to be "consumable". Whereas Adams (1990; 2003) does not focus on chickens specifically, building upon her argument it could be argued that the treatment and depictions of chickens is partly anti-female, therefore shared with women, and partly anti-animal, which arguably is also shared with women. Furthermore, speciesism and patriarchy are likened in the sense that both are perceived as "natural" hierarchies; the social domination of nonhuman animals and women is largely denied and explained by their "innate inferiority by nature".[1]

Whereas speciesism may not be a universally accepted concept, the pioneering philosophical approach has echoed within and outside academia. The sociologist David Nibert (2002) has redefined the term "speciesism" as an ideology emerging from social and economic institutions rather than individual practices and emphasised the economic nature of institutionalised oppression of nonhuman animals. Cudworth (2014), however, has suggested that the notion of speciesism may not be most suitable for a critical account of human-animal relationships; the concept of speciesism and the language of rights have their serious limitations; debates on speciesism are subjected to "drawing and re-drawing of species boundaries in deciding 'which' other animals count as ethical subjects" and fail to account for the diversity of animals and their unique ways of being (p. 25). Cudworth (2008; 2011) has coined the term "anthroparchy" to define and explain a social system of human domination that is co-constituted with other kinds of

[1] Historically, in Western discourses women were seen as having more direct affinity with the natural world and animality, whereas men were largely identified with culture and rationality (Plumwood, 1993, pp. 19–41). Anthropologist Sherry B. Ortner (1974) has claimed that the relationship between "culture" and "nature" is principally the one of control and that women's "pan-cultural second-class status could be accounted for, quite simply, by postulating that women are being identified or symbolically associated with nature, as opposed to men, who are identified with culture" (p. 73). It could, however, be argued that the second-class status is not entirely pan-cultural and that the categories of "nature" and "culture" are not universally accepted — Ortner does not account for non-Western cultures.

complex forms of domination such as patriarchy and capitalism. In anthroparchy, "the incredible diversity of non-human species are homogenized as 'animals', identified as part of 'nature' and dominated through formations of social organization which privilege the human" (Cudworth, 2011, p. 107).

Due to space limitations, it is not possible to include all influential thinking on human-animal relationships. Last but not least, the concept of "animal-industrial complex", first coined by Barbara Noske (1989), must be noted as it is an important organising frame of analysis in CAS. Twine (2012) has developed the notion of the animal-industrial complex (A-IC hereafter) as:

> a partly opaque and multiple set of networks and relationships between the corporate (agricultural) sector, governments, and public and private science. With economic, cultural, social and affective dimensions it encompasses an extensive range of practices, technologies, images, identities and markets (p. 23).

With my focus on chicken farming, the A-IC is a particularly useful frame to the critique of the newspapers' and campaigners' corpora as it helps illuminate the ways governments, science and corporate agribusiness together commodify nonhuman animal bodies.

2.2 Analysis of objectifying language

Adams' (1990) feminist-vegetarian critique and Dunayer's (1995; 2001) critique of speciesism in the English language deserve attention due to a significantly different approach compared with the major works of the late 20th century on the human-animal relationship. Both authors have examined the linguistic aspects in the objectification of animals. In her investigation of the language of animal farming, Adams (1990) highlights euphemisms for farmed animals such as "food producing units", "protein harvester" and "crops" that render them as inanimate objects (p. 58). Similarly, in her book *Animal Equality: Language and Liberation*, Dunayer (2001) demonstrates how ambiguous, illusory, and biased words perpetuate the oppression of nonhuman animals. Attention is also drawn to the terms such as "game", which suggests that the purpose of some animals is to be hunted (although it could be argued that historically this was a term of elevation), or the term "laboratory animals", which implies that the animals are inherently for laboratory use (whereas many "laboratory animals" could actually live outside laboratories). Furthermore, Dunayer (2001) develops linguistic guidelines on grammar, sentence structure and punctuation and an alternative thesaurus of farming, hunting and other animal-related terms. For example, Dunayer (2001) suggests that a "broiler chicken" should be called an "enslaved chicken", "captive chicken", "exploited chicken" or "chicken reared for slaughter", whereas "farm animals" should be called "enslaved nonhumans" or "food-industry captives" and the term "animal agriculture" should be replaced with "food-industry enslavement and slaughter" (pp. 196–197).

The downside of the proposed vocabulary is that it may appear quite odd, if not resembling a parody. The use of a single politically correct vocabulary may not be a viable solution to resist exploitative discourses and practices. It not only might be met with ridicule, but also by proposing only one possible way of speaking about and for nonhuman animals, the invention and development of a variety of alternatives would be made impossible. Moreover, both Adams' (1990) and Dunayer's (2001) works have flaws in their discussions on nonhuman animals and names of meat. They claim that cows were renamed as beef or pigs as pork to conceal the deaths of animals. The authors miss the fact that the terms have their origins in status and linguistic divisions introduced after the Norman Conquest of England in 1066 (Pope, 1994, p. 10). Following the conquest, the Norman aristocracy spoke and referred to meats in French, so the names of meats eaten by aristocracy were replaced with French ones (beef — *boeuf*, veal — *veau*, mutton — *mouton*, pork — *porc*), while the living farmed animals retained their Old English names (e.g. cattle or sheep). The oxtail, for instance, which at that time was considered poor quality meat, maintained its Saxon name (Goody, 1982, p. 136). With regards to chickens, it is also suggested that the word "capun" (*capon*) appeared in the country after the Conquest, reflecting "the preferences of the conquering aristocracy" (Burnley, 1992, p. 87).

Furthermore, Dunayer (2001) fails to explore languages other than English, in which the same word applies to both a nonhuman animal and their flesh or where the lexis for an animal product contains a direct reference to the animal.[2] To illustrate, the Spanish people eat "cerdo", which translates both as "pig" and "pork", or "la carne de cerdo" that would be an equivalent of "meat of a pig". The Germans eat "Schweinefleisch", which literally means "pigs' flesh". Nevertheless, while Dunayer (2001) can be criticised for focussing only on (American) English, imposing "verbal hygiene" and not taking historical aspects into consideration, she makes a strong point setting out speciesist language as the antithesis of animal equality.

Les Mitchell (2006; 2012; 2013) and Stibbe (2001; 2003; 2012a) are two notable scholars who have extensively contributed to the analysis of discourses around animal farming. They have demonstrated that the animal farming industry language shares multiple features with scientific writing such as dry recitation of statistics, technical terminology and distancing through the passive voice and the use of the third person. In *Animals Erased: Discourse, Ecology, and*

---

[2] Of note, Vietnamese-American scholar Hanh Nguyen (2019) has addressed the criticism about the animal rights movement being centred around writing in English and examined the ways south-east Asian languages objectify and marginalize nonhuman animals.

Reconnection with the Natural World, Stibbe (2012a) draws attention to the use of mass nouns (e.g. lamb) as a linguistic manoeuvre to distance us from animals, objectifying them and presenting them as replaceable representatives of a species. If animals are perceived as identical, their value is reduced; one animal can be easily replaced by another without any loss. I shall pause to note that chickens of the same commercial breed have been selected to look almost identical, which further reduces their individuality. While Stibbe (2012a) does not study chickens specifically, he finds that in industry magazines, live chickens are frequently referred to as dead ones, for example, when referring to "bruised carcasses" instead of bruised chickens or when the noun "damage" is used instead of "injury". Mitchell (2006; 2012; 2013) analyses transitivity patterns, the use of personal pronouns, euphemisms, and metonymy to provide insights into the social construction of farmed animals in industry discourse. Giving examples of the terms "weaners, broilers, commercial calves, slaughter lambs", Mitchell (2006, p. 54) emphasises the use of metonymy as a device to erase an animal's identity and agency. In the qualitative analysis of a popular farming magazine *Farmers Weekly,* Mitchell (2013) shows that farmed animals are objectified and constructed as raw materials, parts of the production process, things to be used for profit and products. In 22 articles analysed, 95 instances of instrumental representation of farmed animals are found; examples include "meat cattle", "beef calves", "beef animal", "beef types", "beef breeds" among others (Mitchell, 2013, p. 306). It is concluded that such terms contribute to moral disengagement and the belief that animals exist to be used by humans, so there is nothing morally wrong in their exploitation.

As noted by the sociolinguist Norman Fairclough (2015), a critique of discourse should be "a point of entry for a critique of the existing social order which provides sound reasons for acting to change it in certain ways" (p. 14). After Stibbe (2001; 2003) published several papers on the animal representation in industry discourse, the attention of the scientific community was drawn to the issue. In a paper published in *The Journal of Poultry Science,* animal scientists Candice C. Croney and Richard Reynnells (2008) responded with a call for transparency and accuracy in internal and external industry communication. Croney and Reynnells (2008) questioned whether the industry is deliberately using linguistic ploys, e.g. the term "stalls" for crates or the term "euthanasia" for the killing of piglets by slamming their heads against floors or walls (the practice also called "blunt trauma" in the industry) to obscure violent practices and make them appear more acceptable. They concluded that the industry needs to place under scrutiny the way it treats farmed animals, and attention to the sort of language it uses to describe the practice might encourage such scrutiny. While such feedback does not ensure change, it is an example of how CDA may enable a researcher to examine discourses critically and have an impact beyond their academic field.

2.3 Media representations

I shall start this section with the studies that analyse the representation of animal farming-related issues such as zoonotic diseases and climate change in print, broadcast, and internet media sources, but do not focus on animal ethics. Secondly, I will discuss seminal works that have explicitly grounded their argument within the realm of CAS. As CAS scholar Nick Taylor (2016) notes, "given the centrality of the media in framing discussions and nominating issues to be considered important, research addressing the various mechanisms used to support speciesism is important and, pleasingly, beginning to grow" (p. 47).

Linguist Brigitte Nerlich is a leading scholar in analysing media depictions of zoonotic diseases, namely foot and mouth disease (Nerlich, 2004; 2011), swine flu (Nerlich & Koteyko, 2012) and bird flu (Nerlich & Halliday, 2007; Nerlich et al., 2009; Hellsten & Nerlich, 2010; Nerlich, 2011). Nerlich (2004) analyses the language and policy surrounding the 2001 foot and mouth disease (FMD) in *The Guardian.* One of the key findings is that the journalists and policy actors cited in *The Guardian* conceptualise FMD using war and battle metaphors, e.g. "battle", "frontline", "two fronts", "fighting" and "wartime" (Nerlich, 2004, p. 18). Military metaphors are deployed to encourage support for the government's ruthless slaughter policy (Nerlich et al., 2002; Nerlich, 2004).[3] After the initial support for the "war" against FMD, the uncompromising military frame backfired when it became "too real" and materialised into the killings of millions of animals that news documented in war-like narratives and visuals of "burning pyres and animal carcasses" (Nerlich, 2004, p. 18). Whereas Nerlich (2004) does not focus on animal ethics, she notes that public resistance reframed the policy as "medieval, brutal and misguided" (p. 23). Importantly, Nerlich's work demonstrates that linguistic structures affect the perception and have practical implications.

Frames and metaphor scenarios have been demonstrated to be cognitively, emotionally, and politically important in the depictions of avian influenza and swine flu (Nerlich, 2011; Nerlich & Koteyko, 2012). The quantitative and qualitative analysis of the development of the avian influenza debate in medical articles, newspapers and online discussion groups between 1997 and 2006 indicates that in 2005, reporting turned into a "hype" in the UK, in the sense of being disproportionate in the number of articles and tone to the likely threat posed by the virus (Hellsten & Nerlich, 2010). Another study shows that in early 2005, scientists deployed the rhetoric of fear and warning that was "heated up" by journalists (Nerlich & Halliday, 2007). Importantly, the framing

[3] Of note, alternative policy could have been that of vaccination of animals or vaccination combined with slaughter.

of bird flu as a pandemic or, more precisely, a pandemic "in waiting" in newspapers is identified as a powerful tool in shaping public debates, as well as having practical implications such as increased funding for biomedical research (Nerlich & Halliday, 2007; Hellsten & Nerlich, 2010).

In contrast to the FMD coverage in 2001 and bird flu coverage in 2005, swine flu outbreaks in 2009 were framed in British print media as a "metaphorical pandemic disease of 'panic'" with a reference to "the cliché of 'crying wolf'" (Nerlich & Koteyko, 2012, p. 713). The news media engaged in meta-reporting and used an anti-hype rhetoric, which was further echoed in blogs (Nerlich & Koteyko, 2012). It is concluded that blaming the media for the hype is "a powerful storyline against which 'official' sources have to compete for public attention" (Nerlich & Koteyko, 2012, p. 713). While the processes that lead to a selection of a particular frame or metaphor remain speculative, a key insight from the discussed studies is that the deployed framings inform the understanding and the responses to an issue and translates into "real-life" scenarios with implications to nonhuman animals.

Apart from infectious diseases, the coverage of another key issue linked to animal farming, i.e. the climate crisis, has been extensively analysed.[4] Geographer Keith Lee and others (2015) have analysed the articles on climate change published by major US newspaper the *Los Angeles Times* between 1999 and 2010. Applying the Actor-network theory, Lee and colleagues argue that "actants include humans, nonhumans and objects that have agency in shaping story-networks by contributing to or having a stake in the events or circumstances" and demonstrate that cows are depicted as culpable agents for climate change in the newspaper (Lee et al., 2015, pp. 200-201). As if cows farmed themselves, their agency is boosted to shift the blame for greenhouse gas emissions from the industry onto the "flawed" animal bodies. The authors note that stories focussing on health do not blame animals and their biological features for human medical issues associated with eating meat, such as cardiovascular disease (Lee et al., 2015). In the *Los Angeles Times* climate-change articles, however, cows are responsible and conveniently require "production-oriented technological fixes rather than food system level reform", while their welfare is not reported to be relevant (Lee et al., 2015, p. 210).

In 1990, the patron of animal rights Singer famously critiqued the media for not educating the public sufficiently on the ethical issues surrounding animal farming. Singer (1990) lamented that "the average viewer knows more about the lives of cheetahs and sharks than he or she does about the lives of chickens or

[4] In ecolinguistics, media constructions of climate change have been extensively studied, with many studies blaming the media for giving disproportionate space to climate change deniers (Boykoff, 2013).

veal calves" (p. 216). More recently, the communication scholar Núria Almiron and sociologist Matthew Cole (2015) have observed that the "media's role in manufacturing human consent for the oppression and exploitation of nonhumans is a budding research topic" (p. 3). Some fruitful analyses have taken a qualitative, broadly Foucauldian approach to discourse analysis to critique the representation of nonhuman animals in a wide range of media, including newspapers (Freeman, 2009; Stewart & Cole, 2015; Khazaal & Almiron, 2016) and media aimed at children (Cole & Stewart, 2014). Cole and Stewart (2014) examine the role that the media plays in the cultural construction of human–animal relationships in childhood and demonstrate that heteronormative gender identities and speciesism intersect in children's films and magazines. The term "cutification" is coined to refer to a representational style targeting the caring sentiment of predominantly girl readers; "cutification" deploys the cute aesthetic appeal of an individual animal but obscures the systemic exploitation of other animals.

A particularly relevant CAS study is an analysis of premiere sources of American news in print and broadcast by the cultural and media scholar Carrie P. Freeman (2009). It is the first consistent analysis of representations of farmed animals in the news media. Although the study conflates different species of animals, from tuna to cows, and thus cannot offer a nuanced analysis, it serves a useful parallel for my analysis of British newspapers. Freeman (2009) asks to what extent news media representations of farmed animals reinforce speciesism or challenge the status quo and reveal openings for change. Discursive angles are identified in 106 print and broadcast media stories produced between 2000 and 2003 in the USA. The study concludes that farmed animals are largely constructed as bodies, not beings, and that American print and broadcast media objectify them, neutralise, or trivialise their deaths and overlook their interests and sentience.

In the British context, notable is the study by Stewart and Cole (2015) on the portrayals of urban foxes in British newspapers. Following the story of a fox that allegedly attacked nine-month-old twins, Lola and Isabella Koupparis in 2010, Stewart and Cole (2015) analyse 199 newspaper stories using both qualitative and quantitative methods. The perception of foxes as "vermin" or "killers" is fuelled by the media as foxes are increasingly depicted as "inappropriate" co-residents of urban environments. Natalie Khazaal and Núria Almiron (2016) further analyse media coverage of nonhuman animals in 60 articles from *The New York Times* (United States) and *El País* (Spain) published between 2011 and 2013. Using CDA, Khazaal and Almiron (2016) show that both newspapers are biased against farmed animals; *El País* is characterised by what the researchers call "the crude speciesism" and *The New York Times* is characterised by a camouflaged, more deceptive style, which portrays the animal farming industry with an ethical veneer. Although the study does not distinguish between different farmed animal species, it confirms Freeman's (2009) findings revealing the lack of coverage of the systemic violence against farmed animals and their commodification.

Taylor (2016) points to the proximity of the media and the corporate interests suggesting that "it is hardly surprising that we find support for the carnist status quo through its support of one of the most vertically integrated and fiscally powerful industries, the 'meat' industry" (p. 47). Freeman and biologists Marc Bekoff and Sarah Bexell (2011), however, discuss the representation of animals in the news media in relation to the Society for Professional Journalists' principle to give voice to the "voiceless" and argue that "journalists have an obligation to provide the perspective of nonhuman animals (NHA) in stories that affect them" (p. 2). Freeman and media scholar Debra Merskin (2016a) produce a concrete tool for improvement, notably detailed guidelines for media professionals reporting on nonhuman animals. Some of the key recommendations "to help editors and journalists craft cutting edge, important stories on animal-related issues in ways that meet journalistic criteria of accuracy, fairness, and completeness" are summarised as follows:

- Recognise that nonhuman animals have interests (such as interest in food, safety, and freedom from pain) and include them.
- Represent nonhuman animals as sentient individuals.
- Assign gender pronouns to animals when sex is known and avoid using industry terms. When sex is unknown use "he/she" or "they".
- Explore human-animal interactions while questioning biases and cultural prejudices against certain species.
- Balance industry and government sources with activist sources. Include perspectives of animal advocacy organisations covering the spectrum from more radical to moderate groups.
- Scrutinise animal exploitation in its many forms including legal practices and question the use of animals *per se* (Freeman & Merskin, 2016b).

My analysis of British newspapers is informed by Freeman's and Merskin's (2016a; 2016b) guidelines for journalism in the sense that the articulated tenets are desirable. Although newspapers are not obliged nor expected to take up an animal advocate's perspective, I shall analyse the corpora under the premise that chicken farming is a legitimate social issue and that the interests of groups, in this case of chickens and animal advocates, are worthy of reporting "based on the media's social responsibility obligations to provide all relevant viewpoints" (Freeman, 2009, p. 171).

2.4 Campaigners' rhetoric

In the book *Framing Farming: Communication Strategies for Animal Rights*, which is possibly the most comprehensive analysis of activist discourse, Freeman (2014) analyses the campaigns of five major animal rights organisations in the USA and interviews their leaders. The investigations into how campaigners construct nonhuman animals reveal their motivations, tactics, and belief systems. Drawing from the theories of strategic communication, Freeman (2014) identifies the dilemma between a pragmatic approach, which puts reform and human interests upfront, and an abolitionist approach, which places justice upfront. According to Freeman (2014), choosing the pragmatic approach results in the loss of critical rhetoric and jeopardises the long-term goals of the activists.

Dunayer (2015) analyses 191 editorials and letters written by representatives of American organisations advocating for animals published in American newspapers between 2011 and 2014. In these texts, Dunayer (2015) typically finds a combination of speciesist and nonspeciesist language. She criticises animal advocates for the use of "exploitative labels" such as "farm animals", "dairy calf" or "veal calf" and concludes that "overwhelmingly, representatives of US nonhuman-advocacy organisations failed to communicate the unequivocal anti-speciesism needed to significantly advance animal equality" (pp. 97–104). Arguably, Dunayer (2015) is overly pessimistic and imposes "verbal hygiene". Nonetheless, her findings reveal that most of the analysed texts revolve around animal cruelty and suffering and only two texts (1%) talk about justice.

Cultural geographer Harvey Neo (2015) analyses vegetarian advocacy of the Singaporean Vegetarian Society and interviews its members to investigate their motivations for adopting a vegetarian diet. The interviews reveal that a moral concern for nonhuman animals is the main motive. Yet publicly, when promoting a vegetarian diet, the advocates prioritise normative arguments; the core finding is that:

> notwithstanding their strong personal views about the critical importance of animals in influencing their decision to become vegetarians, all the activists acknowledged that to sell the vegetarianism message through the animal rights approach might not be fruitful. Instead, they have continually emphasised the health and environmental benefits of not consuming meat. This remains a somewhat perplexing contradiction. (Neo, 2015, p. 245)

In addition, intersectional studies have explored the tendency across a number of animal rights organisations to commercially exploit women's sexuality and the conceptual link between women and nature.[5] Scholars have argued that the

---

[5] The term "intersectionality" was probably first introduced by Kimberlé Crenshaw in 1989, when she addressed issues of Black women's employment and highlighted that both gender

exploitation of female stereotypes and bodies became one of the favoured animal rights movement tactics to gain attention from males and media, solicit donations and raise funds (Deckha, 2008; Gaarder, 2011; Glasser, 2011; Wrenn, 2013a). The sociologist Corey L. Wrenn (2013a) suggests that the professionalisation and commercialisation of organisations where advocacy is merged with capitalist interest result in growing sexism. The animal rights/welfare organisations mirror the dominant culture and "prostitute the female body for organisational gain" (Wrenn, 2013a, p. 141). The use of sexist language and imagery not only makes a supposedly animal-friendly discourse unfriendly to women, but also jeopardises the long-term viability of the movement itself (Luke, 2007; Deckha, 2008; Glasser, 2011; Wrenn 2013a). Sexism in animal rights campaigns leads to a situation in which feminism and the animal rights movement are at odds with one another; as sociologist Carol L. Glasser (2011) puts it, "when two oppressed groups argue over whose oppression matters more they reinforce each other's oppression and neglect to work together to fight oppression at its roots" (p. 62).

Studies on PETA conclude that PETA uses sexist imagery to promote animal rights and thereby reinforces both sexist and, counterintuitively, speciesist ideology (Deckha, 2008; Gaarder, 2011; Glasser, 2011; Wrenn, 2013a). Glasser (2011) in her analyses of PETA's advertisements concludes that they utilise images of sexualised, naked, inegalitarian women and perpetuate the misogynistic idea of women as sexual objects. One of the adverts to which Glasser (2011) draws attention promotes veganism. The advert features a photograph of a thin young woman who is naked and has her body sectioned to represent cuts of meat. The advert states that "all animals have the same parts. Have a heart. Go vegan". Glasser (2011) suggests that presenting a sexualised naked female body as meat is objectifying, normalising thinness, and denigrating. Similarly, Wrenn (2013a) criticises PETA's "I'd Rather Go Naked than Wear Fur" campaign of photographs in which sexualised naked women renounce fur. Feminist and CAS scholar Maneesha Deckha (2008) notes that unlike sexualised females, males in PETA campaigns are generally represented humorously, preserving their integrity and social power. The British conservation group Fish Love has also been criticised for its controversial campaign on marine life, which featured photographs of nude female celebrities holding fishes and other sea animals (Wrenn, 2013a).[6] The

---

and race intersect to shape the experiences of Black women (Crenshaw, 1989). Crenshaw (1989) argued for a multidimensional analysis that takes account of the intersections of various social, cultural, and biological categories. Since the concept of intersectionality was coined, it has become one of the major paradigms in women's studies (Yuval-Davis, 2006), whereas CAS (Twine, 2010; 2012) included species into the intersectional matrix to challenge animal oppression.

[6] Other animal rights organisations and companies promoting "cruelty-free" products have

campaign is problematic because sexualised female bodies are exploited to promote the idea of sustainable fishing. Furthermore, nude celebrities are photographed with nonhuman animals of endangered marine species removed from water, thus presumably dead.

To the best of my knowledge, there are currently no studies available on the discourses of CIWF and AA. My own investigation has revealed that in 2003, the London Underground refused to place a CIWF advertisement. The advert intended to draw attention to the suffering of intensively farmed chickens and featured an image of crowded female models dressed in underwear on the left, an image of crowded chickens on the right and the following text:

> Thousands of big-breasted birds packed together for your pleasure. The "birds" on the left either naturally well endowed, or have chosen to have their breasts enhanced. The birds on the right, however, have been selectively bred to have abnormally large, meaty breasts. (BBC, 2003)

The poster asks viewers to contact CIWF "to get your hands on better breasts" (BBC, 2003). One could clearly argue that women (young, thin, conforming to dominant beauty standards) are sexually objectified even if the advert aims at problematising selective breeding and excessively large chicken breasts. Since the advert was considered inappropriate by the London Underground, CIWF organised a "live" version of it, which involved female models and activists dressed as chickens travelling on tube in London. In a text reporting on the action, it is emphasised several times that the event was carried out by "supporters and models" (*Farm Animal Voice*, 2003 [FAV3]), making a distinction between the two groups and potentially using the latter group as attention-grabbing objects.

As will be explained in Chapter 5, no other texts or visuals in the CIWF and AA corpora are found to have sexist, racist or other discriminatory notions. Nevertheless, feminist perspectives must be stressed since gender stereotypes appear in the newspapers' corpora via feminisation of activists and blaming women for "wrong" shopping behaviour. Also, the association between eating flesh and masculinity has been long established in Western cultures and is visible in findings

---

also been accused of sexism. In 2012, LUSH Cosmetics, a bath and beauty product company targeting vegans, featured a performance where a woman in a bodysuit enacted an animal test subject and was tortured by a male "researcher" (Omond, 2012). The woman, a professional artist, endured 10 hours of violent performance in a store window, where she was dragged by a rope tied to her neck, force-fed, given injections and her hair was shaved off. The performance was heavily criticised by feminists (Vegan Feminista, 2013; Wrenn, 2013a; 2013b). While LUSH Cosmetics has defended themselves on the grounds that they were not actually hurting women but rather intended to draw attention to nonhuman animal testing for cosmetic products, their means of campaigning remain controversial.

from my own research. Another key insight from the studies discussed is that animal advocates negotiate between idealism and pragmatism in their advocacy messages. While different in their methodological approaches, the studies highlight that campaigners struggle with their rhetoric and (un)intentionally reproduce normative and unexamined assumptions, and this will be shown to be the case in the CIWF and AA corpora too.

2.5 Shortcomings

The heterogeneity in approaches and methodologies of the reviewed works highlights the shortage of data and comprehensive theories on discursive animal representation. One of the main disadvantages of most discussed studies that make use of linguistic analysis is that only specific cases or small corpora are analysed, and the study timeframes may be too short to observe any temporal change. Although statistical evidence derived from larger bodies of texts could provide stronger support for the study hypotheses, most of the reviewed studies eschew quantitative methods, while the studies that combine quantitative and qualitative methods, such as by Hellsten and Nerlich (2010), tend to leave animal subjectivities and ethics unremarked. Additionally, studies that generalise about nonhuman animals cannot offer a more nuanced analysis. Following the insights from previous research, notably Freeman's (2009; 2014) analysis of the American news media and campaigners' communication, I have chosen to provide an in-depth analysis by working with large bodies of texts over a period of 34 years, combining qualitative and quantitative methods and focussing on chickens under specific conditions (farmed for their flesh and eggs).

3.

Sources of data, analytical framework and methodology

In this chapter, I present the sources of data and explain the processes of data collection. I then discuss how I adopt and adapt CDA as a conceptual framework to analyse discursive framings of chicken farming in the British newspapers and campaigners' magazines. Criticisms of CDA are identified. Other relevant approaches, namely Positive Discourse Analysis (PDA), ecolinguistics and CL, are briefly discussed focussing on the aspects that are integrated to address the shortcomings associated with CDA. Finally, I explain in detail how I develop a specific methodology to suit my research questions and describe the process of analysis.

3.1 Newspapers: tabloid vs broadsheet journalism

The UK print media market could be segmented into broadsheets and tabloids. This segmentation is based on traditional newspaper format with broadsheets being larger.[1] The historical divide relates to more than just size; "tabloid" is associated with lighter content and shorter, crisper stories (Popović & Popović, 2014). Broadsheets are called "elite press", "serious press" and "quality papers" and are associated with a higher-minded approach to journalism (Carvalho, 2007). Traditionally, tabloids have targeted the lower middle classes and the working class, whereas broadsheets have targeted the educated and professional middle classes (Day et al., 2004). The inclusion of two broadsheets and two tabloids in my analysis aids the representation of a more diverse population of readership.

Despite their distinctive formats and the long-standing divide, there is much debate on what features exactly constitute tabloid and broadsheet content and style (Sparks, 2000). As helpfully described by sociologist Clive Seale and colleagues (2007) and media researcher Sofia Johansson (2007), tabloid journalism is characterised by:

---

[1] In January 2018, *The Guardian* switched to tabloid format. Since my study period is between 1982 and 2016, for the purpose of clarity I refer to *The Guardian* as a broadsheet.

- Priority given to "soft news", e.g. human interest stories, entertainment and scandal over "hard news", e.g. economic, social, political events.
- Sensational approach.
- Personalised mode of address and language mimicking conversation.
- Colloquial language.
- Liberal use of humour, puns, wordplays, and metaphors.
- Shorter stories (compared with broadsheets).

Media scholar Martin Conboy (2006) pinpoints that the language of tabloids "lies within the traditions of working-class entertainment and is thereby more connected to everyday life and tends to relegate the serious to a secondary place and foreground the carnival and the colloquial" (p. 212). I shall note that jokes and puns go hand in hand with the focus on national readership, since they may not be decipherable to foreign audiences. Broadsheet journalism, on the other hand, is characterised by:

- Priority towards "hard news" over "soft news".
- Serious and intellectual approach.
- Priority of the public over the private.
- Expert knowledge, authoritative and formal orientation towards source material.
- Elaborated language of argumentation and evidence.
- More complex sentence structures.
- Longer texts (Harrington, 2008).

These simplified descriptions of tabloid and broadsheet newspapers can be contested as they do not account for "increasingly blurred boundaries of journalism" (Harrington, 2008, p. 1). Media scholars have debated the recent phenomenon of "tabloidisation" of the news media.[2] The term "tabloidisation" is predominantly understood negatively as the news media turning to entertainment, sensationalism, consumer culture and the private realm if not simply "dumbing down" (Johansson, 2007, p. 7). Yet pejorative notions of tabloids and tabloidisation have been challenged by scholars suggesting that "soft news" can give a platform for otherwise suppressed perspectives and voices (Glynn, 2000, p. 105). Moreover, the lack of empirical evidence on tabloid coverage "has made it difficult to provide a reliable and valid conceptualisation of tabloidisation" (Uribe & Gunter, 2004, p. 388).

---

[2] For a full discussion see *Tabloid Tales: Global Debates over Media Standards* edited by C. Sparks and J. Tulloch (2000).

It has also been argued that tabloids have themselves undergone changes and that they have become more "tabloidised" (Uribe & Gunter, 2004; Johansson, 2007). Media and communication scholars Rodrigo Uribe and Barrie Gunter (2004) conclude: "If tabloid characteristics are changing over time, the very concept of tabloidisation may also need to be constantly revisited in order to determine whether or not it is describing the actual tendencies followed by popular journalism" (p. 400). Ultimately, Johansson (2007) points out that the term "tabloidisation" is driven by value-judgements and assumptions on what "good" and "bad" journalism entails rather than observations of historical changes in journalism (p. 35). In my study, data is collected electronically and using identical search terms that prevent pre-judgement and help neutralise bias against tabloid and broadsheet newspapers (data collection processes are described in Section *3.1.2*).

3.1.1 Guardian, Mirror, Telegraph and Mail

This book exemplifies the newspapers' role in shaping and policing discourses on chicken farming by investigating broadsheets *The Guardian* and *The Daily Telegraph* and tabloids *Daily Mirror* (including its Sunday edition *Sunday Mirror*) and *Daily Mail* (including its Sunday edition *Mail on Sunday*). The chosen sources are major mainstream dailies and can be regarded as representative British newspapers. They are particularly suitable for research purposes due to their political-cultural stances, high circulation figures and the demographic profiles of their readership that capture different segments of society (See Table 3.1).

The Guardian was founded in 1821 as *The Manchester Guardian* and is a centre-left/liberal paper, whereas *The Daily Telegraph* was founded in 1855 and is conservative. ABC figures for national newsprint media show that in December 2017, the average circulation per issue was 151,625 for *The Guardian* and 393,310 for *The Daily Telegraph*, respectively (ABC, 2017a; 2017b). When combined with digital audiences, the readerships are much higher; 9,636,000 adults monthly for *The Guardian* and to 9,339,000 adults for *The Daily Telegraph* (Table 3.1). Nearly four-fifths of *The Daily Telegraph* (79%) and *The Guardian* (78%) readers are of the upper-middle, middle, and lower middle class. *The Daily Telegraph* has the oldest print readers — 61 years old on average (The Media Briefing, 2017). *The Guardian's* readership is younger; one-third of readers are under the age of 35.

Table 3.1 Readership demographic data

Readership monthly	Guardian	Telegraph	Mirror	Mail
Print and PC	9,636,000	9,339,000	7,875,000	13,072,000
< 35 years old, %	34.2	28.5	30	24.2
≥ 35 years old, %	65.8	71.5	70	75.8
Female*, %	48	49	47	52.5
ABC1	7,555,000 (78%)	7,375,000 (79%)	4,317,000 (55%)	8,946,000 (68%)
C2DE	2,080,000 (22%)	1,964,000 (21%)	3,558,000 (45%)	4,126,000 (32%)
Print circulation daily	151,625	393,310	581,877	1,394,385

Source: www.newsworks.org.uk (data for 2017, updated 10/01/2018)

*Gender demographics data for 2014 via the Media Briefing: www.themediabriefing.com

The *Daily Mirror* is a daily tabloid founded in 1903, which in the 1930s shifted from being a conservative paper targeting middle-class women into a left-wing paper aimed at the working class (Bingham & Conboy, 2009, p. 640). Among the sources selected, the *Daily Mirror* has the greatest share of "skilled working class/working class/non-working" readers (Table 3.1). Interestingly, since the 1950s, the *Daily Mirror* has exploited the claim that Britain is a nation of animal lovers and in 1957, it established the National Pet Club (Molloy, 2011). In her account of the *Daily Mirror's* position as the newspaper for the nation of animal lovers, media scholar Claire Molloy (2011) explains that the tabloid utilised and fostered such a collective identity to create "a relationship between the *Daily Mirror* and its readership, establish a regular advertising space that could capitalise on the commercialisation of the pet market and, at the same time, give the paper an identity that differentiated from its competition" (p. 38).

Founded in 1896, the *Daily Mail* is traditionally conservative in its politics (Conboy, 2010, p. 115). The tabloid caters for a readership which is just over half (52%) female, older and lies somewhere in between tabloids and broadsheets, thus the *Daily Mail* could be considered to be "middle market" (Table 3.1). In November 2016, it had the largest print/digital readership in the UK (The Publishers Audience Measurement Company, 2018). ABC (2017c; 2017d) figures for national newsprint media show that in December 2017, the average circulation per issue was 1,394,385 for the *Daily Mail* compared with 581,877 for the *Daily Mirror.*

3.1.2 Data collection and management

The timeframe for *The Guardian, The Daily Telegraph, Daily Mail* and *Mail on Sunday* and *Daily Mirror* and *Sunday Mirror* was set between 1st January 1982 and 31st December 2016 (34 calendar years). The *Sunday Mirror* and *Mail on Sunday* were included to increase otherwise small tabloid corpora and because of the practicality associated with the electronic databases that do not separate between the weekday and Sunday editions. *The Observer* and *The Sunday Telegraph* were not included since the corpora from the weekday editions were of sufficient size and because the Sunday editions are digitised separately. Data were collected from the LexisNexis, Proquest, Telegraph Historical Archive, Daily Mail Historical Archive and UKPressOnline. The search terms were "chicken" OR "chickens" AND "farm" OR "farming" for all the digital databases. While identical search terms were used for each newspaper, different search engines and algorithms may have affected the search results.

Online archives had a major advantage of making the process of data collection quicker compared to manual collection. Nonetheless, several drawbacks must be noted. First, among the results were a portion of texts in which chicken farming and chickens were mentioned only tangentially, duplicates and irrelevant items such as texts on hen parties. Eliminating duplicates and text items that were far removed from the discussion of chicken farming or chickens as farmed animals allowed me to concentrate on the debates surrounding chicken farming and was done cautiously in an attempt to provide an extensive examination of the newspapers' discourse. However, it kept the corpora from being a true census. The second drawback is that online archives provide metadata for texts (the section, by-line, word count, keywords, etc.) which had to be removed manually to keep the total word count true. Data downloaded from the LexisNexis database were saved as Microsoft Word documents and converted to *txt files for further analysis with the AntConc (3.4.4w) software. Data were provided as scans by the Daily Mail Historical Archive, the Telegraph Historical Archive, the ProQuest and the UKPressOnline. The scanned texts had to be typed up manually or processed using the optical recognition software Readiris and manually edited to convert them into searchable documents and later into plain *txt files.[3]

Quotes may not retain their original formatting features, e.g. new paragraph, and page numbers are not provided by the databases. At the end of each quote, in addition to the title of the newspaper and the publication date, a unique code for the item is provided in square brackets, e.g. "(*The Guardian*, 21/2/2006 [G20])". The code helps to find detailed information on the cited text such as the author and headline in Appendix F. Of note, listing *all* items (1186 texts) would not be feasible due to space limitations, therefore only texts *quoted* in this book are listed in Appendix F. Apart from the references, due to space considerations I shall henceforth use shortened titles to refer to the newspapers' corpora: *Guardian* for

[3] The collection and preparation of corpora for analysis with CL tools proved to be more laborious than anticipated. In future studies, these issues are likely to be resolved as the newspapers' data are currently being digitised. The British Newspaper Archive states that "up to 40 million newspaper pages from the British Library's vast collection" will be digitised "over the next 10 years" (British Newspaper Archive, 2019).

The Guardian, Telegraph for *The Daily Telegraph, Mirror* for both the *Daily Mirror* and *Sunday Mirror,* and *Mail* for the *Daily Mail* and *Mail on Sunday.*

3.2 Campaigners

3.2.1 Compassion in World Farming

CIWF is a UK-based charity focusing specifically on the welfare of farmed animals. The CIWF Master Brand Toolkit states that CIWF is "not a vegetarian organisation and... see[s] higher animal welfare as central to better food" (CIWF, 2015a, p. 5). The core mission of CIWF is "to end factory farming and advance the wellbeing of farm animals worldwide through advocacy, campaigning and engagement" (CIWF, 2015a, p. 5). These statements highlight that the charity endorses a liberal tradition based on welfare reform, where chicken farming is acceptable given welfare is taken into account.

CIWF is chosen primarily due to its visibility in the British media, which has also been observed in my analyses of the *Guardian, Mirror, Telegraph* and *Mail.* Altogether, CIWF is referenced in 111 articles, whereas AA figures in 15 articles spread across the four newspapers. The second reason to choose CIWF is its influence in the process of policymaking. CIWF has more than 50 years of experience in campaigning for the welfare of chickens, which makes the charity particularly relevant. The charity was founded in 1967 by farmers Peter and Anna Roberts and, interestingly, traces its origins to chickens:

> Until 1967 Peter Roberts was a Hampshire dairy farmer who kept free-range hens. One day when Peter was explaining the mass production techniques for broiler chickens being newly imported from America, Anna remarked "well, don't the chickens have any rights?" Soon afterwards, the farm was sold and Compassion in World Farming was born. Peter's first campaign centred on the battery cage for laying hens. (*Agscene,* 1999 [AG12])

Currently, CIWF works internationally, operating in China, Czechia, Belgium, France, Italy, the Netherlands, Poland, Spain, Sweden, the USA, and the UK. One of the most prominent CIWF campaigns on chicken welfare involved a mascot, Rosa, who visited 21 EU countries demanding clear labelling on chicken meat products in 2014. According to the CIWF Annual Review 2014/15 (CIWF, 2015b), the campaign reached 100 million people. Another campaign on chickens in 2014 resulted in a documentary film about Craig Watts, a contracted chicken farmer in the USA, who blew the whistle on his employer exposing the poor conditions for chickens raised for meat in intensive farms (CIWF, 2014a). Other prominent national and European level campaigns between the 1980s and 2010s are presented in Tables 3.2 and 3.3.

Table 3.2 Timeline: Campaigning for the welfare of hens farmed for eggs

1980s	"Welcome to the battery" advertisement	The Directive 88/116/EEC laid down rules for hen keeping. The requirements were to provide hens with at least 450 cm2 of cage floor area, which is less than an A4 page. The advert "Welcome to the battery" was launched to expose the cruelty of battery cages. It was banned from cinemas creating a controversy and gaining media coverage.
1990s	Hetty the Hen	CIWF introduced a mascot, "Hetty" the hen, who travelled around Europe lobbying companies, the European Parliament and Agriculture Ministers with regards to the ban of battery cages.
1999	Phasing out battery cages in the EU	The CIWF campaigned internationally until the European Commission announced that battery cages would be illegal from 1st January, 2012.
2011	Supporting the ban of battery cages	CIWF campaigned to ensure that the battery cage ban was not postponed.
2012	Ensuring compliance with the law	CIWF campaigned for compliance with the battery cage ban. On February 13, 2012, Defra announced that the UK was battery cage-free.

Source: *Farm Animal Voice* (2012 [FAV24])

Table 3.3 Timeline: Campaigning for the welfare of chickens farmed for meat

1980s	The Joint Broiler Campaign	A joint campaign to alert consumers of *Salmonella* and *Campylobacter* threats was launched by CIWF, Chickens' Lib, AA and Friends of the Earth.
1990s	A Bill for protection of broilers introduced in the Commons	In 1998, MP Bill Etherington introduced a Bill, which although did not become law for almost 10 years, had increased Parliamentary awareness.
2000s	Campaigns for the Broiler Directive	As there were no laws to protect chickens raised for meat, CIWF campaigned for new legislation. In 2007, the Broiler Directive was approved by the European Parliament.
2003	CIWF goes to court	CIWF took the UK Government to court to stop the breeding of chickens for meat. The case was based on an EU Directive, which prohibits the breeding of animals that has adverse impact on their health.
2008	Campaign with Hugh Fearnley-Whittingstall	Fearnley-Whittingstall launched a documentary series to raise consumer awareness of intensive farming and to encourage the consumption of meat from free-range chickens.
2014	Rosa the broiler chicken	The mascot Rosa travelled 39 days to campaign for clear labelling of chicken meat products.

Source: *Farm Animal Voice* (2012 [FAV24])

3.2.2 Animal Aid

AA is selected since it is the oldest and the largest animal rights organisation in the UK (Animal Aid, 2016a).[4] It was founded in 1977 in Tonbridge by the primary school teacher and anti-vivisection activist Jean Pink. As AA grew, her successor Mark Gold expanded its scope; the organisation widened its agenda to include hunting, animal farming and other forms of nonhuman animal exploitation (Animal Aid, 2016b). AA is not registered as a charity, but as an NGO, and campaigns on the national level. According to AA, they did not apply for charitable status "to ensure that our campaigns are unconstrained by restrictive charity law and so that we do not feel the need to self-censor" (*Outrage*, 2011 [OU18]). The NGO also carries out educational work in schools throughout the UK and undercover investigations such as on the conditions in intensive and free-range chicken farms. In 2015, they delivered 180 school talks (AA campaigner Ben Martin, personal communication, 2016). In 2016, the NGO employed 16 people and had approximately 20,000 supporters and 37,000 subscribers to their E-Activist list (Deputy Director Mary Shephard, personal communication, 2016). In their webpage, the core objectives of AA are formulated as follows: "We campaign peacefully against all forms of animal abuse and promote cruelty-free-living" (Animal Aid, 2016a).

Since AA proclaims itself to be against "all forms of animal abuse" (Animal Aid, 2016a), it would be assumed to hold a firm position against all types of chicken farming. In contrast to CIWF, AA should construct chicken farming as profoundly unjust and chickens as sentient beings entitled to the possession of their own lives. Despite having different rationales and ultimate goals, CIWF and AA share common interests as they raise the status of nonhuman life and fight the same opponents, i.e. the industry of intensive farming. In the 1980s, AA joined efforts with CIWF for the "Don't Eat a Battery Egg Week" campaign to lobby the government to improve the welfare of hens farmed for eggs. The following extract illustrates how AA urges readers to get involved in the anti-battery cage campaign by CIWF:

> This year the European Directive which covers the battery cage system comes up for review and Compassion in World Farming (CIWF) are putting renewed effort into their campaign to get rid of this cruel practice. As part of the campaign, CIWF have organised a mass lobby of Westminster Parliament on Wednesday 8th July. They need the support of everyone who can attend that day, in order to convince British MPs that the battery cage should be outlawed. (*Outrage*, 1992 [OU7])

[4] The Royal Society for the Prevention of Cruelty to Animals was initially considered, but not chosen due to its welfare rather than animal rights stance.

AA's support for CIWF demonstrates common ground that the campaigners share; to achieve their goals both organisations need to generate mass support and motivate individuals, businesses and institutions into action and change. Thus, the auxiliary motive to include their corpora to the analysis is an expectation to identify clusters of linguistic features and frames that inspire and encourage us to acknowledge chicken sentience and care about them.

3.2.3 Data collection and management

The CIWF flagship magazine was first published in 1979 under the title *Agscene*. In 2001, it changed its name to *Farm Animal Voice*. The magazine was published quarterly until 2011, thereafter three times a year. The data from the magazines *Agscene* and *Farm Animal Voice* were first collected during a visit to the CIWF headquarters in Godalming, Surrey, in December 2014. Since some issues were missing from the archive, in July 2016, I visited the British Library to search for the missing issues and extend the corpus. While collecting every single text on chickens within the period was unachievable, the sample collected is representative as nearly all issues from 1982 onwards were obtained. Altogether I collected 517 texts and 595 images for the period between January 1982 and July 2016. Excluded were nine texts that mentioned chickens or chicken farming peripherally; these texts mentioned chickens among other farmed animals but did not focus on any aspect of chicken farming. The final sample comprised 508 texts.

AA first issued *Animal Aid News* in 1978. The 7th issue came out under the new title of *Outrage* in March 1980. The magazine is sent out to supporters quarterly. The data were collected during a visit to the AA headquarters in Tonbridge, Kent, in July 2016. The special edition *The Uncounted Dead: Farming's Unofficial Victims* (henceforth *The Uncounted Dead*), which was published in 2014, was added to the corpus. Excluded were two images due to poor quality as it was unclear whether they represented chickens or another bird species. The final sample included 60 texts and 76 images published between January 1982 and July 2016.

Data from the campaigners' magazines were scanned and saved as PDF files. The texts were typed up or converted into searchable PDFs using Readiris and into *txt files using AntFileConverter (2016), a free tool that allows batch conversion developed by the applied linguist Laurence Anthony. Extracts and quotes from the campaigners' magazines may not retain their original formatting features, e.g. new paragraph. At the end of each extract, I provide the title of the magazine and publication year. Each text is assigned a unique code in square brackets, e.g. "(*Farm Animal Voice*, 2004 [FAV5])". In Appendix G, the code helps to find detailed information on the campaigners' texts quoted (the headline, title, year, issue, and page). Of note, listing *all* items (508 texts) would not be feasible due to space limitations, therefore only texts *quoted* in this book are listed in Appendix G.

3.3 Critical Discourse Analysis

> It is through language we are able to construct our reality. This is not to argue that an external, independent reality does not exist but rather that our ideas about this reality are socially constructed. (Mitchell, 2012, p. 492)

CDA is informed by a social constructionist approach to meaning-making, particularly, the work of the social theorist Michel Foucault on discourse analysis (Hidalgo Tenorio, 2011). Depending on the discipline, the influence on CDA can be traced back to the Frankfurt School, as well as sociolinguists Norman Fairclough, Ruth Wodak and Teun van Dijk (van Dijk, 1993). Within CDA, power is largely perceived in a Foucauldian sense as a systemic and constitutive feature of society. Power relations can be maintained not only through coercion but "through the recurrence of ordinary, familiar ways of behaving, which take these relations and power differences for granted" (Fairclough, 2001, p. 2).

The concept of discourse is used in a variety of ways by different scholars, such as social theorists (Foucault, 1972) and linguists (Stubbs, 1983; van Dijk, 1993). In this book, the term "discourse" is used in two ways. First, "discourse" refers to different types of language used in different sorts of social situation, such as farming industry discourse. The second meaning of "discourse" is more important to my study; in the Foucauldian sense, discourse is a social practice of producing meaning and power/knowledge (Foucault, 1972). For Foucault (1972), discourses are "practices that systematically form the objects of which they speak" (p. 54). In this way, discourses cannot be neutral; they are ideological and contribute to establishing, perpetuating as well as challenging relations of power (Mitchell, 2012).

CDA is a highly eclectic and broad approach, which does not limit itself to a specific methodology (Wodak & Meyer, 2009). Definitions of CDA are therefore manifold; I adhere to the definition of CDA developed by sociolinguists Wodak and Meyer (2009):

> CDA can be defined as being fundamentally interested in analysing opaque as well as transparent structural relationships of dominance, discrimination, power and control as manifested in language. In other words, CDA aims to investigate critically social inequality as it is expressed, constituted, legitimized, and so on, by language use (or in discourse). (p. 10)

The main principles and assumptions defining CDA are helpfully summarised by Fairclough and Wodak (1997):

- CDA addresses social problems.
- Power relations are discursive.
- Discourse constitutes society and culture.
- Discourse does ideological work.
- Discourse is historical.
- The link between text and society is mediated.
- Discourse analysis is interpretative and explanatory.
- Discourse is a form of social action (pp. 271–280).

Traditionally, CDA, which has variously been taken as a paradigm and analytical technique, has investigated how discourse maintains social domination of one group of people over another and how dominated groups can discursively resist their exploitation (Fairclough & Wodak, 1997; Wodak & Meyer, 2009; Hildago Tenorio, 2011). CDA, albeit a critical approach concerned with oppression and exploitation, has largely ignored nonhuman animals (Stibbe, 2012b; 2014), and until recently, animal farming, which is an excellent example of a practice naturalised in ideology and discourse to the point where it is rarely questioned, has been virtually overlooked by CDA.

One of the most important critical projects of recent years has been CAS, a transdisciplinary field characterised by methodological diversity, including critical ethnography, interviewing and CDA. CAS scholars have extended the scope of cultural studies, "which focuses on the analysis of everyday life, by examining routine human–animal practices" (Deckha, 2011, p. 213), although Taylor and Twine (2014) pinpoint that:

> Any contextualisation of CAS must confront the fact that, in an intellectual sense, it existed before the term was coined, and that it has since become an umbrella term for bringing together scholars who do critical research on human–animal relations. (p. 4)

The analyses of the role of language in the manufacturing of consent for nonhuman animal exploitation such as by Stibbe (2003; 2012a) and Khazaal and Almiron (2016) illustrate the effective application of CDA in CAS. In the words of Almiron and colleagues (2018), "By widening the focus to include human oppression of other animals, a whole new magnitude, depth and complexity of the entanglements of human violence, and of the role of media and communication in it, are revealed to us" (p. 374).

In my study, CDA has been selected as the most appropriate analytical framework due to several reasons. First, CDA is attentive to structural forces and oppression and is characterised by its commitment to social justice, which in this case is extended to farmed animals, namely chickens. The examination of ideology and the emancipatory purposes of CDA fit the issue of chicken farming even though chickens do not have the capacity to speak for themselves in the same way as humans do. While power does not necessarily stem from language, language can perpetuate, challenge, or subvert it, make it transparent and change its dynamics (Wodak & Meyer, 2009). Second, CDA pays attention to the historical, political, and socio-economic context. When interpreting texts about chicken farming, this means taking into consideration factors such as the political economy, social, market and legislative changes and events such as zoonotic disease outbreaks.

To develop a specific methodology best suited for my research questions, it is necessary to further consider the criticisms of CDA. Most work in CDA "is about negative evaluation of discourses which run counter to the analyst's beliefs and values" (Stibbe, 2015, p. 124). CDA tends to critique oppressive discourses, rather than analyse discourses that "do well", rarely focussing on counter-discourses or providing suggestions of what is desirable. However, if the issues arising in and from chicken farming are to be addressed, it is not enough to criticise. Identifying transformative narratives and frames is needed to produce discourses that could become sites of resistance. Given that this book focusses on commercially farmed chickens, finding alternative language has proved to be a difficult task, even within the campaigners' corpora. Nevertheless, liberating perspectives and frames are sought in the sense that identifying "bad examples" should help raise consciousness and move towards a better practice in the hope of shaking the food status of chickens.

Searching for narratives, frames and lexical clusters that offer openings for change is defined by some researchers as PDA. Linguists Jim Martin and David Rose (2003) coined the term PDA for studies that acknowledge positive, emancipatory discourses and are oriented towards constructive social action. Essentially, PDA does not replace CDA, but instead extends "the focus of CDA beyond texts which are implicated in oppression, exploitation and the abusive power relationships" (Stibbe, 2018, p. 168). PDA (without necessarily using this term) has been applied in the field of ecolinguistics in the search for a "correct" lexis. Since the early 1970s, two approaches have been developed under the single name *ecological linguistics*, or *ecolinguistics* (Steffensen & Fill, 2014). I shall refer to the tradition that was developed predominantly by the linguist Peter Mühlhäusler (2003). Mühlhäusler encouraged ecologically concerned linguists to approach linguistic practices in the context of an ecological crisis (Steffensen & Fill, 2014). This paradigm of linguistic research draws upon CDA, examines the role of language in the present ecological situation and seeks a broader understanding of the relations between discourse, power, and the nonhuman world. Whereas ecolinguistic studies vary in form, Stibbe (2015) identifies five general characteristics of the ecolinguistic approach to discourse analysis. These features closely resemble those of CDA, but add the ecological focus, the search for *alternative* language and the applicable research aim:

1. Discourses which have a considerable impact on ecosystems are analysed.
2. The analysis of discourses demonstrates how clusters of linguistic features construct worldviews.
3. Worldviews and discourses are judged against the explicit or implicit ecological philosophy of a researcher.
4. Ecologically destructive discourses are exposed, and alternative discourses are sought out and promoted.
5. The study has an applicable goal through raising awareness, informing policy or has other practical applications (Stibbe, 2015, pp. 118–119).

Ecolinguistics promotes language awareness in the context of ecology just as other CDA researchers raise awareness regarding social inequalities such as sexist or xenophobic bias. Nonetheless, with a few exceptions such as Stibbe (2003; 2012a) or Mitchell (2006), most ecolinguists and critical discourse analysts do not focus on farmed animals, even less on chickens. Given that both environmental issues and farmed animal exploitation are consequences of the human supremacy ideology and that the former are structurally tied to the latter, I argue that it is short-sighted to neglect the issue of farmed animals. I borrow from more-than-human geographies (MTHG) the focus on *entanglement* and therefore address chicken farming not as a singular issue, but as a relational phenomenon where chickens and humans are inextricably entangled with one another. There is no space to do full justice to MTHG, but the approach must be noted as it has some serious implications for the ways we think about nonhuman animals. According to the geographer Beth Greenhough (2014), humans are not treated independently from nonhuman entities, hence "neither should they be represented politically as autonomous of the world around them" (p. 104). In a world where boundaries between humans and nonhumans are progressively blurred, nonhuman entities "are subject to and productive of political agency and to whom therefore politics should be rendered accountable" (Greenhough, 2014, p. 97).

As such, MTHG may call for a critical engagement with speciesism, an abandonment of exceptionally human rights and, simultaneously, an expansion of political and ethical communities to what the philosopher and anthropologist Bruno Latour (1993) calls a "parliament of things". Nonetheless, the idea of more-than-human entanglement and human-nonhuman assemblages does not invariably lead to animal-centred ethics. Entanglement might as well justify the rearrangement of the nonhuman world for human advantage. MTHG have been critiqued for thinking without ethical and political nuance, ignoring structural forces and the relationship between space and power (Panelli, 2010). Thus, for my study purposes, CDA is more helpful in revealing relationships of exploitation.

The final criticism to be addressed is that typically only a small number of texts are analysed in CDA (McEnery & Hardie, 2011), for, as discourse analyst Ruth Breeze (2014) explains, CDA requires a detailed, contextualised interpretation and illumination of a small body of texts "with an emphasis on reading between the lines" (p. 242). Corpus linguists Tony McEnery and Andrew Hardie (2011) note that since the 1990s, researchers have attempted to incorporate CL into CDA. However, a multitude of studies that successfully deployed corpus tools largely ignored CDA theory and, *vice versa*, CDA studies made only very limited use of corpus tools, eschewing quantitative analyses and statistics (McEnery & Hardie, 2011). Whereas researchers have a clear argument to avoid working with large corpora since qualitative analysis is highly laborious, hypotheses that are derived from the in-depth analyses of small amounts of data can be tested over large bodies of text using corpus tools and make CDA less susceptible to accusations of "cherry picking". Corpus tools are particularly useful to identify lexical regularities and systematic patterns, which otherwise would be difficult to detect manually (Breeze, 2014).

It is agreed that CL is useful when checking intuitions and providing statistical quantitative information when texts are electronically available (Fairclough, 2015). Yet, the incorporation of CL into CDA should be conducted with caution since CL does not have a theory of language (Fairclough, 2015, pp. 19–26). CL is not capable of providing a broad qualitative interpretation and contextualisation of the findings and even less so a critique of social relations. Its lack of theoretical concepts creates a risk of reduction of research to a software-assisted exercise. Therefore, there is a concern that CL has "strictly limited usefulness for analysts as a tool but can lead to illusions and mistakes if it comes to be seen as more than that" (Fairclough, 2015, p. 23). In my study, I use CL as a tool, subservient to CDA, to provide statistical evidence, reveal patterns and address the issue of "cherry picking".

Since CDA is more of a theory and "a critical perspective" and is not limited to specific methodology (van Dijk, 2015, p. 466), I develop an original methodology most suitable for my study and capable of adding to the research on discursive representation of farmed animals. My analysis of the newspapers' and campaigners' corpora follows a three-step process described by cultural theorist Stuart Hall (1975):

1. A long preliminary soak in the text, which allows the analyst to focus on particular issues while preserving the "big picture".
2. A close reading of the chosen text and preliminary identification of discursive strategies and themes.
3. Interpretation of the findings within the larger framework of the study (p. 15).

3.3.2 Step 1 "Big picture"

After an initial reading of the collected texts, I gather descriptive data. Texts are categorised by year, topic, and other relevant factors, e.g. type of content (news/opinion). Descriptive statistics such as the size of the corpora, word count and distribution of texts over the period are produced. Prevailing narratives, discursive angles and major temporal changes are identified. CL tools are applied to the newspapers' and campaigners' corpora to produce exploratory frequency comparisons. As pinpointed by the corpus linguist Costas Gabrielatos (2018), "exploratory frequency comparisons are not motivated by particular hypotheses, and any research questions that motivate them are expected to be quite general (e.g. what topics are mentioned more frequently in the two corpora?)" (p. 227). Exploratory frequency comparisons are performed by deriving a list of key items, or *keywords*, i.e. unusually frequent words that reveal the "aboutness" of a corpus. The AntConc (3.4.4w) software identifies keywords by making wordlists for a corpus of interest ("study" corpus) and a "reference" corpus and comparing the frequencies of each lexical item. Keywords are ranked according to a keyness metric (Rayson, 2003, p. 51).

Whereas keyness metrics vary between CL studies, the log-likelihood (LL) significance test is commonly used and is available in the AntConc (3.4.4w) software. The LL significance test takes into account the sizes of two corpora (the total number of words) and the actual frequencies of the word (Baker, 2010, p. 63). The test produces a log-likelihood score. A score of 3.84 or more means that there is a 5% "chance that we would get the same or a larger frequency difference when, in reality, no such difference exists" (Gabrielatos, 2018, p. 6). A score of 6.63 or more means that there is a 1% chance; a score of 10.83 or more means a 0.1% chance and a score of 15.13 or more means a 0.01% chance. Importantly, Gabrielatos (2018) emphasises that "statistical significance does not reveal the size of a frequency difference, but, indirectly, the level of confidence we can have that the difference we have observed (however large or small) is dependable" (pp. 5–6). When the analysis is based on statistical significance only, discursively uninteresting words may be among the top items (Gabrielatos, 2018). High absolute frequency words, such as pronouns, articles, and prepositions as well as rare words, such as proper names, units, initials, and abbreviations may appear among top keywords, but may not reveal much about ideology.

It is necessary to provide a commentary on what a "study" and "reference" corpus are. Traditionally, the "reference" corpus is a large corpus representative of language use in general, such as the British National Corpus, or a comparable specialised corpus (Branum & Charteris-Black, 2015). However, as Gabrielatos (2018) pinpoints:

> In fact, the terms "study" and "reference" corpus might be misleading. There is nothing intrinsic in a corpus that renders it a good selection for a "study" or "reference" role. Any two corpora can be compared, as long as their characteristics (nature, content, time-period) help address the particular research questions or hypotheses. (p. 29)

In the exploratory keyword analyses, I use all four newspapers against one another and CIWF/AA against one another to identify salient differences between the sources. For example, I use the *Telegraph* corpus as a "study" corpus and compare it with the *Guardian, Mirror,* and *Mail* corpus as a "reference", and *vice versa.* The corpus of CIWF is compared against the corpus of AA, and *vice versa.* I provide a list of the top 100 keywords (which include ideologically uninteresting items) for each pair in Appendices A, B, C, D and E.

3.3.2 Step 2 Close reading examination

In the second stage, I take a closer look at the discursive construction of chickens and identify which aspects of chicken farming are problematised and/or foregrounded and what aspects are backgrounded. I investigate the ways in which different actors are constructed, who is allowed to speak with authority or whose voices are silenced, what culpable agents are identified and what solutions are suggested. Text extracts and quotes are introduced to allow a closer examination. The quotations can never be fully representative, but they expose prevailing narratives, frames, and angles. Atypical quotations may also be included to illustrate exceptional frames. On the linguistics level, the choice of words, e.g. adjectives, pronouns, and verbs, is examined. Grammatical structures such as active and passive voice and nominalisations, and punctuation such as scare quotes are considered.

In addition, the exploratory frequency comparisons described in Step 1 help generate hypotheses, thus leading to a targeted approach where I select items to examine (Gabrielatos, 2018). The targeted frequency comparisons help support (or reject) insights by identifying over/underuse or similarity of lexical items. For example, I analyse whether the adjective "painful" comes up equally frequently in the newspapers. The lexical items analysed can be words or lemmas (base forms). Using a lemma allows a search for word-forms. For example, the frequency comparisons for the lemma *suffer** includes "suffer", "suffered", "suffering", etc.; asterisk indicates a string of 0 or more characters excluding space or punctuation.

To identify over/underuse or similarity I establish keyness using an effect-size metric that reflects the size of a frequency difference (Gabrielatos, 2018). I use ratio, the simplest of the effect-size metrics, which compares the normalised frequencies in two corpora. Gabrielatos (2018) helpfully notes that the values of ratio are directional:

> A value of "1" indicates that the item has equal normalised frequency in the two corpora; higher/lower values indicate higher/lower NF [normalised frequencies] in C1 [corpus 1] — for example, a value of "4" indicates that the item is four times more frequent in C1 than C2 [corpus 2]. However, it must be noted that the values are directional; i.e. they depend on which corpus is used as the study corpus. To use the example above, if C1 is the study corpus, then the value is "4", whereas, if C2 is the study corpus, then the value will be "0.25". (p. 14)

Focussed frequency comparisons are presented in tables that provide absolute frequency (AF), normalised frequency (NF) per 10,000 words, the log-likelihood score (LL) and ratio. Over/under-use is indicated by "+" or "-". For the purpose of clarity, when relative underuse is identified and the ratio is lower than 1, I present the ratio from the perspective of the "reference" corpus in brackets, e.g. "0.8 (1.2)". If a word or lemma is not found in a corpus, a ratio is not provided as division by zero is disallowed; this is marked as "div" in the frequency analysis tables. Calculations of NFs, LLs and ratios are made using Paul Rayson's Excel spreadsheet (Rayson, 2009); the spreadsheet maintains 15 figures in its numbers for calculations. In the tables, however, the numbers are reported rounded to one decimal place.

Occasionally, I apply concordance analysis, "identifying short spans of text in which a target word or phrase occurs, and centering that 'node item' in a table of such short spans" (Cook & Ancarno, 2019). Concordances provide insights about the most prominent ideas related to the "node" and help investigate the semantic relationships between the "node" word and its collocates (co-appearing words). Gabrielatos and Baker (2008) emphasise the synergy between CDA and CL in concordance analysis:

> Concordance analysis is where corpus-based and CDA methodological approaches overlap. A concordance is a list of a given word or word cluster with its co-text on either side. Concordances can be sorted alphabetically on the left/right side of the word/cluster under investigation, and can thus facilitate the examination of different patterns or semantic/discourse prosodies. (p. 14)

3.3.3 Step 3 Interpretation

Critical theories, including CDA, aim at producing critical knowledge. In the words of Wodak and Meyer (2009), such theories "are aimed at producing 'enlightenment and emancipation' [and] seek not only to describe and explain, but also to root out a particular kind of delusion" (p. 7). My aim in this book is to raise awareness of the ways in which discourses shape our attitudes towards chicken farming and chickens. Rather than merely identifying discourse structures, I interpret and explain them as embedded in social and cultural context. Framings and representational choices are examined and critiqued from their ideological potential to normalise or problematise chicken farming. Attention is paid to how and what meanings are constructed, and what implications they might have on readers' minds and consequently on chickens' lives. Finally, I compare dominant ideas identified in the newspapers' and campaigners' corpora and situate my findings within a broader scholarship.

4.

Newspapers

4.1 Overview of the newspapers' corpora

A summary of the descriptive details of the *Guardian, Mirror, Telegraph* and *Mail* corpora is presented in Table 4.1. The *Guardian* corpus is the largest, immediately suggesting that the broadsheet dedicates the most space and interest to chicken farming. Table 4.1 shows that the *Guardian* corpus is 2.7 times larger in the number of articles and three times larger in total word count than the *Telegraph* corpus. The *Mirror* articles are on average shortest in length, which corresponds with the aforementioned characteristic of tabloid texts being shorter. This, however, does not apply to the *Mail* corpus, which is the second largest and the average length of texts is comparable to that of the broadsheets.

Table 4.1 The sizes of the newspapers' corpora

	Guardian	Mirror	Telegraph	Mail
Total number of items	434	254	159	339
News	230	189	80	256
Opinion/feature	178	54	76	71
Letters	26	11	3	12
Word count	345,505	79,927	115,255	248,339
Average length of an article	796 words	315 words	725 words	733 words

While newspapers consist of multiple sections such as news, editorial, opinion, feature, reviews, column and more, I treat the newspapers' corpora as consisting of two major spaces 1) "news" and 2) "opinion/feature" articles. Letters are distinguished to illustrate the engagement and feedback from readers. Although the blurred line and changes in journalism fall beyond the scope of this book, it is noteworthy that differentiating between "news" and "opinion" can be difficult (Esser & Umbricht, 2014). Clear labelling is not always provided; for example, articles can be labelled thematically, e.g. "environment", but such a caption does not inform the readers which type of article it is. Under "news", I place items that are labelled as news and/or are characterised by an apparently detached point of view and "emphasis on verifiable facts and attributed sources" (Esser & Umbricht, 2014, p. 230). In tabloid news, however, value judgements are more likely to be present in an explicit manner.

Under the category "opinion/feature" fall items other than news such as editorials, reviews, features, comments, and others. Opinion/feature items do not aim at simply reporting on an event or phenomenon, but rather discuss questions from a variety of standpoints. They tend to be longer, written in first person and overtly attitudinal. Unlike news, which are supposed to be written under the code of journalistic impartiality or factuality, opinion/feature articles can be intentionally controversial and express opinions polemically. Some articles, however, lie somewhere in between news and opinion as they mix information, analysis, and interpretation. These articles are not "straight" news reports, but rather analyses that cover local and global events, include facts, do not have a personal voice, but provide value judgement. In my study, these articles are placed under the "opinion/feature" category.

Recurrent topics are listed in Table 4.2. A "topic" here refers to a general subject area of an article. For example, 139 *Guardian* articles cover chicken farming with regards to public health issues. Where articles cover more than one topic, they are categorised under the dominant topic. For example, some articles discuss the impact of avian influenza on business and public health. If public health is emphasised and attributed more space than the business aspect, the text is categorised under the thematic domain "public health". If an article focusses on financial losses caused by the epidemic, it is placed under the topic of "business/economics". "Public health/food safety", "chicken welfare" and "business/economics" are the top three topics across the newspapers (Table 4.2, highlighted in grey).

Table 4.2 Newspaper articles by topic

Topic	Guardian	Mirror	Telegraph	Mail
Public health/food safety	139 (32%)	66 (26%)	22 (14%)	111 (33%)
Chicken welfare	124 (29%)	60 (24%)	35 (22%)	75 (22%)
Business, economics	29 (7%)	36 (14%)	32 (20%)	49 (14%)
Cultural and social issues	16 (4%)	14 (6%)	17 (11%)	33 (10%)
Organic/free-range farming	23 (5%)	9 (4%)	19 (12%)	23 (7%)
Backyard farming/chicken companions	23 (5%)	9 (4%)	19 (12%)	11 (3%)
Human interest/sensational stories	0 (0%)	43 (17%)	0 (0%)	17 (5%)
Ethical vegetarianism/veganism/direct action	31 (7%)	14 (6%)	6 (4%)	12 (4%)
Extensive debate over chicken farming	24 (6%)	0 (0%)	4 (3%)	1 (0%)
Environmental issues	16 (4%)	1 (0%)	1 (1%)	0 (0%)
Miscellaneous	9 (2%)	2 (1%)	4 (3%)	7 (2%)
Total	434	254	159	339

As we shall see later in the chapter, across the four newspapers emerge four consistent discursive themes. Chicken farming is perpetually normalised through (1) defining chickens as means of production or commodities; (2) ignoring their sentience; (3) failing to link chicken welfare with human welfare and environmental issues; (4) excluding sources that could provide an alternative view. Normalisation and objectification are most prevalent in "factual" and "straight" news reporting that embraces an apparently detached stance and adopts the scientific/industry vocabulary. When problematising chicken farming, two major discursive themes emerge across all sources, including the campaigners' corpora: (1) presenting chickens as victims, and (2) drawing upon self-centred concerns such as public health issues. The three less-common discursive themes are: (1) positively depicting chickens as individuals; (2) questioning the moral acceptability of killing and farming other animals; (3) providing a holistic critique of chicken farming that recognises the link between chicken, human and environmental health.

4.1.1 Temporal peaks

Figure 4.1 presents data distribution over time. All four newspapers react to the global spread of avian influenza in 2006 and 2007. As we shall see, bird flu news stories predominantly focus on the threat to humans. In 2008, there is a notable growth in the *Guardian*, *Mirror* and *Mail* coverage of chicken farming due to high-profile campaigns by the celebrity chefs Fearnley-Whittingstall and Oliver. Because of their involvement in chicken welfare campaigns, the chefs are cited and talked about in the newspapers. Moreover, Fearnley-Whittingstall authored several *Guardian* articles promoting free-range farming. His campaign and stance can be well-illustrated with the following extract where the chef presents free-range farming idealistically:

> the outdoor life is the best and fairest way to raise a chicken for meat. The birds live with the sun and the rain on their backs and grass under their feet, and they are fully able to express their natural behaviour. (*The Guardian*, 19/1/2008 [G26])

In the *Telegraph* corpus, there is no increase in the number of texts published in 2008, but six out of eight articles published during the year mention (positively or negatively) Oliver and/or Fearnley-Whittingstall in the context of their chicken welfare campaigns. Overall, there is a minor increase in the number of articles across the four newspapers, but fluctuations suggest that interest in chicken farming is sporadic rather than sustained over the period of 34 calendar years. Only in the *Guardian*, has the topic of chicken farming become increasingly prevalent during the last two years, i.e. 2015 and 2016, which relates to the newspaper's growing awareness of global intersections between chickens, humans, and the planet.

Figure 4.1 Newspaper data distribution over time

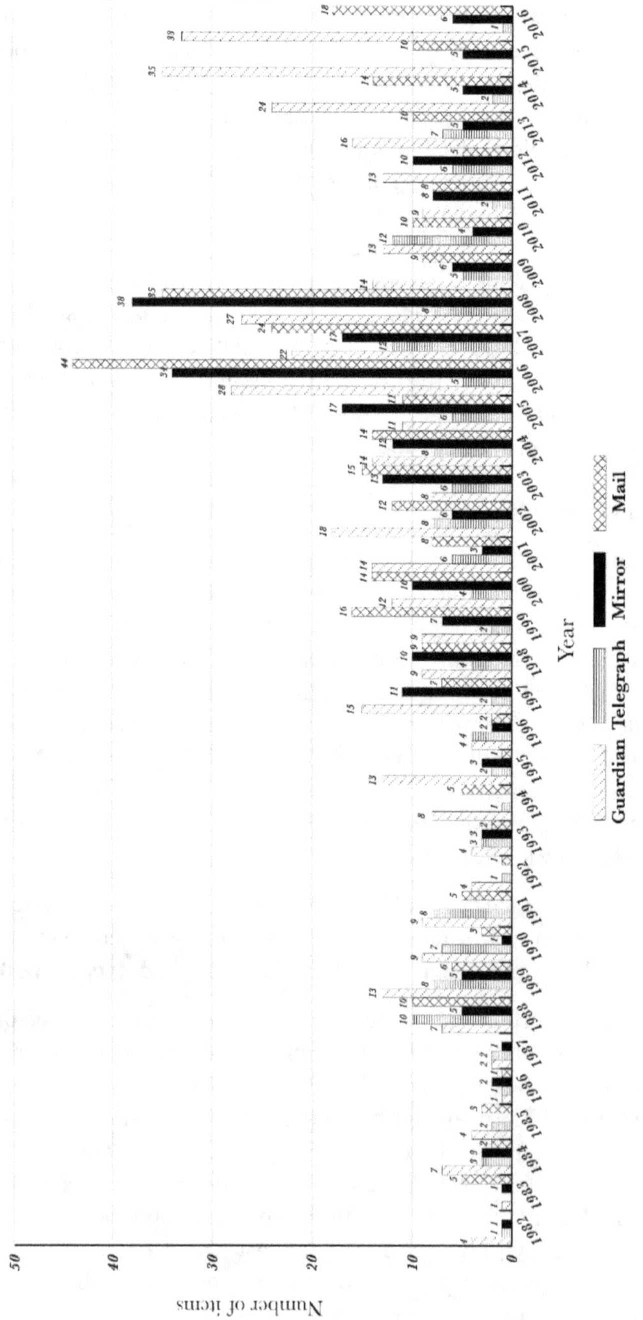

4.1.2 CIWF and AA in the newspapers

Before moving towards the detailed analysis of the newspapers, I shall note how much the voices of CIWF and AA feature in their corpora. CIWF receives the most coverage in the *Guardian* corpus; the search for "Compassion in World Farming" resulted in 56 texts (13% of all items). Whilst 13% may at first appear trivial, it should be reiterated that the *Guardian* corpus is the largest and comprises a variety of texts, ranging from comments, opinion pieces to reviews and news. Furthermore, none of the *Guardian* texts ridicules or presents CIWF in a negative light. Typically, their spokesperson is cited as an expert in chicken farming, for example:

> "Broilers are particularly vulnerable to disease for many reasons," says Dr Lesley Lambert, of Compassion in World Farming. "The birds are genetically very similar because they have been bred to put on rapid muscle growth, however this compromises their immune, skeletal and respiratory systems…" (*The Guardian*, 7/6/2006 [G23])

In the *Mail* and *Telegraph* corpora, the search for "Compassion in World Farming" resulted in 30 texts (9%) and 12 texts (8%), respectively. In the *Mirror* corpus, 13 texts (5%) mention the charity. In these newspapers, CIWF is also typically referenced as a credible and authoritative source which supports my initial hypothesis that the charity holds a position of authority and influences public discourse about chicken farming. For instance, a *Telegraph* feature investigates the claims behind food labels and cites a CIWF report on farmed animal welfare standards in egg production: "The Compassion in World Farming report scored the minimum Lion code standards 'very poorly' and said they generally ensured compliance only with minimum standards" (*The Daily Telegraph*, 9/3/2013 [T29]). Compared with other relevant organisations referred to in chicken farming-related stories, CIWF stands in the middle; on average CIWF is mentioned more frequently than Greenpeace, PETA, or AA, but less frequently than the RSPCA or the Soil Association.

AA is mentioned in eight *Guardian* texts (1.8% of all texts). The coverage is even smaller in the *Mail* (five texts, or 1.5%), *Mirror* (two texts, or 0.8%) and *Telegraph* (no texts, or 0%), indicating that the animal rights organisation is comparatively ineffective in engaging with the newspapers or that the newspapers do not perceive the NGO and their agenda as legitimate and newsworthy. As we shall see in this chapter, the newspapers can be hostile towards activists; in most texts, however, AA actions are presented neutrally. Journalists refer to undercover investigations and footage produced by AA, quote their spokespersons, or publish their letters. To illustrate, in a news story on the government plans to scrap farmed animal welfare regulations, the director of AA Andrew Tyler expresses his concerns: “Suffering and exploitation are already integral to animal farming. To deregulate and dilute what slender protection currently exists would have been monstrous” (*The Guardian*, 7/4/2016 [G50]). In the *Mirror* corpus, two letters written by AA activists problematise intensive chicken farming and ask readers to stop supporting the industry: “Please show you care by boycotting battery chicken and battery eggs” (*Daily Mirror*, 31/7/2005 [M6]).

4.1.3 A comment on visuals

Visual culture, a worthy topic in its own right, is largely beyond the scope of this book. Images are not provided by the digital database LexisNexis, therefore a brief comment on qualitative observations is provided for the newspapers. In the campaigning magazines, however, images are readily available, thus, a more detailed commentary on the visuals is provided in Chapter 5.

For each newspaper, 20 images were identified using the Google search engine; the timeframe was set between 1982 and 2016 and the search terms were “chicken farming” and the site of the newspaper. Images are not reproduced due to copyright issues. Campaigners’ images are reproduced in black and white rather than in original colour. The first immediate finding is that all four newspapers use stock images from suppliers such as Alamy, Getty Images, East News or Shutterstock. This indicates that images do not necessarily add authenticity to texts, though they may appear to do so. Stock photographs depict free-ranging chickens in aesthetically pleasant images, and caged hens in clear bright colourful images that do not suggest cruelty. As the same images are used repeatedly, they better reflect the availability of chicken-related images in stock photography agencies than accurately illustrate the narratives developed in the stories. Additionally, “standard” visually appealing press photos of celebrity chefs Oliver and Fearnley-Whittingstall are identified.

Original photos produced by photojournalists working for the newspapers are also found. Photojournalists document events as well as characters; for example, stories on farmers and backyard chicken keeping are told in words and images. Gritty images from undercover investigations are identified in all newspapers except the *Telegraph*. Gritty images are known to play an important role in the current visual media environment; they help draw attention to the story and recruit activists (Jasper, 1997). In the case of chicken farming, they add emotional value and serve as evidence of cruelty and/or unsanitary conditions. For example, photographs captured in chicken farms, slaughterhouses or during live transportation help problematise the industry practices as they bring the reader closer to the lived realities of chickens. Moreover, the “shock value” of graphic imagery may increase the sales of the newspapers. A quantitative study would be required to determine whether the tabloids are displaying a larger proportion of graphic chicken-related images than the broadsheets.

4.1.4 Structure of the chapter

Bearing in mind the underlying assumptions of broadsheet and tabloid journalism and the political orientation of the sources, I organise the chapter as follows. I open with the analysis of the left-leaning broadsheet *Guardian*, which has the largest corpus and therefore is predicted to offer the most insight. This is followed by a section on the left-leaning tabloid *Mirror*. I then move on to the right-leaning broadsheet *Telegraph* and tabloid *Mail*. The analysis of each newspaper corpus follows the same structure. First, dominant themes and narratives are outlined. In Section *Normalising chicken farming*, I investigate how a newspaper reproduces the dominant ideology and instrumentalises chickens. In Section *Problematising chicken farming/alternative discourses*, I analyse how a newspaper offers openings for change. I identify the angles and frames deployed to sensitise the reader to the issue of chicken farming and challenge the objectification of chickens. This division is deployed for the purpose of structure and convenience; in practice, the line is often blurred as stories can provide a range of views. Journalistic texts may reproduce the underlying assumptions of exploitative ideologies while also introducing alternative angles or they may at first appear sympathetic to chickens but do not challenge the status quo. Supplementary subsections such as on chicken agency are added. Finally, I summarise and discuss my findings comparing the sources.

4.2 The Guardian

More than half of all *Guardian* texts (230 texts, or 53%) are news. Opinion/feature pieces occupy two-fifths (178 texts, or 41%) of the corpus. There are 26 letters (6%) authored by members of the public, industry representatives and activists. Table 4.3 shows the thematic distribution of articles over time. Public health is the focus in 139 *Guardian* texts. This places the *Guardian* corpus, alongside the *Mail*, as having the highest proportion of articles covering chicken farming in relation to public health issues (32% and 33%, respectively). The second-largest thematic domain in the *Guardian* corpus is chicken welfare (124 texts, or 29%).

The foremost findings after a close reading of the *Guardian* corpus are that opinion pieces are generally characterised by the inclusion of an animal welfare perspective and that an anti-intensive farming attitude increasingly dominates opinion pieces over the analysed period. The primary rationale against intensive farming varies from public health and other human-centred motives to chicken welfare and multiple arguments combined. The lemma *factory farm** has become ever more prevalent in the newspaper throughout the period, replacing the more neutral or even positive synonyms such as "modern farm" or "commercial farm". In addition, the broadsheet carries out its own investigations on topics such as welfare standards.

Among the four newspapers, the *Guardian* corpus stands out for having 24 texts (6%) under the category "extensive debate over chicken farming" (in comparison to 3% in the *Telegraph* and 0% in the *Mirror* and the *Mail*). These texts discuss multiple aspects of chicken farming in depth. Moreover, the *Guardian* does not shy away from discussing veganism. The exploratory keyword analysis of the *Guardian* corpus against the *Mirror, Mail* and *Telegraph* corpora identifies *vegan* among the top 100 keywords (Appendix A online). Table 4.4 shows that the lemma *vegan** is not found in the *Mirror* corpus. Table 4.6 demonstrates that the absolute frequency (AF) of the lemma *vegan** in the *Guardian* corpus is 62 and in the *Mail* corpus it is 10. The normalised frequencies (NFs) per 10,000 words are 1.8 and 0.4, respectively; the ratio is 4.5 which indicates that *vegan** is 4.5 times relatively more frequent in the *Guardian* than in the *Mail* corpus. The Log-likelihood score 25.8 shows that the difference is significant at $p < 0.0001$. Table 4.5 analogously demonstrates that the lemma *vegan** is three times relatively more frequent in the *Guardian* than in the *Telegraph* corpus.

Environmental issues are the focus in 16 *Guardian* texts (4%), which is considerably more compared with the other newspapers; one text is found in the *Telegraph* and the *Mirror*, whereas none are found in the *Mail* corpus. Environment-related words are identified in the exploratory keyword analysis of the *Guardian* corpus (Appendix A). Absolute (AFs) and normalised (NFs) frequencies of topical words and lemmas *climate, environment*, emissions, planet, sustainab** and *pollution* are compared in Tables 4.4, 4.5 and 4.6. Table 4.4 shows that in the *Mirror* corpus, *climate, emissions*, and *planet* do not feature; AFs equal zero. Table 4.5 demonstrates that the words *climate* is 5.6 times relatively more frequent and *emissions* is 4.4 times relatively more frequent in the *Guardian* than in the *Telegraph* corpus. Table 4.6 compares the *Guardian* with the *Mail* and shows that *emissions* is 38.1 times relatively more frequent, *sustainab** is 8.2 times relatively more frequent and *climate* is 5.4 times relatively more frequent in the *Guardian* corpus.

Table 4.3 Distribution of the thematic domains in the Guardian corpus

	public health/food safety	*welfare of chickens*	*ethical vegetarianism/veganism/direct action*	*business/economics*	*extensive debate over chicken farming*	*backyard farming/chicken companions*	*organic/free-range farming*	*environmental issues*	*cultural and social issues*	*miscellaneous*	*total per year*
1982				2		1	1				4
1983			1								1
1984		1	1	2			1		2		7
1985	1	3									4
1986				1							1
1987		1		1							2
1988	5	2									7
1989	7	2	3							1	13
1990	1	3		1		1	1	2			9
1991		3	2	1	1		1	1			9
1992		2	1	1							4
1993	2	1				1					4
1994	2	2		1	2	1					8
1995	2	7	2				1	1			13
1996	2	1			1						4
1997	5	4		1	1		1	1		2	15
1998	3	3	1				1		1		9
1999	5		1	1	1		1				9
2000	2	3	1				3			3	12
2001	7	2	2	1		1				1	14
2002	3	5	1		2		4		1	2	18
2003	3		2		1	1			1		8
2004	9	2		1			2				14
2005	5	4				1	1				11
2006	18	5	3			1		1			28
2007	8	11				2		1			22
2008	1	13	2	3		4	1	1	2		27
2009		9	2	2				1			14
2010	2	3	3	2	1	1			1		13
2011	2	3		2	1		1				9
2012	1	4		2		3	2		1		13
2013	9	4			1	1		1			16
2014	15	3	1	2	1			1	1		24
2015	9	9	1	2	5	2	1	3	3		35
2016	10	9	1		6	2		2	3		33
TOTAL	**139**	**124**	**31**	**29**	**24**	**23**	**23**	**16**	**16**	**9**	**434**

Table 4.4 Frequency analysis: Guardian and Mirror

	Guardian		Mirror		Keyness		
Word or lemma	**AF**	**NF**	**AF**	**NF**	**Over/under-use**	**LL**	**Ratio**
climate	67	1.9	0	0.0	+	27.9	div
environment*	320	9.3	35	4.4	+	21.6	2.1
emissions	53	1.5	0	0.0	+	22.1	div
planet	49	1.4	0	0.0	+	20.4	div
vegan*	62	1.8	0	0.0	+	25.8	div
sustainab*	80	2.3	2	0.3	+	21.2	9.3
pollution	46	1.3	2	0.3	+	9.2	5.3
Total word count	**345,505**		**79,927**				

Note: (+) indicates "overuse"; (-) indicates "underuse"; (div) indicates "division by 0 disallowed"; LL of 3.84 or higher is significant at the level of $p < 0.05$

Table 4.5 Frequency analysis: Guardian and Telegraph

	Guardian		Telegraph		Keyness		
Word or lemma	**AF**	**NF**	**AF**	**NF**	**Over/under-use**	**LL**	**Ratio**
climate	67	1.9	4	0.3	+	18.9	5.6
environment*	320	9.3	48	4.2	+	32.3	2.2
emissions	53	1.5	4	0.3	+	12.6	4.4
planet	49	1.4	9	0.8	+	3.1	1.8
vegan*	62	1.8	7	0.6	+	9.8	3.0
sustainab*	80	2.3	13	1.1	+	6.8	2.1
pollution	46	1.3	5	0.4	+	7.6	3.1
Total word count	**345,505**		**115,255**				

Table 4.6 Frequency analysis: Guardian and Mail

	Guardian		Mail		Keyness		
Word or lemma	**AF**	**NF**	**AF**	**NF**	**Over/under-use**	**LL**	**Ratio**
climate	67	1.9	9	0.4	+	27.0	5.4
environment*	320	9.3	138	5.6	+	21.6	1.7
emissions	53	1.5	1	0.0	+	22.1	38.1
planet	49	1.4	10	0.4	+	20.4	3.5
vegan*	62	1.8	10	0.4	+	25.8	4.5
sustainab*	80	2.3	7	0.3	+	21.2	8.2
pollution	46	1.3	5	0.2	+	25.8	6.6
Total word count	**345,505**		**248,339**				

4.2.1 Normalising chicken farming

In the *Guardian* corpus, 40% of all items are not inclusive of the animal welfare or rights perspectives, which is the smallest proportion among the four sources. There is a considerable difference between the *Guardian* news and opinion/feature articles. Although no texts overtly say that chickens' interests or suffering do not matter, 60% of the *Guardian* news articles (138 texts) and 19% of opinion/feature articles (34 texts) demonstrate discursive *erasure.*

The absence of chickens' perspectives and *common-sense* objectification of them as resources can be as (or more) powerful in normalising chicken farming as overt statements. First, I shall demonstrate how chickens are objectified as soon as economics are introduced. Across all four newspapers, chickens are defined as commodities or means of production when economic concerns are present. Business-related news items are usually upfront about their economic focus in their headlines, e.g. "Organic sales slump for first time: Bread, meat and chilled meals hit hardest. The sector hopes to reverse downward trend in 2010" (*The Guardian*, 12/4/2010 [G31]). These articles are aligned with the discourses of neoliberal economics where the commodity status of chickens is taken for granted. Chickens appear in units, numbers and profits: "sales have dropped off a cliff. Normally, the farm sells 10,000 chickens a day, but now they are selling fewer than a dozen" (*The Guardian*, 11/4/2013 [G30]). An exception could be a feature on intensive farming divestment. While the text focusses on the economic aspect of chicken farming, the quoted businessperson points to an ethical motive for moving away from intensive farming: "We don't want to invest in companies where the animals are not able to reflect their natural behaviours" (*The Guardian*, 5/4/2016 [G48]).

Interestingly, a third of texts focussing on organic farming are framed around economic factors (e.g. demand, supply, growing or dropping sales), organoleptic characteristics of organic products and the impact on human health. The appeal to self-interest triumphs over the improved conditions for chickens in organic farms. An illustrative example demonstrates how organic farming is defined solely through the sensory qualities of the meat as it is lamented that the chickens' corpses are not hung for better flavour: "What is the point of a chicken, particularly an organic one, that doesn't taste of anything?" (*The Guardian*, 15/7/2000 [G12]). Readers are implicitly assumed and encouraged to choose organically produced meat based on self-centred motives such as taste; chicken welfare is not the key motivation.

When human beings are most anxious about their own wellbeing, chicken suffering is least visible, even despite the vast numbers of chicken deaths. News stories on public health risks typically fail to engage with the animal welfare or rights perspectives or make connections between human and chicken welfare, and this will be the case for all four newspapers. Across the sources, avian influenza generated a considerable number of stories that revolved around the threat to public health and economic risks such as trade restrictions and financial losses. The fact that chickens (and not the economy or humans) are the primary and direct victims of the virus and its control measures (i.e. mass killing) is largely neglected. Word choices tend to trivialise and neutralise chicken deaths describing these in euphemisms such as *destruction, disposal,* or *cull.* Chickens are referred to in commercial terms and largely remain faceless reservoirs of the virus and objects of economic calculation, although the loss of life is staggering: "The outbreak could cost the economy up to $380m (£218m) according to Emmanuel Ijewere, one of the country's biggest poultry farmers. He said 5,000 to 6,000 birds were being slaughtered on his farm every day" (*The Guardian,* 21/2/2006 [G20]).

Avian influenza stories are also characterised by a "rhetoric of fear", which is tangible in the headlines such as "China bird flu scare: 'My family and I don't dare to eat anything these days'" (*The Guardian,* 11/4/2013 [G30]), "Avian flu: As the danger moves closer" (*The Guardian,* 11/1/2006 [G18]) or "Europe on high alert over avian flu: Turkey begins culling as 2,000 birds die at one farm: Romania seals off villages while tests continue" (*The Guardian,* 10/10/2005 [G17]). The world news story on the bird flu epidemic in Vietnam further illustrates that concerns revolve around public health, livelihoods and the economy, but not chickens: "As well as transforming medical practices, challenging traditional methods of farming and rewriting countless restaurant menus, the H5N1 virus has ravaged the rural economy" (*The Guardian,* 16/5/2005 [G15]). "Traditional methods" figure in the article solely in relation to human communities, whereas what "traditional" farming means for chickens is not discussed.

Government and industry representatives such as Defra, the Ministry of Agriculture, the National Farmers' Union (NFU) and the British Poultry Council (BPC), scientists and officials such as the WHO are repeatedly cited in bird flu news. For example, the French agriculture minister calls for support for chicken farmers and encourages the consumption of chicken meat: "In France, the agriculture minister Dominique Bussereau urged people to continue eating chicken. 'The first step consumers can take in solidarity (with chicken farmers) is not to stop eating chicken,' he told Europe 1 radio" (*The Guardian,* 20/2/2006 [G19]). Yet steps that consumers could take in solidarity with chickens are not identified. The voices of stakeholders such as activists, campaigners or animal welfare experts who could put the epidemic in the context of the lived realities of chickens are rarely introduced.

Feature articles, on the other hand, demonstrate that empathy towards chickens can be introduced by citing a variety of sources. A feature on the avian flu outbreak in the USA accounts for farmers' emotions rather than chickens' and describes chickens as property. However, a veterinarian also scrutinises the killing methods and challenges the scientific language describing them. He expresses welfare concerns noting what the foam suffocation method would feel like to a human being:

> "...each [avian influenza] outbreak incident is unique and involves site specific conditions that need to be considered in making the best disposal decision for the situation at the site," reads a 2006 paper by the Environmental Protection Agency. The reality is often much more emotional than that language might imply. "These farmers spend their entire careers caring for their animals and to see the disease affect their flocks... is an emotionally devastating event"... Not all agree that using foam is humane. "We could do better," says Michael Blackwell, chief veterinary officer at The Humane Society of the United States, who likens death by foam to "cuffing a person's mouth and nose, during which time you are very much aware that your breathing has been precluded". (*The Guardian*, 6/8/2015 [G40])

Other public health news articles, such as on *Campylobacter, Salmonella*, drug residues or chemicals in eggs and chicken flesh and antibiotic resistance also typically ignore the experiences of chickens and fail to engage with the animal welfare or rights perspectives. Food safety and public health not only take an obvious priority, but the fact that diseases, drugs, or chemicals primarily affect chickens is obfuscated. These articles seldom investigate how viruses or bacteria affect chickens as living beings and forget to raise questions such as why the antibiotics are being used in the first place or how chickens get infected with bacteria such as *Salmonella* or *Campylobacter*. The poor treatment of chickens is not regarded as relevant. For instance, stories on *Campylobacter* tend to ignore that chickens get ill themselves and instead focus on the safety of "end products": "*Campylobacter* affects about 280,000 people — and leads to around 100 deaths — annually. Contaminated poultry is a major cause of infection and tests have found that up to two thirds of fresh chicken are affected" (*The Guardian*, 22/12/2015 [G44]).

Deliberately or not, the erasure of chickens as sentient beings and instrumentalisation of them through the *detached* vocabulary of industry and medical/veterinary science result in the concealment of their lived realities. As argued by Stibbe (2015) and Mitchell (2013), the choice of words, such as "destroy poultry", embed the perspective of chickens as objects rather than subjects and produce moral disengagement: "Under the Zoonosis order, inspectors are empowered to destroy poultry suspected of carrying the *Salmonella* bacterium" (*The Guardian*, 10/5/1990 [G3]). Consider the headline "Why two out of three supermarket chickens could still make us sick: Entrails blocking drains, meat on the floor, water left unchanged. The *Guardian* investigates industry still plagued by food poisoning bug" (*The Guardian*, 24/7/2014 [G32]). The investigation focusses on *Campylobacter* contamination and describes in detail the appalling conditions and violations of hygiene regulations in a slaughterhouse, where chickens are "processed": "the scald tank was left uncleaned for two nights, so that three days of birds — more than 250,000 chickens — were processed through the same dirty water" (*The Guardian*, 24/7/2014 [G32]). The practices in the slaughterhouse are condemned as unsanitary and the overcrowding of chickens in farms is briefly noted, but the link between the poor treatment of chickens and infections that ultimately affect humans is not made. The sole occasion when chicken welfare is mentioned in a 2,540-word article is superficial. The company uses chicken welfare as an excuse for not stopping the slaughter line after "the breakdowns"; the sceptical reader might imagine that loss of profit is a more likely reason for not halting "production", but the story does not challenge "the firm":

> The firm said it and the vets had to make difficult decisions when there were breakdowns in the evisceration, defeathering and scald tank parts of the line. These required weighing up contamination risk against the welfare of chickens awaiting slaughter. (*The Guardian*, 24/7/2014 [G32])

Stories that report on labour-related issues (e.g. migrant workers or modern slavery) similarly miss out on an opportunity to draw a link between the appalling conditions for workers and poor chicken welfare. For example, a feature on gangmasters exploiting Lithuanian workers highlights the harsh working conditions in chicken farms, but barely touches upon what it means to be a chicken in the same unhealthy environment. While the exploitation of workers is condemned, the exploitation of chickens goes unnoticed. Lived realities of chickens are not seen as problematic beyond their impact on workers:

> Some of the biggest farms house more than a million birds on one site. It is a labour-intensive job — a catcher can collect around 6,000 birds an hour — and it needs to be done in the dark to keep the birds as calm as possible. The chickens are liable to flap, peck, claw, vomit and defecate. By its nature, it is dirty and dangerous work. (*The Guardian*, 11/8/2015 [G43])

With some exceptions, articles focussing on the environmental impact of chicken farming also tend to overlook the direct effects on chickens. We might expect that care for animal welfare would sit comfortably with concerns over environmental impact, but this may not necessarily be the case. Consider a feature discussing the issue of food waste in the USA and the impact of animal farming on the environment. The text notes that chicken farming has considerably intensified since the 1950s but does not remark on any resulting welfare issues. Instead, chicken flesh is seen as sustainable food: "In terms of climate pollution, the switch to chicken is a plus as it has a far lighter carbon footprint than beef or dairy farming" (*The Guardian*, 14/7/2016 [G52]).

4.2.2 Problematising chicken farming/alternative discourses

Almost two-thirds of all *Guardian* texts (60%) contain at least one sentence on chicken welfare, which is the highest proportion among the analysed newspapers. Opinion/feature articles are much more likely to be inclusive of chicken welfare perspectives than news stories (81% vs 40%) and therefore will be the focus in this section. The counter-narratives originate from the authors of texts — journalists, celebrities, activists, and other prominent public figures who write for the broadsheet — and from citing those in favour of animal welfare or rights. The list of authors that have debated chicken farming and advocated for chicken welfare in the *Guardian* include George Monbiot (environmentalist), Philip Lymbery (the Chief Executive Officer of CIWF), Zhou Zunguo (the CIWF spokesperson in China), Peter Singer (philosopher), Alison Hills (philosopher), Julian Baggini (philosopher), Yuval Noah Harari (historian), Clare Druce (an activist who formed an animal rights organisation Chickens' Lib), Hattie Ellis (activist and author of *Planet Chickens*, a book condemning chicken farming), Linda Turvey (an activist who runs a sanctuary for hens rescued from battery farms), Ben Martin (campaigner at AA), Audrey Eyton (animal welfare campaigner and writer) and Fearnley-Whittingstall.

The *Guardian* opinion/feature articles typically write chickens in as objects of cruelty and victims, a frame which, we shall see, features in all four newspapers, and dominates the campaigners' corpora. The following extract is illustrative of a vivid emotive account of the lives of chickens raised for their flesh: "They are 19-days-old. They have nothing to perch on or peck at except the cereal-based feed that moves by on a conveyor belt, or their nearest neighbour. They will never see the light of day..." (*The Guardian*, 15/10/1991 [G5]). A recurrent trait of the *Guardian* opinion/feature articles and, as Chapter 5 will show, the campaigners' corpora is balancing an emotional account of chickens' realities and a knowledgeable tone based on facts. Emotive claims (e.g. chickens *succumb* and *die*) are incorporated into a knowledgeable narrative characterised by statistics and veterinary science terminology (e.g. *chronic respiratory disease* and *colisepticaemia*):

> Six hundred million of these chickens are bred and slaughtered every year. Three and a half million of these birds succumb each year to one of the diseases of intensification, chronic respiratory disease, heart attacks, fatty liver and colisepticaemia. They die in their infancy, for at seven weeks of age they have not yet reached sexual maturity. (*The Guardian*, 6/7/1991 [G4])

When critiquing intensive farming, the *cheapness* of intensively produced food is subjected to scrutiny and this will be the case in the *Mail* and CIWF corpora, too. Table 4.7 presents illustrative concordance lines for "cheap" using context words "meat", "food", "egg(s)" and "chicken(s)". Concordances reveal the negative connotation the adjective carries. It is typically argued that there is no such thing as *cheap* food as the *real* price of *cheap* products is environmental destruction, public health, and animal welfare issues (Table 4.7). It is also repeatedly stated that intensive farming methods have created a *culture of cheap food*, in which humans are alienated from food production. On the other hand, the adjective *cheap* is used positively when suggesting plant-based alternatives to animal products as a more sustainable option. Illustrative examples are highlighted in grey in Table 4.7.

Table 4.7 Extract from "cheap" concordance using context words "meat", "food", "egg(s)" and "chicken(s)"

sacrifice animal welfare in the name of	**cheap** meat, future generations will pay the price
show the heavy price some pay for	**cheap** chicken. Then there's pesticide use. Numer
of supermarket poultry. A heavy price for	**cheap** chicken But the drive to clean up
on earth can ultimately afford food this	**cheap**? If we factor in the hidden costs
for each time we opt for unfeasibly	**cheap** food. Having quantified the damage, the ide
or more varied. The real cost of	**cheap** food grown by factory farming methods is
buy. Battery egg production has always been	**cheap** and ugly. This page of the Guardian
circles, that when it comes to meat, "	**cheap**" equals "bad". Not only does this imply
to avoid chicken, pork and salmon in	**cheap** food, from green motives and from a
something, has to pay the price for	**cheap** meat and dairy products and all too
brutal demonstration of the real cost of	**cheap** food. The price is not paid at
Campylobacter revelations show, the cost of	**cheap** food is a lurch back to 19th-
done. I agree with you that the	**cheap** food culture is one that has dogged
rom anyone who could provide something red,	**cheap** and meat-like promised to examine their
a new era of fake meat — nutritious,	**cheap** and indistinguishable from the real thing,
special offer will run for a week	**Cheap** food damages the environment, says Waitro
public health and farming The culture of	**cheap** food has damaged public health, farming
is calling on retailers to stop selling	**cheap** meat from chickens reared in poor conditio
will sort it out. Don't buy	**cheap** chicken. Part 3 of our investigation into
war, Britain has slowly turned into a	**cheap** -food culture, a society in which we
at last becoming aware that all this '	**cheap**' food has its downside, though one that
hidden costs of industrial agriculture, then the '	**cheap**' food in our shops no longer looks
from plants, this could be the new	**cheap** food. No wonder then that the sales

Challenging the industry rhetoric of *care* is a recurrent trait of the *Guardian* opinion/feature articles. In the following extract, the fast-food chain McDonald's is scrutinised. Industry rhetoric is dissected demonstrating the power of language to shape rather than simply to mirror, e.g. "environmentally-controlled houses" evoke a more appealing image in our minds than windowless crammed sheds. Industry depictions of farming methods are "translated" in such a way that exposes the commodification of chickens whose only purpose is to reach "table weight as fast as possible":

> "Chickens are reared on deep litter, in environmentally-controlled houses which minimise distress to the birds. Temperature and ventilation are constantly monitored, as is the supply of food and drink." Described thus, a McChicken may appear to live a life of uncommon luxury. But dissect this dressed up public relations jargon, and you discover that the described conditions deviate not one jot from the intensive methods of rearing deplored by animal welfare groups. Thousands of McChicks are put into large sheds when just a few days old. They will never again see natural daylight. At first they have plenty of room, and will always have plenty to eat and drink because the name of the game is to get them up to table weight as fast as possible. (*The Guardian*, 31/7/1993 [G6])

"Higher welfare" farming is typically juxtaposed with intensive farming, which produces *cheap* products and is seen as emblematic of cruelty to sentient beings. The most frequently offered solution, thus, is replacing intensive farms with "higher welfare" farms, which are usually (although not invariably) depicted through renewed images of pastoral farming, while overt suggestions to abstain from all chicken products are rare. Consider the following extract where the engaging, emotive voice of Professor Webster condemns intensive chicken farming as immoral and constructs humans as being "inhuman" for the cruelty inflicted upon sentient beings:

> Take chicken, currently Britain's best-selling meat. The broiler chicken industry is probably the most sordid in the country. *Unless the label says free-range* [italics added], you can assume your chicken has spent its entire life indoors, densely packed in windowless sheds, walking over litter which becomes caked with faeces… Professor John Webster, head of the Veterinary School at Bristol University has denounced this as "the single most extreme example of man's inhumanity to another sentient creature". (*The Guardian*, 18/11/1995 [G11])

The term "high welfare" with regards to chicken meat or eggs first appears in the corpus in 2006 and becomes a buzzword from 2007 due to the public engagement of celebrity chefs Fearnley-Whittingstall and Oliver. The chefs are predominantly presented in a neutral or positive light. Around 2008 and 2009, the effect that their chicken welfare campaigns had on public attitudes and shopping behaviour is widely reported, e.g. due to the chefs' social influence the sales of battery eggs begin to fall: "the trend has accelerated with the help of high profile television campaigns, including a Channel 4 documentary in which the food writer Hugh Fearnley-Whittingstall cried on a visit to a battery farm" (*The Guardian*, 16/5/2009 [G29]).

Nevertheless, while a positive attitude towards "higher welfare" systems is commonly expressed, "higher welfare" farming also receives some scrutiny. A feature on sustainable food illustrates how the welfare rhetoric is challenged. The idyllic representations and terminology are scrutinised, resembling, as we shall see, the critique found in texts produced by animal rights activists as it draws upon scientific research to argue that those hens are suffering:

> Terms like "organic" and "cage-free", however, don't mean that hens spend their days bathed in sunshine and pecking at grass in a farmyard. "Cage-free" means only that hens are not kept in cages; they can still spend all their lives indoors. The organic label requires that farmers need to use organic feed and create access to the outdoors, but big farms can comply by building small porches around hen houses with as many as 150,000 to 200,000 birds. The Cornucopia Institute is especially critical of large farms that use the organic label, but give birds extremely limited access to the outdoors... The researchers took aerial photographs of large organic egg farms and found few, if any, hens outside. (*The Guardian*, 28/12/2015 [G45])

The writer Jenna Sten deconstructs the idyllic representation of "higher welfare" farms by eschewing euphemisms when describing the hens who have their beaks "sliced off" and are not allowed to "grow old" and the male chicks who do not stand a chance in the egg industry (*The Guardian*, 6/4/2016 [G49]). The author is not only sceptical about welfare claims of free-range farming, but also argues that the animal welfare rhetoric legitimises chicken exploitation by making the industry and consumers look or feel good. For Sten, it is not enough to stop consuming intensively farmed eggs, her solution to the ethical dilemma is stopping eating eggs altogether:

> Stop eating eggs. Like, all of them. Every single brand is doing bad things to hens. "Free-range" is a feel-good term. Businesses use it to create a generous reputation for themselves, and it makes us feel kind. But any large or small scale farming system harvesting eggs from hens is not letting them grow old in green pastures once their productivity levels drop, no matter how many nice words are on the box. Male chicks are routinely killed in both conventional and free-range hatcheries because they do not lay eggs, and are therefore not profitable. "Debeaking", a process in which hens have part of their beak sliced off with a hot blade is also standard practice; debeaking prevents hens from injuring one another in the overcrowded spaces they live in, but it also prevents them from performing healthy social behaviours such as preening, and sometimes eating. The process is, as you might imagine, painful. (*The Guardian*, 6/4/2016 [G49])

Revealing problematic aspects of chicken farming, such as the killing of male chicks, in such a blatant manner may lead the *Guardian* reader to a conclusion that a vegan diet is the only just diet. This conclusion is reached by philosophers

Peter Singer and Jim Mason (2006) in their book *The Way We Eat: Why Our Food Choices Matter.* Singer and Mason (2006) point to the pragmatism of veganism since it is difficult to *be sure* that farmed animals indeed have good lives on "humane" farms (p. 257). Moreover, conscientious omnivores are faced with the questions of how "humane" is "humane" enough. Therefore, "drawing a clear line against eating animal products may be the best way to ensure one eats ethically" (Singer & Mason, 2006, p. 257). Furthermore, in the *Guardian* opinion piece, Sten's critique of "higher welfare" farming goes beyond the focus on suffering. Sten makes appeals to *fairness*; the author refers to chickens as *people*, thereby including them in the moral community and denouncing commodification of farmed animals as morally wrong — "animals aren't products":

> Choosing not to eat eggs is a viable option, and removes the need to "be sure" that the animals are being treated right. Animals + money = profit is a pretty inhumane system to begin with. A fellow commenter noted that within the structure of capitalism, "ANY food product + money = profit". But animals aren't products. This may sound like sentimental fiction to some — but animals are people... Legalities aside, animals are irrefutably, scientifically sentient — which means they feel feelings, good and bad ones. When we turn them into products, and refer to them as such, it distances us from this fact, and turns our relationship with them into something we can comfortably commodify or wilfully ignore. (*The Guardian*, 6/4/2016 [G49])

Of note, Sten acknowledges that her claims may be perceived as a "sentimental fiction" by some; this theme, namely the juxtaposition of sentiment and rationality grounded in science, reappears across all sources in different situations. As we shall see, animal advocates are mocked as sentimental and thus feel obliged to counter this narrative by relying on scientific "truths". The following extract further illustrates the prevailing rationalist approach; the British writer and campaigner Eyton argues that animal suffering is not "just a sentimental concern of the soft-hearted" but a "scientifically and statistically" proven fact (*The Guardian*, 10/7/1994 [G8]). Such framing, unintentionally, echoes the supposed opposition between reason and emotion. Nevertheless, animal suffering is placed before the impact on the environment and human communities. The A-IC is problematised as Eyton points out to the vested corporate and institutional interests:

> Against intensive farming there is a vast and ever-mounting dossier of scientifically and statistically proven evidence. The chronic suffering endured by animals in many intensive systems is not just a sentimental concern of the soft-hearted. It is a scientifically proven fact. The loss of the hedgerows which contained farm animals, the loss of wildlife sustained by that habitat, the pollution of the waterways, the loss of rural employment, the loss of traditional

> small farms and the plight of those who ran them (suicide is the second most common cause of death among farmers) are all proven facts. Yet Britain's intensive farming policy goes on, supported and sustained by vested interests and the Ministry of Agriculture. (*The Guardian*, 10/7/1994 [G8])

Importantly, in the *Guardian* opinion/feature pieces, intensive chicken farming is not only situated within the scope of social, political, or environmental issues but also framed around the principles of justice and deplored as harshly as "avian concentration camps" (*The Guardian*, 8/1/2008 [G25]), "concentration-camp chicken unit[s]" (*The Guardian*, 7/7/2007 [G24]) or "apartheid" (*The Guardian*, 10/7/1994 [8]), echoing the tactics of animal rights activists and scholars to appropriate human rights rhetoric. The emotive descriptions of chicken farms through the prism of the Holocaust or racial discrimination may sensitise the *Guardian* reader and open a debate on animal ethics. For example, intensive chicken farming is challenged by raising an ethical question, — "[is it] morally justifiable to impose concentration camp conditions on these living creatures?" (*The Guardian*, 2/12/1989 [G1]). In addition, consider how the term "apartheid", which draws analogies to institutionalised racial discrimination, is employed by Eyton to address the prejudice against farmed animals as a systemic abuse:

> Cracks are beginning to show in our long-practised animal apartheid system, in which we have convinced ourselves, against all evidence, that the animals we eat are less intelligent, in need of space, exercise, exploratory behaviour etc than are those we pat, ride or watch. (*The Guardian*, 10/7/1994 [G8])

As previously noted in Section 2.1, comparisons to human oppression can be traced back at least to the accounts on speciesism by the patron of animal rights Singer (1975) and activist Spiegel (1988), but in the words of Still (2015), are "often treated as unthinkable by those concerned with philosophical ethics more generally" (p. 26). The analogies may seem too simplistic and reductive if not insulting from the perspective of human victims, as the ideological underpinnings of human oppression and the economic exploitation of farmed animals are different. Substantial differences should be acknowledged to avoid controversy; for instance, farmed animals do not experience humiliation in the same way as humans do and chicken farming does not aim to exterminate chickens, whereas the Holocaust was aiming at genocide. The enslavement analogy arguably fits better than the Holocaust as farmed animals are bred to be exploited (or bred to be killed). The counterargument could be that while the conflicts and *experiences* certainly differ, the analogies fit on the conceptual level because *mechanisms of oppression* have some important parallels through property status, denial of bodily integrity and killing. Importantly, being provocative, "appropriated" human rights rhetoric produces moral shock and conveys the message that animal farming may in the future become as equally morally unjustifiable as genocide, enslavement and racism are today.

The debate whether chickens are ends in themselves or means are brought up by the philosopher Baggini, who is a regular contributor to the *Guardian.* Baggini interrogates the idea of animals as "replaceable things" (*The Guardian,* 2/5/2006 [G22]). He analyses eating meat and the consumption of "higher welfare" products from a philosophical utilitarian perspective, but candidly weighs up animal lives against gustatory pleasures. Admitting that in western societies cost-benefit calculations are biased in favour of human interests, Baggini bluntly states that if one considers the life of a farmed animal more valuable than their enjoyment of meat, they should not eat meat:

> Given that meat-eating is not essential — at least not in modern western countries — you can quantify its relative worth by saying that there is more value in our enjoyment of a carcass's worth of juicy steak than there is in the life of the cow that involuntarily donated it. If that sounds brutal, live with it or pass the tofu. So-called ethical consumers have a tendency to tinker with their purchasing decisions in order to feel virtuous, rather than grasp head-on the fundamental issues that require hard choices. In the case of meat, good though it is to try to avoid needless suffering, the fundamental issue is whether animals are replaceable things that can be killed by the million to secure their meat for us. If you can't swallow that, perhaps you need to reconsider what you're prepared to chew. (*The Guardian,* 2/5/2006 [G22])

Another article by Baggini questions longstanding cultural prejudice for and against different nonhuman animal species when discussing China's dog meat festival (*The Guardian,* 23/6/2015 [G39]). The philosopher argues that protesters are hypocrites if they are not equally disgusted by the intensive farming conditions for pigs and chickens. Although Baggini replaces pigs with the end product — "pork and chicken farming", he calls for consistency in views and behaviour, therefore suggesting protesters boycott meat coming from intensive farms:

> Others might have been motivated by the pictures of dogs crammed together in cages. This is indeed cruel, but this is how animals are abused in many parts of the world. If you don't like how the Chinese treat their dogs, then protest against their pork and chicken farming, too. Remember also that in westernised industrial farming, animals are often kept in similar conditions all their lives, not just on market day. So do sign the petition, just as long as you also campaign against intensive farming and studiously ignore any meat that comes from it. (*The Guardian,* 23/6/2015 [G39])

Another philosopher, Hills, engages with the reader as a moral being and draws attention to the comfort of ignorance (*The Guardian,* 30/3/2005 [G14]). She suggests that intensive chicken farming is crueller and larger in scale than fox hunting, but it is not opposed due to self-serving interests; consumers conveniently "turn a blind eye" to intensive chicken farming. Hills' offered solution is to reform and stop consuming products from intensive farms:

> Factory farming involves millions more animals than foxhunting, and the prolonged ordeal of a broiler chicken probably causes more harm to each creature, too... Anyone concerned for animal welfare should put the reform of farming right at the top of their priorities. We should no longer support factory farms by buying the food they produce... We like to think that our treatment of animals shows us at our most civilised and compassionate. In reality, it shows us at our most squeamish. We don't like to see animals suffering in front of us, but are quite prepared to turn a blind eye to whatever goes on behind the factory doors. (*The Guardian*, 30/3/2005 [G14])

The following extract illustrates how *Guardian* is confronting the government over chicken suffering. The government is blamed for not taking appropriate measures. The following extract shows that both "experts" and "counter-experts", namely a Conservative Minister and CIWF, are given a chance to speak. The feature is, however, stylistically, and ideologically closer to that of CIWF, since the position of CIWF occupies more space and is supported by the journalist's conclusion about the *living miseries* and commodification of chickens in intensive farming. Chickens' sentience and interests are highlighted by pointing to behaviours they are not able to perform and experiences they are not able to enjoy under the confinement of intensive farming:

When in July 1992 members of CIWF went to Parliament to lobby MPs, it argued that it was a crime to imprison birds in cages anyway. Unable to stretch their wings, flap them or fly, unable to make a nest in which to lay eggs, unable to peck or scratch in the ground for food, unable to enjoy a dust bath, forced to stand or squat on sloping wire mesh, they were the miserable victims of mankind's greed and exploitation. The lobbyists got little support from John Gummer, then Minister for Agriculture. "I do not believe," he said, "it would be fair to place more unilateral welfare restrictions on farmers in Britain." Two years later the government was still energetically supporting battery farming... However nasty, brutish and short life may be in the wild, it must rate as a paradise compared with the living miseries of industrial farming, where animals have been robbed of their freedom and reduced to production units in a relentless food machine financed by pharmaceutical companies, and controlled by accountants. (*The Guardian*, 10/7/1994 [G9])

The famous reference to philosopher Thomas Hobbes in imagining "life in the wild" as "nasty, brutish and short" is deployed paradoxically to make a point that chickens in intensive farms are horribly abused by and for humans. Intensive farms *imprison* birds, *robbing* them of "their freedom", which could be an implicit comparison to enslavement. The prison analogy further exposes chicken farming to ethical critique as chickens are "forced to stand or squat on sloping wire mesh", which evokes what the literary scholar Elaine Scarry (1985) describes as the most effective torture technique of using prisoners' bodies against themselves by making them stand for long hours. The coercive relationship, confinement and violence affecting farmed animals in intensive farms and slaughterhouses have long been critiqued by activists and scholars as analogous to the human condition in a prison, psychiatric asylum and other sites of confinement (Coppin, 2003; Novek, 2005; Cole, 2011).[1] Drawing upon Foucault's work on the governance of humans, sociologist Dawn Coppin (2003) analyses the shift from traditional free-range pig farming to intensive farming in total confinement as comparable to the advent of the disciplinary institutions such as prisons, schools and asylums, which all are characterised by control. Cole (2011) defines intensive farming systems as troubling disciplinary institutions that produce "docile bodies" through spatial distribution, surveillance, and "correction" (p. 86). In addition, the story criticises intensive farming not only for disciplinary control, but also for what could be described as the violence of the A-IC, which is tangible in the expression "a relentless food machine financed by pharmaceutical companies, and controlled by accountants" (*The Guardian*, 10/7/1994 [G9]). Without using the term "A-IC", the journalist maps the interconnections between overlapping sectors. The neoliberal production system that feeds upon the productive capacities of chickens' bodies and transforms subjects (chickens) into objects (units in a machine) is problematised; shared corporate interests between agribusinesses and pharmaceutical companies, which are "pharming" nonhuman animals to control disease and to increase feed conversion and profits, are highlighted.

The following extract further illustrates how anthropocentric attitudes towards chickens are challenged. It is argued that chickens do not receive much attention because of their low "likeability" in comparison to other animal species such as horses and due to being less friendly. While both male and female chickens are used in meat production and it could be disputed whether hens are indeed unfriendly, it is important that attention is drawn to biases built upon aesthetics and subjective perceptions of an animal:

> Calves, like the horses before them which were being sent to European slaughterhouses, have won wide-spread public support. Yet there is hardly a public peep against the conditions of broilers. Who's interested in hens, even when they are being crammed into dark sheds by the thousands and force-fed so they become four pound chickens within 42 days? ...But hens are neither furry nor friendly. (*The Guardian*, 13/1/1995 [G10])

---

[1] The American activist and CAS scholar Davis (1996) titled her book on chicken farming as *Prisoned Chickens, Poisoned Eggs*.

Importantly, the extracts from the opinion pieces demonstrate how prejudice against farmed animals is tackled and how discourse of intensive farming is extended from suffering to justice and the morality of animal farming from a philosophical perspective. The common argument against concerns for animal welfare, which is that one should ignore animal welfare because of "bigger" or "worse" social issues, is rejected. The treatment of nonhuman animals is seen as a moral issue, symptomatic of our attitudes towards *all living beings*:

> And before anyone starts moaning about me banging on about animal welfare while humans are homeless, dying, starving, drowning in search of asylum and fleeing wars, death and destruction, it seems to me that the way we treat animals is just a symptom of our brutish attitude towards all living beings. (*The Guardian*, 29/3/2016 [G47])

It could be argued that the questions about human morality and what it means to be *human(e)* shift the focus away from chickens as these questions are more concerned with what the treatment of animals tells us about ourselves, rather than chickens' entitlement to the possession of their own lives. Nonetheless, the opinion pieces demonstrate an effort to critically explore the human-farmed animal relationship and *denormalise* intensive farming. Unlike news items that report on events refraining from any further discussion or interpretation, the *Guardian* opinion pieces can raise the questions about the ways chickens figure in human worlds and humans figure in chicken worlds.

4.2.3 Growing awareness: 2015–2016

The number of *Guardian* texts is highest in the end of period, i.e. in 2015 and 2016. This increase suggests a growing concern over chicken farming; however, further research is needed to examine whether it continues after 2016. The coverage in 2015 and 2016 is linked to multiple events and characterised by an understanding of chicken farming as a global far-reaching issue. Concerns over food safety and antibiotic-resistant bacteria due to the overuse of antibiotics in animal farming and a continuous threat of avian flu are all prominent topics in the last two years of the analysed period. Importantly, while *Guardian* news stories on public health continue to background chicken welfare, the end of period shows an increase in news items that include chicken welfare perspectives when covering topics such as government policies on chicken farming, legal definition of free-range farming, and the industry seeking deregulation and so on. These news articles betray the human-centred ideology; for example, a news story on Defra's planned reform to deregulate chicken farming foregrounds chicken welfare by citing CIWF and RSPCA campaigners:

> In a change that has caused concern with the RSPCA, Compassion in World Farming, and opposition parties, the government has already quietly tabled a draft order to scrap the official code on farming chickens for meat and breeding... The RSPCA said it has been voicing concerns for the past three years about the "downgrading" of the guidelines from statutory codes to industry-led guidance and criticised the lack of transparency around the process. (*The Guardian*, 26/3/2016 [G46])

Furthermore, the two years contain the highest number of opinion/feature stories and letters questioning the very idea of intensive animal farming and its consequences and discussing chicken farming holistically (12 items out of 35 in 2015 and 12 items out of 33 in 2016). A feature on an avian flu outbreak in the USA links the influenza virus to the lived realities of intensively farmed chickens and questions the sustainability of "the system" by introducing the critical voice of the American Society for the Prevention of Cruelty to Animals (ASPCA):

> "It's reasonable when we see these outbreaks to wonder if they are a manifestation of the unsustainability of the system," says Suzanne McMillan, senior director of the farm and animal welfare campaign at the American Society for the Prevention of Cruelty to Animals (ASPCA). "Bird flu is a window into how today's poultry flocks live day to day, in intensive confinement and unsanitary conditions. It's an unnatural, unsustainable situation." (*The Guardian*, 6/8/2015 [G40]).

In the following extract, intensive chicken farming is situated in the context of consumerism. Poor chicken and workers' welfare can be read "symbolically" as representing the underlying problem of the industry's greed, the consumerist ideology and the government's inability or unwillingness to control. The vivid description strengthened with the mild profanity "shit", the image of "a gas chamber" evoking the concentration camps and the reference to genocide "poultrycide", paints a grim picture of chicken farming for both chickens and workers:

> an ugly picture of greed and ravenous consumerism fuelled by miserable wages for its workers and miserable lives for its chickens? ...No natural light, 34,000 birds in one shed, a tide of chicken wading around in its own shit (soaked up by the sawdust, admittedly), then sent to the gas chamber — more poultrycide than countryside. (*The Guardian*, 19/3/2015 [G35])

As this chapter has shown, the *Guardian* commissions some philosophical articles. In 2015, an introduction to the new edition of Singer's *Animal Liberation*, written by the historian and philosopher Harari, was published in the broadsheet. Harari positions intensive farming as an important social issue and a *crime*, immediately placing the practice in the context of justice. Consider the dramatic tone and urgency expressed in the headline:

> Industrial farming is one of the worst crimes in history; The fate of industrially farmed animals is one of the most pressing ethical questions of our time. Tens of billions of sentient beings, each with complex sensations and emotions, live and die on a production line. (*The Guardian*, 25/9/2015 [G41])

Harari considers the numbers of chickens exploited and points out that the numbers of farmed animals are markedly higher than the numbers of free-living “large creatures”. Of note, the recent study by Bar-On and colleagues revealed that of all mammal biomass on Earth, only 4 percent are wild animals, 36 percent are humans and 60 percent are farmed animals, whereas “the biomass of domesticated poultry (≈0.005 Gt C, dominated by chickens) is about threefold higher than that of wild birds” (Bar-On et al., 2018). Harari’s use of the disturbing statistics shifts the narrative and moves animal farming from margin to centre. The author also emphasises nonhuman animal sentience and paraphrases Singer’s comparison of animal suffering in agribusiness and human suffering caused by war:

> In 2009, there were 1.6 billion wild birds in Europe, counting all species together. That same year, the European meat and egg industry raised 1.9 billion chickens… This is why the fate of farm animals is not an ethical side issue. It concerns the majority of Earth’s large creatures: tens of billions of sentient beings, each with a complex world of sensations and emotions, but which live and die on an industrial production line. Forty years ago, the moral philosopher Peter Singer published his canonical book Animal Liberation, which has done much to change people’s minds on this issue. Singer claimed that industrial farming is responsible for more pain and misery than all the wars of history put together. (*The Guardian*, 25/9/2015 [G41])

Harari’s article questions intensive farming, in a sense reproducing the famous question “Can they suffer?” raised by one of the earliest proponents of animal welfare paradigm Jeremy Bentham (1789). Harari’s construction of chickens as being able to be happy diverges from the vast majority portrayals of chickens as solely victims and objects of cruelty: “They may not be as intelligent as us, but they certainly know pain, fear and loneliness. They too can suffer, and they too can be happy” (*The Guardian*, 25/9/2015 [G41]). Ultimately, the historian talks about the future and how technologies may impact on the nonhuman world. He challenges anthropocentrism and favours ethics based on sentience: “When we come to design this brave new world, we should take into account the welfare of all sentient beings, and not just of *Homo sapiens*” (*The Guardian*, 25/9/2015 [G41]).

Examples of writing that interrogates chicken farming, places it in the context of sustainability and effectively engages the reader are found in opinion articles produced by the environmentalist Monbiot. Since Monbiot is a prominent public figure with a position of authority and a regular contributor to the *Guardian*, his articles deserve attention. Six articles published in 2014, 2015 and 2016 were collected in the *Guardian* corpus under the "Comment is free" and "Environment" sections. Consider the following headlines that urge readers to eat less meat by highlighting chicken welfare and linking animal farming to environmental and public health issues: "Faeces, bacteria, toxins: welcome to the chicken farm; Whether it's welfare standards, environmental impact or the emerging threat to human health, we've got to change our insatiable greed for this meat" (*The Guardian*, 24/5/2015 [G36]) and "If you must eat meat, save it for Christmas; From chickens pumped with antibiotics to the environmental devastation caused by production, we need to realise we are not fed with happy farm animals" (*The Guardian*, 16/12/2014 [G34]). In the latter article, Monbiot places conditions for farmed animals as the top argument against intensive farming before public health risks and the devastating impact on the land and sea. Furthermore, the rosy portrayals of animal farming in children's books are problematised:

> It begins with the stories we tell. Many of the books written for very young children are about farms, but these jolly places in which animals wander freely, as if they belong to the farmer's family, bear no relationship to the realities of production. (*The Guardian*, 16/12/2014 [G34]).

Monbiot engages with the socialisation of children in meat culture, or in his own words, "the sanitation of childhood, in which none of the three little pigs gets eaten" (*The Guardian*, 16/12/2014 [G34]). There is an affinity here with the argument by sociologists Cole and Stewart (2014) in *The Cultural Construction of Human-Animal Relations in Childhood* that children's sensibility to exploitative practices is reduced, while simultaneously empathy is cultivated "through imagined relationships with representations of other animals, such as toys or sympathetic characters in children's literature" (p. 8). Moreover, children learn about animal welfare "in ways which build on the empathy cultivated in the family and mass media, but which do not question the morality of using other animals, and which mask the most violent practices involved in exploiting other animals" (Cole and Stewart, 2014, p. 10). Monbiot unravels violent practices in another article by engaging with the reader and deglamorising the industry as cruel and greedy; referring to "children's tales" serves a dual purpose, it pushes the reader to question the image of bucolic farms and touches upon the socialisation of children into meat culture:

> It's time to wean ourselves off the fairytale version of farming; Children's tales bear no resemblance to the cruelty of most modern farms, yet this image enables us to turn a blind eye to animal welfare and is exploited by the industry for profit... (*The Guardian*, 29/5/2015 [G38])

After an examination of mass production of chickens from the welfare perspective, Monbiot continues to link chicken farming to environmental damage such as water and air pollution, and the destruction of rainforests due to soya production for farmed animal feed.

Monbiot's articles also illustrate that ideologies are not internalised in a fixed and uniform way; they are subject to change. His writing is particularly interesting to analyse in relation to animal ethics since his attention to farmed animal suffering fluctuates and his stance on veganism is variable throughout the period. Due to the time and space limitations, it will not be possible to analyse Monbiot's articles in detail, but it must be noted that some of his writing constructs farmed animals instrumentally, as either efficient or inefficient converters of feed; his stance on veganism has been critiqued for the focus on efficiency and lack of engagement with animal ethics (Cole, 2015).

The following extract illustrates how Monbiot is caught up between reproducing cultural norms about meat and challenging the status quo. He takes a chicken as an example of cruelty and reminds the reader that brutal realities of intensive farming exist to satisfy our gustatory pleasures. Monbiot vividly depicts the painful experiences of chickens, reveals the gory details of what happens to their *bodies* rather than "carcasses" and thereby challenges their objectification:

> Inside chicken factories are scenes of cruelty practised on such a scale that they almost lose their ability to shock. Bred to grow at phenomenal speed, many birds collapse under their own weight and lie in the ammoniacal litter, acquiring burns on their feet and legs and lesions on their breasts. After slaughter they are graded. Those classified as grade A can be sold whole. The others must have parts of the body removed, as they are disfigured by bruising, burning and necrosis. The remaining sections are cut up and sold as portions. Hungry yet? (*The Guardian*, 24/5/2015 [G36])

Nevertheless, meat is presented as essential to humans assuming that they are not ready to "quit" it: "I know that most people are not prepared to stop altogether" (*The Guardian*, 24/5/2015 [G36]). Although Monbiot's perspective could be seen as realistic, it perpetuates the dominant assumptions about meat-eating as a prerequisite and desirable and, implicitly, about veg(etari)an diet as difficult. Despite being nostalgic about the days when consuming animals was "rare and special", the environmentalist candidly connects meat to the lived reality of an animal. His offered solution to unsustainable and cruel meat production is thus to reconnect with food, understand what meat production entails and ultimately eat less of it:

> To recognise that an animal has been sacrificed to serve our appetites, to observe the fact of its death: is this not the least we owe it? Knowing what we do and what we induce others to do is a prerequisite for a life that is honest and meaningful. We owe something to ourselves as well: to overcome our disavowal, and connect. (*The Guardian*, 24/5/2015 [G36])

In 2016, Monbiot's position becomes more radical as he confesses he had "converted to veganism to reduce... [his] impacts on the living world" (*The Guardian*, 9/8/2016 [G53]). Whereas the primary motive to go vegan is not animal suffering, and Monbiot focusses on food scarcity and environmental issues, he condemns the government's support for animal farming and engages with readers inviting them to make the right choice — to withdraw their consent to the A-IC by cutting out meat, dairy and eggs: "When there's a choice between protecting the living world and appeasing powerful lobby groups, most governments will take the second option. But we can withdraw our consent from this corruption" (*The Guardian*, 9/8/2016 [G53]).

Monbiot's "conversion" to veganism may not reflect a bigger trend, yet it demonstrates how behavioural changes can be inspired by multiple arguments against intensive farming. Opinion pieces such as these by Monbiot and Harari demonstrate an awareness of various aspects of chicken farming and effectively combine different motives, such as sustainability and animal welfare to address chicken farming. Moreover, an editorial on the topic of antibiotic resistance reveals the newspaper's perception of intensive animal farming as a global, multifaceted problem that involves animal cruelty:

> The use of antibiotics in agriculture is a much greater scandal still. Animals are routinely dosed so that they can tolerate the overcrowding essential to factory farming. This is not only cruel but enormously shortsighted... As more of the world eats more meat, farming will become more economically efficient, which is to say more cruel and more dependent on routine antibiotic dosage. This is a global problem and it will become a global health crisis, too. (*The Guardian*, 11/4/2016 [G51])

Overall, the years 2015 and 2016 do not show radicalisation with regards to chicken farming and the editorial reminds us of the prevailing assumption that the world inevitably "eats more meat" (*The Guardian*, 11/4/2016 [G51]). Nevertheless, the *Guardian* stands out from the other newspapers for its articles in the end of period demonstrate an awareness of the far-reaching impact of chicken farming and thereby a discursive shift towards chicken farming as a global and complex issue.

4.2.4 Industry response

While the *Guardian* largely positions itself against intensive farming in opinion/feature articles, there is room for different, opposing voices in the broadsheet. The industry's response to critique is visible in letters written by industry representatives and in news articles that quote them. In this section, I shall briefly explore how the industry stakeholders construct themselves, chickens, and chicken welfare.

Monbiot's authority in shaping public discourse is evidenced by the fact that industry representatives feel the need to respond to his critique. For instance, in 2015, the *Guardian* published a response letter to Monbiot's article on chicken farming. Andrew Large (Chief Executive, BPC) combines the industry lexis with the animal welfare lexis to justify farming practices. His letter is a prototypical illustration of the industry claiming to be a proponent of chicken welfare, if not a pioneer of it:

> George Monbiot also gets it wrong on welfare. In the UK 90% of all chicken is produced to Red Tractor standards and this demonstrates that the chicken has met production standards developed by experts on animal welfare, safety, hygiene and the environment. Farmers take the welfare of their birds extremely seriously, and therefore to accuse the sector of cruelty is absolutely unfounded. (*The Guardian*, 24/5/2015 [G37])

Indeed, around 90% of "broiler" chickens are farmed under the Red Tractor scheme (de Castella, 2014), but the Red Tractor is not an animal welfare assurance scheme. Farmers are concerned with the welfare of *their birds* as long as it maximises their profits. As Monbiot correctly points out in his response to Large, welfare standards by Defra (2013) recommend the stocking density of 34 kg/m^2, but "the standard for broiler chickens set by the Red Tractor scheme is actually worse: planned stocking densities must not exceed 38 kg/m^2 for broilers" (*The Guardian*, 29/5/2015 [G38]). Furthermore, in *Farm Assurance Schemes & Animal Welfare* report issued by the CIWF and OneKind (2012), the Red Tractor scored lowest compared to all other UK schemes.

Similarly to Large, the Executive Officer of BPC Jeremy Blackburn appeals to the value of science and combines the industry lexis ("stockmen", "national flock", "poultry producers") with the welfare lexis ("cruel", "look after") when defending the Red Tractor (*The Guardian*, 19/1/2008 [G27]). In a letter to the *Guardian*, Blackburn professes the industry's commitment to chicken welfare and public health:

> British Poultry Council members rear chickens to the Assured Chicken Production Red Tractor standard that promotes good health, welfare and food safety. We were one of the main players in negotiating the EU welfare directive for chickens kept for meat. To describe animals reared under these scientifically developed standards as cruel is an insult to the stockmen who look after the national flock. Animal welfare is the top priority for poultry producers because their birds are their livelihood. (*The Guardian*, 19/1/2008 [G27])

Participating in the negotiations on the welfare directive does not make the BPC chicken welfare advocates. It is likely the council was seeking to loosen regulations and lower the standards. Furthermore, the argument that chicken welfare is "the top priority" for farmers can be contested. If chickens died *en masse*, farmers would experience a financial loss. Yet behavioural and emotional needs of chickens can be routinely neglected without paying any economic price. In fact, chickens suffer, but most survive and (re)produce under intensive "scientifically developed" conditions.[2]

4.2.5 Chickens as agents

The representations of chickens as agents are noticeably less common than instrumental representations or representations of chickens as objects of cruelty in the *Guardian* corpus and this will be the case for all the corpora. Nevertheless, such representations are important for they invite readers to be interested in and empathise with chickens. In the *Guardian* corpus, agentive representations are found in stories on chickens rescued from intensive farms, chickens in "higher welfare" farms and backyard chickens, who occupy a middle position between providers of protein and companions.

Features on backyard chicken keeping show that there can be a strong emotional bond between humans and chickens. To illustrate, the human-chicken relationship is compared to that between a shepherd and a sheepdog (rather than shepherd and a sheep):

> Still, it's easy to get hooked on chickens. With their well-ordered social life, and early to rise, early to bed hours, they are enthralling creatures. People have lived with chickens for more than 2,500 years. Owning a flock of them throws you into a relationship with an animal that is as real and functional as that of the shepherd and his sheepdog. (*The Guardian*, 8/10/2005 [G16])

---

[2] "Normal" mortality rates in chickens raised for meat is 4.8% in USA (National Chicken Council, 2016). Statistics for the UK could not be provided as the industry does not share this information with the public.

Another illustrative example comes from an article on keeping companion chickens by the British novelist Emily Barr (*The Guardian*, 15/4/2006 [G21]). Barr's text is exceptional since it revolves around avian influenza and most bird flu stories lack the sense of justice and compassion towards chickens. Barr shows affection for her backyard chickens. While chickens are Barr's property "obediently laying eggs where we'd intended them to", their lives are valued beyond their economic worth and their deaths are seen as unfair and tragic (*The Guardian*, 15/4/2006 [G21]). Although predestined to be killed due to the risk of virus transmission, chickens have agentive roles and become creatures in their own right:

> The chickens had the run of the garden, and spent their days cruising, pecking, giving themselves dust baths, and obediently laying eggs where we'd intended them to… they would jump the ditch and meander blissfully over the fields of the farm next door, pecking as they went… They reminded me why we were here… Our chickens pecked out their window a few days ago, in a heartbreakingly courageous attempt at escape. They managed to wander their old strutting grounds for a few hours. Now they are back in their shed, the window boarded over. Their life is no life at all. Their slaughter is scheduled for Friday. I haven't told the boys yet. I'm not sure how I'm going to get through the day myself. (*The Guardian*, 15/4/2006 [G21])

The following extract on rescued ex-battery hens emphasises the joyfulness of chickens, which becomes a reward to people who rescue them. Chickens are assigned positive emotions and characters and being compared to other companion animals such as cats and dogs. The risk with this account is that it can be seen as patronising; it re-spins the power relations of "pet" keeping (which is problematic, especially considering the chickens exploited in the "pet" food industry):

> "People adore them," she [the founder of the Battery Hen Welfare Trust] says. "They love to get these little animals into a free-range environment, just to see the birds enjoying themselves, running freely. They can come in all sorts of conditions, so it's very satisfying to see them going off to their free-range retirement. Chickens have real characters: they can be very curious and cheeky. They're like little cats and dogs with feathers." (*The Guardian*, 7/8/2008 [G28])

While it could be argued that backyard chicken keeping is yet another *kinder* form of animal exploitation, the majority of the representations of chickens in backyard farming indicate appreciation of them as doers and sensers who act according to their own nature. The features on backyard and rescued chickens go beyond the reductionist constructions of chickens as objects of cruelty; they speak through an affectionate and compassionate voice and show chickens as leading joyful lives for themselves.

Nevertheless, chicken agency is exploited to create the concept of "higher welfare" farming. Distancing language of efficiency and the notion of chicken-machines are replaced with familiarity and visibility of chickens to create, in a Baudrillardian sense, a simulacrum of farming. Communication and cultural studies scholar Cathy B. Glenn (2004) has analysed the American advertising campaign for "Happy Cow" cheese and demonstrated how the advert creates an image of farmed animals as happy, talking and consenting to farming practices. In the "Happy Cow" advert, living animals had disappeared and had been replaced by virtual joyful cows that willingly provide humans with their "products". While the primary aim of the advertising is simply to sell a product, the advertisement, as Glenn (2004) puts it, involves "doublespeak", which serves the purpose of obscuring farmed animal exploitation and suffering (p. 65). Like Glenn (2004), Cole (2011) draws attention to the contemporary depictions of pastoral power in the marketing of eggs. The UK-based Happy Egg Company uses "the 'win-win' slogan: 'happy hens lay tasty eggs'" and attributes happiness to hens as well as eggs (Cole, 2011, p. 94). Since chickens are my study objects, I have looked at the company's website to see whether their rhetoric has changed. In agreement with Cole (2011), I found that anthropomorphised and feminised portrayals of hens are deployed to create an idyllic image of farming: "The wind in their feathers and the earth at their feet, our girls love exploring. So we give them as much space as possible to do just that" (The Happy Eggco, 2017a). Without providing concrete information (e.g. how much space?), the website provides a handful of tenuous welfare claims such as the "girls on our farms love football, so the farmers will often give them a ball to have a peckabout" (The Happy Eggco, 2017b). These claims are accompanied by aesthetic photographs of hens in fields. Yet, as Cole (2011) highlights, numerous parameters of chickens' lives in these farms such as the killing of male chicks or hens that are not considered productive remain hidden.

In all the newspapers including the *Guardian* corpus, stories that support "higher welfare" farming deploy *naturalness* and visibility to create a markedly different image from the one of a filthy factory farm which is hidden from the public eye. A consumer is invited to learn about chickens in subject position as actively enjoying these *renewed pastoral* farms. Moreover, "higher welfare" stories are characterised by an assumption that improved welfare results in improved taste. To illustrate, it is suggested that the closer the behaviour of chickens resembles their ancestors the red jungle fowl, the better the flavour of their flesh is:

> I have to say that Home Farm still does not compare in texture and flavour to the Les Landes chicken which Tesco imports. The environment of these birds — small flocks in a huge wooded area — reflects the habitat of their wild ancestors, and the proof that this environment creates the best flavour seems undeniable. (*The Guardian*, 5/5/1990 [G2])

The consumption of chickens' bodies farmed in these idyllic farms is celebrated. Consumers of "higher welfare" chicken products are given not only a reward of *improved* taste, but also a moral affirmation through chicken happiness. Chicken happiness becomes an *add-on* to consume and locks human use of chickens as benevolent: "Slow growing, happy free-range chickens simply taste better" (*The Guardian*, 21/10/2015 [G42]).

4.2.6 Summary and discussion

Although a strong bias towards human interests is evident in the *Guardian* corpus as in all the newspapers, the human-centred ideology is not fixed. The *Guardian* corpus is the largest, immediately revealing that chicken farming receives more attention than in the *Telegraph*, *Mirror*, and *Mail*. Nearly two-thirds of *Guardian* texts (260 texts out of 434, or 60%) include at least one sentence on chicken welfare. A notable distinction between news and opinion/feature articles is observed, with the latter typically being welfare-inclusive (81%). Nearly two-thirds of news items (60%), however, "objectively" exclude the experiences and interests of chickens in situations and events where they are affected participants.

As the sociologist Ulrich Beck (2010) notes, "the news media do not only function in terms of global focussing of events; rather the news media adopt a more performative stand" (p. 261). In other words, the *Guardian* chooses issues to report on and actors and perspectives to validate as important. Except for the high-calibre welfare campaigns such as the ones led by Fearnley-Whittingstall, chickens are more likely to appear in news when they are problematic to humans, threaten the economy and public health rather than for their own sake. The *Guardian* news stories appeal to objectivity and factuality and rely upon scientific "truth" claims and official sources. Yet "truth" claims and "facts" are likely to echo the ideology which neglects animal sentience to effectively instrumentalise and commodify chickens. The terminology deployed to refer to chickens constructs them as resources, e.g. "livestock" or "poultry". Chickens are calculated as loss or gain to the economy or inscribed as a threat to public health.

It may not be surprising that chickens are predominantly instrumentalised and depersonalised in the *Guardian* news. Chickens are primarily viewed through the lens of the A-IC — as food animals or flocks defined by geography or ownership. Individual chickens could hardly be identified in the articles that focus on issues such as the economy and are upfront about their non-animal welfare focus. Nonetheless, a greater inclusion of voices of people who question chicken farming, such as activists and campaigners, could ensure that instrumental portrayals do not become the sole representations of chickens. Articles such as the one on factory farming divestment demonstrate that the welfare perspective can be introduced even in rather unlikely places such as economy-focussed stories.

As we shall see, failing to acknowledge the inextricable connection between chicken and human welfare issues is a major method of discursive erasure in all the newspapers. In the *Guardian* bird flu, *Salmonella* or *Campylobacter* news stories, chicken sentience and experiences are rarely considered despite the virus and bacteria affecting chickens directly and indirectly, when they are killed in staggering numbers as a "control measure". *Guardian* articles on slaughterhouse workers offer a perfect yet rarely taken opportunity to interrogate the conditions for chickens and make a link between the exploitation of birds and workers.

By contrast, a philosophical debate on whether it is ethical to use chickens for our needs can be found in opinion/feature articles such as those by Baggini and Sten. The instrumental relationship between humans and chickens is challenged by constructing intensive farms as horrible wrecking places. Rhetorically, intensive chicken farming is presented as abhorrent and atrocious through referring to chickens as *victims of mankind's greed and exploitation* or *prisoners* and to farms as *concentration camps* and farming as *apartheid*. The "appropriation" of human rights rhetoric exposes biases towards chickens and invites readers to perceive the relationship between humans and farmed animals as the one between the oppressors and the oppressed. Readers, in a sense, become the "bystanders" and are reminded that they participate in animal cruelty as consumers and citizens.

Furthermore, a recurrent trait of *Guardian* opinion pieces is an extensive critique of chicken farming from multiple standpoints, notably chicken welfare, public health, sustainability, and climate change. This extensive critique is particularly visible between 2015 and 2016, the years that show an increase in coverage of chicken farming. Opinion pieces produced in the end of the analysed period indicate a growing awareness of farming practices and a discursive shift that repositions chicken farming as an important global issue. This coincides with an overall growing concern over sustainability and farmed animal welfare in the EU and with a growing "higher welfare" product market in the UK (European Commission, 2016).

It could be argued that merging chicken welfare problems together with socio-political, cultural, environmental or public health issues can be muddling and distracting from a specific cause (e.g. banning cages) as texts move away from being solely about farming and the wellbeing of farmed animals. Nonetheless, the holistic framing has the potential to open a far-reaching debate that goes beyond minor welfare improvements since it scrutinises animal farming as a systemic problem. As pointed out by Singer (Spira & Singer, 2006) with regards to the Belgian-American animal rights advocate Henry Spira's successful animal activism, it is important to look out for "vulnerabilities to public opinion" and "put your adversary on the defensive" (pp. 2016–2021). The critique of chicken farming linking animal ethics, environmental destruction, impact on public health and less privileged humans such as slaughterhouse or farm workers redefines "normal" chicken farming as abuse of nonhumans, humans and the planet and opens possibilities for alliances between activists.

The *Guardian* features on backyard and rescued chickens construct them as persons and companions. While remaining inevitably anthropocentric, I suggest that representations such as in the illustrative example from the opinion piece by Barr (*The Guardian,* 15/4/2006 [G21]), where her backyard chickens are personalised, are helpful in reinstating chicken agency and balancing out the view of chickens as objects (produced, slaughtered, abused, etc.). They provide an alternative discursive angle for chickens as ends in themselves rather than means or victims of cruelty. One could argue that such an angle may not be suitable for news reporting, but chickens are sentient beings and therefore should not be portrayed as nonliving things, units or merely reservoirs of disease either.

On the other hand, chicken agency and (positive) emotions are exploited in discourses of "higher welfare" farming to sell the products and the very idea of "higher welfare" farming. The sociologist Mara Miele (2011) interrogates "what is happiness for a chicken" and argues that farmed animal happiness is a political technique (p. 2076). Miele (2011) suggests that the invention of the happy chicken is a step towards better, more compassionate chicken farming. But she also points to marketing strategies and notes that chicken happiness is instrumental to the supposedly improved taste of their flesh — an argument that is also found in the *Guardian* features on "higher welfare" farming. I reiterate that chicken happiness in agriculture is also problematic since the *unhappy* parts of chicken lives remain invisible to consumers. The invention of the concepts such as "higher welfare" or "free-range" primarily serves the industry as chickens are further inscribed as (value-added, better-tasting) products and our domination of them as kind and thus ethically acceptable. Consumers are provided with moral affirmation as they are fed with renewed *pastoral* images of farming, which translate *naturalness* into the domesticated environment of chicken farms. Furthermore, chicken-centred narratives construct farming as a potential site of chicken *happiness* and the consumption of chicken products as enabling this *happiness*.

Here one might return to the analogy of human enslavement in antebellum America. Thomas Jefferson claimed that amelioration of enslavement would bring about abolition. However, amelioration presented slavery as progressive and improving and thereby elevated the institution rather than threatened it (Dierksheide, 2008). As argued by historian Christa Dierksheide (2008), amelioration became an end in itself. Enslaved Black people were presented as "happy", childlike and in need of *care* from their benevolent owners. Returning to the question of chickens, the examination of the industry's welfare claims shows that welfare lexis is exploited and manipulated to defend and elevate industry practices, which, if not sugar-coated in this way would be seen as cruel. The industry moves away from the notions of factory and efficient production towards what Khazaal and Almiron (2016) call "camouflaged speciesism", i.e. the notions of *happy* chickens and *caring* farming. The debate is shifted away from the legitimacy of chicken farming in favour of welfare improvements and taste preference.

Whilst "higher welfare" farming does not receive as much criticism as intensive farming, occasionally it is placed under scrutiny in the broadsheet. The analyses of welfare rhetoric and investigations of the lived realities of chickens in "higher welfare" farms reveal openings for a more radical change, such as reducing the consumption of animal products, abstaining from certain products or turning to a vegan diet. In contrast to campaigners' corpora, where, we shall see in Chapter 5, the emphasis is placed on chicken suffering, the *Guardian* opinion pieces offer framings that go beyond suffering and lifestyle choices and thus have a stronger ideological potential for transforming dominant human-chicken relationships. Returning to the enslavement analogy, the reader can assume abolition rather than reform.

To conclude, as may have been expected from a left-leaning quality paper known for its educated readership, social democratic ideology and attention to sustainability issues (Carvalho, 2007), the *Guardian* provides a platform for a critical debate on intensive chicken farming and is open to animal rights and welfare perspectives in opinion/feature articles. Opinion pieces vary in degree from fundamentally deploring intensive farming to criticising its various aspects. Most revolve around discussions of "humane" treatment and condemn intensive farms as miserable factory-like places, presenting chickens as sentient beings with emotions and interests. Such narratives are voiced by journalists, activists, and public figures such as Monbiot. Nevertheless, opinion/feature articles can be perceived precisely as opinion, up for debate or even deliberately controversial, whereas news is seen as an objective account of global and local events. A more balanced representation of chicken farming could be produced in the *Guardian* if the voices of animal advocates would be more pronounced in news. Since news items occupy a greater share of the *Guardian* corpus than opinion/feature pieces (230 vs 178 texts), adding critical voices to news reporting would make animal welfare/rights agenda more legitimate and remind the reader that chickens are sentient beings rather than things.

4.3 The Mirror

News stories occupy nearly three-quarters of the *Mirror* corpus (189 texts, or 74%). One-fifth (54 texts, or 21%) are opinion/feature articles. The corpus contains 11 letters (4%). Table 4.8 shows thematic distribution of *Mirror* articles between 1982 and 2016. As in the *Guardian* and *Mail* corpora, the largest thematic domain (66 texts, or 26%) is public health risks and food safety. The majority of these texts are news reports on the bird flu epidemic. The keywords associated with the epidemic, i.e. *flu, virus, strain, outbreak* and *Tamiflu*, are identified in the top 100 keywords of the *Mirror* corpus (see Appendix B online). Tables 4.9, 4.10 and 4.11 compare the frequencies in the *Mirror* corpus against the *Guardian, Telegraph* and *Mail* corpora. The ratios of topical words *flu, virus, strain* and *outbreak* are highest when the *Mirror* corpus is compared with the *Telegraph* corpus; *flu* is used 3.9 times relatively more frequently in the *Mirror, strain* 5.7 times, *virus* 4.4 times and *outbreak* 4.3 times, respectively.

The second-largest thematic domain in the *Mirror* corpus is chicken welfare (60 texts, or 24%). The term "high welfare" in relation to chicken farming first appears in the corpus in 2002. It is used synonymously with "higher welfare", which is popularised through the campaigns by the celebrity chefs. Furthermore, as the *Guardian* and *Mail*, the *Mirror* carries out its own undercover investigations into the treatment of chickens raised for their flesh or eggs and reports on the investigations of other organisations. Although veganism does not feature in the corpus, a joint undercover investigation into a chicken farm was carried out with the vegan-run animal rescue Hillside Animal Sanctuary in 2002.

Unlike the broadsheets, the *Mirror* and *Mail* corpora contain articles that clearly prioritise sensation and therefore are placed under the category "human interest stories/sensational stories". In the *Mirror* corpus, 43 stories (17%) are found, covering events such as chickens burned alive in a farm fire or a hen laying banana-shaped eggs. Articles that would question chicken farming from multiple perspectives, as a moral, environmental, and public health issue, are virtually absent in the *Mirror* corpus, whereas they occupy 6% of the *Guardian* corpus. Only one article is dedicated to environmental issues, indicating that environmental concerns in relation to chicken farming are invisible in the tabloid.

Table 4.8 Distribution of the thematic domains in the Mirror corpus

	public health/food safety	*welfare of chickens*	*human interest/sensational stories*	*business/economics*	*cultural and social issues*	*ethical vegetarianism/direct action*	*organic/free-range farming*	*backyard farming/chicken companions*	*miscellaneous*	*total per year*
1982								1		1
1983			1							1
1984		2				1				3
1985										0
1986		1	1							2
1987			1							1
1988	1	1	2	1						5
1989	4	1								5
1990	1									1
1991										0
1992										0
1993			2			1				3
1994										0
1995		1					2			3
1996	2									2
1997	3	3	2	3						11
1998	1	1	3	3					2	10
1999	1	2	2		2					7
2000	3	4	1			1			1	10
2001		1	1				1			3
2002	2	3	1							6
2003		7	3		1	1	1			13
2004	5	3	1	1	1			1		12
2005	8	4	3				1	1		17
2006	13	1	3	12	1		3	1		34
2007	9	2	1	3	1	1				17
2008	6	12	4	8	3	2	1	2		38
2009	1	3	1					1		6
2010	1			2		1				4
2011	1	1	2		3			1		8
2012		3	2	2	1	1		1		10
2013	1		2	1		1				5
2014			3			2				5
2015	3	1			1					5
2016		3	1			2				6
TOTAL	**66**	**60**	**43**	**36**	**14**	**14**	**9**	**9**	**3**	**254**

Table 4.9 Frequency analysis: Mirror and Guardian

	Mirror		Guardian		Keyness		
Word or lemma	**AF**	**NF**	**AF**	**NF**	**Over/under-use**	**LL**	**Ratio**
flu	230	28.8	320	9.3	+	154.6	3.1
virus	97	12.1	188	5.4	+	37.1	2.2
strain	71	8.9	101	2.9	+	46.3	3.0
outbreak	74	9.3	121	3.5	+	38.9	2.6
tamiflu	9	1.1	5	0.1	+	13.9	7.8
killer	11	1.4	9	0.3	+	13.0	5.3
dead*	115	14.4	147	4.3	+	86.5	3.4
rotting	11	1.4	4	0.1	+	21.1	11.9
horrific	12	1.5	5	0.1	+	21.6	10.4
sickening	7	0.9	3	0.1	+	12.4	10.1
shock	17	2.1	12	0.3	+	22.5	6.1
Total word count		**79,927**		**345,505**			

Note: (+) indicates "overuse"; (-) indicates "underuse"; (div) indicates "division by 0 disallowed"; LL of 3.84 or higher is significant at the level of $p < 0.05$

In addition, one of the most immediately noticeable differences between the *Mirror* corpus and the other newspapers lies in linguistic style. The language in the *Mirror* is more colloquial and emotive. The avian influenza virus is more likely to be sensationalised as a *killer* virus in the *Mirror* corpus rather in the other newspapers (Tables 4.9, 4.10 and 4.11). The hype around bird flu and other chicken and human health issues is created by using emotional descriptors such as *dead**, *rotting, horrific, sickening* and *shock*. Tables 4.9, 4.10 and 4.11 show the relative overuse of these keywords. For example, *rotting* is used 11.9 times relatively more frequently in the *Mirror* corpus than in the *Guardian*, 4 times than in the *Telegraph* and 11.4 times than in the *Mail*. *Sickening* is used 10.1 times relatively more frequently in the *Mirror* corpus than in the *Guardian*, 3.4 times the *Telegraph* and 21.8 times the *Mail*. Furthermore, the *Mirror* uses humour extensively. As the critical linguist Roger Fowler (1991) notes, humour and wordplay are the chief rhetorical devices deployed by tabloids to engage the reader's interest (p. 45). Puns and wordplay, recurrently found in headlines, set a light-hearted tone. Examples of homophones and figurative language used to create puns are "eggciting", "eggcellent", "egg-static", "farmer's so unclucky" or "vet cries fowl over birds cull".

Table 4.10 Frequency analysis: Mirror and Telegraph

	Mirror		Telegraph		Keyness		
Word or lemma	**AF**	**NF**	**AF**	**NF**	**Over/under-use**	**LL**	**Ratio**
flu	230	28.8	86	9.3	+	131.3	3.9
virus	97	12.1	32	5.4	+	62.4	4.4
strain	71	8.9	18	2.9	+	56.1	5.7
outbreak	74	9.3	25	3.5	+	46.6	4.3
tamiflu	9	1.1	0	0.0	+	16.1	div
killer	11	1.4	0	0.0	+	19.6	div
dead*	115	14.4	31	2.7	+	87.0	5.4
rotting	11	1.4	4	0.3	+	6.5	4.0
horrific	12	1.5	5	0.4	+	6.1	3.5
sickening	7	0.9	3	0.3	+	3.4	3.4
shock	17	2.1	12	1.0	+	3.7	2.0
Total word count	**79,927**		**115,255**				

Table 4.11 Frequency analysis: Mirror and Mail

	Mirror		Mail		Keyness		
Word or lemma	**AF**	**NF**	**AF**	**NF**	**Over/under-use**	**LL**	**Ratio**
flu	230	28.8	332	13.4	+	74.6	2.2
virus	97	12.1	200	8.1	+	10.4	1.5
strain	71	8.9	119	4.8	+	15.9	1.9
outbreak	74	9.3	115	4.6	+	20.2	2.0
tamiflu	9	1.1	8	0.3	+	6.4	3.5
killer	11	1.4	10	0.4	+	7.6	3.4
dead*	115	14.4	175	7.0	+	33.1	2.0
rotting	11	1.4	3	0.1	+	18.2	11.4
horrific	12	1.5	5	0.2	+	16.1	7.5
sickening	7	0.9	1	0.0	+	14.3	21.8
shock	17	2.1	14	0.6	+	13.2	3.8
Total word count	**79,927**		**248,339**				

4.3.1 Normalising chicken farming

Around one-half of *Mirror* texts (51%) are not inclusive of animal rights or welfare perspectives, which is the highest proportion among the newspapers' corpora. In comparison to the *Guardian*, the division between news and opinion articles is less pronounced; chicken welfare is entirely omitted in 104 news stories (55%) and 23 opinion/feature articles (43%). Since news items occupy a greater share of the *Mirror* corpus, I shall predominantly focus on news articles in this section.

The anthropologist Gary Marvin (2001) highlights that representations are necessarily immersed in cultural meanings; they are manifestations of human concerns, desires, and imaginings. As is observed in all four newspapers, economy-focussed news items calculate chickens in monetary terms and deny their sentience. For example, a news story on the chicken business of Prince Charles personifies the business by attributing it an ability to *suffer* (*Daily Mirror*, 8/5/2014 [M31]). Meanwhile, hens are constructed as *stock* and receive attention because they are the *stock* of the Prince, but not for their own sake: "Prince Charles's business is suffering after 24 of his egg-laying hens were slaughtered by a fox. The attack on the organic coop leaves the prince without any stock to supply his local farm shop" (*Daily Mirror*, 8/5/2014 [M31]).

Consider the economic focus in the news headline: "185,000 hens destroyed; *Salmonella* bug hits top egg producer" (*Daily Mirror*, 9/11/2012 [M27]). The verb "destroy", used for material objects in its basic meaning, obscures the killing of hens and the construction of a passive voice removes the human actor. *Salmonella* infection is not necessarily lethal to chickens and a vaccination is widely available and has been used in the industry since 1998 (British Egg Information Services, 2018a; 2018b). Yet the story reports on how *Salmonella* "hits" the *producer* (instead of hens), for whom the mass killing is an easy fix to the "problem":

> Charles Crawford, director of Ready Egg Products, said his birds started dying about four weeks ago and the company culled about a third of the flock to stop the disease spreading. He added: "We have had a problem and we have dealt with it. There is no danger to human beings." (*Daily Mirror*, 9/11/2012 [M27])

In the *Mirror* corpus, sensational bird flu stories markedly increase the total of texts that do not mention chicken welfare. Consider the joke in the headline "Bird flu: don't get in a flap" (*Daily Mirror*, 19/10/2005 [M7]) for a news story on the first EU case of bird flu. Such new stories give little or no attention to practices of intensive farming and do not perceive the virus as an issue related to intensification or poor conditions for chickens. The loss of life is considered as wholly an economic loss. An illustrative example comes from a news article which, although uses the verb "kill", equates chickens' lives to sums of money:

"All chickens on 600 farms in the Suphan Buri province will be killed. The area raises one billion chickens a year and earns more than £1 billion in exports" (*Daily Mirror*, 26/1/2004 [M5]).

The pervasiveness of the A-IC is tangible in the exclusion of critical voices such as the ones of campaigners. The exclusion ensures that violence against chickens, although visible, remains unremarked in news reporting. An illustrative example comes from a news report on an "experimental" killing of chickens. The voices of campaigners, who could provide an ethical judgement or at least raise welfare concerns regarding a staggering number of healthy chickens being killed in testing precautionary measures, are absent. The verb "exterminate", the generic term "poultry" and the pronoun "none" instead of "no one" trivialise and neutralise the mass killing of 6,000 sentient beings (*Daily Mirror*, 26/11/2005 [M8]). The authorities, i.e. the Department of Agriculture, on the other hand, are personalised using the relative pronoun "who":

> More than 6,000 chickens have been slaughtered to test emergency response to an outbreak of avian flu. The poultry were taken from a farm in Co Monaghan, by fire service crews who exterminated them using gas. The Department of Agriculture, who ordered the slaughter, stressed none of the flock had any infection and the exercise was to test the authorities' response and the effectiveness of the gas. (*Daily Mirror*, 26/11/2005 [M8])

Another news story on the "experimental exercise" of gassing 6,000 chickens points to the dangerous conditions for firefighters involved. The identification with firefighters (which could be expected in the tabloid with a largely working-class readership) could be leveraged to build awareness about the exploited animals too. However, it is not questioned whether the method of killing or conditions are acceptable for chickens or whether such an "experiment" is justifiable at all:

> Six thousand chickens are to be gassed today in an experiment to see how quickly they die... The Fire Officers' Association has told members not to take part in the slaughter because it claims it does not comply with the standard procedures for a hazardous material incident. It maintains it was not consulted and claims its members' lives would be at risk. (*Daily Mirror*, 16/5/2006 [M10])

In these stories, there are no adjectives describing the events as *tragic, sad,* or *depressing,* nor are chickens' lives mourned. Chickens' experiences are completely erased; they disappear in what is aridly referred to as a *material incident.* One could ask whether a *Mirror* reporter would keep an equally detached instrumental tone if animals of a culturally important species such as horses, dogs or cats were affected. While a separate study is required to thoroughly compare the representation of different animals, it would be surprising to find a news story on a mass killing of dogs or cats without at least a hint of compassion or an inclusion of an empathetic voice of an animal advocate. For example, a *Mirror* news story dramatises the killing of unwanted, old, or simply no longer "good" racing dogs:

> Animal lovers who packed the public gallery gasped in disbelief as 47-year-old David Smith, who charged £10 a time to put down unwanted racing dogs, was spared jail. Smith could have been locked up for up to five years had he been found guilty of animal cruelty. (*Daily Mirror*, 17/3/2007 [M13])

While the greyhounds are essentially working dogs rather than "pets" and the story informs readers that the dogs are killed "humanely" (using a gun) and the killer is not charged for animal cruelty, but for breaching environmental rules by burying dogs on his land, the events are immediately situated in the context of animal cruelty. Consider the use of the verb "slaughter" which is preferred over "shoot" to evoke emotions in the headline: "Barking; this man slaughtered up to 10,000 greyhounds. Yesterday he was fined just 20p for each one that he killed" (*Daily Mirror*, 17/3/2007 [M13]).

Moreover, the *Mirror* corpus is characterised by sensational humorous representation, which undermines chicken welfare issues. A light-hearted tone makes "soft" news stories that are problematic from an ethical point of view seem fun. Consider the wordplay in the headline "The great eggscape; it's no yolk as 7,000 chickens cross the road to go on the run after lorry crashes" (*Daily Mirror*, 16/12/2005 [M9]). The comical headline matches the text, which presents the road accident in an equally entertaining manner. Colloquial and idiomatic language, and a reference to the comedy-drama film *Chicken Run* obscures the gravity of the situation.[3] Although the news story notes that the chickens are terrified, the events are portrayed as amusing:

> Thousands of chickens brought mayhem to a busy road yesterday when the lorry they were travelling in crashed. The clucking fugitives attempted their own Chicken Run on the main N55 Cavan Road when the truck came off at a bend and ploughed into a ditch at around 5.40 am. And just like the hens in the box office smash the runaway birds didn't let their one shot at freedom in Ballinagh, Co Cavan, pass them by. Shocked motorists were in a flap as the terrified birds scrambled across the road laying eggs in every direction. (*Daily Mirror*, 16/12/2005 [M9])

Another news story on a lorry accident similarly uses wordplay in the headline "Shell shock for drivers" (*Daily Mirror*, 6/10/2006 [M11]). The headline shows that the disturbance caused to drivers is the main issue of concern. Idiomatic

[3] *Chicken Run* is an animated film telling a story of farmed chickens who decide to escape the farm so that they do not get turned into chicken pies. At the end of the film, the chickens escape and live happily.

phrasing "to cause a flap" and "pecking order" and a common riddle joke "why did the chicken cross the road" put a light-hearted, humorous tone on the events where chickens are hurt. In a situation where chickens have no culpability and little agency, they are called an "errant flock":

> Why did thousands of chickens cross the road yesterday? Because their lorry overturned. The birds caused a flap on a country road near Carrickmacross, Co Monaghan, during the lunchtime spill. But the pecking order was soon restored when nearby farm workers rounded up most of the errant flock on the Ballybay to Shercock Road. (*Daily Mirror*, 6/10/2006 [M11])

Overall, unsurprisingly, the *Mirror* prioritises shock or entertainment over analysis. A feature reporting on a planned killing of chickens who have escaped from intensive farms and managed to survive in the isle of Bermuda illustrates how the lack of critical voices results in a biased representation. While chickens inhabiting the isle are equated to *plague*, it is not specified what harm chickens do or what environmental or social implications their colonisation has (*Daily Mirror*, 24/8/2012 [M25]). The story of chickens in Bermuda could equally be situated as a success story if it were written from a perspective of an animal advocate since it proves that chickens can successfully adapt to living freely in local environments. Yet colloquial language, humour and the advice of the author to "trap" chickens "for the pot" demonstrate an entirely anthropocentric perspective on the events; in addition, the advice shows that even backyard chickens are ultimately regarded as *meat*:

> The idyllic isle of Bermuda cowers under a plague of wild creatures. Hens, to be precise. Many escaped after Hurricane Emily destroyed their battery farms, and they're breeding like, well, like chickens. One feral hen can produce up to 198 chicks in a year. They must have very busy cockerels in Bermuda. A cull has been ordered. As a former hen keeper, I suggest they throw down some corn and trap them for the pot. (*Daily Mirror*, 24/8/2012 [M25])

In the *Mirror* corpus, headlines are more likely to be attention-grabbing and light-hearted, whereas the content of a story may differ in style. This could be explained by the common practice of headlines being written by the editors instead of the authors of texts. Consider the pun which exploits the idiomatic phrase "one hell of a" to create a humorous headline "It's one hen of a storm" (*Daily Mirror*, 4/2/1999 [M3]). The headline sets a light-hearted tone, but the news story accounts for the deaths of chickens in a more serious tone, for the loss of lives means a financial loss:

> More than quarter of a million chickens have been killed by gale force winds in Uruguay. Gales of up to 80 mph cut electricity and flattened buildings, including a number of huge chicken barns. Farmer Ariel Lencina said he alone had lost 200,000 hens. (*Daily Mirror*, 4/2/1999 [M3])

A mix of styles in the headline and the body of text may produce a narrative that is not consistently objectifying. To illustrate, the headline for a news story on a fire in a chicken farm is sensational and ironic: "12,000 chickens roasted; Blaze 'no big deal' insists farmer" (*Daily Mirror*, 25/3/2011 [M22]). The reporter further describes chickens burned alive in a funny way ("barbecued"), but the event is simultaneously presented as *horrific* and *sad* and chickens' experiences are considered:

> Thousands of helpless month-old chickens were barbecued in a horrific inferno early yesterday morning. More than 12,000 birds were burnt alive when the fire broke out at the farm in Monalena, Co Limerick, at around 3.30 am. It took five units of the fire brigade three hours to bring the blaze under control, but sadly they couldn't save the terrified chicks. (*Daily Mirror*, 25/3/2011 [M22])

Nonetheless, the perspectives of the farmer, who does not see the event as newsworthy, and the local councillor, who focusses on the *suffering* of the farmer and "his business", trivialise the loss of lives. The fire is called *bird bonfire,* a rather "creative" word choice to describe events that are neither controlled nor celebratory:

> Farmer Connie Nash, who owned the chickens, insisted the bird bonfire was no big deal. He said: "This doesn't warrant anything in newspapers. This is a chicken house that got burnt down."... Local Fine Gael councillor Damien Reidy said: "I was very upset to hear about the terrible fire at Connie Nash's farm. I hope he and his business make a full recovery." (*Daily Mirror*, 25/3/2011 [M22])

Another illustrative example of a combination between light-hearted "tabloid-speak" and a more serious tone which includes an animal welfare perspective comes from a "soft" news story on hens bought from a farm for a stag party prank. Consider the headline "Call the RSPCA... the stag do's become a hen party; Two birds die in boozy lads' prank" (*Daily Mirror*, 30/6/2012 [M24]). The article is written in a sensational entertaining manner, using colloquial language, idiomatic expressions and puns; the individuals who purchased the hens and then abandoned them without food and water in a hotel room are mocked: "Two bird-brained brothers fell fowl of the law" (*Daily Mirror*, 30/6/2012 [M24]). The adjective "bird-brained", however, reproduces the stereotype of birds being unintelligent. Ultimately, the RSPCA prosecutor brings seriousness back by declaring that "using animals for the purposes of entertainment or a prank has long been a criminal offence in this country" (*Daily Mirror*, 30/6/2012 [M24]).

The story on the stag party prank also illustrates how the language in the *Mirror* can be irreverent. When reporting on a campaign against cages for hens launched by a British teenager, the tabloid chooses the headline "Clucky teenager takes on Tesco" (*Daily Mirror*, 20/4/2016 [M33]). Another news story on the same campaign calls the female activist a "plucky teenager" (*Daily Mirror*, 26/6/2016

[M34]). Nonetheless, in both texts, support for the young activist rather than the supermarket giant is expressed. The tabloid sides with the "underdog" as the teenager's message is conveyed through a direct quotation and her campaign is presented as successful: "A new petition on the website www.Change.org has already had more than 176,000 backers" (*Daily Mirror*, 26/6/2016 [M34]).

The representation of campaigners can help as well as undermine the cause. The celebrity chef Oliver receives slightly more coverage than his colleague Fearnley-Whittingstall; Oliver features in 13 stories and Fearnley-Whittingstall in eight stories, respectively. The depictions of Oliver are more neutral or positive; Oliver is humanised by referring to his age or family status, e.g. "father-of-two Jamie" (*Daily Mirror*, 7/1/2008 [M14]) or "delighted Jamie, 33" (*Daily Mirror*, 6/8/2008 [M19]). Fearnley-Whittingstall is more likely to be ridiculed: "There was a great clip on TV Burp of Hugh Fearnley-Whittingstall on Hugh's Chicken Run, viewing the conditions of an intensive chicken farm and sobbing: 'What kind of animal would want to live here?!' Harry Hill: 'A fox?'" (*Daily Mirror*, 22/1/2008 [M17]).

Fearnley-Whittingstall receives more criticism in the tabloid due to associations with a class position and elitism. A feature on the celebrity's Channel 4 programme "Hugh's Chicken Run" illustrates a conflict between classes. In the series, Fearnley-Whittingstall promotes free-range chicken farming on the basis of welfare and taste and attempts to change the consumption habits of the residents of Axminster, Devon. He encourages residents on the working-class council estate to raise their own free-range chickens on unused allotments. A local woman, Hayley, becomes central to the series. The single mother of two enthusiastically participates in the experiment but challenges the chef. Hayley is the only participant who by the end of the campaign refuses to buy meat from free-range farms on the grounds of cost. The *Mirror* feature on the programme emphasises the chef's class position. Fearnley-Whittingstall is described using loaded adjectives "double-barrelled TV toff", as bossing around and struggling to charm "the cash-strapped locals":

> Over the next three nights, we'll also see him [Fearnley-Whittingstall] try to convert Axminster in Devon into Britain's first free-range town. Here he really has an uphill struggle charming the cash-strapped locals who are sceptical about being bossed around by a double-barrelled TV toff. Single mum Hailey, who rises naturally to the top of the pecking order, clearly has Hugh's number. "Do you think if you were just Hugh and you owned a corner shop, you'd get the response you got today?" she asks. (*Daily Mirror*, 7/1/2008 [M15])

It might seem that in the TV show, Hayley's refusal to transform into an "ethical" consumer is presented as a moral failure associated with the working class. Therefore, Fearnley-Whittingstall's approach can be seen as condescending and may not appeal to the large share of the *Mirror* working-class readers. Without stating it explicitly, the journalist mocks the campaign as revolving around middle-class habits and suggests that not eating chicken flesh is a better alternative:

> And while I admire Hugh's intentions, I can't quite ignore the little voice in my head saying that if you really cared about the welfare of chickens you wouldn't eat them, full-stop — even if they had spent their entire lives sunning themselves by a swimming pool in Marbella. (*Daily Mirror*, 7/1/2008 [M15])

This suggestion, however, seems to be more of a stick to beat Fearnley-Whittingstall rather than a genuine call to remove chickens from our diet. The ironic tone and focus on the personality of the celebrity makes the story ambivalent. It is also worth noting that only two texts in the *Mirror* corpus bring up the idea that one should not eat chicken flesh at all, if they care about chickens (the second one is analysed in the following section).

Consider the humorous headline "Chicks out of cluck" for a TV preview on Fearnley-Whittingstall's television programme Hugh's Chicken Run (*Sunday Mirror*, 13/1/2008 [M16]). In the story, the chef's physical appearance ("badhair") is attacked *ad hominem*. His emotional response to killing chickens is presented ironically, as hypocrisy is assumed. Furthermore, gender stereotypes manifest in feminisation of sentiment; Fearnley-Whittingstall is stripped of his masculinity as he is being called a "*boy*":

> I don't doubt that badhair boy Hugh Fearnley-Whittingstall wept genuine tears as he prepared to exterminate another feathered victim of his harrowing TV experiment revealing the shocking truth about poultry farming. Luckily the cameras happened to be pointing at him. But, unfortunately, he cries exactly like a bad actor. (*Sunday Mirror*, 13/1/2008 [M16])

Fearnley-Whittingstall's fellow campaigner Oliver is referred to as an *accomplice*, a term retaining its connotation to crime. Nonetheless, the feature ultimately draws attention not only to "cheap shots", but also "cheap chicken" and acknowledges the effort of the celebrity chefs, concluding that consuming eggs and meat from intensive farms supports cruelty:

> Chicken week on Channel 4 and, cheap shots aside, good for Hugh and his accomplice Jamie Oliver for taking a stand. ...Guest Ricky Gervais wasn't joking when he said: "Buying the cheapest eggs and chickens is buying into cruelty." He's right. It's a question of compassion. (*Sunday Mirror*, 13/1/2008 [M16])[4]

Nevertheless, the narrative that *cheap* food has hidden costs is less prevalent in the *Mirror* corpus than in the *Guardian* and the *Mail*. It does not permeate the *Mirror* corpus, although some instances are found. The illustrative extract from

---

[4] Ricky Gervais is a British celebrity.

the concordances for "cheap" in Table 4.12 demonstrates that the adjective carries a negative connotation primarily due to animal cruelty and the impact on local economy. *Cheap* could be condemned less because of the tabloid's primary working-class readership, who could be assumed to be critical contributors to the consumption of *cheap* chicken meat and eggs.

Table 4.12 Extract from "cheap" concordance using context words "meat", "food", "egg(s)" and "chicken(s)"

on the appalling methods used to raise	**cheap**, battery-farmed chickens. You appl
out of business as buyers bring in	**cheap** chicken from abroad, where welfare
the myth that factory farming gives us	**cheap** food." M & S BANS BATTERY FARM
rmers also face savage competition from	**cheap** imported chicken. Supermarkets are
yesterday urged stores to stop selling	**cheap** meat from poorly reared chickens.
actory-farmed chicken. When it comes to	**cheap** meat, it's the animals that pay
FSA is now urging families who have	**cheap** Spanish eggs to avoid eating runny
ercrowded factory farms. Please boycott	**cheap** supermarket chicken and ask your M

The *Mirror* feature stories on organic farming, on the other hand, foreground the benefits to human health rather than chicken welfare. An illustrative example demonstrates that better conditions for chickens are seen as instrumental to the quality of chicken bodily products; the focus is placed on the end product rather than chickens in their live state:

> Chicken is full of essential nutrients and is an excellent, low-fat food containing high levels of protein and a variety of vitamins and minerals. Why it's bad: Nutrition expert Patrick Holford, www.patrickholford.com, says: "But if chickens don't get enough exercise and eat too many carbs, they get fatter faster and then pass this fat on to us." But that's not the only problem. "If chickens aren't kept in good conditions, that helps create superbugs that put our health at risk," adds Patrick. Swap for: Chickens reared organically. Patrick says: "These chickens have to be given top-quality feed so it's often worth spending a little extra..." (*Daily Mirror*, 16/4/2013 [M28])

4.3.2 Problematising chicken farming/Alternative discourses

Less than one-half of the *Mirror* texts contain at least one sentence on chicken welfare (49%, compared to 60% in the *Guardian* corpus). Chicken welfare is included in 85 news stories (45%) and 31 opinion/feature pieces (57%). Voices bringing the perspectives of chicken welfare/rights belong to Fearnley-Whittingstall, Oliver, Lymbery (CIWF), Joyce D'Silva (CIWF), Elisa Allen (PETA), the Advocates for Animals, the British Hen Welfare Trust, the Alliance for Animal Rights, and others.

Animal welfare perspectives are most pronounced in investigative journalism pieces. Investigative journalism stories are lengthy, hard-hitting, written in a serious tone and construct chickens as victims. When reporting on undercover investigations carried out by animal rights groups and by the tabloid itself, the *Mirror* uses similar rhetoric to the one of activists to demystify the rosy picture of both intensive and "higher welfare" farms. An illustrative example comes from a *Sunday Mirror* investigation into free-range farming titled "So you think 'free-range' hens spend their days just clucking happily round a field? This is the reality...; consumer check; investigation into treatment of free-range hens" (*Sunday Mirror*, 19/10/1997 [M1]). The journalist challenges the readers' idyllic perceptions of free-range farming: "So next time you pick up half a dozen free-range eggs in the supermarket, the hens who laid them might not have been scratching around in a picture-book farmyard" (*Sunday Mirror*, 19/10/1997 [M1]). The feature also includes commentary from a spectrum of sources, namely CIWF, PETA and a free-range farmer, that critically evaluate free-range farming from the perspective of chicken welfare. Both animal advocacy organisations challenge free-range as a feel-good term, with PETA expressing a more uncompromising stance against free-range systems:

> The term free-range is often a sick joke. It's incredibly misleading. There's a whole range of suffering that these hens go through in the name of free-range production. For the public, it is a way of appeasing its conscience when there is really nothing comforting in the way these eggs were produced. (*Sunday Mirror*, 19/10/1997 [M1])

PETA's language is punchy. In another news report which questions free-range farming, a PETA representative slams egg production by using emotive language and humanising chickens through their family bonds. Referring to the sibling bond not only appeals to readers' emotion but also reflects the commercial practices of breeding chickens who are genetically related: "Male chicks are suffocated or ground up alive and their sisters have beaks cut without pain relief" (*Sunday Mirror*, 27/3/2016 [M32]).

Whereas philosophical debate on the treatment of chickens is absent, consumers are not kept comfortably detached in investigative journalism stories. An illustrative example comes from a news report on an undercover film shot by a worker in a chicken farm. The news story describes distressing scenes in detail and reminds readers that chickens in the footage are farmed for British consumers:

> Sick and deformed chickens with raw patches of skin flap around the corpse of a bird too weak to survive. In seconds they are pecking away at its flesh as hundreds around them, unable to stand and with most of their feathers gone, drag themselves along by their wings. All are crammed into a huge windowless shed.

> And soon they will all be dead... skinned and ready for dinner tables across Britain… (*Sunday Mirror*, 23/9/2012 [M26])

The actor Martin Shaw, who is a patron of the film, equates chicken sheds to concentration camps. The public is not assumed to be "bystanders" turning a blind eye on chicken suffering. On the contrary, their outrage is expected to have an impact on business practices: "I hope and trust those shopping outlets that make use of these animal concentration camps will rethink their buying policy. If not, public outrage will make the decision for them" (*Sunday Mirror*, 23/9/2012 [M26]).

Apart from investigative journalism, constructions of chickens as victims are also found in reports on political events and legislation, such as the directive passed by the EU to ban battery cages. Despite the playful headline "We are clucked; Farmers are 'not prepared' for EU ban on all battery egg production", the subheading defines the life of a hen as "a year of hell" (*Daily Mirror*, 21/1/2009 [M21]). Intertextual borrowing from campaigner discourse manifests in a vivid, emotive description of the battery cage system:

> Battery hens live in awful conditions for most of their lives. They are put into the cages when they are around 18 weeks old, just before they start laying eggs. Tiny cages are arranged in rows of three to six tiers high inside huge, windowless sheds. On average, a battery hen shed in Ireland contains 7,500 birds who lay 300 eggs a year each. After a year the hens lay fewer eggs and most farms will then remove them for slaughter. (*Daily Mirror*, 21/1/2009 [M21])

Another way in which animal ethics can find their way into the content of the *Mirror* is through letters. In letters, readers respond, react, and engage in public debate. For instance, the *Sunday Mirror* investigation into the conditions in a battery farm owned by the chairman of the NFU's Egg Committee Ian McHardy elicited strong reactions from readers. A reader shames McHardy, who claimed that his hens were happy in battery cages (*Sunday Mirror*, 16/4/2000 [M4]). More specifically, the reader considers battery farming as the country's moral disgrace referring to the identity of Britain as a nation of animal lovers. The letter is one of the few examples that include the narrative of chicken farming as a moral issue and asks what cruelty tells about us as human beings:

> Shame on those who condone this evil trade. Well done Sunday Mirror for exposing the brutality of battery hen farms. Battery farmer Ian McHardy should hang his head in shame. How can anybody condone suffering on this massive scale and actually insist that the hens are happy?... Mahatma Gandhi once said: "The greatness of a nation and its moral progress can be judged by the way its animals are treated". We're supposed to be a nation of animal lovers. What happened? (*Sunday Mirror*, 16/4/2000 [M4])

The ethics of eating meat are explored in a feature on the TV programme "Jimmy and the Giant Supermarket". The feature is exceptional as it finds the realities of intensive chicken farming "barbaric" and calls the animal welfare ideology into question (*Daily Mirror*, 12/6/2012 [M23]). Scare quotes for "spent" and "high welfare", the personal pronoun "who" for hens as well as the term "factory" for an intensive farm immediately challenge the rhetoric of the industry. Finishing the piece with a question about killing and eating farmed animals has a rhetorical role rather than information-seeking intent; it performs a function in communicating with the reader:

> Celebrity chef uses "spent" egg-laying hens to produce affordable kievs: Jimmy's version will use older hens who have come to the end of their laying life—another example of the double-edged sword that is "high welfare" farming. I don't doubt Jimmy is sincere when he says he cares passionately about animal welfare. But anyone who is truly passionate about animal welfare will find the scenes in the chicken factory barbaric. Likewise, Jimmy's ongoing campaign for rose veal. Yes, it's shocking to shoot male dairy calves at birth because they're of no use. But is it really any less shocking to kill them when they're a year old and then eat them? (*Daily Mirror*, 12/6/2012 [M23])

Another exceptional feature revolves around cloning and other ways in which humans "design animals" and nature (*Sunday Mirror*, 1/11/1998 [M2]). The story deplores "factory farming" as causing animal suffering and environmental damage; chickens are mentioned to exemplify farmed animal welfare issues associated with selective breeding and intensive farming:

> Selective breeding has in itself, led to serious animal welfare problems such as the modern broiler chicken which reaches slaughter weight in just six weeks, but is prone to painful leg problems and heart conditions... Factory farming, which generates an enormous amount of farm animal suffering, has also caused serious environmental problems, such as water pollution. (*Sunday Mirror*, 1/11/1998 [M2])

Overall, however, positioning chicken farming as a global multifaceted issue or linking it to environmental issues are uncommon in the *Mirror* corpus of 34 years. Moreover, it is worth reiterating that as the tabloid corpus contains shorter texts on average, lengthy opinion pieces that would develop moral debates on chicken farming are not found. In addition, chickens are rarely the "doers" of actions in all the corpora, including the *Mirror*. The representations of chickens as agents and sensers of positive emotions are predominantly found in rescue stories or stories on backyard/companion chickens. These stories may be seen as trivia, sensationalised by a funny narrative and exaggeration. However, they present alternative discursive angles through direct quotations. The "soft" news story headlined "Plucky hen's escape plan is fowled up; runaway" (*Daily Mirror*, 24/4/2013 [M30]) tells an adventurous yet compassionate story about a hen, Agatha, who travelled 40 miles by sneaking into a van. The story depicts a compassionate human-chicken relationship, where both the human and the chicken are emotionally invested. Agatha is patronised, but valued and presented as having positive emotions and interests:

> "I'm so pleased to have found Agatha," said Melanie, 50. "I know she's a chicken, but she means as much to our family as a dog or a cat. She probably enjoyed her adventure, but I think she's glad to be home." (*Daily Mirror*, 24/4/2013 [M30])

Quoting people who care about chickens gives authenticity. Since journalists themselves tend to avoid challenging the legitimacy of chicken farming, quotes can become a way of shaking the status quo. For instance, a news story on a campaign to save hens from battery cage farming launched by the Battery Hen Welfare Trust cites a volunteer Margie Mackay, who frames battery cage farming as morally wrong: "No animal deserves to be caged for all its life. It's just not right" (*Daily Mirror*, 30/6/2008 [M18]).

While a separate study would be required to investigate fully the language of the tabloid and its changes over time, my research clearly demonstrates that entertainment is an important feature of the *Mirror* (and, as we shall see, the *Mail*) corpus. In the *Mirror* corpus, an inspiring story on an animal activist who saves battery hens uses the idiomatic expression "down on one's luck" to create a pun; the headline is "I take in hens who are down on their cluck; Caring Jane has saved 400,000 battery chickens" (*Daily Mirror*, 28/10/2013 [M29]). A "soft" news story titled "Nice cardig-hen" (*Daily Mirror*, 23/9/2008 [M20]) tells a story about a hen rescued from battery cage farming. The hen is personalised through a proper name, vivid description of her physical appearance and by assigning an emotional state ("stressed-out"). Through quoting the foster carer, the news story depicts Buffy the hen not only as an object of cruelty but as an agent. Punning (e.g. "plucked her to safety"), however, keeps the story light-hearted:

> A stressed-out hen who lost all her feathers at a cramped battery farm found a new way to keep warm yesterday — a knitted jumper. One-year-old Buffy was almost entirely bald and 1 kg underweight when the RSPCA plucked her to safety three weeks ago… [The foster carer] said: "Sadly, we occasionally find hens in this state when we rescue them and when Buffy arrived she looked like she was oven-ready. But now she's bold enough to peck and scratch about and tries to join the other chickens sunbathing in her little jumper." (*Daily Mirror*, 23/9/2008 [M20])

4.3.3 Summary and discussion

Chickens' experiences are erased in just over half of the *Mirror* texts (51%). Most public health and economy-related news items inscribe chickens as means of production or commodities. The vast majority of bird flu stories in particular overlook the negative effects on chickens. The events are rarely questioned from an animal welfare perspective, even less so from an animal rights position, despite the mass killings. The exclusion of voices of animal advocates who could provide an alternative narrative leaves violence against chickens unremarked.

Nonetheless, it should be acknowledged that the *Mirror* maintains some room for serious investigative journalism. The tabloid carries out its own investigations and reports on the undercover investigations by animal rights groups and activists. Alternative narratives where chicken farming is openly and forcefully criticised are produced. Readers are exposed to the unpleasant realities of intensive, as well as "higher welfare" chicken farming, which is shaken off the "moral pedestal". Even if it is the shock value of exposed cruelty that appeals to the tabloid, the undercover stories deliver a strong educative message which may have a "real-life" impact. Studies have shown that once exposed to information about farmed animal suffering, members of the public are more likely to take political action, and change their consumption behaviour (Tiplady et al., 2012).

Overall, "hard" news and political debate give way to "soft" news and stories for human interest with little urgency or political substance in the *Mirror* corpus. Accidents involving chickens, their deaths, cruelty cases and rescue operations are reported more frequently in the tabloid than in the *Guardian*, whereas structural factors to chicken exploitation remain undebated. This indicates that the *Mirror* favours the coverage of separate events rather than more abstract political moral discussion. A holistic critique of chicken farming that would combine arguments regarding ethics, environment, public health, and welfare of workers is virtually absent. This corresponds with the identified features of tabloid journalism to prioritise the private realm, entertainment, and a short format, which may prevent ideas from developing and taking hold.

Trivial journalism concerns "mundane" events and incidents in the lives of celebrities (e.g. a story of Prince Charles' hens killed by a fox) as well as "extraordinary" events and incidents in the lives of ordinary people (e.g., a road accident involving chickens). Typically, "soft" news and human interest stories are presented humorously. As the linguist Deborah Schaffer (1995) notes, "since tabloids cannot rely on the hard-news value of their stories (or the reputations of their reporters) to sell copies, they must make use of other attention-getting devices to lure readers" (p. 28). Headlines are especially characterised by sensationalism and shock value. Puns, colloquialisms, exaggeration, irreverent language, and adjectives evoking powerful, emotional connotations are deployed to arouse or entertain the reader.

One could point out that humour and puns are not exceptional for chicken stories and do not invariably create hegemonic messages. They could be read as a joke in itself, used for entertainment value in order to *sell* news. Headlines designed to excite may draw the reader's interest in chicken farming and chickens' lived realities. As illustrative examples have shown, rescue stories arouse sympathy for chickens and restore chicken agency by combining information and entertainment. Light-hearted stories such as on Buffy are of little political relevance and do not debate the very idea of chicken farming, but they do present an intimate and compassionate human-chicken relationship. Chickens and their experiences are placed centrally. However, even if playful language is a general characteristic of the tabloid, in situations that are considered tragic or upsetting (as observed in the story on the killing of racing dogs or on the human victims of the bird flu virus), humour is not deployed at the expense of the victims. In the case of chickens, constructing them as not-so-serious animals perpetuates an ideology, which already regards them as derisory.

In the depictions of Fearnley-Whittingstall, humour is deployed to belittle his personality and undermine his message. However, unlike chickens, who are preconceived as "birdbrained" and cannot respond to assaults in ways humans can, Fearnley-Whittingstall can be considered as occupying a position of power. The stories revolving around the chef point to issues of social identity. Fearnley-Whittingstall's welfarist position, where he uses chicken welfare as a mechanism of taste delivery, is vulnerable to being reduced to the question of taste and luxury afforded by the upper and middle classes. Considering the tabloid's readership, it is unsurprising that the chef is perceived as imposing upper-middle-class values onto the working class.

The final point for discussion is that more change throughout the period of 34 years could have been expected. In the *Guardian* corpus, chicken farming is increasingly placed in "the big picture". In the *Mirror*, the interest in chicken farming is sporadic. It depends on global events such as the epidemic of avian influenza, campaigning efforts and *(extra)ordinary* events that are sensationalised. Awareness of chicken farming as a global multifaceted issue does not seem to be increasing. Given the ever-growing knowledge on the climate crisis and environmental destruction, it is striking that environmental problems rarely come up in the context of chicken farming.

4.4 The Telegraph

In the *Telegraph* corpus, 50% of all texts are news items (80 texts). Opinion/feature articles occupy the other half of the corpus (76 texts, or 48%) and three texts (2%)

are letters. The thematic distribution over 34 years is presented in Table 4.13. In contrast to the *Guardian, Mirror* and *Mail*, the largest thematic category in the *Telegraph* corpus is not public health, but chicken welfare (35 texts, or 22%). While this finding might seem positive, one must note that the *Telegraph* corpus is the smallest and more importantly, that these texts may not be written from an animal advocate's perspective. Chicken welfare may be discussed only to dismiss any concerns; some texts defend intensive farming as maintaining sufficient welfare standards and providing affordable food. In addition, when describing farms and farming methods, the more neutral or positive synonyms such as "modern" are preferred to "factory", suggesting a more approving attitude towards intensive chicken farming. Compared to the *Guardian* corpus, *factory* is used 1.9 times relatively less frequently, to the *Mail*—1.7 times and the *Mirror*—1.5 times (Tables 4.14, 4.15 and 4.16). The terms "high welfare" and "higher welfare" in relation to chicken farming appear in the *Telegraph* corpus later than in the other newspapers. They first appear in 2008 due to campaigning by Oliver and Fearnley-Whittingstall. Furthermore, the term "welfare" is significantly underused in the *Telegraph* corpus in comparison to the *Guardian* and *Mail* (see Tables 4.14 and 4.16 for frequency analyses). When compared with the *Mirror* corpus, the difference is statistically insignificant, and the ratio is close to 1 (Table 4.15).

Proportionally, organic/free-range farming receives the most coverage in the *Telegraph* corpus (19 texts, or 12%, compared to 4% in the *Mirror*, 5% in the *Guardian* and 7% in the *Mail*), but it is seldom criticised or praised from the chicken welfare perspective. Texts vary between idyllic and critical representations of these farming systems, but the focus is typically on human factors such as price or taste. Chicken keeping as a hobby and chickens as companion animals feature in 19 texts, or 12%, which is also proportionally higher than in the *Guardian* (5%), *Mirror* (4%) and *Mail* (3%) corpora. This category also includes pro-farming texts on school farms that teach children about animal farming.

The *Telegraph* corpus contains a considerably higher proportion of texts that demonstrate the identification with business/farmers and revolve around economic factors such as price, costs, profits, sales, losses, business innovation and imports (32 texts, or 20%, compared to 7% in the *Guardian*, 14% in the *Mail* and 14% in the *Mirror*). The exploratory keyword analysis of the *Telegraph* corpus identifies *economy* as one of the top 100 keywords (see Appendix C online). The term *economy* is used 5.5 times relatively more frequently in the *Telegraph* corpus compared to the *Mirror*, 3.8 times compared to the *Guardian* and 3.2 times compared to the *Mail* corpus (Tables 4.14, 4.15 and 4.16).

Table 4.13 Distribution of the thematic domains in the Telegraph corpus

	welfare of chickens	*business/economics*	*public health/food safety*	*organic/free-range farming*	*backyard farming/chicken companions*	*cultural and social issues*	*ethical vegetarianism/veganism/direct action*	*extensive debate over chicken farming*	*miscelaneous*	*total per year*
1982	1									1
1983										0
1984	1	1		1						3
1985	1	1								2
1986		1								1
1987		1			1					2
1988		3	4	1					2	10
1989	2	2		1	1	1	1			8
1990	1	1	1	4						7
1991	3	1	1		1	1			1	8
1992	1									1
1993	1		1				1			3
1994	1									1
1995		1			1					2
1996		1				2		1		4
1997		1	1							2
1998	1	1				2				4
1999			1	1						2
2000	2				1	1				4
2001	1	1				3	1			6
2002	1	1	1	1	3	1				8
2003	2	2			1				1	6
2004	3		1	3						7
2005	1	2	2			1		1		7
2006	1	1	2				1			5
2007	3	1	4	2	2					12
2008	3	1			1	1	1	1		8
2009	1		1		1	1		1		5
2010	1	2	1	3	2	1	1		1	12
2011				1		1				2
2012	1	2			3					6
2013	2	3			1	1				7
2014		1	1							2
2015										0
2016				1						1
TOTAL	**35**	**32**	**22**	**19**	**19**	**17**	**6**	**4**	**5**	**159**

Public health is a less prominent topic in the *Telegraph* corpus (22 texts, or 14%, compared to 26% in the *Mirror,* 32% in the *Guardian* and 33% in the *Mail*). Bird flu stories, for example, tend to focus on the impact on the economy rather than on public health risks. Tables 4.14 and 4.16 show that the lemmas *Campylobacter* and *antibiotic** are relatively underused in the *Telegraph* corpus compared to the *Guardian* and the *Mail.* The difference between the *Telegraph* and *Mirror* corpora is statistically insignificant (Table 4.15). The term *Salmonella,* however, is relatively more frequent in the *Telegraph* corpus. This is because the *Telegraph* provides an extensive coverage of the *Salmonella* scandal in relation to Currie. The broadsheet enjoys the story of the junior Health Minister Currie, who in 1988 infamously claimed that most British eggs are infected with *Salmonella,* sparking outrage from the industry.

"Cultural and social issues" are covered in 17 texts (11%). Topics such as the welfare of workers in the chicken business, food traditions, food poverty, and fox hunting and pheasant shooting as opposed to chicken farming are discussed. Interestingly, chicken farming is claimed to be crueller and therefore used as an alibi to defend fox hunting and pheasant shooting. As we shall see later in this chapter, it is an interesting paradox since when it comes to the UK farmers' profits and provision of affordable food, chicken farming is less likely to be presented as cruel.

Overall, not only does chicken farming receive less attention in the *Telegraph* corpus than in the *Guardian,* but also within the small number of items that mention chicken farming it receives markedly less criticism. Four articles (3%) discuss chicken farming at length, incorporating multiple arguments against intensive chicken farming. Only one article (0.6%) focusses on the sustainability of egg production in the corpus of 34 years. Ethical vegetarianism and veganism remain underexplored; only one sceptical piece is found on the vegan American novelist Jonathan Safran Foer. Unlike in the *Guardian, Mirror* and *Mail* corpora, animal rights organisations PETA and AA do not feature in the *Telegraph* corpus, which immediately suggests no space for the animal rights agenda. There is no general increase in the number of articles throughout the period. In fact, the years 2015 and 2016 contain none and one item, respectively.

Table 4.14 Frequency analysis: Telegraph and Guardian

	Telegraph		Guardian		Keyness		
Word or lemma	**AF**	**NF**	**AF**	**NF**	**Over/under-use**	**LL**	**Ratio**
economy	24	2.1	19	0.5	+	18.4	3.8
factory	55	4.8	313	9.1	-	22.2	0.5 (1.9)
welfare	107	9.3	539	15.6	-	26.9	0.6 (1.7)
antibiotic*	21	1.8	496	14.4	-	168.1	0.1 (7.9)
Campylobacter	6	0.5	182	5.3	-	68.3	0.1 (10.1)
Salmonella	91	7.9	163	4.7	+	14.6	1.7
Total word count	**115,255**		**345,505**				

Note: (+) indicates "overuse"; (-) indicates "underuse"; (div) indicates "division by 0 disallowed"; LL of 3.84 or higher is significant at the level of $p < 0.05$

Table 4.15 Frequency analysis: Telegraph and Mirror

	Telegraph		Mirror		Keyness		
Word or lemma	**AF**	**NF**	**AF**	**NF**	**Over/under-use**	**LL**	**Ratio**
economy	24	2.1	3	0.4	+	11.8	5.5
factory	55	4.8	57	7.1	-	4.5	0.7 (1.5)
welfare	107	9.3	92	11.5	-	2.3	0.8 (1.2)
antibiotic*	21	1.8	20	2.5	-	1.0	0.7 (1.4)
Campylobacter	6	0.5	10	1.3	-	3.0	0.4 (1.4)
Salmonella	91	7.9	45	5.6	+	3.6	1.4
Total word count	**115,255**		**79,927**				

Table 4.16 Frequency analysis: Telegraph and Mail

	Telegraph		Mail		Keyness		
Word or lemma	**AF**	**NF**	**AF**	**NF**	**Over/under-use**	**LL**	**Ratio**
economy	24	2.1	16	0.6	+	13.5	3.2
factory	55	4.8	198	8.0	-	12.4	0.6 (1.7)
welfare	107	9.3	324	13.0	-	9.8	0.7 (1.4)
antibiotic*	21	1.8	428	17.2	-	205.0	0.1 (9.5)
Campylobacter	6	0.5	144	5.8	-	73.2	0.1 (11.1)
Salmonella	91	7.9	155	6.2	+	3.1	1.3
Total word count	**115,255**		**248,339**				

4.4.1 Normalising chicken farming

Animal welfare or rights perspectives are entirely excluded from 42% of all *Telegraph* items. More than one-half of the news articles (46 texts, or 57%) and just above one-quarter (21 texts, or 27%) of the opinion/feature articles entirely omit chicken welfare. As observed in other newspapers, the instrumentalisation is particularly visible in economy-focussed stories that value chickens in terms of profit or loss. An illustrative example comes from a news story concerned with product labelling. Farmed animals disappear as the final product — *meat* (instead of live animals) is *reared*: "It is misleading labelling to say something is produced in Britain, and imply it came from Britain, if the meat is reared overseas" (*The Daily Telegraph*, 22/9/2009 [T21]).

In 1988, five stories depict the *Salmonella* scare following Currie's statement that most British eggs were infected with the bacteria. The right-leaning broadsheet has used the scandal as an opportunity to criticise internal Conservative Party politics and a female minister. Support is expressed for farmers, whereas killing methods and the conditions in intensive farms remain excluded from political and moral debate:

> The industry is still reeling from a catastrophic drop in sales after Mrs Currie's warning 17 days ago about the *Salmonella* danger from eggs. The government has agreed to deal with the entire unsold "mountain" of nearly 400 million eggs by paying packing station, 30p a dozen to destroy up to 1,100,000 cases, each of 360 eggs, at a cost of nearly £10 million... The Government is also paying £1.50 a hen for up to four million young hens aged 18-30 week to be killed, about a tenth of the total laying flock. This will take place under the supervision of the agricultural departments. (*The Daily Telegraph*, 20/12/1988 [T2])

The *Telegraph* pays more attention to business and economics at the expense of chicken welfare and public health issues. In bird flu stories, concerns are predominantly expressed with regards to the impact on the economy. *Farmers and processors* are constructed as the primary victims of the virus and conditions are threatening them instead of chickens: "The UK poultry industry has warned that the bird flu outbreak in Suffolk 'could not have come at a worse time', threatening to make already tough conditions even more difficult for farmers and processors" (*The Daily Telegraph*, 6/2/2007 [T15]). When chicken welfare is considered, it is done superficially. For instance, a modal verb "might" conveys low probability of welfare problems when chickens on free-range farms are confined indoors as an effort to halt the spread of avian influenza: "One of the concerns with free-range is that if you shut them up together for a long time you might have animal welfare problems" (*The Daily Telegraph*, 8/4/2006 [T13]).

The connection between chicken welfare, human wellbeing and the health of the planet remains largely unexplored in the *Telegraph* corpus. For instance, a news story covers a dispute between the celebrity Sir Ridley Scott and a neighbouring chicken farm. Sir Ridley complains about the chicken farm which intrudes into his idyllic rural surroundings. The news story constructs chickens as a nuisance and does not question the living conditions in these farms. Chickens are limited to "aural and visual pollution" and the only identified environmental problem is bad odour: "Horrified by the cackling chickens and allegedly unseemly smell that wafted into his property, Sir Ridley, 72, took his neighbours to court, complaining that their chickens caused 'aural and visual pollution and bad odours'" (*The Daily Telegraph*, 15/12/2009 [T22]).

As in the *Mirror* corpus, the discursive method of employing humour to disengage from the problematics of chicken farming is identified in the *Telegraph* corpus. Particularly, it is visible when reporting on campaigning and activism. Overall, campaigners and activists do not receive as much coverage and credibility as in the *Guardian* and the *Mirror.* There is no coverage of undercover investigations in the *Telegraph* corpus. A feature on the American novelist Foer, who authored a book promoting veganism and animal rights *Eating Animals,* depicts him as an unhealthy individual with *pale skin,* and potentially malnourished — a common bias against a vegetarian diet (Varner, 1994). Foer mentions that chickens "are bred to put on weight so fast their bones snap" and is juxtaposed with Oliver and Fearnley-Whittingstall, meat-eating (and thus preferable) campaigners for chicken welfare (*The Daily Telegraph,* 6/3/2010 [T24]). As Foer does not eat meat, he is assumed to be a cheerless individual, which again reproduces the stereotype of a veg(etari)an diet as ascetic or difficult, while Foer's book is described as incendiary, further positioning him as controversial if not an "enemy":

> unlike Jamie Oliver and Hugh Fearnley-Whittingstall, he [Foer] finds no joy in eating animals — two words that provide the title to his incendiary new book. In person, he looks as if he doesn't find joy in eating much else, either. He's shortish, thin, with pale skin and dark circles beneath his eyes. The only solid sustenance he accepts while we're together at the London hotel where he's staying — on a trip from New York to promote the book — is a single slice of lime in a glass of fizzy water. I resist the temptation to conclude that he's not getting enough protein, because in his book Foer states that vegetarians, and even vegans, have no such problem — and quotes plentiful research to back that up. (*The Daily Telegraph,* 6/3/2010 [T24])

It is important to account for the representation of vegetarians and vegans when their motive for the diet is based on animal ethics (rather than health benefits, for example), since biases towards these individuals reflect biases towards their political stance. The sociologists Cole and Morgan (2011) have analysed 19 British newspapers (including the *Guardian, Telegraph, Mirror* and *Mail*) and found that all the papers tended to discredit veganism through ridicule, constructed vegans as faddists, sentimentalists, extremists or ascetics and neglected the core ethics behind veganism — the fundamental objection to nonhuman animal exploitation.[5] Cole and Morgan (2011) note that veganism is framed as asceticism explicitly and implicitly by referring to vegans as "strict", "staunch" or "ardent". In the *Telegraph* article on Foer, the novelist is depicted as having "a single slice of lime in a glass of fizzy water", which

[5] Only 22 out of 398 newspaper articles, or 5.5%, were positive about vegans or veganism (Cole & Morgan, 2011).

implicitly frames him as ascetic and perhaps modish since lime can be seen as less traditional than lemon (*The Daily Telegraph*, 6/3/2010 [T24]). The use of "single" is an exaggeration to emphasise the simplicity of the drink, although having one slice of lime in a drink is rather standard. Details such as "shortish" or having "dark circles beneath his eyes" serve as red herrings, whereas the fact that the author could be simply dehydrated after a flight from New York to London is omitted. Through the ironic portrayal, Foer's influence as a major author who could threaten the status quo is warded off.

Another feature of animal activism depicts an activist entirely in a negative light. The activist's attempt to rescue chickens from an intensive farm is ridiculed as a fatuous act committed "out of compulsion" as if he were an addict or a madman (*The Daily Telegraph*, 13/5/2006 [T12]). The feature focusses on the illegal activities rather than dealing with questions such as why one might want to rescue chickens. The activist is constructed as an irrational and pathetic individual who cannot even properly rescue chickens. At the same time, "Keith" is a dangerous person who served 14 years in prison, a sentence which is given for crimes such as murder. Furthermore, an unwarranted generalisation is made about all activists; they are animalised by their deeds as *animal voices*:

> Keith came triumphantly towards me through the gloom, with two bulging, clucking sacks — but you could hardly call it a raid. He had captured eight chickens out of a total of 25,000 — birds that had simply fallen through the waste-pits under the sheds. He cleaned them up and took them to a sanctuary, but that was not the point. The real point was that Keith — a 39-year-old, firebomb-making, criminally active liberationist who had already served 14 years in prison — was acting out a compulsion. Like all the others, he was escaping from his "animal voices." (*The Daily Telegraph*, 13/5/2006 [T12])

Whereas using the example of Keith to make conclusions about all activists is a logical fallacy and there is a contradiction in the depiction of the activist (pathetic and yet very dangerous), the ideological implications are no less potent. The animalisation of Keith adds to the strategy of negative other-presentation and perpetuates the human-animal dichotomy. As in the case of Foer, an *ad hominem* attack is used to negate the problematics of chicken farming. Discourses that could potentially shake the speciesist ideology are disarmed.

Whimsical language and a bullying tone undermine the efforts of Oliver and Fearnley-Whittingstall to improve chicken welfare. The celebrities are tacitly accused of hypocrisy or seeking publicity as they are said to have been "moved to prime-time tears" (*The Daily Telegraph*, 30/1/2008 [T17]). As observed in the *Mirror*, patriarchy and speciesism intertwine in the *Telegraph* feature article;

the chefs are belittled as less masculine through calling them "emoting boy chickies", which reproduces a gendered discourse of sentimentality (*The Daily Telegraph*, 30/1/2008 [T17]). The negative emotional twist of the animal metaphor projects the features of humans on to chickens, while also being derogatory to the chefs. The aggressive irreverent tone continues as the author expresses a desire to "dry their tears" with a cloth to drain butter, and then "get the skewers ready", — an unclear insinuation of threading chicken flesh or perhaps of violence towards the chefs:

> On television, Hugh Fearnley-Whittingstall and Jamie Oliver have been urging British consumers to spend more on better-quality chickens that have lived better-quality lives. It has been quite a drama, with both men moved to prime-time tears at the plight of intensively reared poultry in this country. Poor little emoting boy chickies! How one yearns to dry their tears with butter muslin and get the skewers ready. (*The Daily Telegraph*, 30/1/2008 [T17])

Later, the columnist acknowledges that "agribusiness is not pretty" but intensive chicken farming is defended as providing accessible food (*The Daily Telegraph*, 30/1/2008 [T17]). Food is equated with meat, therefore implying that meat is a necessity. Furthermore, crowded conditions in hospitals are compared to conditions in chicken sheds, but overcrowding is only problematic when experienced by humans. The treatment of humans is seen as similar but (therefore) worse. Oliver's emotional response to chicken suffering is ridiculed and his concerns of chicken welfare are played down:

> Yet how else could we provide food for all? When human beings have to live in high-rise coops and patients in hospitals are crammed into mixed-sex wards, I can't get too upset over the quality of life of our nation's poultry, even if Jamie Oliver is howling into his hankie over the fate of Hetty Hen in the background. (*The Daily Telegraph*, 30/1/2008 [T17])[6]

Similarly, a rather sympathetic feature on Chicken's Lib, an organisation dedicated to chicken rescue and welfare, ultimately dismisses the cause as unimportant in comparison to other social issues and emphasises the necessity of food:

> I admire Mrs Druce's persistence, and have sympathy with her aims [to outlaw battery cages]. But I cannot escape the conclusion that there are more important things to worry about, organisations such as Chickens' Lib are a luxury that can only be indulged once the necessities of life — such as food — are secure. (*The Daily Telegraph*, 16/12/1985 [T1])

---

[6] Here Hetty Hen could be a reference to the CIWF mascot Hetty Hen which was used to campaign against battery cages.

The conflict between human and nonhuman animal welfare seems rather fabricated into an either-or situation. While it is true that an individual is able to participate in activism such as Chicken's Lib only when their primary needs such as food are satisfied, one should also note that in Britain, the majority of people are enjoying food security (Taylor & Loopstra, 2016). The argumentation that "there are more important things to worry about" can be used against almost any cause, e.g. why worry about the climate crisis when there is a threat of terrorism and so on. Compassion does not have to be a zero-sum game; treating chickens better or simply not eating them does not require putting aside other social issues such as poverty. In addition, concern with poverty is not characteristic to the *Telegraph* corpus generally, suggesting that food scarcity might be used as an alibi to ignore welfare issues in intensive farming.

In the broadsheet, whimsical language is used to defend intensive farming and thereby criticise organic farming. Consider the pun of *organoholic* in the headline; the reference to Alcoholics Anonymous in the opening "confession" puts a light-hearted tone and helps dismiss concerns for farmed animal welfare:

> My name is Clive, and I used to be an organoholic... but I'm all right now; After years of chemical-free eating, Clive Aslet admits that he has given up organic produce in favour of cheaper, local and even (whisper it) intensively reared food. (*The Daily Telegraph*, 20/5/2010 [T26])

The author *whispers* that he eats meat from intensively farmed animals as if eating such meat would require secrecy. Implying that the pressure from the organic/animal welfare lobby is high, the author constructs eating the intensive produce almost as a courageous act. More so, the opinion piece uses exaggeration to claim that chickens' needs are met under the conditions of intensive farming; in a humorous tone, intensively farmed chickens are said not to "have read Spinoza or been taught to water-ski" (*The Daily Telegraph*, 20/5/2010 [T26]). The text also describes chickens as having *brainless existences*, implying that they are not suffering. Chickens' *brainless* existence in intensive farms is juxtaposed with the existence of humans who are metonymically referred to as *souls*. Ultimately, intensive farming is defended based on a practical economic argument of efficiency:

> The chickens, during the six weeks they were alive, may not have read Spinoza or been taught to water-ski, but they appeared to live the physically comfortable, brainless existences that may well be chicken heaven. Efficient agriculture of this kind produces an awful lot of food, at low prices; and as a nation of 60 million souls, we do eat an awful lot of food. (*The Daily Telegraph*, 20/5/2010 [T26])

Another opinion piece critiques organic farming as unsafe and raises concerns about the type of chickens used and their feed. The opinion piece could use the argument that "conventional" breeds of hens cannot fully benefit from free-range environment due to their poor leg strength, but the critique does not stem from the farmed animal welfare perspective. Whimsical language and the ironic comparison of the production of eggs through organic means and the fairy-tale of Cinderella perpetuate the derogatory image of organic farming:

> To eat an organic egg with your organic ham you must first find an organic chicken. This is simpler than might be imagined. You start by buying a conventional hen. You are then instructed to keep this bird for six weeks, during which time (and indeed for the rest of its life) at least 80 per cent of its food must be organic. The balance can be "drenched with poisons". And this is where it gets exciting. On the stroke of midnight at the end of the sixth week, just like Cinderella's coach turning into a pumpkin, the ayatollahs decree that your chicken becomes an organic chicken. It certainly helps if you believe in miracles because the egg you eat for breakfast the next day is an organic egg. (*The Daily Telegraph*, 28/3/2002 [T6])

First, consider the term "organic" for nonhuman animals reared in an organically managed farms; although the term is widely accepted, it defines not only the end products but also living beings ("organic chickens") through production methods. Second, note that hens are degendered and depersonalised by referring to them as "it" as advised in the *Telegraph* style guide. Third, 20% of the diet of hens is dramatically described as potentially "drenched with poisons" (*The Daily Telegraph*, 28/3/2002 [T6]). Whereas the point of such a description is to criticise the regulations which at the time allowed one-fifth of the feed to be nonorganic and therefore assumingly "drenched with poisons", one must note a potential ideological inconsistency, — is the feed in intensive farms then assumed to be entirely poisonous? Another question could be how much organic production actually resembles a religion, since the term for religious authorities among Shiite Muslims "ayatollahs" is chosen to depict the drive for organic farming as fanatical and dangerous.

Organic farming is dismissed in a feature on an authority on animal farming and welfare, Professor Sir Colin Spedding, who from 1988 to 1998 served as a chairman of the Farm Animal Welfare Council, an advisory body to British government (*The Daily Telegraph*, 22/2/2013 [T28]). Spedding defends intensive farming by comparing battery cage farming to companion hamster keeping. The comparison between a hamster cage and a battery cage is misleading at best, and at worse completely invalid: "Many people feel that battery cages are evil, but when you ask them how they keep hamsters, they realise there is little difference, he observed. He himself, he admitted gleefully, did not buy organic food" (*The Daily Telegraph*, 22/2/2013 [T28]).

The conditions, which hens and companion hamsters are subjected to, differ radically. A battery cage provides 550 cm^2 floor space per hen (RSPCA, 2005). The lack of space prohibits hens from expressing the simplest natural behaviours such as preening or flapping their wings. The "enriched" cage, which has replaced the battery cage in the EU since 2012, provides 750 cm^2 per hen, but only 600 cm^2 have to be usable, which still severely restricts movement (RSPCA, 2005). Hamsters are typically housed alone in a space they can move around. Among many other differences between the lived realities of hamsters and hens, a hamster is kept for companionship, is not subjected to a specific light regime to increase their productivity, nor is forced to stand on a wire mesh like hens are. But when an animal welfare expert draws an analogy between the two practices and *gleefully* admits he does not opt for products from organically managed farms, the message delivered is that battery cages are perfectly acceptable.

On the other hand, in *Telegraph* texts that are supportive of "higher welfare" farming, one can spot the influences of economic interests and the inscription of chickens as value-added commodities. Although chickens become agents to some extent, the representations of "higher welfare" farms can also be excessively idyllic and romanticised. The welfare of chickens is instrumental to the organoleptic characteristics of their products and fetishised in what could be perceived as the middle-class "foodie" culture; French breeds of chickens ("poulet noir and poulet de Bresse") evoke an image of "French holidays", i.e. an elite experience and culture:

> Chickens on this Lancashire farm roam within the protection of an old walled garden, sheltering in houses at night. Richard and Susie Charles specialise in French breeds, mainly the black-legged poulet noir and poulet de Bresse. Fed on grains, mainly wheat, and mashed vegetables, the flavour of the meat is reminiscent of that eaten on French holidays. (*The Daily Telegraph*, 31/1/2004 [T7])

A feature on a farming co-operative attributes agency and positive emotions to chickens and produces a pleasant picture of a farm. The so-called chicken "nursery" is described as some sort of luxury (*The Daily Telegraph*, 31/3/2007 [T16]). Yet what is implied must be incubation in a "hatchery", a prerequisite to commercial farming, since allowing hens to rear their own chicks is not economically viable. Chickens are claimed to have comfortable lives for 14 weeks, which is considerably longer than in intensive farms but still very short if compared to the potential lifespan of 10 years:

> Nearby, scratching contentedly in the grass for worms, are the chickens, a cross-breed of Rhode Island Reds and Ross-Cobbs. Until their demise at 14 weeks, they are comfortably accommodated in environmentally friendly huts; there is even a "nursery", or brood hut, for the day-old chicks, who are gradually acclimatised with heat lamps. (*The Daily Telegraph*, 31/3/2007 [T16])

Furthermore, as in the *Mirror*, in the *Telegraph* corpus, humour is used to trivialise chicken deaths. For example, a feature on backyard chicken keeping starts with a confession by the author for killing eight hens. The flippant attitude to the birds immediately manifests itself through the funny names given to them such as Lunch and Dinner. While overall sympathetic towards chickens, the article trivialises animal deaths through a light-hearted tone and presenting chickens' experiences and emotions as comical. Chicken deaths are defined as a human failure rather than a loss of life of sentient beings:

> I am a mass murderer. In the course of a year, I have been responsible for eight corpses. The only plus side of this appalling slaughter is that at least my offences are not likely to land me in prison, because the victims have all been hens. Lunch and Dinner, Ole and Olay, Lion and Tiger, plus two others who didn't last long enough even to be named, have all passed through my inept hands. This trail of destruction is so mortifying that I daren't return to my local rare-breeds centre for new supplies and must search ever farther afield for enlightenment and new victims… I've had one who hurt her leg and lost the will to live. Another became alarmingly like a teenage girl, refusing to leave her bedroom. Whenever I tried to get her to eat or drink she would fluff up her feathers and peck me. (*The Daily Telegraph*, 3/4/2010 [T25])

Another feature, on chicken keeping at a private school, is equally anthropocentric in that it defines the activity as meaningful exclusively for the benefits of pupils. It is likely that caring for animals is assumed to be a gendered practice as pupils are girls. Yet what this human-chicken relationship means to a chicken's life, and what impact teaching girls about chicken farming could have on their attitudes towards the animals, is not addressed: "At Wycombe Abbey in Buckinghamshire, junior house girls keep chickens and sell the eggs to staff. Tending the flock eases homesickness at the start of term, says assistant housemistress Bridget Kilfeather" (*The Daily Telegraph*, 14/3/2015 [T30]). In Cole's and Stewart's (2014) account on British school farming projects, it is argued that such projects present the use of animals "as both inevitable and necessary" (p. 121). In their analysis of "Living Eggs" programme, which involves hatching eggs in British schools, the sociologists conclude that children are not taught to *care* but to control animals' bodies, thus "school hatcheries duplicitously train children in moral indifference to the instrumentalization of other animals" (p. 117).

Ambivalent discourses are produced when chickens and their suffering are used as an alibi to defend other practices that involve nonhuman animal exploitation. Strikingly, a thorough critique of intensive chicken farming is found in pro-hunting articles. A *Telegraph* opinion piece describes the lived realities of chickens farmed for their flesh in intensive farms in a compassionate tone. The alienation from food production and the effect of sterile packaging in masking the brutal realities of farmed animals are brought to light. Although the pronoun "it" is used to refer to a pheasant, speciesism is tackled by raising the question of why different species of nonhuman animals are treated differently:

> Every year, we eat 900 million chickens, whose average age at slaughter is 39 days. They spend their lives crammed together in sheds, and stuffed full of antibiotics to stop infections running rampant. Not a great life — but no one seems too upset about our children gobbling them up, because out of sight is out of mind (and when they're in sight, they come in such lovely packaging). Compare that with the life of a pheasant. Once it is old enough to fend for itself, it is released into a wood to do as it will. For a few months, it can fly anywhere it chooses. Then, if it hasn't been eaten by a fox, someone shoots it and eats it. Can someone explain to me why — as most Labour MPs seem to believe — that is more immoral than the lives we allot to those chickens? (*The Daily Telegraph*, 12/2/2010 [T23])

The rhetoric is deployed to contest the Labour Party's policy on pheasant shooting rather than the conditions for chickens. Such argumentation resembles a tactic observed in the media to silence Western feminist voices, when Western feminists are presented with the fact that in other geographical locations, women are more oppressed (Valenti, 2014; Warren, 2017). Analogously, the life of a pheasant might indeed be of a better quality than the life of a chicken farmed for flesh in an intensive farm, but that does not make pheasant shooting morally right nor animal-friendly. Suggestions to improve the conditions for chickens, to stop or reduce the consumption of intensively produced chicken products, are not found. Thus, the ideological objective is at best ambivalent.

Another *Telegraph* piece which also passionately denounces intensive chicken farming in light of hunting is authored by the present Prime Minister Boris Johnson. The column stylistically constructs intensive chicken farming in ways that resemble campaigning discourse; a vivid and emotive account of the misery of chickens farmed for their flesh is provided. Hunting can be described by anti-hunting campaigners in gory detail — against *pretty* and *fluffy* creatures — therefore, a horrifying account of chicken farms serves as a "matching" distraction. Labour is accused of hypocrisy and a disingenuous concern for animal welfare, but Johnson's interest in chicken farming does not seem genuine either. Cruelty in chicken farming is deployed to criticise the members of Labour for their anti-hunt campaign:

> But I don't believe for one second that Blair and his ministers are interested in animal welfare. If they were, they might take an interest in the sufferings of broiler chickens, whose diet is designed to make them grow as fast as possible, causing abnormalities of the bones and joint problems so severe that, given the chance, the poor corpulent fowls select pain-killing drugs in their feed. According to yesterday's Guardian, a quarter of broiler chickens are in pain for a quarter of their lives. Immediately before death they are suspended from shackles, hung upside

> down and electrocuted. Think of that, Mike Foster, Labour MP for Worcester and leading anti-hunt campaigner, next time you chomp on a chicken tikka sarnie from Sainsbury's (and the Labour minister Lord Sainsbury might think of it, too). (*The Daily Telegraph*, 18/1/2001 [T3])

Chicken farming is also juxtaposed with hunting in a letter to the editor. The reader points out that British consumers support the killing of chickens by buying chicken products. However, it is not implied that consumers should change their behaviour; on the contrary, consuming nonhuman animal bodies for food is seen as an excuse for hunting and enjoying the kill:

> There is a lot of hypocrisy in the urban view of hunting. Most of the anti-blood sport activists eat meat. While the hygienic plastic-packed chicken does not show the blood and gore, buying a chicken means you have paid someone to kill it and draw it. So it seems that it is all right to kill a chicken so you can enjoy eating it, but wrong to enjoy killing a fox. (*The Daily Telegraph*, 18/3/2002 [T5])

The reader points to hypocrisy with regards to the treatment of nonhuman animals, but himself provides assertions rather than arguments in favour of hunting. First, there is no evidence that the majority of anti-hunting activists eat meat. Secondly, it could be argued that most people do not find pleasure in killing animals and that there is a moral difference between killing for food and for sport.

4.4.2 Problematising chicken farming/Alternative discourses

More than one-half of the *Telegraph* texts contain at least one sentence on chicken welfare (58%, compared to 60% in the *Guardian*, 49% in the *Mirror* and 51% in the *Mail*). As in the *Guardian*, opinion pieces in the *Telegraph* corpus are more likely to be inclusive of welfare (55 texts, or 73%) compared to news items (34 texts, or 43%). However, chicken welfare is more likely to be introduced superficially rather than addressed in-depth. Philosophical articles debating chicken farming as a moral issue are virtually absent in the corpus of 34 years. Consequently, this section will focus on pieces of journalism that are the exception rather than the rule. The prominent figures that have introduced the chicken welfare perspectives include Oliver, Fearnley-Whittingstall, D'Silva, Ellis and Turvey.

I start by focussing on opinion/feature articles that are sympathetic to chickens and activists. Although activists are more likely to receive criticism and mockery rather than supportive coverage, three articles sympathetic to animal advocates are found in the *Telegraph* corpus. A feature on the campaigner D'Silva from CIWF portrays her positively and authoritatively and delivers her compassionate message on farmed animal welfare. Consider the headline "Crusader at the farm gate: Joyce D'Silva's call for more compassionate farming has never resonated more strongly" (*The Daily Telegraph*, 2/6/2001 [T4]). D'Silva is depicted as an expert in farmed animal welfare and her stance on chickens as victims of the cruel and greedy industry is reproduced with accuracy:

> Broiler houses are another story. Day-old chicks are brought in — about 20,000 to a shed — on clean wood shavings. They are bred to grow incredibly fast; 2 kg in six weeks. They become top heavy, suffer lameness, leg problems, sudden death syndrome, degenerative heart disease and fluid in the abdomen. But still the industry wants more. It is trying to reduce the present 41-day life span of these benighted birds: faster growth, bigger profits. (*The Daily Telegraph*, 2/6/2001 [T4])

The feature on the animal activist Turvey, who dedicated her life to rescuing battery hens, could be considered the most moving text in the *Telegraph* corpus. The piece accounts for Turvey's compassionate relationship with chickens and the journalist is open about his own emotions concluding that a human-chicken relationship can be loving. The final sentence, however, reveals the preconceptions about chickens and undermines the message; the adverb "even" positions chickens low in the hierarchy of what humans can love:

> Linda knows her facts, too: 60 million chickens born each year; 30 million (males) immediately killed; battery hens live 72 weeks... But it is the emotion, rather than cold facts, that stays with me as I leave. According to Linda, chickens have a large vocabulary; they are characters; they have feathers shot through with beautiful colour; and they start life with wonderfully smooth skins that only wrinkle with age. It seems there's nothing we can't love if we try. Even chickens. (*The Daily Telegraph*, 1/3/2008 [T18])

The headline of a feature on Fearnley-Whittingstall constructs farmed animals as end products. It is *food* that is *reared* and *slaughtered*, not the living animals: "Hugh Fearnley-Whittingstall is on a mission — to educate consumers that it is their moral responsibility to know under what conditions their food is reared and slaughtered" (*The Daily Telegraph*, 1/5/2004 [T8]). The feature is nonetheless sympathetic to chickens and introduces Fearnley-Whittingstall's ethical stance on the production of chicken meat by referring to his book and citing him directly:

> In Hugh's book — which articulates with fierce indignation the dull litany of horrors involved in factory-farming meat — that role is probably taken by the "hock burns". Look at your supermarket chicken, he says. See that dark mark on its leg? That's where, while it sits crippled by genetic obesity and knee deep in faeces-soaked litter, the ammonia from the excrement has burned its own flesh. (*The Daily Telegraph*, 1/5/2004 [T8])

Exceptional representations are also found in a few features on backyard and rescued chickens who are assigned human traits and anthropomorphised. A feature on the French countryside constructs a loving human-chicken relationship, where chickens are valued beyond their economic value. Unlike in the feature on backyard chickens "Lunch and Dinner, Ole and Olay, Lion and Tiger" (*The Daily Telegraph*, 3/4/2010 [T25]), in this story the backyard chicken keeper mourns the chicken's death, anthropomorphising her through an idiom "put oneself to bed" and a poetic euphemism for death "eternal sleep":

> A few days later, when I go to put the chickens to bed, there are only three chickens on their perches, and I can see at once who is missing. Milly. Milly who limped, but now can walk. Milly who was sick, but now is strong. My heart sinking, I make a cursory search for her, though I know it is in vain. I have learnt that when a chicken hasn't put herself to bed by nightfall, it is because she will be sleeping elsewhere for eternity. (*The Daily Telegraph*, 28/8/2010 [T27])

A feature on the photographer Kevin Foord, who was invited to take photographs of a farm for the jacket of the book *The Farm* by the writer Richard Benson, demonstrates how animal welfare and chicken agency can be introduced in seemingly unlikely places (*The Daily Telegraph*, 11/10/2008 [T20]). The feature describes how Foord, who is a city dweller, is genuinely interested in chickens. As he takes photographs of old baths used as drinking troughs for chickens, Foord raises concerns about chicken wellbeing:

> I was trying to explain the practicalities of recycling to Kevin as he photographed this bath, but he was interested only in the fact that the chickens looked happy. "That's the main thing I worry about with farms," he said. "Are the animals miserable? You don't like to think they are. If old baths make chickens happy, I say use more old baths." (*The Daily Telegraph*, 11/10/2008 [T20])

The *Telegraph* corpus, however, contains very few articles offering an extensive debate on chicken farming and incorporating farmed animal welfare, environmental and socio-cultural issues. Only four exceptional occasions in 34 years corpus are found; three texts are reviews of books that thematically revolve around industrial food production. This demonstrates that the broadsheet, which overall seems reluctant to denounce intensive farming, cannot shield itself from the volume of publications and evidence against intensive farming. Before criticising *Last Chance to Eat: the Fate of Taste in a Fast Food World* by Gina Mallet, the journalist offers an introduction to industrial food production where he likens chicken farms to concentration camps, draws attention to environmental and public health issues and engages the reader through the adjective "together" and pronoun "we":

> Chickens have been consigned to concentration camps, and herbivorous creatures have been turned into cannibals. The food chain has been contaminated, the wells poisoned. And instead of eating freshly cooked food together, we graze, sadly and separately, on chemical junk out of cartons. Food has become alien and dangerous. (*The Daily Telegraph*, 7/5/2005 [T11])

When discussing Paul Roberts' *The End of Food*, the journalist problematises chicken farming as unsustainable and invites readers to take action through their consumption behaviour (*The Daily Telegraph*, 26/7/2008 [T19]). The book review is characterised by "rationalist" arguments and an economic emphasis; the term "cost(s)" is repeated seven times in the 647-word article. Animal suffering is not the main motive against "cheap factory-farmed chickens" and campaigners Oliver and Fearnley-Whittingstall are once again emasculated as "sentimental". Nonetheless, the reviewer constructs chicken farming as having far-reaching implications for the environment, chicken welfare and public health and suggests paying premium for chicken meat from organic farms:

> It helps, when considering, say, the difference between expensive free-range organic and cheap factory-farmed chickens (as expounded by sentimental cooks such as Jamie Oliver and Hugh Fearnley-Whittingstall), to be alert to the unanticipated side effects of practices such as factory farming, "costs that don't show up in the retail price of the product or practice, but that eventually must be paid by someone — and that ultimately may make the practice or product unsustainable". The case for paying more to buy a virtuous chicken is easily made, when you realise that the side-effects (beyond considerations of animal welfare, though these have costs, too) include the cost of preventing a potential avian flu epidemic, and *Salmonella* and *E. coli* infections, as well as the costs of higher energy consumption and repairing any environmental damage. Non-taxpayers aside, these costs are all borne by the same people who consume the intensively farmed chickens. You might as well save this part of the cost of your roast chicken and pay the full price in the first place of a much better-tasting ethically sourced bird. (*The Daily Telegraph*, 26/7/2008 [T19])

Compared to the *Guardian* and *Mail* corpora, the narrative that *cheap* food has hidden costs is less pronounced in the *Telegraph* corpus. The extract from the concordances for "cheap" in Table 4.17 illustrates that the adjective carries a negative connotation primarily due to animal cruelty and public health issues; environmental issues are largely omitted.

Table 4.17 Extract from "cheap" concordance using context words "meat", "food", "egg(s)" and "chicken(s)"

argued book, Roberts points out that "food is	**cheap** because we ignore many of the real costs
hell. From here we get the kind of	**cheap** chicken that is piled high in supermarkets a
action — for example, a widespread boycott of	**cheap** chicken? The giant supermarkets would ha
currently suffering is caused by our demand for	**cheap** eggs. If we want **cheap** eggs, we will
versial that consumers have refused to buy the	**cheap** eggs that the system has produced so reliabl
our demand for **cheap** eggs. If we want	**cheap** eggs, we will get mass production, by metho
find it extraordinary that chicken has become a	**cheap** filler on our plates — they were once regard
publicity." So should we be saying no to	**cheap** food? "Absolutely." Joyce is also campaigni
da Turvey, see www.henheaven.org. Reality of	**cheap** food is not for the chicken-hearted JAN
treatment of animals; which is more important,	**cheap** food or animal welfare? Enter, at this poin
ociety, and farmers, had been "paying twice" for	**cheap** food. the disease would have cost taxpayers
misunderstanding or ignoring the true costs of "	**cheap**" food. The speech, at the Banqueting Hous
from Salmonella and Campylobacter. we want	**cheap** food we also want convenient food. One ty
chicken which was a treat and not just	**cheap** food. What the birds are fed on is
Colquhoun We are living in the era of	**cheap** food, when you can pick up a chicken
should stop trying to buy large quantities of	**cheap**, mass-market meat and go for smaller amo
know why." Can Jamie wean us off	**cheap** meat? As two top TV chefs begin a

Suggestions to abstain from animal products altogether are virtually absent in the *Telegraph* corpus but urging to choose "higher welfare" products is found, especially in the "Food and Drink" section. For example, a feature discusses eggs, their nutrition and safety and advises against buying eggs from caged hens:

> Which eggs should I buy? Avoid eggs from caged hens — this will send a strong message to the industry. Boxes containing these eggs are labelled simply Fresh Eggs. All supermarkets sell free-range and organic eggs and some sell eggs from specialist breeds such as Cotswold Legbar, Burford Browns, Chaucer Gold, Black Rock and Columbian Blacktail. (*The Daily Telegraph*, 1/1/2005 [T10])

Although humour is predominantly used to obscure welfare issues in chicken farming, two *Telegraph* features stand out as they use humour to address the problematics of chicken farming. The following extract illustrates how marketing techniques are challenged using a dose of humour and irony. An advert for chicken ready meals is mocked as dishonest and attention is brought to a serious welfare issue in chicken farming, i.e. ammonia-induced burns:

> A new blitz of adverts promoting the natural "goodness" of a range of steam-in-the-microwave chicken ready meals is illustrated with a picture of a fluffy chicken nosing out of a rustic-looking hutch into the sunshine. If Captain Birds Eye can put his hand on his hoary old nautical heart and promise that his SteamFresh Meals are made with outdoor-roaming birds — rather than factory-farmed broilers with ammonia-burns on their legs — I'll eat my hat or, if I have to, a SteamFresh Meal. I think my hat may be safe. (*The Daily Telegraph*, 26/11/2004 [T9])

A feature on bird flu starts with a rather humorous introduction. The journalist uses the words from the Book of Revelation (6:8), replacing "Death" with "Bernard", a reference to Bernard Matthews from Norfolk, the founder of one of the largest British chicken and turkey businesses (Bernard Matthews, 2017). The feature was published soon after the avian influenza virus was detected at a Bernard Matthews's intensive farm in the UK in the beginning of 2007.[7] Although the cause of the outbreak was not found, the government investigated a possible link between Bernard Matthews's farms in the UK and Hungary, where an identical strain of the avian influenza virus was identified earlier. In a playful way, using a quote from the New Testament, the *Telegraph* journalist assigns blame for the bird flu epidemic to Bernard Matthews' farms:

> "And I looked, and beheld a pale horse: and his name that sat on him was Bernard, and Hell followed with him. And power was given unto them over the fourth part of the earth, to kill with sword, and with hunger, and with death, and with the beasts of the earth." And he did come from the place that is called Norfolk. (*The Daily Telegraph*, 5/2/2007 [T14])

The feature is an exception among bird flu stories not only because of the style, but also because on a more serious note, it references Fearnley-Whittingstall and constructs intensive chicken farming as cruel: "The horrors of intensive rearing of poultry — the ammonia burns on the legs, the obesity, the 'smothers' — were well exposed in Hugh Fearnley-Whittingstall's River Cottage Meat Book" (*The Daily Telegraph*, 5/2/2007 [T14]).

---

[7] A nonlethal strain of the bird flu virus was found again at Bernard Matthews' farms in 2009 and in 2013 (BBC, 2009; 2013).

4.4.3 Summary and discussion

As the sociologist and media researcher David Croteau notes (2014), "the ideological influence of media can be seen in the absences and exclusions just as much as in the content of the messages" (p. 163). Essentially, chicken farming and suffering are less newsworthy for the *Telegraph*. This is first observed through the meaningful difference in the quantitative data as the *Telegraph* corpus is 2.7 times smaller than the *Guardian* corpus (159 vs 434 texts). At the qualitative level, one can spot substantial differences in meanings given to chicken farming across the newspapers. While the corpora of the broadsheets are not homogeneous, a markedly less critical approach in representing intensive farming practices is observed in the *Telegraph*. More space and support are given to the pro-industry perspectives. In addition, the *Telegraph* less frequently than the *Guardian* problematises intensive chicken farming through public health issues, which could further reflect its support for agricultural and pharmaceutical industries. With the exception of bird flu stories, chicken farming is rarely framed as having far-reaching consequences. Although the link between the climate crisis and animal farming is indisputable, the impact of chicken farming on climate and the environment is poorly disseminated, if not concealed.

Similar to the *Guardian*, the *Telegraph* news reporting on global and local events related to chicken farming appears detached, but more than one-half of news stories (57%) provide unbalanced representations of chicken farming, concealing cruelty and bureaucratising chicken exploitation. The main discursive methods in the objectification of chickens in the *Telegraph* are the same as in the other newspapers; chicken sentience is denied, chickens are commodified; campaigners' voices are excluded and the link between chicken welfare, human and environmental health is unacknowledged. When included, chicken welfare is likely to figure superficially. A brief note on the opposing views might be added so that the journalist could not be accused of one-sidedness or for the sake of making the story more interesting and could be termed "dominance through mentioning" (Davis, 2018).

In contrast to the *Guardian* and the *Mirror*, in the *Telegraph* corpus, an overtly pro-intensive farming stance is expressed by individuals who do not represent the industry, as well as those who do. The speciesist ideology can be forthright, e.g. when referring to chickens' lives as a *brainless existence*, or more nuanced, as in the case of Sir Spedding, who reassures that keeping hens in battery cages is as acceptable as keeping "pet" hamsters. The figurative analogy between hamster and hen cages is fallacious yet memorable and persuasive. Moreover, the opinion/feature articles that defend intensive farming use a rhetoric that seemingly prioritises consumer interests such as the price of food. The access to affordable food is a valid and important issue to address but denying farmed animal suffering and ignoring the public health and environmental issues constrains the debate in favour of the industry rather than consumers, let alone chickens.

Interestingly, when convenient, chicken farming can be constructed as deeply cruel. Three features use chicken farming as an alibi for other forms of animal exploitation (i.e. fox hunting and pheasant shooting). These texts compare the lives of chickens to other animals and address the apparent hypocrisy in the treatment of nonhuman animals. Nonetheless, from the perspective of an animal advocate, these stories are counterproductive. They switch the narrative from one issue to another without genuinely aiming at improving chicken welfare or calling for abolition, even though chicken welfare issues are brought to light. Intensive chicken farming is deployed politically as an excuse for hunting and shooting animals, which is then presented as acceptable by comparison.

For example, in the column authored by Boris Johnson, the political motive is tangible; Johnson's lament for the fate of intensively farmed chickens is a discursive trick in an ideological struggle against Labour. As noted by van Dijk (2006), word choice can be automatic, yet when it comes to communication from a politician, "each word is chosen as a function of its ideological and communicative presuppositions and implications" (p. 128). In addition, conflicts dominated by class distinctions can be identified; fox hunting and pheasant shooting are traditional rural (and expensive) activities associated with the upper classes, whereas the consumption of *cheap* chicken products is associated with the urban modern working class.

With regards to style, the *Telegraph* allows a tone of voice that somewhat resembles the *Mirror* or *Mail* corpora, not in its quest for sensationalism but in its humour, aggression and irreverence deployed for readers' pleasure. The rhetoric used in the portrayal of the campaigners Fearnley-Whittingstall and Foer reveals the hostility to their positions on animal ethics. Exaggerations and red herring deployed to describe the campaigners are linguistic manifestations of a negative other-presentation, which generally organises ideological discourse (van Dijk, 2006, p. 126). *Ad hominem* attacks and ridicule show that populist tactics are deployed by a major "quality" newspaper to negate animal ethics and preserve the status quo. Other tactics to dismiss animal advocacy include positioning activist work as less important compared to other social issues as well as situating care for animals and humans as an either-or situation.

As the psychologist Jared Piazza and others (2015) note in their account of rationalisation of meat consumption, when an ideology such as meat-eating is so embedded culturally, it goes unchallenged unless presented with an alternative viewpoint. An American study on media representations of farmed animal welfare found that the coverage of welfare issues impacted negatively on meat demand (Tonsor & Olynk, 2011). Moreover, a study by animal welfare scientists Jesse Robbins and others (2016) shows that when people are made aware that information on animal farming is withheld from them, their trust in industry decreases, whereas support for farmed animal welfare increases.

These studies indicate that media have the power to affect behaviours and consequently, the lived realities of farmed animals.

With regards to the *Telegraph* corpus, I suggest that the broadsheet does not sufficiently educate the readers on the negative effects of intensive chicken farming. The *Mirror*, *Guardian* and *Mail* expose the gritty realities of intensive as well as "higher welfare" chicken farming by carrying out their own and reporting on the investigations of others; the *Telegraph* shies away from openly and willingly criticising chicken farming as investigative journalism stories are not found. It must be acknowledged, however, that alternative voices are occasionally heard in the *Telegraph* corpus. Animal rights organisations such as AA or PETA do not feature in the corpus, but 12 texts refer to CIWF as experts, which suggests that a reformist position is given a little space in the broadsheet.

Overall, texts constructing chickens as victims of intensive farming are found, but chicken farming is never framed through the concept of justice. The feature on the activist Turvey could be considered the most transforming text in the *Telegraph* corpus since it depicts her standing up for chickens and entirely dedicating her life to chicken rescue (*The Daily Telegraph*, 1/3/2008 [T18]). In this altruistic human-chicken relationship chickens are ends in themselves. Nonetheless, the story does not debate whether it is morally right to use chickens for food nor suggests any changes to consumption behaviour. Similarly, a few features on backyard chicken keeping, such as the one on Milly the chicken, or the feature on a photographer interested in chicken happiness depict a compassionate human-chicken relationship. Mostly, however, constructions of backyard chicken keeping or "higher welfare" farming are *ambivalent* as chickens remain of instrumental value. As observed and discussed with regards to the *Guardian* and *Mirror* corpora, "higher welfare" farming can be romanticised, and chicken welfare is constructed as functional to the taste qualities of their bodily products. Seemingly benevolent, discourses of "higher welfare" farming cement chickens' status as food commodities.

With regards to changes over time, it is important to note that temporal peaks differ from the other newspapers analysed and that the *Telegraph* does not show an increasing interest in chicken welfare over the period. While the campaigns by Oliver and Fearnley-Whittingstall resonate in the broadsheet between 2008 and 2010 (although at times in a controversial way), they do not seem to have a continuous effect. Little conversation and engagement with the reader shows a degree of ideological resilience to change and offers little moral progress. Here I must refer back to the demographics of the *Telegraph* readers, who are on average older than the readers of the other newspapers.

My findings confirm the expectations that the two broadsheets represent different political perspectives on chicken farming — the *Telegraph* being conservative and the *Guardian* being liberal and left-leaning. The *Telegraph* is supportive of the status quo and the British chicken industry and shows a greater interest in chicken farming as a business, livelihood, or a middle-class hobby. As Croteau (2014) notes, "if media texts can normalise behaviours, they can also set limits on the range of acceptable ideas" (p. 156). The analysis of the *Telegraph* corpus shows that while the idea of chicken welfare is occasionally acceptable in the conservative newspaper, it remains a sideshow, whereas the idea of chickens' entitlement to their lives remains unacceptable.

4.5 The Mail

Three quarters of the *Mail* corpus are news items (256 texts, or 76%), which immediately indicates that chicken farming attracts more attention in news reporting. One-fifth of the texts are opinion pieces (71 texts, or 21%) and 12 texts are letters (4%). Thematic distribution between 1982 and 2016 is presented in Table 4.18. The *Mail* has the highest proportion of articles covering food safety and public health threats such as *Campylobacter* infections, antibiotic resistance and avian influenza (111 texts, or 33%, compared to the lowest proportion, or 14%, in the *Telegraph*). The exploratory keyword analysis of the *Mail* corpus shows the term *superbug* in the top 100 keywords (see Appendix D online). The term *superbug** informally describes pathogenic bacteria, or *bugs*, resistant to antibiotics; it is used 10.1 times relatively more frequent in the *Mail* corpus compared to the *Mirror*, 7.3 times compared to the *Telegraph* and 2.1 times compared to the *Guardian* (Tables 4.19, 4.20 and 4.21). The relative overuse highlights the *Mail*'s interest in the topic of antibiotic-resistant bacteria, as well as exemplifies its colloquial language.

Chicken welfare issues are the focus in 75 texts (or 22%, the same percentage as in the *Telegraph* corpus). The term "high welfare" in relation to chicken farming first appears in the *Mail* corpus in 2002. Its synonym "higher welfare" is used more frequently from 2003 when describing chicken products and farming standards. The ethics of chicken farming are addressed in lengthy opinion/feature articles that highlight chicken sentience and the cruelty of intensive farming. Our role as consumers and our responsibility for chicken welfare is a common subtheme in opinion/feature stories criticising *cheap* chicken products. The exploratory keyword analysis of the *Mail* corpus shows *cheap* in the top 100 keywords (see Appendix D). Frequency comparisons are presented in Tables 4.19, 4.20 and 4.21. In addition, the *Mail* investigates chicken farming undercover and reports on the investigations by activists, leaving the *Telegraph* as the only corpus with no undercover investigation stories. Frequency analyses of keywords *die*, *death** and *painful* demonstrate that the tabloid gives more coverage to the *painful* experiences and deaths of chickens and humans compared with the *Guardian* and *Telegraph* (Tables 4.20 and 4.21, also see Appendix D). The difference between the *Mail* and *Mirror* corpora for *painful*, *die* and *death** is statistically insignificant (Table 4.19), suggesting that both tabloids are more likely to provide an emotional account of events.

Table 4.18 Distribution of the thematic domains in the Mail corpus

	public health/food safety	*welfare of chickens*	*business/ economics*	*cultural and social issues*	*organic/free-range farming*	*human interest/sensational stories*	*ethical vegetarianism/veganism/direct action*	*backyard farming/chicken companions*	*miscellaneous*	*extensive debate*	*total per year*
1982											0
1983		1	2			2					5
1984			1	1							2
1985		2							1		3
1986				1							1
1987											0
1988	3	2	1	3					1		10
1989	1		5								6
1990		2	1								3
1991	1		3		1						5
1992							1				1
1993			1					1			2
1994		1		1	1	1			1		5
1995			1								1
1996		2									2
1997	1	2			1	3					7
1998	3	2	1	1	1	1					9
1999	9	1	3	3							16
2000	4	7		1		1			1		14
2001	3	1		1	1		1		1		8
2002	3	7		1		1					12
2003	4	10				1					15
2004	7	5	1				1				14
2005	5	1			2		2	1			11
2006	23	5	7	5	2	1		1			44
2007	6	1	4	3	4	1	1	2	2		24
2008	8	7	8	5	2	1	3	1			35
2009	2	2	1	1	2		1				9
2010		5		1		1		3			10
2011	4	1	2		1						8
2012				2	1	1		1			5
2013	3	2	1	1	1		1	1			10
2014	7	2	1	1		2			1	1	14
2015	6	1	2				1				10
2016	8	3	3	1	3						18
TOTAL	**111**	**75**	**49**	**33**	**23**	**17**	**12**	**11**	**7**	**1**	**339**

Business and economic aspects are the dominant topic in 49 texts (14%, the same proportion as in the *Mirror*). Foreign competition, sales, financial losses, and the economic pressure on farmers to cut costs and produce *cheap* chicken meat and eggs are examples of topics reported on. The *Mail* corpus contains fewer "human interest/sensational stories" than the *Mirror* (17 texts, or 5%, compared to 43 texts, or 17%, respectively). These articles typically report on accidents involving chickens, such as farm fires, or depict trivia and sensationalise it, e.g. chicken escape stories. Extensive debate that would draw upon multiple arguments such as public health issues, environmental problems, human and chicken welfare is scarce; one article authored by a CIWF representative in 2014 provides an extensive analysis of intensive animal farming. Environmental concerns emerge in the *Mail* corpus only tangentially.

Table 4.19 Frequency analysis: Mail and Mirror

	Mail		Mirror		Keyness		
Word or lemma	**AF**	**NF**	**AF**	**NF**	**Over/under-use**	**LL**	**Ratio**
cheap	147	5.9	21	2.6	+	14.8	2.3
painful	31	1.2	6	0.8	+	1.5	1.7
die	76	3.1	21	2.6	+	0.4	1.2
death*	136	5.5	38	4.8	+	0.6	1.2
superbug*	63	2.5	63	0.3	+	23.0	10.1
Total word count	**248,339**		**79,927**				

Note: (+) indicates "overuse"; (-) indicates "underuse"; (div) indicates "division by 0 disallowed"; LL of 3.84 or higher is significant at the level of $p < 0.05$

Table 4.20 Frequency analysis: Mail and Guardian

	Mail		Guardian		Keyness		
Word or lemma	**AF**	**NF**	**AF**	**NF**	**Over/under-use**	**LL**	**Ratio**
cheap	147	5.9	130	3.8	+	14.2	1.6
painful	31	1.2	9	0.3	+	21.1	4.8
die	76	3.1	46	1.3	+	20.7	2.3
death*	136	5.5	118	3.4	+	14.1	1.6
superbug*	63	2.5	42	1.2	+	14.0	2.1
Total word count	**248,339**		**345,505**				

Table 4.21 Frequency analysis: Mail and Telegraph

	Mail		Telegraph		Keyness		
Word or lemma	**AF**	**NF**	**AF**	**NF**	**Over/under-use**	**LL**	**Ratio**
cheap	147	5.9	49	4.3	+	4.2	0.5
painful	31	1.2	5	0.4	+	6.1	1.5
die	76	3.1	9	0.8	+	21.2	2.0
death*	136	5.5	21	1.8	+	28.4	1.6
superbug*	63	2.5	4		+	26.9	7.3
Total word count	**248,339**		**115,255**				

4.5.1 Normalising chicken farming

In the *Mail* corpus, 49% of all texts exclude the chicken welfare and rights perspectives (compared with 40% in the *Guardian*, 42% in *Telegraph* and 51% in the *Mirror*). Chicken welfare is entirely omitted in 146 news stories (57%) and 19 opinion/feature articles (27%). As in the other newspapers, economy-focussed and public health stories typically deny chicken sentience and define them as a means of production. Critical voices are absent in news stories on *Campylobacter* or *Salmonella* infections. The suffering of chickens from bacteria, from the living conditions that allow bacteria to thrive in the first place and from control measures, i.e. slaughtering, is obscured. Furthermore, avian influenza, as observed in all the newspapers, is hardly ever constructed as an animal welfare issue despite the staggering number of chicken deaths. When it comes to counting the "death toll", humans typically are the only victims of the virus, whereas chickens are simply a reservoir of infection. Compassion or mourning over the millions of chicken lives lost to control the spread of virus is imperceptible:

> The latest victims were in Vietnam, where the deaths of an eight-year-old girl and a 13-year-old boy brought the number of fatalities to seven... Europe has banned imports from Thailand where an estimated seven million chickens have been slaughtered in an attempt to halt the outbreak. (*Mail on Sunday*, 25/1/2004 [MA17])

Avian influenza predominantly is an issue of "poultry sales", "devastating" to *everyone* except chickens themselves:

> There is no doubt that it [bird flu] will be every bit as devastating to poultry farmers (and, in fact, everyone in the countryside) as foot and mouth disease was... It is already clear that it has the potential to have the same impact on poultry sales as BSE [bovine spongiform encephalopathy] did on beef sales in Britain. (*Daily Mail*, 14/2/2006 [MA21])

Discourses of efficiency and production also normalise experiments on chickens, if not construct them as inherently positive. For example, a news story takes scientific practices, which are clearly subjected to socio-economic forces, for granted. The story titled "Cloned chickens on the menu" depicts an experiment on growing chickens from stem cells from an entirely economic perspective: "Cloned chickens that all taste exactly the same could soon be on the dinner table. They would revolutionise factory farms, which dream of disease-resistant birds that grow faster on less food…" (*Daily Mail*, 16/8/2001 [MA12]).

While natural science disciplines could claim to have the closest and the most objective engagement with nonhuman animals, there is never an objective animal "undistorted by the optics of cultural perspectives" (Marvin, 2001, p. 275). The nature of knowledge depends on the power relationships among the groups that produce it. Like in the *Telegraph* corpus, Professor Sir Colin Spedding appears in the *Mail* corpus arguing for the battery cage system (*Daily Mail*, 25/7/1997 [MA6]). The chairman of the Farm Animal Welfare Council, Spedding claims that if hens are allowed more space, they become more aggressive and attack each other. His argument is based on an interesting assumption that neither hens nor humans can be trusted with freedom: "Greater freedom of expression of animal behaviour does lead to this vicious behaviour developing. Unfortunately, a hen responds to total freedom no better than humans" (*Daily Mail*, 25/7/1997 [MA6]). Here, hens are conveniently aligned with humans, whereas making an analogy between human and hen emotional responses from the animal rights perspective would likely be dismissed as sentimental, anthropomorphising, or unscientific. Furthermore, a free-range system is far from *total* freedom and the environmental and managerial factors that are linked to aggressive behaviour in hens are left out of the discussion.

In the *Telegraph* and *Mirror* corpora, I identified the use of humour to deliver hegemonic messages and deny the problematics of chicken farming. In the *Mail* corpus, puns, idiomatic and derisive language, a light-hearted tone, and irony are also found, but deployed differently. Puns and idiomatic phrases are common in headlines, while the tone in the body of an article tends to be more serious. In addition, in the *Mail* corpus, humour is found more frequently in the first half of the period analysed.

Two business-focussed articles published in the 1980s deserve to be examined in more detail for they "humorously" articulate oppressive power relations. The stories report on declining beef consumption and growing chicken meat consumption. Farmed animals are presented as wanting (and competing) to be eaten. One text uses a light-hearted tone and personifies cows suggesting that they feel worried and humiliated because of the growing consumption of chicken flesh: "The cow's ruminations this morning ought to concern the terrible humiliation of being ousted from America's affections by, of all things, that feathered fool, the chicken" (*Daily Mail*, 11/12/1984 [MA2]). A clear bias against chickens is visible in referring to "the chicken" as a "thing" and "fool".

The second feature "When beef comes second to video" notes that in response to a changing market, "beef producers are attempting to breed leaner cuts of beef", as if it would be possible to breed meat cuts rather than living animals (*Daily Mail*, 9/12/1983 [MA1]). Turkeys and chickens are said to be looking forward to ending up in meals:

> Turkeys, along with chickens are not only more popular… but their fate is more varied than ever before. Instead of appearing only at Christmas they can look forward to being a year-round delicacy as turkey burgers, turkey sausages or turkey scallops. (*Daily Mail*, 9/12/1983 [MA1])

The idea that farmed animals compete to be eaten is strengthened by a cartoon illustration showing a cow, a pig and a sheep protesting against the popularity of chickens and turkeys. The pig asks, "Why not us?", i.e. why are pigs not being consumed. Adams' (2010) has argued that images in advertising frequently exploit "the idea that meat animals desire being desired, that is, that animals figured as female bodies are sexually available and want to be ravished/consumed" (p. 309). In the words of Adams, the animals being consumed "are made to appear cartoonish" and sexualised, "as though cartoons aren't doing heavy loading for cultural constructions" (Adams, 2010, p. 310). In the *Mail* cartoon, the intersection between the oppression of animals and women is visible as the sheep, ironically, demands *equal rights*. Such an illustration could be interpreted as a mockery of animal and women's rights discourses, especially bearing in mind the date of the publication; the year 1983 opened the second term for Margaret Thatcher as Prime Minister and Tom Regan published *The Case for Animal Rights*. Furthermore, the story discusses the role of women in declining beef consumption. Derogatory gendered constructions are noticeable in blaming women for poor cooking skills and for choosing convenience:

> Fewer women now know the old methods of pot roasting and braising that their mothers were familiar with. And even if they do, few nowadays have the time or patience to keep turning and basting a joint for the longer length of cooking time… And it must be convenience which explains the dramatic rise in the popularity of chicken and turkey pieces in the past few years. (*Daily Mail*, 9/12/1983 [MA1])

Without overt statements, the narrative builds a domestic stereotype of women, where women are responsible for shopping and cooking for the family. "Few nowadays have the time or patience" must refer to working women who apparently cannot be bothered to cook, implicitly shaming women for abandoning the traditional role of home keeping. Whereas the journalist does not explicitly call for a return of traditional values, he refers to *their mothers* as knowledgeable. The feature ends by presenting then-current housewives as profoundly ignorant of farmed animal welfare as well as culinary skills: "Meanwhile, the complaints of the anti-factory farming lobby and the complaints of tastelessness in modern chickens have little effect on the housewife compiling her shopping list" (*Daily Mail*, 12/9/1983 [MA1]).

The narrative of female guilt is tangentially repeated in three more articles published in 1988, 1999 and 2000, of which I will cite two. They are noteworthy since the *Mail* has a large female readership and yet is infamous for misogyny and has received strong criticism from both members of the public and the academic community for sexism and racism.[8] The articles are apparently sympathetic to chicken welfare, but proclaim industry helplessness in the face of "housewives' penny-pinching". The gendered narrative originates from citing industry representatives who use gender stereotypes to defend intensive farming, for instance: "The great British housewife... is concerned with one thing and one thing only — price" (*Mail on Sunday*, 31/10/1999 [MA10]). The use of a singular noun in the stereotyping phrase "the great British housewife" (further in the text also "the average housewife") has an implication of constructing women as a homogenous group.

A feature on the slaughtering of male chicks in the egg industry cites an industry representative who constructs housewives as hypocrites. Housewives are concerned about farmed animal welfare but do not shop accordingly: "The housewife has a firm set of morals in her mind when it comes to animal welfare — until she opens her purse" (*Daily Mail*, 15/3/2000 [MA11]). The singular noun again stigmatises the women as a singular other, whereas the reference to a *purse* could have a sexual connotation.[9] In addition, the industry representative defends the practice of killing male chicks in the egg industry by using hunting as an alibi: "It is wrong to talk about cruelty. I couldn't kill for pleasure like many people who go hunting. We only kill chicks because we have to" (*Daily Mail*, 15/3/2000 [MA11]). The "not as bad as" rhetoric is used to

---

[8] The *Mail* was criticised in the media for focussing on the physical appearance of British actress Emma Watson when she was giving a speech for the United Nations HeForShe campaign, aimed at the advancement of gender equality in 2014 (iMediaEthics, 2014). In 2017, the tabloid was also criticised for the front page headline "Never mind Brexit, who won legs-it" and the following article that discussed the physical appearance of Prime Minister Theresa May and first Minister of Scotland Nicola Sturgeon (Martison, 2017). Scholars have also criticised the *Mail* for misogyny, e.g. for constructing rape involving alcohol as a problem of women drinking (Meyer, 2010). Linguist Majid Khosravinik (2009) analysed the discursive representation of refugees, asylum seekers and immigrants (RASIM) in the *Mail*, concluding that the tabloid perpetuates negative stereotypes of RASIM.

[9] *Purse* in jargon can refer to female genitalia.

excuse killing for "need" as less cruel than killing for pleasure, regardless of whether "blood sports" bear relevance to the debate on intensive farming. By contrast, in the *Telegraph*, whose readership is of a higher social class, fox hunting and pheasant shooting (activities associated with the upper classes) are excused as less cruel than chicken farming for food.

Just like the appeal to "worse" problems can be used to condemn or defend intensive farming, the argument of taste can be deployed to argue both for and against "higher welfare" farming. The construction of taste as a physiological and social sense deserves unpacking. As my findings in other newspapers show, the improved taste is typically constructed as a reward for "ethical" shopping behaviour. However, in the *Mail* corpus, both types of claims can be found — 1) that "higher welfare" is superior and 2) that intensive produce is superior taste-wise. A story reports on a blind experiment during which five types of chicken meat cooked in an identical way were served unidentified to a panel of jury; Hugh Fearnley-Whittingstall Special Label is the winner whereas chicken meat from an intensive farm scores the lowest (*Daily Mail*, 7/2/2008 [MA31]). In another feature, it is claimed that "organic poultry is actually less nutritious, contains more fat and tastes worse" than "battery farmed meat" (*Daily Mail*, 4/12/2006 [MA24]). Articles claiming that "higher welfare" products do not taste better typically neglect the welfare aspect. In addition, technically, it is inaccurate to refer to chicken meat as "battery farmed"; with the exception of birds used for breeding purposes, chickens raised for their flesh are not kept in cages, but in sheds.

In the *Mail* corpus, Oliver features in 21 stories on "higher welfare" farming, whereas Fearnley-Whittingstall features in 24 stories. As previously observed in the *Mirror*, "higher welfare" farming can be reduced to the "foodie culture" of the middle classes. In the *Mail* corpus, however, such narratives are rather uncommon; four out of 24 texts mock Fearnley-Whittingstall by association with an upper-class position. A column on a Channel 4 series stands out for its sarcasm and criticises the chef and his campaign as elitist and patronising:

> The posh double-barrelled one [Fearnley-Whittingstall] went beetling down in the Land Rover from his delightful farm to the local council estate, where he set the ignorant natives straight about their nasty poultry habit... I bet I wasn't the only one who cheered when a single mother murmured that Hugh had some nice ideas about animal welfare, but he should try feeding a family on her budget. In an ideal world, every chicken would be raised in the sun-ripened pastures of South-West France with its own Jacuzzi and personal acupuncturist. But, back here on earth, many hard-working mums have to decide whether their families matter more than their feathered friends. If it's miracles you want, try pulling a wishbone, boys. In the meantime, please stop ladling out the guilt. (*Daily Mail*, 9/1/2008 [MA28])

The phrase "nasty (poultry) habit" might have the connotation of drug or tobacco addiction. The readers can enjoy being reminded of the stereotype of council estates as places of addiction and yet it is Fearnley-Whittingstall, a member of the liberal elite, who is condemning the "habit" and "guilt mongering". A conflict between classes and between a traditional feminine form of caring and a less gendered form of caring, i.e. social responsibility, can be identified. Saying that "hard working mums" have to choose between their family and chickens implies that chicken meat is necessary to the human diet. Caring for children and chickens thus becomes an "either/or" situation, although *care* is not a zero-sum game.

Surprisingly, another *Mail* feature uses concerns for chicken welfare *against* vegetarianism as the author argues that vegetarians do not care about farmed animals. The article is not a prototypical *Mail* text, but interesting for its ambivalence in what it is "really about" and for illustrating that animal welfare can be rhetorically exploited for different purposes. Consider the headline "Free-range chickens and the hypocrisy of being vegetarian as Marks & Spencer stop selling battery laid eggs" (*Daily Mail*, 7/10/1997 [MA7]). The feature starts with a journalist confessing his admiration of the will power of vegetarians to refuse meat: "For years… I admired the self-restraint of vegetarians, the dedication to their cause which led them to pass up the delights of a succulent chop or a good roast. But no longer" (*Daily Mail*, 7/10/1997 [MA7]). Immediately the reader is presented with a stereotype of vegetarian diet as ascetic and restrictive and meat as highly desirable. The author then suspects *self-righteous vegetarians* of bogus concern for farmed animal welfare: "Now, having investigated animal welfare, I find it very hard to swallow the claims of all those millions of self-righteous vegetarians who say they care deeply about the protection of farm animals" (*Daily Mail*, 7/10/1997 [MA7]). The guilt of *vicious vegetarians* lies in that they do not exclude all animal products:

> The stark truth is that they [vegetarians] are often more cruel, and less honest, than meat-eaters. Notions such as "free-range" are not the only delusions these people weave for themselves… A tiny minority has also learned how to eat deliciously and nutritiously while avoiding animal products altogether — the vegans. But let's turn to the group I now call the "vicious veggies". In what way, exactly, are they vegetarians? For what is "vegetable" about milk, yoghurt, butter, cheese? These are animal products. And what is "vegetable" about eggs? (*Daily Mail*, 7/10/1997 [MA7])

While the journalist makes a valid point that eggs and dairy products are derived from animals and free-range is a feel-good term, omnivores also "buy" the concept of free-range and the aforementioned products. The accusation of vegetarians being crueller seems far-fetched and ideological. Nonhuman animal suffering is reported to be one of the major motives to consume fewer animal products and/or choose a vegetarian diet (Fox & Ward, 2008). The journalist perhaps feels threatened by vegetarians or defensive as he goes on arguing which is crueller — the production of eggs or chicken meat. He concludes that egg production is crueller since the misery of a hen lasts longer:

> The standard broiler chicken lives a very nasty life stuffed into a windowless barn for virtually the whole time. But it lives, on average, just 42 days from hatching to slaughter, so is put out of its misery very quickly. (*Daily Mail*, 7/10/1997 [MA7])

The journalist then claims that "chickens we eat must, by definition, reach the slaughterhouse in reasonable shape or we wouldn't want to eat them" (*Daily Mail*, 7/10/1997 [MA7]). Yet many chickens die before reaching slaughter age and during transportation (Vecerek et al., 2006), and those who do not reach a slaughterhouse in a *reasonable shape* can go for "pet" food industry. It appears that welfare issues in chicken meat production are conveniently omitted in order to vilify egg-eating vegetarians.

It is then assumed that vegetarians eat more dairy products than omnivores, but no data are presented to support the claim. Whereas all dairy consumers are rightfully held accountable for the deaths of male calves in the dairy industry, only vegetarians are targeted and "guilt mongered". In addition, a chicken's life in the meat industry is presented as less miserable because it is shorter. But when talking about male calves, the journalist laments the killing of new-born calves, whereas according to his logic it should be crueller to prolong their suffering by raising them for veal and then exporting to other countries for slaughter:

> Aren't all users of dairy products, and those vegetarians who generally eat more of them, guilty [of veal production]? And now that veal exports have been blocked by the BSE beef ban, these infant male dairy calves are being slaughtered in Britain days after they're born. Can vegetarians really expect to escape blame for that, too? (*Daily Mail*, 7/10/1997 [MA7])

Although the feature seems to be sympathetic to hens, acknowledges their suffering and correctly points to the remaining cruelty in the lacto-ovo-vegetarian diet, the exaggerations and assumptions create an unreasonably negative portrait of vegetarians and the vegetarian diet, leading to an impression that farmed animal welfare issues are deployed to negate this group of people, rather than to improve chicken welfare. No actual vegetarians or vegans are cited in the article, leaving their perspectives out.

Finally, it is worth noting that a nonsensical article is found in the *Mail* corpus, which indicates that the tabloid gives a platform for arguments lacking a sound basis. This article revolves around the Irish celebrity chef Kevin Thornton who equates chicken meat from intensive farms to poison. In the article, Thornton makes absurd comments about eggs:

> I was reading something a while ago, they were making vegetarian eggs and I was thinking how are they going to make vegetarian eggs. I was boggled. I read up about it and what they were doing was feeding the chickens only vegetables, so I don't know technically how this will work. Therefore the chick is going to hatch out of a pure vegetarian egg. If you feed the chicken a grain, whatever type of grain it is, depending on where the grain is from, the chicken is stressed out, it doesn't have wings. They catch cold the whole lot of them. It's not a very good environment. (*Daily Mail*, 22/1/2008 [MA29])

Thornton's narrative is difficult to follow and yet it is left unquestioned. There is no explanation about the types of vegetarian diet or that eggs are considered vegetarian by ovo-vegetarians irrespective of the chickens' diet. The fact that having wings does not depend on whether chickens eat grain or vegetables is not introduced either. Thornton's arguments are presented without trying to make sense of them or providing explanations.

4.5.2 Problematising chicken farming/Alternative discourses

At least one sentence on chicken welfare or animal ethics is found in 51% of all *Mail* texts. Like in the broadsheets, the distinction between opinion and news items is tangible; 52 opinion/feature items (73%) and 110 news items (43%) include chicken welfare/animal ethic. The voices who speak on behalf on chickens belong to Oliver, Fearnley-Whittingstall, Ellis, Eyton, Lymbery, the animal behaviourist Marian Dawkins, Viva, Advocates for Animals and the Battery Hen Welfare Trust.

Like in the *Guardian*, in the *Mail* corpus chicken welfare is assigned space and depth in lengthy argumentative articles. The majority of opinion pieces describe chickens as objects of cruelty and victims of intensive farming. The narrative of personal responsibility and the notion that *cheap* chicken products are *bad* permeate the corpus. Illustrative concordance lines for "cheap" in Table 4.22 demonstrate that the adjective carries a very negative connotation. The idiomatic phrases "paying the price" or "true cost" construct *cheapness* of chicken products as deceptive. Consider the headline of a feature on avian influenza: "Horrific price of food on the cheap" (*Daily Mail*, 5/2/2007 [MA25]). The main argument is that *cheap* chicken products have hidden costs which are externalised on chickens, humans, and the environment:

> The inconvenient truth is that cheap food comes at a price a cost to the environment and health. More and more people are realising this and turning to organic produce: sales in Britain rose by a third last year alone to £ 1.6 billion. (*Daily Mail*, 5/2/2007 [MA25])

The following illustrative example comes from a feature discussing a roast chicken meal. Despite the article focussing on food quality, the production and consumption of *cheap* chicken meat are primarily criticised on welfare grounds. The suffering of chickens is detailed using a mix of veterinary science register, everyday language, and affective language (e.g. "piteous", "cruelly cramped", "suffocating", "suffer" and "abuse"):

> The lot of the average broiler is a piteous one. Most chickens eaten in this country are intensively reared and raised as fast as possible with little concern for their welfare. Conditions in sheds are cruelly cramped and the stench of excrement and ammonia suffocating. As the barns are not generally cleaned for the six-week period of growth (a traditionally reared chicken can take up to six months), the birds suffer from hock burns (hocks are the upper joints of the legs) caused by contact with ammonia in faeces, respiratory diseases, broken limbs, skeletal defects, weakened immune systems and bronchitis. All this abuse, just so we can buy a cheap, insipid bird with little texture and a complete lack of flavour. It's a heavy price to pay for second-rate meat. (*Mail on Sunday*, 30/4/2006 [MA22])

Another illustrative example comes from a feature which compares different chicken meat products from the animal welfare perspective. Marketing language is deconstructed to expose the conditions in intensive farms producing *cheap* chicken meat:

> Cheap supermarket bird Tesco £1.99 label: uses suppliers "like Fred Maxwell... who has been rearing chickens on his family's farm for over 20 years. Fred understands the importance of flock husbandry... with his approach to bird welfare he ensures he meets the high standards required by Tesco". Reality: This chicken will probably have been intensively-reared in a vast shed packed with 17 birds to a square metre, and raised to maturity in just 39 days, 17 days quicker than the minimum required for free-range birds by using artificial light to make the birds feed for far longer per day. (*Daily Mail*, 7/2/2008 [MA31])

In contrast to the other newspapers, consuming *cheap* chicken flesh and eggs is likened to addiction and obsession in the *Mail* corpus (Table 4.22). "Addiction" and "obsession" are more negative metaphors than a "culture of cheap food" identified in the *Guardian*. Although this "obsession" is presented as a national problem, the *Mail* speaks to an individual; their addiction is personal, while culture is shared. Three prototypical narratives are found in the *Mail* corpus, which all assume that British consumers are ignorant and greedy — 1) they do not want to know, 2) they are aware of chicken welfare issues but do not care and 3) they can afford "higher welfare" products but choose cheaper products produced intensively.

Table 4.22 Extract from "cheap" concordance using context words "meat", "food", "egg(s)" and "chicken(s)"

as they eat. One group was addicted to	**cheap** and cheerful chicken; the second to ready
ask of our chickens is that they be	**cheap** — cheaper, pound for pound, than bread. It
brings us to the next truth behind your	**cheap** chicken. According to producers, the reason
st focal point of our national obsession with	**cheap** chicken. If planning permission is granted,
enemy, but only as a form of revenge.	**Cheap** chicken is bad food in the sense that
ecause the British simply cannot get enough of	**cheap** chicken. Last year, we consumed 35.4kg of
. In Britain, consumers can't get enough of	**cheap** chicken. On average, we eat 31 kilos per per
The true cost of our obsession with	**cheap** chicken? The lethal bacteria that can lurk i
problem is that we have become addicted to	**cheap** dairy products, fish and meat and in the
The price (IN SUFFERING THAT IS) of	**cheap** eggs; 24 hours of hell in the life of
had just paid; just as if we want	**cheap** eggs, male chicks will pay the price as
erything. Rather than treating the chicken as a	**cheap**, everyday staple, it should be something you
itical correctness and our insatiable demand for	**cheap** food are inflicting a terrible toll on our
ich caused BSE? The inconvenient truth is that	**cheap** food comes at a price a cost to
. But we consumers, addicted as we are to	**cheap** food, don't help. Every time the price
a very high price, so to speak, for	**cheap** food. Factory farming is all about producing
NATURE'S REVENGE; Our desire for	**cheap** food has led us to accept farming techniques
against profligate, greedy man whose desire for	**cheap** food has led to such cruel and inhumane
security about what we eat. The price of	**cheap** food is simply too high. Corrigan's Family
thing and one thing only — price. People want	**cheap** food. Nobody wants to know where the mea
understand the true cost of this abundance of	**cheap** food. Unless we have the proper informatio
of all the evils is our desire for	**cheap** food, which obliges producers to cut corner
, by a hen each year The curse of	**cheap** food; Why pay good money to put your

moral implications raised by the production of	**cheap**, mass-produced meat. There is an increasin
for years of cruelty in the pursuit of	**cheap** meat? ON SUNDAY mor
and thousands of farmed chickens intended as	**cheap** meat for the supermarkets, all crammed tog
I co-wrote, exposing the true cost of	**cheap** meat. While the food and farming industry
chicken is that we have become addicted to	**cheap** white meat and, in the long term, the

The *Mail* opinion piece "Cockfights, battery farms and now crossbred bald mutants. Why are we so cruel to the poor chicken?" by the British science writer Michael Hanlon is fully dedicated to "the chicken's misfortune in the history of mankind" (*Daily Mail*, 22/5/2002 [MA13]). Among many issues, it tackles the ethics of genetic development of featherless chickens for hot climate countries. This "scientific development" has also been depicted in the *Guardian*: "The fast-growing, featherless bird may look a little foul, but it was hailed as the environmentally friendly future of chicken farming" (*The Guardian*, 21/5/2002 [G13]). The *Guardian* article emphasises sustainability but simultaneously ignores situational or structural causes of such genetic experiments; in this sense, it can be compared to the aforementioned *Los Angeles Times* climate-change articles, which uncritically suggest technological fixes of the *flawed* bodies of cows to reduce carbon footprint (Lee et al., 2015). In the *Mail* article, however, a sceptical attitude towards breeding bald chickens is expressed. Intensive chicken farming is problematised as causing suffering and turning chickens into *cheap* commodities. Speciesism is addressed by comparing the status of chickens to other animals, namely rats, mice, geese, foxes and whales; the exploitation of chickens is underlined by adjectives "captive" and "abused":

> few worry about the chicken, arguably the most abused animal in our care. Admittedly, rats and mice suffer more in scientific research laboratories, and unspeakable procedures are performed on geese to make foie gras, but when the sheer number of birds is taken into account, the cruelty inflicted upon the world's hundreds of millions of captive broilers and layers probably tops it all... But then, few of us seem to care. While the plight of the fox is enough to move Parliament and there are international commissions to protect the whale, no one gives much thought for a bird that has been acting as humanity's portable protein factory for as long as civilisation has existed. All we ask of our chickens is that they be cheap — cheaper, pound for pound, than bread. (*Daily Mail*, 22/5/2002 [MA13])

Humans who turned chickens into ever-cheaper commodities, — *humanity's portable protein factory* — are constructed as indifferent to cruelty. Consumer guilt permeates the opinion piece which ultimately concludes that the consumer is willingly ignorant: "[it] is possible to buy, at a price, free-range meat that has been produced with a modicum of humanity, but most of us choose not to" (*Daily Mail*, 22/5/2002 [MA13]).

Another feature article by Hanlon similarly tackles speciesism by highlighting hypocrisy in the treatment of different species of animals (Daily Mail, 16/8/2005 [MA20]). Hanlon emphasises the magnitude and intensity of chicken farming and addresses commodification of chickens by again calling a chicken farm *a protein factory:*

> Whatever the protestations of the poultry industry, the life of a typical broiler chicken is not a pleasant one. Producing protein that can be sold for £1 a pound or less, for a profit, means that animal welfare is never going to be high on the agenda. If cows, sheep or pigs were kept in similar conditions, there would be an outcry. But somehow we choose to turn a blind eye to what happens to poultry. A poultry farm is in effect a protein factory. Of course, the same can be said for a field full of beef cattle or gambolling lambs. But it is the intensity of chicken rearing that really sets this type of farming apart. (*Daily Mail*, 16/8/2005 [MA20])

Hanlon addresses bias towards chickens not only by comparing their treatment to other farmed animals (cows, lambs, and pigs), but also to other free-living animals. Like Baggini in the *Guardian*, Hanlon argues that criticizing foreign practices while "turning a blind eye" to chicken farming is "cant". Note that British farmers are seen as perpetrators of chicken suffering, yet consumers are the main culpable agents, — they desire *cheap* protein, are ignorant about the realities of intensive farming and hypocritical in their assumed identity of "animal lovers":

> We are amazingly ignorant — perhaps willingly so — of what goes on in the name of cheap protein. We consider ourselves to be a nation of animal lovers. We have banned fox hunting, gibber with indignation at the annual slaughters of Canadian seal pups and pour scorn on barbaric foreign practices, such as the production of fois gras in France. But most of this is cant and hypocrisy. (*Daily Mail*, 16/8/2005 [MA20])

Nevertheless, Hanlon's solution to chicken suffering and public health issues, predictably, revolves around "humane" treatment rather than abolition; the author encourages the consumption of free-range products that are seen as kinder and healthier for us:

> There is an answer to all this, of course. Not necessarily to go vegetarian, or even organic, but to buy the best meat you can, and that usually means free-range. Free-range chickens will probably have led a far more natural life, and will have needed far less prophylactic medicine to prevent the infections associated with overcrowding... (*Daily Mail*, 16/8/2005 [MA20])

The depicted world of the *Mail* opinion reader is predominantly of (aspirational) middle-classness. The desirable lifestyle and responsible citizenship are enacted through the consumption of "good" (quality) products. It is argued that "we are what we eat" and that most British consumers can afford "higher welfare" chicken products. The extract illustrates that poor people belong to the "other" group; they are outside the ingroup of the *Mail* readers:

> You are what you eat. There is much truth in that old cliché… People who would never dream of buying a secondhand car or clothes from Dunnes Penneys, cheerfully snap up chickens for £2.99… Poor people need affordable food. But we are not a poor country and the vast majority of us can well afford to pay premium for the real thing, the non-industrial, non-intensive real thing. The fact that most of us choose not to tells us a great deal about ourselves and where our priorities lie. (*Daily Mail*, 23/1/2008 [MA30])

The opinion piece finishes with a rhetorical question: "What does the food that you buy for yourself and for your loved ones tell you about how much, or how little, you care" (*Daily Mail*, 23/1/2008 [MA30]), suggesting that consumption habits are integral to one's moral identity.

As the *Mail* favours self-responsibility and consumption as a form of embodied social action to progress human and chicken wellbeing, the government and institutional bodies are rarely held accountable. It is possible that chicken farming is framed as a private issue intentionally, assuming that the reader is not interested in macro-politics. Regardless of whether such framing is deliberate or not, the focus on personal consumption depoliticises chicken farming. This can be further illustrated with the headline of an opinion piece "Who's to blame for this food crisis? You are" (*Mail on Sunday*, 31/10/1999 [MA10]). A variety of topics underlying the *crisis* are noted: political (action from the government); commercial (intensive farming methods, imports) and social (consumer desires and behaviour). The latter is identified as the major cause of the *crisis*. Consumer ignorance and greed are blamed for the impact on farmers, farmed animals, and consumers' own health:

> Now things have gone wrong and we look for someone to blame. There are plenty of targets. There's the last Tory Government, under which BSE was allowed to flourish. There's modern farming methods. There's the French. There's Europe and the European Commission. There's Tony Blair. All nonsense, I say. I tell you who I blame. I blame you and I blame myself. We've been sleepwalking to disaster. Unthinkingly, uncaringly and, I'm sorry to say, greedily, we have filled our supermarket trolleys to overflowing with cheap produce from who knows where, not caring a fig for the effect of our actions on our farmers, the animal world or our wellbeing. (*Mail on Sunday*, 31/10/1999 [MA10])

The term "crisis" deserves further unpicking. The abstraction "crisis" suggests that the real subject may not be an objective phenomenon related to farmed animal welfare, regulation, or commercial realities. Instead, the "crisis" points to social anxieties and nostalgia to the past. In opinion articles, nostalgia typically manifests itself through lament for the loss of traditions and "real food", alienation from nature, devaluation of food and farming as a livelihood, moral decline, consumer ignorance and lack of personal responsibility. In the opinion piece "We fed this crisis" (*Daily Mail*, 13/12/2008, [MA33]), which revolves around a contaminated meat scandal, the journalist laments the loss of the "old-fashioned way" and "respect for real food" and speaks out against the growing distance between the consumer and producer. Not only health, but also the mind and morality of the consumer are at risk — intensive farming "corrupted the way we think about food" (*Daily Mail*, 13/12/2008 [MA33]).

Similarly, in response to the *Salmonella* scare in 1988, a *Mail* reader "prays" to see the end of battery farming and encourages the consumption of "higher welfare" eggs. The reader draws a direct link between hen welfare, the quality and safety of eggs and the price, and shames poor consumers for spending on tobacco, alcohol, and fast foods. Note that the hens are constructed as having a "contract" with us — they "repay us with fresh, disease-free" eggs in exchange for a free-range life:

> I pray that *Salmonella* scare will bring an end to the horror of battery-caged hens so that they may once again live as nature intended. So what if eggs cost more! People spend vast sums on tobacco, drink, sweets and fast foods. Give the hens their right to a free-range, normal life and they will repay us with fresh, disease-free food. (*Daily Mail*, 7/12/1988 [MA3])

The idea of animals consenting to our use, albeit "humane", can also be well-illustrated with a quote from a participant in Fearnley-Whittingstall's TV show. The participant is sensitised to animal welfare through an image of pastoral farming; the verb "give up" suggests that chickens voluntarily sacrifice their lives for us: "these animals give up their lives so we can eat, so we have to respect them" (*Daily Mail*, 4/11/2006 [MA23]). The common notion of "the animal contract" is prominently discussed in the biologist Stephan Budiansky's (1992) book *The Covenant of the Wild: Why Animals Chose Domestication.* Budiansky (1992) has claimed that the "animal contract" was developed through the historical process of domestication, in which animals voluntarily associated with humans. According to Budiansky (1992), farmed animals are better off than their "wild" counterparts; the populations of farmed animals are growing, while "wild" animals are disappearing. The argument, however, comes from a "species perspective" rather than a viewpoint of an individual animal, who during his or her short existence on a farm does not consent nor benefit from the "contract". Nibert (2013) rejects this idea of a "natural partnership" between humans and domesticated animals and argues that the domestication, or in Nibert's terms "domesecration", brought violence, displacement and exploitation to many humans and nonhumans for the benefit of a few.

In the following illustrative example, concerns do not revolve around chicken welfare *per se* but around British family traditions. Readers are constructed as responsible citizen-consumers, if only they "make a stand" through appropriate shopping behaviour (*Daily Mail*, 28/3/2005 [MA19]). Such framing, however, remains reductive, since the importance of macro-politics and the industry actors are underestimated:

> Like most families, I sat down yesterday to a traditional roast lunch—a wonderful ritual that is part of the British way of life. But factory-farmed meat, eaten in the vast quantities we are accustomed to, is not only an insult to that tradition, it is an abomination that is both cruel to the animals and dangerous for our own health... It is perfectly possible for farmers to find ways of producing meat in a humane way, if there was sufficient demand for it and not so much pressure to drive down prices... if enough people are prepared to make a stand for better food, then the corporate suppliers — and the Government — will take note and change bad practices. (*Daily Mail*, 28/3/2005 [MA19])

While political institutions and leaders are nearly excluded from the conversation, the role of the retail sector is tangible, but typically overshadowed by consumer responsibility. For example, a news story on the supermarket price war on eggs highlights that low-cost eggs targeted at those with low income come at the expense of farmers' and hens' welfare: "the cost of a half-dozen box [of eggs] is the lowest in years welcome news for poorer families in search of nutritious food. But the consequences for egg producers, human and hen, are not necessarily so positive" (*Daily Mail*, 6/4/2016 [MA34]). The impact that supermarket policies have on hen welfare is further addressed by criticising battery and colony cages. Note that colony cages are not called "enriched":

> Colony cages are a minor improvement on battery cages. Battery hens were each crammed into a space equivalent to an A4 piece of paper; in colony cages, they get the equivalent of one piece of A4 plus a beer mat. This means they still can't flap their wings or take dust baths, resulting in distress. It is these colony-caged hens that supply the 50p-for-six boxes. So the price war is helping to perpetuate cage farming. (*Daily Mail*, 6/4/2016 [MA34])

The news story finishes with the idea that consumers should be able to make an informed decision and pay more, formulated by campaigners. While the supermarkets are identified as culpable agents for pressuring farmers and perpetuating low welfare standards, the responsibility of consumers is underlined:

> Carol McKenna, of Compassion in World Farming, urges consumers to spend a bit more on higher welfare eggs ideally free-range or organic. Indeed, Jane Howorth, of the charity British Hen Welfare Trust, says consumers must take their share of the blame as they benefit from the price war. She says too much emphasis is placed on farmers' treatment of hens and not enough on the responsibility of the consumer. (*Daily Mail*, 6/4/2016 [MA34])

The headline "Tesco is a supermarket, not the guardian of our livers and morals" (*Mail on Sunday*, 24/2/2008 [MA32]) speaks for itself; supermarkets are seen as perpetuating social problems by selling cheap chicken meat (as well as cheap alcohol), but the root cause lies with consumers: "Supermarkets don't cause social ills, they respond to them and, OK, they perpetuate them" (*Mail on Sunday*, 24/2/2008 [MA32]). The idea that "if we buy something, we must take our share of responsibility for the way in which it has been produced" (*Daily Mail*, 12/4/2007 [MA27]) is reiterated by different voices, including journalists, readers and activists, and in different contexts. Some *Mail* articles redefine the idea that when humans treat farmed animals poorly for the sake of *cheap* products, public health risks become a punishment: "let's hope that we do not pay the price for this carelessness in years to come — in the hospital ward" (*Daily Mail*, 16/8/2005 [MA20]). The notions of "paying the price" and "nature's revenge" resonate with the concept of sin and punishment in religious thinking. Zoonotic diseases are perceived as a punishment for our alienation from *nature* and unnatural treatment of farmed animals: "As long as we keep them [farmed animals] so isolated from nature, nature has a way of striking back" (*Daily Mail*, 18/5/1990 [MA4]). Of note, an industry representative responded to this critique by embracing, or perhaps hijacking welfare discourses: "A well cared for bird is a healthy bird. It is therefore in no one's interests, especially the producers, to neglect the welfare of their chickens" (*Daily Mail*, 29/5/1990 [MA5]). Chicken welfare, however, is only given value inasmuch as it contributes to productivity and the meaning of "a well-cared bird" remains vague.

Nearly a decade after, *Salmonella*, *E. coli*, and antibiotic resistance are constructed as nature's revenge for what, in Biblical terms, would be gluttony and avarice. Consider the headline which uses the Biblical reference of the plague to describe the phenomenon:

> Nature's revenge: Our desire for cheap food has led us to accept farming techniques which treat our fellow creatures with utter contempt. But are we now all in danger of paying the ultimate price — being destroyed by a terrible plague which those methods have helped to create? (*Daily Mail*, 28/8/1999 [MA9])

The story starts with placing antibiotic resistance in a theological discourse of justice, where humans deserve a punishment for being cruel, ignorant and greedy: "There is simple Biblical justice in the warning by Government scientists that antibiotics vital in human medicine are being ruined through overuse in the feed of farm animals" (*Daily Mail*, 28/8/1999 [MA9]). Religious narratives are rewritten with nature as the punisher. Citizen-consumers and their biggest "sin" — *desire for cheap food* lie at the root of the problem: "The main source of all the evils is our desire for cheap food, which obliges producers to cut corners" (*Daily Mail*, 28/8/1999 [MA9]). Nearly a decade later, the biblically-inspired narratives are repeated. The opinion article "Nature's revenge: Is bird flu the price we're paying for years of cruelty in the pursuit of cheap meat?" depicts intensive farming as going against nature (*Daily Mail*, 6/2/2007 [MA26]). Our relationship with the natural world is conceptualised as nature's struggle against human control advanced by scientific developments and fuelled by greed; nature, thus, is exacting revenge on humanity in the form of avian influenza:

> But there is indeed something both surreal and biblical about these increasingly familiar scenes: nature, fed up with the way we have treated it, fighting back against profligate, greedy man whose desire for cheap food has led to such cruel and inhumane treatment of animals...We have treated animals as inanimate raw materials which we can bend to our will, always confident that science — and our wills — can successfully triumph over Nature's laws. But Nature is fighting back. (*Daily Mail*, 6/2/2007 [MA26])

Another reference to Judaeo-Christian theology is found in a letter from a reader who keeps hens. The reader legitimises our use of chickens (and other animals) under the premise of *good* (pastoral) care. An interpretation of the Great Chain of Being, which places men at the apex (just beneath God) and nonhuman animals below, is deployed as an argument for "humane" treatment of animals:

> As humans who now live by farming not by hunting, there is an urgent, ethical question; is it right to mistreat animals in the name of food? I keep hens. I know they don't want to live in a cage smaller than your newspaper. Your average roasting chicken lives locked up for 12 weeks, stuffed full of meal that includes animal waste and antibiotics, then, usually with a broken wing or a deformed foot, it is decapitated by machine and sold as "farm fresh". Don't get me wrong; I can wring a chicken's neck and eat the bird the same night... I know that we live in a chain of being, but I want my part to be humane and without hypocrisy. It is not wrong to eat meat. It is wrong to tether pigs in concrete stalls, rear veal in cages and feed animals their own remains. (*Daily Mail*, 10/7/2003 [MA14])

As this extract illustrates, the *Mail* gives substantial coverage to welfarist messages that revolve around "humane" pastoral farming in opinion/feature articles and letters. I shall also include an extract from an atypical text to show that the arguments of human superiority and care for animals can lead to an entirely different conclusion. In a review of the book *The Pig Who Sang to the Moon* by Jeffrey Moussaieff Masson, it is suggested that a human lives *naturally* if s/he *protects* nonhuman animal lives rather than eats them:

> In the wild, both hens and cocks elude their enemies, form intense friendships, protect their brood and greet dawn with a burst of song. This is how chickens were meant to live. No chicken is happy in battery cages... humans are meant to protect animal life, to take delight in it and to appreciate its pure wildness. (*Daily Mail*, 23/1/2004 [MA16])

This book review is an exception in the *Mail* corpus since it sympathises with the vegan vision of the writer: “Above all, he says, we owe all farm animals the deepest of apologies. Anyone who has a heart will be reduced to tears, if not to vegetarianism, by his argument” (*Daily Mail*, 23/1/2004 [MA16]). This is a sole example in the corpus of 34 years, which suggests that like the *Telegraph*, the *Mail* remains largely isolated from more radical views that support veganism.

As is the case with the *Mirror*, the *Mail* pays attention to chicken deaths, accidents, and cruelty cases rather than questions farming *per se*. A prototypical example comes from a news story on the deaths of more than a million chickens on British and French intensive farms due to overheating. While the article notes the economic loss, it also includes the voices of campaigners PETA and AA who construct the event as shocking and brutal:

> “To the farmer, chickens dying from trauma and heat exhaustion is an acceptable loss. But to the chicken languishing in a broiler shed, it’s a living hell.” Andrew Tyler, of Animal Aid, said: “Farmed animals suffer appallingly in the heat.” (*Daily Mail*, 13/8/2003 [MA15])

While it could be argued that the tabloid seeks sensational stories and thus employs vivid and graphic descriptions, from the perspective of an animal advocate such representations are welcome as they encourage readers to perceive chicken deaths as a loss of life of sentient beings. Another exceptional news story describes the killing of chickens due to the avian influenza risk from the perspective of the birds. The news story is titled “Tossed into bin bags, the tiniest victims of Hong Kong flu panic. The cull of the chicks” (*Daily Mail*, 30/12/1997 [MA8]). Of note, the event takes place in a faraway foreign country; if the virus were posing a threat in the UK, concerns over public health would likely overshadow compassion to chickens in news reporting:

> Their [chickens’] short, undignified lives were even shorter and less dignified than usual. These tiny chicks were scooped up by the armful, tossed into black binliners then taken to the gas chamber in their thousands yesterday as health workers began slaughtering every chicken, duck, pigeon and quail in Hong Kong in an attempt to wipe out a killer flu bug. (*Daily Mail*, 30/12/1997 [30/12/1997])

Lastly, I shall note that as in the other newspapers, the representations of chickens as agents and sensers of positive emotions are infrequent. The scarcity of such representations in the newspapers' corpora can be partly explained by my search query, which focusses of chicken *farming* rather than chicken *keeping* as a hobby or in sanctuaries. Texts on chicken keeping, however, are interesting as they typically construct chickens as persons. In the following extract, the language is patronising, yet chickens are presented as charismatic. The feature on a rescued hen Albert gives a detailed account of a loving human-chicken relationship and Albert's attractive personality traits:

> Albert basked in our love. She moved her head from side to side to look at these strange humans. From battery farm hell to this Eden… We came to love Albert as much as any dog or cat we ever had. She had immense character. She was a comic. She made us laugh with her jerky, Max Wall run across the lawn. She let us stroke her, too. She loved a gentle finger running down the back of her neck and across her wings. She would cluck gently just as a cat would purr and drift into a gentle trance. (*Mail on Sunday*, 22/2/2004 [MA18])

4.5.3 Summary and discussion

My analysis demonstrates that the division into broadsheets and tabloids is helpful as a starting point but is insufficient to account for individual differences in the newspapers' coverage of chicken farming. Both tabloids, the *Mail*, and the *Mirror*, have overall higher proportions of texts that omit chicken welfare (49% and 51%, respectively) than the broadsheets (40% in the *Guardian* and 42% in the *Telegraph*). Yet, despite the conservative bias of the paper, the *Mail* comes second after the *Guardian* corpus with regards to the depth of argument in opinion/feature articles.

As for the characteristics of tabloid journalism, the *Mail* takes a less scientific approach than the *Guardian* or the *Telegraph*. As is the case with the *Mirror*, a formal orientation and evidence-based approach give way to a moral(ising) or sensational orientation. "Soft" news stories on chicken deaths and human interest stories which sensationalise trivia have little political substance. Furthermore, texts providing inaccurate information are found. Humour, a light-hearted tone, ridicule, and puns, however, are less prevalent in the *Mail* than in the *Mirror* corpus. Aside from eye-catching headlines and some exceptions, chicken farming is more likely to be constructed as a serious issue in the *Mail*. Urgency and dramatisation are observed in the stories that frame zoonotic diseases as *nature's revenge* upon humanity. The narrative of punishment for a sin is reframed with nature as the punisher; public health issues become a sort of "revenge" for suffering inflicted upon chickens. The overall attention attributed to environmental problems in the *Mail* corpus, however, does not reflect the scale of effects chicken farming has on the environment.

In the *Mail* corpus, 73% of opinion/feature articles touch upon chicken welfare. One can find lengthy opinion/feature articles that discuss intensive chicken farming from the perspectives of chicken suffering, ethics, and public health. By comparison, in the *Telegraph* corpus, chicken welfare is frequently noted in a superficial manner, perhaps as an effort of journalists to report both "sides". Opinion articles and letters in the *Mail* also indicate a differentiated construction of readership identity. They tend to be characterised by a middle-class aspiration, an anti-cheap (thereby anti-intensive) farming attitude, adherence to family traditions and concern for morality. *Cheap* chicken is a signifier of social anxieties and symbolic of ethos to which the *Mail* generally does not aspire (poor, irresponsible, immoral). One could argue that the articles are about social anxieties (hypocrisy, ignorance, greed, alienation from nature) and the British identity rather than the commercial realities to which chickens are subjected. Nonetheless, they sensitise readers to chicken welfare issues by providing detailed descriptions of chicken suffering.

The *Mail* prioritises the "personalised" realm where the power of the consumer is assumed to be greater than the power of state. This finding is in line with the aforementioned characteristic of tabloid journalism to prioritise the private realm. The voice of the *Mail* can be moralising, judgemental and express scepticism about consumers (unlike in the campaigners' magazines, where, as we shall see in the following chapter, personal responsibility is also emphasised, but readers are constructed positively). In the *Mail*, readers are blamed for the demand of *cheap* chicken meat and eggs and reminded that cruelty is collateral to the consumption.

While consumers are blamed for being greedy and ignorant, the chicken industry is constructed as merely responding to consumer demand for cheap protein. Such reductive framing overestimates the economic power consumers have over the industry and underestimates the power that the animal farming industry, perpetuated by marketing and lobbying has on the consumer. The emphasis on individual consumption obfuscates corporate and institutional accountability and limits the public understanding of what can be done about chicken farming on the level of micro and macro-politics. The readers are restricted to behavioural change (consumption) rather than political action (e.g. pressuring the government and industry bodies). The importance of structural change and large-scale institutional processes relating to subsidies, taxes, regulation, catering in public sector, education or product labelling are undermined.

The importance of democratic participation and political leadership is backgrounded in the *Mail* corpus. The reason why could lie in the entertainment value of tabloid journalism. My study shows that the *Mirror* also largely eschews from political debate on chicken farming, but so does the broadsheet *Telegraph*, suggesting that the format alone cannot provide a satisfactory explanation. It could be worth looking at the *Mail*'s readership demographics; the tabloid has the largest female readership among the four sources. The focus on the private and domestic rather than the public and political realm could originate from a gendered presupposition. Four articles stand out from the corpus for their derogatory constructions of women as housewives responsible for food purchases and cooking for the family. If the tabloid assumes the readers of articles about chicken welfare to be female, then "guilt-mongering", moralising and suggesting shopping as a solution may result from gendered discourses. In addition, the large female readership could potentially explain why the *Mail* is more sensitive to chicken welfare than the *Mirror* or the *Telegraph.* In the UK, women have been associated with the animal rights movement since its start in the nineteenth century (Ferguson, 1998; Gaarder, 2011). In her accounts of gender and the political paths of activists in the animal rights movement, the sociologist Emily Gaarder (2011) notes that female activists markedly outnumber males. Largely female animal activism is known to clash with traditionally male-dominated activities of hunting, experimentation on nonhuman animals and slaughtering (Luke, 2007).

Furthermore, previous studies have associated the *Mail* with the (highly debatable) concept of "middle England" (Moran, 2005; Seale et al., 2007; Meyer, 2010). Social and cultural historian Joe Moran notes that the *Mail* "sees itself as the voice of middle England and is more explicit than most in identifying this region with the suburban, southern white middle class" (p. 239). Moran (2005), however, concludes that middle England is not a geographic region but a rhetorical device:

> The myth of middle England... defuses difficult issues about class, money and power through vague allusions to lifestyle: home makeovers, Delia Smith recipes, Tesco, Radio 4, Marks and Spencer and school runs. It combines long-standing motifs about the British middle classes with the unique brand of populism initiated by Thatcherism, which aimed to short-circuit traditional political processes and speak directly to nominally homogenous, but actually carefully targeted, "people". In short, middle England is a rhetorical strategy... (p. 239)

My findings suggest that the *Mail* coverage of chicken farming reflects the rhetoric of "middle England", especially with regards to the Thatcherist discourse of personal responsibility, where individual lifestyle solutions are given political resonance. The analysis also demonstrates that the *Mail* can be positioned somewhere between the tabloid and the "quality" newspapers for its coverage of chicken farming. The distinction between the middle market *Mail* and the down-market tabloid *Mirror* is palpable, as in the *Mail* corpus, chicken farming is more likely to be addressed as a serious issue in lengthy polemic articles. The conservative position of the *Mail* does not preclude the perception of chicken farming as newsworthy.

5.
Campaigners

5.1 Overview of the campaigners' corpora

A large difference in corpus sizes led to the decision to discuss the CIWF and AA corpora together rather than separately and allocate more space for CIWF in the analysis. Table 5.1 provides the descriptive information and shows that the CIWF corpus contains eight times as many texts and is nearly seven times larger in total word count. The average length of a text, however, is larger in the AA corpus.

Table 5.1 CIWF and AA corpora

	CIWF corpus	AA corpus
Number of texts	508	60
Total word count	171,742	25,975
Average length of an article	338	433
Number of images	595	76

The campaigners' magazines include news reports, features, interviews, shopping guides, book reviews and so on. Tables 5.2 and 5.3 present data distribution thematically between 1982 and 2016. The largest thematic domain for both corpora is, unsurprisingly, "campaigning, lobbying and action" (237 texts for CIWF, or 47%, and 27 texts for AA, or 53%). The exploratory keyword analysis of the CIWF corpus reveals a number of Europe-related keywords (see Appendix E online). Table 5.4 shows that topical abbreviations *EU* and *EEC* (for European Economic Community) and lemmas *Europe** and *Commission** are relatively overused in the CIWF corpus. For example, *EU* is used 20.1 times relatively more frequently in the CIWF corpus than in the AA corpus. This indicates that CIWF perceives chicken welfare issues as stretching beyond national boundaries and recognises the importance of the EU institutions in decision-making.

Table 5.2 Data distribution in the CIWF corpus

	campaigning/lobbying/direct action	*chicken welfare issues*	*business/economics*	*legislation/regulation/policy*	*labelling/advertising/marketing*	*free-range farming*	*cultural and social issues*	*public health/food safety*	*miscellaneous*	*chicken deaths and accidents*	*total per year*
1982			5							1	6
1983	1		1		1						3
1984	4	6	7	6	1	1	1		1		27
1985	4	8	8	3	1		1	1		2	28
1986	6	3	1	2		1	2				15
1987	6	2	4	4	2	1	1				20
1988	11	3	1	3	1		3				22
1989	4	8	2	3	2	2	2	2	2		27
1990	5	7	8	1	3	3		5		3	35
1991	3	4	3	1		3		1			15
1992	10	6		1							17
1993	5	4		1	1						11
1994	3	1		1		1					6
1995	3	2			3						8
1996	2	4	1	1	1			1		1	11
1997	1	2		2							5
1998											0
1999	25	3	1	3		1	1	1			35
2000	6	3		1			1				11
2001	3	1	4	2	1		1				12
2002	7	4		1				1			13
2003	8	3	1	3			1		1		17
2004	5		1		3	2					11
2005	5	3	2	3				2			15
2006	11	4	3		1				1		20
2007	5	1	2	2					1		11
2008	8	1	7	1					1		18
2009	10	1	3	1	3		1				19
2010	4	2	8	2	1	1					18
2011	5		3	1			1	1			11
2012	3		3	1	2						9
2013	4				2	1					7
2014	3	2	2			1	1		1		10
2015	1	4	1	1							7
*2016**	3		2	2					1		8
TOTAL	**184**	**92**	**84**	**53**	**29**	**18**	**17**	**15**	**9**	**7**	**508**

*Corpus for the first six months

Table 5.3 Data distribution in the AA corpus

	campaigning/lobbying/direct action	*chicken welfare issues*	*labelling/advertising/marketing*	*legislation/regulation/policy*	*chicken deaths and accidents*	*public health/food safety*	*miscellaneous*	*business/economics*	*total per year*
1982	3						1		4
1983	3	2							5
1984	3	1					1	1	6
1985		1		1					2
1986	3		1						4
1987	1		1						2
1988			1		1				2
1989		1					1		2
1990				1					1
1991								1	1
1992	2	1	1						4
1993									0
1994	1								1
1995									0
1996		1		1					2
1997									0
1998									0
1999	1			2					3
2000	1	1							2
2001									0
2002	1								1
2003									0
2004		1	1						2
2005									0
2006						2			2
2007						1			1
2008	3								3
2009	1								1
2010									0
2011	1								1
2012									0
2013									0
2014		1			3				4
2015		1							1
*2016**	3								3
TOTAL	**27**	**11**	**5**	**5**	**4**	**3**	**3**	**2**	**60**

*Corpus for the first six months

Table 5.4 Frequency analysis: CIWF and AA

	CIWF corpus		AA corpus		Keyness		
Word or lemma	**AF**	**NF**	**AF**	**NF**	**Over/under-use**	**LL**	**Ratio**
Europe*	505	28.8	10	3.8	+	81.7	7.5
Commission*	139	7.9	2	0.8	+	25.6	10.3
EU	272	15.5	2	0.8	+	59.6	20.1
EEC	81	4.6	1	0.4	+	15.6	12.0
supermarket*	201	11.4	2	0.8	+	41.2	14.9
consum*	263	15.0	5	1.9	+	43.3	7.8
Sainsbury*	52	3.0	0	0.0	+	14.4	div
Tesco	110	6.3	0	0.0	+	30.4	div
Total word count	**175,613**		**25,975**				

Note: (+) indicates "overuse"; (-) indicates "underuse"; (div) indicates "division by 0 disallowed"; LL of 3.84 or higher is significant at the level of $p < 0.05$

Texts on specific chicken health and welfare issues constitute the second-largest thematic category in both corpora (92 texts for CIWF, or 18%, and 11 texts for AA, or 18%). Business and economic aspects of chicken farming are discussed in 84 texts (17%) in the CIWF corpus. The exploratory keyword analysis of the CIWF corpus highlights the charity's attention to consumers and supermarkets (See Appendix E). The lemmas *consum** and *supermarket** are relatively overused in the CIWF corpus (Table 5.4). CIWF identifies the retailers when congratulating or shaming them for poor welfare standards; the chains *Tesco* and *Sainsbury** feature 110 and 52 times in the CIWF corpus. AA does not lobby supermarkets and the names of retailers are not found (Table 5.4). Only two texts (3%) in the AA corpus are dedicated to the topic of chicken business suggesting that the NGO does not focus on nor support industry perspectives.

"Labelling, advertising and marketing of chicken products" occupy a similar share of the CIWF corpus (29 texts, or 6%) and the AA corpus (5 texts, or 8%). Free-range farming and its benefits are covered in 18 texts (4%) in the CIWF corpus. In the AA corpus, there are no texts dedicated to the topic showing that AA, as an animal rights organisation, does not promote free-range farming. On the other hand, texts on chicken deaths and accidents occupy a greater share of the AA corpus (4 texts, or 7%, in comparison to 7 texts, or 1%, in the CIWF corpus), which indicates the attention to the loss of life.

Compared to the analysed newspapers, the campaigners seldom problematise chicken farming from social, cultural, public health or environmental perspectives. Table 5.2 shows that the category "cultural and social issues" contains 17 texts (3%) in the CIWF corpus, while the AA corpus does not comprise texts on cultural and social factors (Table 5.3). Public health and food safety (e.g. antibiotic resistance, *Salmonella* food poisoning, and avian influenza) are given priority in 15 texts (3%)

in the CIWF corpus and three texts (5%) in the AA corpus. Strikingly, environmental concerns feature only tangentially in both corpora.

Distribution of texts over 33.5 calendar years is presented in Figure 5.1. No major increases in the coverage of chicken farming are identified in the AA corpus. An increase in CIWF coverage in 1990 cannot be attributed to a single event. Texts published in 1990 cover various chicken welfare issues, provide industry news and report on legislation and campaigns. A peak in 1999 revolves around the announcement made by the European Commission that battery cages would be illegal from 1st January 2012. Interestingly, in contrast to the *Guardian, Mirror* and *Mail* corpora, the coverage of chicken farming does not peak due to the bird flu epidemic. Furthermore, neither of the activist corpora demonstrate a general increase in coverage since 1982, although the sheer number of animals affected in the ever-expanding chicken industry could rightfully warrant a growing interest from the campaigners.

Figure 5.1 Data distribution over time in CIWF and AA corpora

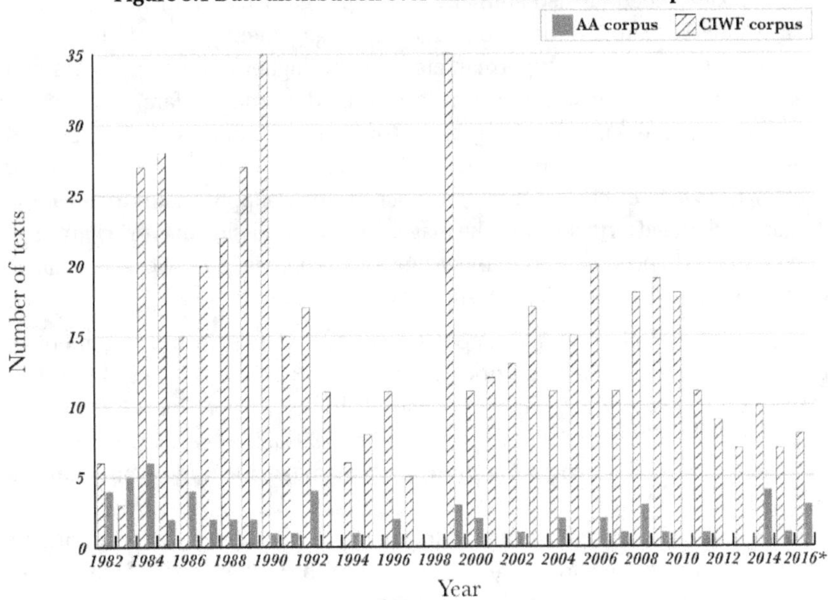

*Data for the first six months

Discursive shifts over time are reflected in the changes of the title and tagline of the CIWF flagship magazine. It is worth reiterating that CIWF was founded by farmers. Before 1992, the tagline of *Agscene*, short for *Agricultural Scene*, had been "News and comment on agriculture and the environment", which de-emphasises nonhuman animals by placing them alongside the cultivation of crops under the generalised term "agriculture". *Agscene* defined itself as a newsletter and contained multiple brief news reports aimed at farmers alongside longer articles on campaigns. In 1992, *Agscene* changed its tagline to "The journal of Compassion in World Farming" and in 1994 to "The quarterly magazine of Compassion in World Farming". The magazine underwent changes in design, style, and content. An increase in the number of photographs and illustrations could be explained by technological advances, and a heightened focus on celebrities and fundraising suggests changing audience (from farmers to consumers).

In 2001, the CIWF flagship magazine changed its title to *Farm Animal Voice*, which emphasises their assumed role of speaking on behalf of farmed animals, and its tagline to "Better lives for animals and us", which underlines the charity's welfarist approach. The 2000s brought further design changes, which enhanced the magazine's visual appeal, a greater focus on consumer and shopping tactics, and a greater amount of world news as CIWF expanded internationally. In 2007, the tagline was changed to "Passionate people for compassionate farming", which again backgrounded farmed animals. The same year CIWF launched the Good Farm Animal Welfare Awards to celebrate their engagement with the industry. For example, CIWF pressures supermarkets to stock "higher welfare" products and presents awards to those that commit to farmed animal welfare. The awards programme includes the Good Egg Award for companies that use eggs from non-caged hens in their supply chain and the Good Chicken Award for companies that use "higher welfare" chicken meat products in their supply chain. In 2009, the magazine changed its tagline to "The magazine of Compassion in World Farming" and in 2010, it became "Your magazine of Compassion in World Farming" emphasising the relationship with supporters.

As for AA, the title *Outrage* suggests a strong reaction to the treatment of nonhuman animals. The magazine's taglines also reflect the NGO's ideological stance. In the 1980s, the tagline emphasised abolition: "For Those Committed to the Total Abolition of Animal Abuse". In the 1990s, the tagline was softened to "The Animal Aid Journal for Action" and the magazine underwent changes in the design and layout. Since 1997, the magazine has become thicker, more colourful, and visually appealing. At first glance, it may appear that the content of the magazine became "lighter". The number of images, features on celebrities, and, as the range of vegan products expanded over the period, the number of vegan recipes and adverts for vegan clothing, food and cosmetics increased. Yet, alongside the emphasis on cruelty-free products, all types of chicken farming systems have increasingly received scrutiny in the magazine.

The following sections are organised by themes. I start with the narratives of intensive farming. This is followed by the representations of "higher welfare" farming, challenges to "higher welfare" and human-centred motives against intensive farming. I then analyse the ways campaigners hold the government accountable and involve readers as citizens. A separate section is allocated to the analysis of texts that make space for chicken agency. Additionally, visual representation of chickens and its intersection with linguistic texts are briefly discussed.

5.2 Intensive farming

Despite their different end-goals, CIWF and AA approach intensive chicken farming similarly. Texts are built on the assumption that their readers agree that chickens suffer and that their suffering matters. This is a logical assumption since the flagship magazines are sent out to the existing supporters of CIWF and AA. The following extracts on battery cages epitomise the key similarity in the narratives produced by CIWF and AA, namely constructing chickens as victims of cruelty. Caged hens are depicted as suffering physically as they are forced to stand in discomfort and psychologically as they are unable to behave according to their nature:

> Their cages are so small that they [hens] cannot stretch their wings. They are forced to stand on an uncomfortable sloping wire floor. The lack of space and barren environment prevents the birds from performing their natural behavioural patterns, such as perching, dustbathing and wing flapping. (*Agscene*, 1993 [AG10])

> Unable to spread their wings, over 40 million hens exist, five to an 18 inch by 20 inch cage. The battery hen will never see daylight, feel fresh air or perform any of its natural instincts — to scratch, dust bathe or nest. (*Outrage*, 1985 [OU2])

Emphasising confinement, crowded conditions, and the inability of chickens to express natural behaviours under intensive farming conditions, both CIWF and AA argue that chickens deserve to live in environments that allow freedom of movement and are more natural to them. The values of freedom and naturalness are juxtaposed with the artificial environment of intensive farming by the CEO of CIWF Philip Lymbery:

> Factory farming is essentially producing animals on an industrial scale; it's mass farming. It's about keeping animals often in close confinement, often in cages where, for example, battery hens can't stretch their wings or where pigs can't even turn around. Or it's keeping them in huge numbers in windowless, barren sheds. It also involves making the animals grow or produce beyond their natural limits: using breeding techniques and using feeding techniques that take them beyond their physiological limits. (*Farm Animal Voice*, 2010 [FAV18])

Victimising chickens is identified in 93% of texts in the CIWF corpus (472 items out of 508) and in 89% of texts in the AA corpus (54 items out of 60). In both corpora, chickens lack agency and are rarely presented as subjects of material, behavioural, relational, and mental processes unrelated to their poor treatment. Through the passive voice and nominalisations such as "chicken suffering", "chicken suffocation", "chicken slaughter" or "chicken transport", chickens are grammatically realised as objects to whom something is being done. Cruelty and pain experienced by chickens are stressed. Table 5.5 presents the frequency comparisons for the lemmas *pain** and *cruel**. Log-likelihood scores below 3.84 indicate that there is no significant difference between the CIWF and AA corpora. The ratio equals 1, confirming that the lemmas occur at a similar frequency in both corpora.

Table 5.5 Frequency analysis: CIWF and AA

	CIWF corpus		AA corpus		Keyness		
Word or lemma	**AF**	**NF**	**AF**	**NF**	**Over/under-use**	**LL**	**Ratio**
Pain*	110	6.3	17	6.5	-	0.0	1.0
Cruel*	138	7.9	20	7.7	+	0.0	1.0
Total word count	**175,613**		**25,975**				

The second key similarity between the CIWF and AA corpora is that CIWF and AA balance an emotive tone of voice with a knowledgeable tone. Comparably to investigative journalism stories, CIWF and AA seek truthfulness in their communications by relying on scientific knowledge and official sources. The narrative forms presenting chickens as victims typically include extensivisation, i.e. describing actions and situations in detail and adding as much subsidiary information as possible (Khosravinik, 2009, p. 485). Engaging, affecting, change-driven voices are interspersed with factual details on farming practices such as animal densities or mortality rates. The following extracts demonstrate how specialist knowledge of chicken health issues in the meat industry is borrowed and integrated in campaigning discourse. Chickens are presented as victims; they "succumb" to various illnesses and the ones that are kept for breeding become "chronically hungry":

> Modern broilers have been selectively bred to grow very quickly, but their legs and hearts cannot keep pace with the rapid body growth. All too often the legs buckle under the strain of supporting the overdeveloped body; as a result, each year millions of chickens suffer from painful leg disorders. Millions a year also succumb to heart failure. The breeding flock cannot be allowed to grow so quickly otherwise many would die before sexual maturity and others would be too unhealthy to breed. To slow down their growth rate, the industry gives them such tiny rations that many suffer from chronic hunger for weeks to end. (*Farm Animal Voice*, 2004 [FAV5])

> Modern broiler chickens have been selectively bred to eat vast amounts of high protein food, and therefore put on weight extremely quickly, leading to the syndrome of birds who are fully grown at 6 to 7 weeks of age, yet still cheeping like the young chicks they are. The parent stock (the breeders) must, therefore, also have these "greedy" tendencies. However, if they ate as much as they wanted to, many would die early from obesity-related illnesses and there would be a great reduction in fertility, because the overweight males would find it difficult to mount the females. Females would also be prone to multiple ovulations and soft-shelled eggs, which would be useless for hatching purposes. To prevent these problems, feed for broiler breeders is heavily restricted, meaning that the birds become chronically hungry. This regime is particularly harsh during the birds' first few months, and some will resort to eating litter from the floor of the sheds. (*Outrage*, 1996 [OU10])

CIWF and AA use knowledge to challenge and construct the industry and industry-related bodies as cunning, dishonest or at least secretive about farming methods. CIWF identifies "factory farming", "industrial chicken farming", "industry" or "intensive poultry farming" as culprits for chicken suffering in 60% of texts. With regards to AA, industry-related culprits are found in 90% of texts. This difference in proportion is because AA pays less attention to political actors. In addition, since AA is more involved in direct action, it more frequently identifies specific industry-related culprits on the national level rather than the industry *per se*. Industry *truths* are challenged by exposing the (potentially disturbing yet routine) practices in chicken farming. The following extracts illustrate how the CIWF and AA campaigners examine the British Egg Information Service's claim that cages are hen-friendly and better than free-range systems:

> we believe that the welfarists can definitely point the finger at the British Egg Information Service and their resource "The Egg Story"... Of battery hens, a very rosy picture is painted: "The number of hens to a particular size of cage is controlled by the law so that nobody can put too many hens together in too small a space." (*Agscene*, 1992 [AG9])

> The British Egg Information Service aims to leave pupils in no doubt that battery is best. In their 12 page booklet Egg Farming they simply take all the criticisms of the battery cage and apply them instead to the free-range system. Free-range hens, exposed to "adverse weather conditions," are disease and parasite ridden. Far from being an advantage, the fact that they have an opportunity to develop a pecking order means that the hens are prone to feather pecking and cannibalism to such an extent that "beak trimming may become necessary". The booklet also argues that free-range hens "tend to suffer from hysteria so that when danger threatens they may crowd together and suffocate each other" (!). (*Outrage*, 1992 [OU8])

The tone of voice in the CIWF corpus appears to be more authoritative and formally orientated, which could be explained by their ambition to effectively lobby authorities and industry players. CIWF positions themselves as knowledge producers and distributors by citing scientists, researchers, and expert bodies. The keywords *scientific* and *Dr* demonstrate the greater reliance upon scientific evidence and expert knowledge (see Appendix E). The lemma *scien** is used 14.1 times relatively more frequently and *Dr* is used 10.1 times relatively more frequently in the CIWF corpus compared with the AA corpus (Table 5.6).

Table 5.6 Frequency analysis: CIWF and AA

	CIWF corpus		AA corpus		Keyness		
Word or lemma	**AF**	**NF**	**AF**	**NF**	**Over/under-use**	**LL**	**Ratio**
Scien*	95	5.4	1	0.4	+	19.2	14.1
Dr	68	3.9	1	0.4	+	12.4	10.1
Total word count	**175,613**		**25,975**				

A veterinary science vocabulary (e.g. *osteoporosis, viral arthritis, ascites, Salmonella enteritidis, coccidiosis*) is extensively used when referring to chicken health issues. An illustrative quote comes from a text on welfare issues affecting chickens farmed for their flesh: "Ascites, an effusion of non-inflammatory liquid into the abdominal cavity, for no apparent reason is becoming increasingly common in 4-week-old birds. Losses up to 40% of some flocks have been reported" (*Agscene*, 1985 [AG3]). The quote also highlights the dilemma CIWF faces; CIWF uses knowledge and scientific claims to effectively challenge (and lobby) the industry, but at the same time slips into further objectifying chickens and normalising the A-IC. The scientific view of chickens is closely entangled with the industry perspective: chicken deaths are defined as (financial) *losses*. In the words of the feminist human-animal scholar Birke (2008), scientific language not only leads to considerable ambivalence in the ways nonhuman animals are portrayed, but also to denial of animal agency and the production of knowledge that is based on domination over nonhuman animals. Technical terms (e.g. "growth rate", "stocking density", "broiler", "breeding flock" or "poultry") and the vocabulary of production economics (terms such as "output" or "losses") may be convenient when referring to industry practices and standards. However, if used uncritically, such terminology constructs chickens as parts of a commercial enterprise and their bodies as predisposed for production: "birds which have good feet, strong legs and good walking and foraging abilities are selected for breeding to produce other chickens with similar favourable traits" (*Farm Animal Voice*, 2010 [FAV17]).

The linguist Mary Kahn argues that in "hard sciences", the scientific writing style masks the unethical treatment of animals; when nonhuman animals under experimentation are being "housed", "dosed", "processed", "relocated" and "translocated", these terms are replacing potentially unpleasant and disturbing, but perhaps more accurate descriptions of animals being "caged", "drugged", "killed" and "banished" (Kahn, 2001, p. 243). An uncritical use of the science and industry jargon, as exemplified in the extracts via terms such as "the parent stock" or "breeders", is more prevalent in the AA corpus in the 1980s and 1990s. Afterwards, with the exception of the key terms such as "broiler" and "poultry", objectifying terms and euphemisms are increasingly challenged using scare quotes: "Many [chickens] had been 'culled' because of leg problems or simply because they were too small or weak to be profitable" (*Outrage*, 2008 [OU15]). The NGO repeatedly highlights the link between the terminology and industry practices: "Hens considered to be 'end of lay' by battery farmers are neither 'old' nor 'spent'" (*Outrage*, 1989 [OU6]). Vivid empathic language is contrasted with functional industry terms: "It was clear that birds with painful joints or any other illnesses could not possibly fight their way through to the food and water containers. These poor creatures are known in the chicken meat industry as 'starve-outs'" (*Outrage*, 2008 [OU15]). Other examples of AA's tactic to use scare quotes include:

- "productive life" (for the period a hen is considered profitable in commercial farming)
- "processing plant" (for slaughterhouses)
- "table birds" (for chickens farmed for meat)
- "enriched cages" (for colony cages that replaced battery cages in 2012)
- "macerators" (for shredding machines used for killing of male chicks in the egg industry)
- "disposed" (for killing of male chicks in the egg industry)
- "culled" (for killing of chickens that are too small or weak to be profitable in the meat industry)
- "rejects" (for male chicks in the egg industry)
- "eradication" (for killing of chickens in the event of avian influenza).

CIWF, on the other hand, pays more attention to *truthful* marketing and consumer rights creating partly chicken-centred and partly consumer-centred narratives. As mentioned earlier in Chapter 3, one of the biggest campaigns the charity had launched was about clear labelling of chicken meat. In 2014, their mascot Rosa travelled Europe for 39 days appealing to the value of honesty and consumer right for information: "Our Labelling Matters mascot, Rosa the chicken, undertook a 39-day, 21-country journey, rallying support for clear and honest labelling of chicken meat across Europe" (*Farm Animal Voice*, 2015

[FAV29]). The consumer is constructed as naïve (assuming that if they knew about chicken suffering, they would not choose meat or eggs from intensive farms) and warned about the potentially misleading packaging: "Words such as 'farm fresh' and 'quality assured' or images of animals outdoors on idyllic landscapes are commonly used to mask the dark truth about factory farming" (*Farm Animal Voice*, 2012 [FAV25]).

Furthermore, CIWF emphasises and problematises the *cheapness* of intensively produced chicken meat and eggs. Illustrative concordance lines for "cheap" in Table 5.7 demonstrate a strong negative connotation attached to the adjective. The prevailing argument that *cheap* chicken products have hidden costs has been previously observed in the newspapers, most notably in the *Guardian* and the *Mail*. In the CIWF corpus, however, the most attention is given to chicken suffering (e.g. "the price in misery of cheap factory farmed chicken" and "the real price of cheap chicken is shocking cruelty") and to economic issues as *cheap* products undermine farmers' livelihoods (Table 5.7). The *Mail*, on the other hand, extends the economic meaning of *cheap* to a moral one by emphasising consumer responsibility and guilt, as observed through phrases such as "the British simply cannot get enough of cheap chicken" or "the true cost of our obsession with cheap chicken?" (presented previously in Table 4.22). While both the *Mail* and CIWF foreground consumption, in the CIWF corpus, positive rhetoric is prioritised over criticism to promote "higher welfare" farming.

Table 5.7 Extract from "cheap" concordance in the CIWF corpus

the price in misery of	**cheap** factory farmed chicken? One glimm
to death the price of	**cheap** chicken is mass misery on
Alternative The real price of	**cheap** chicken is shocking cruelty. But
real cost of the supposedly "	**cheap**" battery egg is immense suffering
them vulnerable to imports of	**cheap** eggs produced in battery cages
to the realities of buying	**cheap** chicken. CHANNEL 4'S FOOD WEEK
-range poultry and to switch	**cheap** chickens to higher welfare chicken
as its farmers risk being undermined by	**cheap**, low-welfare imports. The EU has banned
factory farming can often be	**cheap** and cheerless is the case
huge cost to that apparently	**cheap** piece of meat. The other
farmers risk being undermined by	**cheap**, low welfare imports. One way
— How Come It's So	**Cheap**? Armed with all our persuasive
problem A devastating indictment of	**cheap** meat and factory farming it
labelling and higher prices for '	**cheap**' meat — prices that reflect the

5.3 "Higher welfare"

As expected, "higher welfare" farms are approached differently in the CIWF and AA corpora. CIWF, a charity founded by farmers, presents "higher welfare" systems idealistically, thereby normalising chicken farming and the consumption of chicken flesh and eggs. A clear distinction between *bad* (intensive and cheap) and *good* chicken farming emerges in the CIWF corpus over the period. *Good* farming is considered to be organic, free-range or "higher welfare" indoors for chickens raised for meat. The following extract illustrates a chicken-centred narrative of free-range farming:

> Raising chickens on pasture means a chicken is allowed to be a chicken. They are given the space and enrichment to scratch, peck and flap their wings. It means a slower growing breed is used that is better for their welfare and appropriate for pasture, as compared to conventionally raised broilers. It means they are not just given "access to outdoors", but rather the pasture is a permanent and central part of their life. (*Farm Animal Voice*, 2013 [FAV27])

With regards to egg production, *good* systems are considered to be organic, free-range or indoor barn, whilst battery and "enriched" cages are perceived as cruel: "Many farmers, both in the UK and the rest of the EU, plan to replace the banned conventional cage with 'enriched' cages rather than going over to good free-range and perchery systems" (*Farm Animal Voice*, 2002 [FAV1]). Since around 2006, the term "higher welfare" is used as an umbrella term for organic, free-range, and indoor farming above the legal standard in the CIWF corpus.

The key difference between the CIWF and AA corpora is that CIWF lobbies the industry players and celebrates companies that produce or supply "higher welfare" products, implying that once minor improvements to chicken welfare are achieved, the consumption becomes unproblematic. A pun in the headline "Egg-ceedingly good welfare" sets a cheerful tone; CIWF congratulates a brand of baked goods for committing to use free-range eggs: "The UK's number 1 cake brand has gone free-range across its entire range! Mr Kipling, one of the flagship brands of Premier Foods, has made the fantastic move to use only free-range eggs" (*Farm Animal Voice*, 2011 [FAV20]). The charity praises a supermarket for selling chicken meat products that comply to RSPCA welfare standards and applauds the increasing demand for these products: "UK supermarket giant Sainsbury's, pledged to sell chicken that met RSPCA Freedom Food™ standards or equivalent and UK demand for free-range chicken went through the roof" (*Farm Animal Voice*, 2008 [FAV16]). The following extract illustrates how supermarkets that do not sell eggs from caged hens are praised claiming that eggs from non-cage systems are "produced without cruelty" rather than with less cruelty:

> At the top end of the market, with Waitrose and Marks & Spencer, not a single shell egg they sell comes from a chicken kept in a cage… the Co-op is aiming to match its up-market competitors by 2007 and deserves a hearty pat on the back for offering all their customers eggs produced without cruelty. (*Farm Animal Voice*, 2005 [FAV8])

Readers of both CIWF and AA magazines are expected to make "ethical" shopping choices. The fundamental difference is that CIWF ask their supporters to maintain moral integrity through the consumption of "higher welfare" chicken products: "Now it's over to you. If you eat meat, we hope you are already converted to buying free-range" (*Farm Animal Voice*, 2008 [FAV14]), and the AA supporters are encouraged to abstain from chicken products: "Animal Aid offers a free Go Vegan pack, which contains a number of delicious egg-free recipes, including quiche and chocolate cake" (*Outrage*, 2015 [OU20]). CIWF supporters are urged to buy "higher welfare" products openly and implicitly by providing detailed information on products. Their involvement as consumers has increased over the period. Urging to choose the "right" chicken products has become more frequent since the 2000s. The use of lemma *shop** peaks in 2008, the year when CIWF published its *Compassionate Shopping Guide* and contributed to chicken welfare campaigns by Oliver and Fearnley-Whittingstall.

Celebrity status is used by CIWF to raise awareness of intensive farming: "Thanks to Channel 4 and celebrity chefs Hugh Fearnley-Whittingstall and Jamie Oliver, the cruel conditions in which 800 million chickens reared every year for meat in the UK were well and truly exposed" (*Farm Animal Voice*, 2008 [FAV15]). As observed in the newspapers, the celebrities function as cultural intermediaries and ambassadors for chicken welfare. The chefs convey information on chicken farming in anthropocentric, yet accessible and persuasive way. For instance, Oliver promotes "higher welfare" farming through family values, stating he seeks food which is *good* for his own family:

> I support the Better Chicken Initiative because I want to raise the bar of standard chickens to a totally different level — one that is affordable, accessible and that I would feed to my own kids. If it is successful, this initiative will improve the lives of millions, perhaps billions, of chickens and create a healthier food and farming system. (*Farm Animal Voice*, 2014 [FAV28])

The positive rhetoric delivers a message that what is *good* for chickens is also *good* for you on a practical (healthier product) and moral basis (kinder). CIWF supporters are made to feel good about themselves and empowered as making a difference, being significant, *being pioneers*: "Be a pioneer! Only buy free-range and organic chicken — even if you're buying ready-meals" (*Farm Animal Voice*, 2007 [FAV13]).

Nevertheless, an optimistic "win-win" narrative is instrumentalising and obscuring. Typically, when the benefits of "higher welfare" farming are discussed, the readers are not confronted with the remaining issues or the deaths of chickens. One text promoting "higher welfare" chicken meat in 1990 stands out as an exception in the CIWF corpus of 33.5 years. Although the text inadvertently normalises intensive farming by calling an intensively farmed chicken "a normal broiler", it, more importantly, acknowledges that regardless of "humaneness" of a farming system, the chickens will eventually be killed:

> The Landais chicken, reared in pine forests in S.W. France are slow growing — 12 to 13 weeks when killed instead of the 7 weeks of a normal broiler. They have a drug-free diet and plenty of exercise. It is these factors that are designed to make the difference. Animal welfare and a tastier chicken are consumer demands that could spell the end of the intensive broiler industry eventually — but at the end of the day they still have to be killed. (*Agscene*, 1990, 99 [AG7])

As observed in the newspapers, better living conditions are glamorised and linked to better taste and quality of chicken products. The following extract illustrates how chicken welfare is instrumental for public health and for economic ends; chickens are referred to in commercial terms and inscribed as value-added products. The farmer is morally elevated as she is described positively and personalised by referring to her through characteristics of age and family status:

> A young Cape Town mother of two is taking the market from under the noses of the organised poultry industry in South Africa, by producing table chickens (broilers) on free-range… It is her passion to produce quality chickens without poisoning the earth with antibiotic residue… free-range, drug-free broilers can be found in most supermarkets and cost about R2 (equivalent of £0.18) more per kilo. She hopes to be marketing 32,000 broilers a week by next year. (*Farm Animal Voice*, 2004 [FAV6])

In another text on free-range farming, the "Smith brothers, one-time army officers in bomb-disposal" are presented nearly heroically, whereas chickens are referred to in terms of profitability; they are instrumentalised as a part of "livestock enterprise", determined by "return" and "output":

> The Smith brothers, one-time army officers in bomb-disposal, have 6,500 hens on free-range and they make the staggering claim that Free-range Egg production represents the best return on invested capital open to the farmer — of any crop or livestock enterprise… Output per bird has never fallen below 75% even in the winter snow. (*Agscene*, 1983 [AG2])

In the CIWF Master Brand Toolkit, it is claimed that their "role is not to promote animals as food" (CIWF, 2015a), but throughout the CIWF corpus, chickens are constructed through "what they are for", i.e. as "broiler chickens" or "laying eggs". According to the CIWF Master Brand Toolkit, the charity "celebrate[s] those who make real progress for animal welfare, for example within the food industry, and promote[s] humane alternatives to factory farmed food, but... [is] not an assurance scheme and do[es] not endorse individual livestock products" (CIWF, 2015a). My findings, however, highlight a conflict, if not a contradiction to the stated approach. While intensive farming is deplored, the "higher welfare" farmers who profit from chickens' bodies are presented as *caring guardians* and the "celebration" of these bucolic farms, brands or supermarkets is very close to endorsement, if not advertising. In addition, bringing linguistic aspects back in, "factory farmed food" is a euphemism since it is not food that is factory farmed — the nonhuman animals are. Moreover, the term "livestock products" immediately places farmed animals as resources rather than sentient individuals.

In 1991, an exceptional text discusses the horror of chicken slaughter and rightfully acknowledges that the best way to help chickens is to reduce the consumption or stop eating them, whereas welfare reform comes second:

> The best way to reduce the misery of poultry slaughter would be for people to eat less (or no) poultry. The next best way is for the welfare laws to be rigorously enforced and for slaughtermen to be licensed and properly trained. (*Agscene*, 1991 [AG8])

This, I must reiterate, is an exceptional text as suggestions to eat fewer chicken products are infrequent in the CIWF corpus. This finding is perhaps unsurprising as the charity holds an overall pro-farming stance. Nonetheless, it does not concur with the stated approach in the CIWF Master Brand Toolkit (CIWF, 2015a) where CIWF recommends "reducing global meat and dairy consumption and consuming only humanely produced animal products". There are two interesting points to make, — 1) reducing consumption is listed before the "higher welfare" consumption, highlighting its importance and 2) eggs are not mentioned, thereby erasing hens and egg production from discourse. Ultimately, the loss of the "reduction" message in the CIWF corpus is problematic on a practical level; due to pressure on land, free-range farms simply cannot supply the quantities of chicken meat and eggs we consume today. Thus, the message to consume less should not be a sideshow, but a prerequisite if intensive farming is to be eradicated.

5.4 Challenges to "higher welfare"

In the AA corpus, a discursive shift towards a vegan cruelty-free lifestyle is identified. In the early 1980s, the AA magazine did not oppose "higher welfare" farming. A published letter from an AA supporter urges "readers to buy free-range eggs and not battery eggs. Surely the extra few pence is worth it to save so much misery?" (*Outrage*, 1984 [OU1]). However, in the late 1980s, it is already suggested to abstain from eggs and follow a vegan diet:

> Many vegetarians still depend very much on eggs as a substitute for meat in their meals. However, eggs are not a necessary ingredient in cooking. There are many substitutes that you can use instead of eggs in traditional dishes such as cakes, quiches, pancakes, etc. (*Outrage*, 1989 [OU5])

Essentially, AA challenges "higher welfare" farming for two main reasons. The first one is philosophical; "higher welfare" deceptively provides moral approbation to consumers: "…the supposedly less intensive systems — barn and free-range. Are these completely cruelty-free, or do the friendly sounding names deliberately disguise the harsh reality of egg production?" (*Outrage*, 2004 [OU13]). The second and more prevailing reason is pragmatic; "higher welfare" farms are considered not "high" enough and therefore still causing suffering:

> "free-range" birds are transported and slaughtered in exactly the same cruel way as battery hens, to be processed for use in poultry convenience foods such as frozen curries or pies. They are also crowded together, thousands in a single shed. So although they enjoy a better deal than battery birds, free-range hens on commercial farms still suffer. (*Outrage*, 2000 [OU12])

In the AA corpus, the term "high welfare" is used on only three occasions (Table 5.8). In these texts, "high welfare" farms are criticised. The related term "higher welfare" is not found, suggesting that the NGO does not approve of the terminology and what it entails. Interestingly, animal rights philosophers such as Singer are not cited to advance the animal rights debate; nonetheless, the same conclusions are reached — that the best way to avoid animal suffering is to adopt a vegan lifestyle: "Good reasons to give veganism a go… Male chicks are useless to egg producers, and are considered the wrong (uneconomic) breed to be fattened for meat. Millions are gassed or shredded alive soon after birth" (*Outrage*, 2014 [OU19]).

To support their claims, AA investigates and exposes cruelty and presents evidence of suffering to media representatives, authorities, and the public. AA activists have entered chicken slaughterhouses as well as intensive and "higher welfare" farms to document crowded, poor welfare conditions and troubling numbers of injured, diseased, and dead chickens. In the following extract, an undercover investigation deromanticises "higher welfare" farming by exposing the conditions that chickens are subjected to in an RSPCA approved chicken farm. The vegan diet is framed as the only "humane" diet:

> The RSPCA's Freedom Food scheme is not as humane as the organisation claims… according to Lloyd Maunder's website, every Millard Poultry chicken "gets the best possible attention, enjoying a carefree existence…" Animal Aid

> visited the farm three times — when the birds were seven, 36 and 47 days old. They were kept in an immense hangar-like shed, no different from those used by "standard" intensive chicken operations. In this huge warehouse, there were over than 30,000 birds. None had access to the outside... Our investigation, which followed hot on the heels of a shocking FF [Freedom Food] egg-rearing expose by Hillside Sanctuary, has shown that "high welfare" initiatives cannot necessarily be trusted, and reinforces our view that the only humane diet is one free from animal products. (*Outrage*, 2008 [OU16])

In the AA corpus, both intensive and "higher welfare" farming are more likely to be challenged by emphasising the loss of life. AA continuously documents and mourns the slaughter of chickens for meat, the slaughter of hens whose productivity fall, deaths of chickens due to accidents and natural disasters, killing of male chicks in the egg industry and mass killing of chickens during avian influenza events, and the list is not exhaustive. It is stressed that chickens suffer and are destined to cruel deaths in all farming systems, including the ones that are above the legal standard. Table 5.8 presents frequency comparisons for keywords *die*/dying*, *dead* and *death** (see also Appendix E). The LL scores -22.5, -33.7 and -23.3 alert us to a significant underuse of these items in the CIWF corpus (Table 5.8). Table 5.8 shows that the adjective *dead* is 4.9 times relatively more frequent and the lemma *death** is 3.4 times relatively more frequent in the AA corpus than in the CIWF corpus.

Table 5.8 Frequency analysis: CIWF and AA

	CIWF corpus		AA corpus		Keyness		
Word or lemma	**AF**	**NF**	**AF**	**NF**	**Over/under-use**	**LL**	**Ratio**
Die*/dying	76	4.3	33	12.7	-	22.5	0.3 (2.9)
Dead	37	2.1	27	10.4	-	33.7	0.2 (4.9)
Death*	56	3.2	28	10.8	-	23.3	0.3 (3.4)
High* welfare	94	5.4	3	1.2	+	11.5	4.6
Total word count		**175,613**		**25,975**			

Nonetheless, problematising cruel deaths does not automatically extend the discourse to the question of chicken entitlement to the possession of their own lives. Let me first illustrate this with an example from the CIWF corpus. The mass slaughter of chickens during an avian influenza outbreak is problematised due to cruel killing methods, but not intrinsically: "The spread of avian influenza, particularly in South East Asia, has led to mass slaughter of many millions of birds and killing methods have often been extremely inhumane, with birds burned or buried alive" (*Farm Animal Voice*, 2006 [FAV9]). Similarly, AA focusses on suffering and pain inflicted by farming and slaughter, but it remains unarticulated whether killing chickens is acceptable if it is not painful:

> But no-one should imagine that either regulated or unregulated suffering can be banished from animal farming and slaughter. These are pitiless, bloody activities that are predicated on industrial-scale animal exploitation and killing. Our report is intended to reinforce that point, while opening up to public scrutiny a rarely discussed aspect of the industry—the millions of sheep, chickens, cows, pigs and other farmed animals whose often chaotic, agonising deaths are unrecognised, uncounted and unlamented. (*The Uncounted Dead*, 2014 [UD1])

One exceptional article on chicken deaths during a flood gets closer to the animal rights debate. The loss of chicken lives is lamented focussing on the poor treatment of chickens as commodities rather than sentient beings:

> A staggering 700,000 birds drowned in the 20 broiler sheds spread across both farms, making it by far the single largest loss of life found during the research for this report… Ultimately, the 700,000 chickens who drowned in the sheds in Winteringham on 5 December 2013 lost their lives because, like all farmed animals, they were treated as commodities rather than as sentient individuals. (*The Uncounted Dead*, 2014 [UD3])

Apart from this exceptional quote, the AA corpus is characterised by the lack of debate on the rightness or wrongness of chicken farming as such. Our right to farm chickens or chickens' right not be farmed are not discussed on a philosophical basis. Furthermore, AA eschews discussion of social and cultural issues. The topics of food traditions, food socialisation or social structural influences on meat consumption could be expected in the AA corpus, since the NGO is not restricted by any ties to the industry profiting from chickens. Nevertheless, the socio-cultural causes of consumer demand for chicken flesh and eggs are virtually unaddressed in the corpus. There is only one text on live animal markets that blames sellers as well as buyers of nonhuman animals. The "ignorant" sellers and buyers of live animals are outside the in-group of AA and its supporters:

> the overall atmosphere of Henley market remains sordid and the treatment of animals by both buyers and sellers is a disgrace. The market seems to attract the unfeeling and ignorant. There are persistent rumours of illegal activities associated with regular dealers at Henley, including cockerels bought for cockfighting… (*Outrage*, 1994 [OU9])

5.5 Harm to humans

In the CIWF Master Brand Toolkit (2015a), it is claimed that the charity "recognise(s) the interrelatedness between animal welfare, environmental protection, human health and sustainability" (p. 5). However, the argument that intensive chicken farming harms humans (via environmental, public health or socio-economic issues) remains tangential in the CIWF as well as AA corpora. In the CIWF corpus of 508 texts, only nine texts pay substantial attention to environmental concerns in relation to chicken farming. An exceptional text in the CIWF corpus combines concerns about chicken welfare, the environment and public health. A joint action among concerned citizens, environmentalists and animal welfare advocates is encouraged. While ideologically it is still very much a humanist discourse, farmed animal welfare and vegetarianism find their place among human-centred arguments against intensive farming:

> Thus caged poultry… is under stress and is susceptible to disease, which requires the constant application of veterinary drugs. In areas where there is a concentration of intensive farming it is no longer possible to drink local water; midwives and obstetricians warn mothers there not to give their babies tap water… increasing numbers of consumers are becoming vegetarian or boycotting certain animal products. Animal welfarists, consumers and environmentalists have common cause in demanding action… Wherever you have contacts abroad, please tell them that Europe is turning away from battery and broiler farming methods, because of disease and environmental damage as well as cruelty involved. (*Agscene*, 1990 [AG6])

Overall, not only are environmental issues given little space in the campaigners' corpora, but also environmental concerns are predominantly expressed through the lens of self-interest. In the AA corpus, the argument of environmental impact appears once to promote a diet free of chicken flesh and eggs. After listing farmed animal welfare issues, it is highlighted that animal farming is environmentally unsustainable as it cannot feed the human population:

> 70 per cent of all agricultural land — just under a third of the earth's entire land surface — is used for rearing farmed animals… Put simply, we can feed far more people on a plant-based diet, cause far less pollution and use far less land and water. (*Outrage*, 2014 [OU19])

Apart from avian influenza, public health risks are typically deployed peripherally in the campaigners' magazines. For example, antibiotic-resistant bacteria or food poisoning due to *Salmonella* are noted as an additional argument against intensive chicken farming. The spread of avian influenza, however, draws stronger connections between chicken and human welfare. In 2006, when the avian influenza virus reached the UK, attention was drawn to the threat the virus poses to humans and "terrible human and animal suffering" (*Farm Animal Voice*, 2006 [FAV11]). In contrast to the newspaper news stories that erase chickens, the campaigners use bird flu as an opportunity to progress advocacy combining human-centred arguments and chicken welfare. In both corpora, it is implied that to protect human and nonhuman animal health, one needs to move away from intensive farming. Avian influenza is seen as a consequence of poor treatment of farmed animals:

> Treating animals as if they were unfeeling machines and pushing them to their biological limits was bound to impact on human health. But the industry — mindful only of profits — ploughed on, cramming animals in even tighter, growing them even faster and feeding them on trash. (*Outrage*, 2007 [OU14])

Moreover, a change in the CIWF corpus is identified with regards to a social critique of the chicken industry. In the 1980s, *Agscene* covers the issues of hunger and poverty and blames the industry for unsustainable practices in developing countries:

> Over the last ten years they [chicken industry] have spread like a plague across the oil-rich nations of the Middle East, but the most shameful direction of all must be that in which they are now targeting the under developed nations of the Third World. (*Agscene*, 1989 [AG5])

When public interests are in conflict with the industry's interests, a critique of neoliberalism is tangible. The chicken industry is depicted as "the world's most powerful multinationals", uncontrolled and uncaring of human wellbeing as it creates grain shortages:

> The USDA figures show a fall of 149 million tonnes in the world grain harvest in the last two years with a 35% reduction in carryover stocks. This is a gigantic problem that is being ignored carefully because to do otherwise would mean curtailing the activities of some of the world's most powerful multinationals. It cannot however be denied that the world harvest is getting less, and the world's grain-eating livestock more numerous, and there is no plan to counter the commercial dictates that, when those two graph-lines cross, this will take the food out of the mouths of children to feed it to profitable chicken. (*Agscene*, 1989 [AG5])

Interestingly, three texts tackling the issue of hunger assign some blame for grain shortage onto the nonhuman animals. In the article "Priority: chicken or children?" (*Agscene*, 1988 [AG4]), chickens are constructed as competitors of humans for grain: "ravenous chicken all eager to compete with our own species". The metonymic use of *chicken* sets the birds against *the starving children*, appealing to emotion and obscuring the responsibility of the actual business enterprises and humans running them: "It will not be the starving children that will have first call of the world's harvest, but the factory farmed chicken in the West, the Middle East, Japan, India, Africa" (*Agscene*, 1988 [AG4]). The topics of hunger and poverty do not feature in the AA corpus, confirming the aforementioned disengagement from the critique of socio-economic factors.

5.6 The government and political action

The second most blatant culprit for chicken suffering identified in the CIWF and AA corpora after the industry itself are government institutions. The "British government", "Ministry of Agriculture", "MPs", "The EC Agriculture Ministers", "European Commission" and other European and British institutions are held accountable for chicken suffering in one-third of texts in the CIWF corpus and in one-tenth of texts in the AA corpus. CIWF blames government institutions, but it also seeks solutions through political action and lobbying. CIWF calls upon "those with power to enforce animal welfare legislation" to create new regulations or strengthen the existing ones (CIWF, 2015a). The exploratory keyword analysis highlights their focus on regulation and reform (see Appendix E). The topical lemma *lobb** is 2.9 times and the term *legislation* is 14.9 times relatively more frequent in the CIWF corpus than in the AA corpus (Table 5.9). The words *directive* and *ban* are 10.4 and 13.0 times relatively more frequent in the CIWF corpus than in the AA corpus (Table 5.9). For AA, welfare reform constitutes a step forward, whereas the vegan lifestyle is the ultimate solution to chicken suffering. In addition, the lemma *rescue** is used 7.7 times relatively more frequently in the AA corpus, suggesting the importance of direct action (Table 5.9).

Table 5.9 Frequency analysis: CIWF and AA

	CIWF corpus		AA corpus		Keyness		
Word or lemma	**AF**	**NF**	**AF**	**NF**	**Over/under-use**	**LL**	**Ratio**
Legislation	101	5.8	1	0.4	+	20.7	14.9
Lobb*	139	7.9	7	2/7	+	10.9	2.9
Directive	140	8.0	2	0.8	+	25.8	10.4
Ban	351	20.0	4	1.5	+	69.4	13.0
Rescue*	15	0.9	17	6.5	-	29.6	0.1 (7.7)
Total word count	**175,613**		**25,975**				

In only a few cases, CIWF appeals to British pride presenting Britain as a front-runner in farmed animal welfare that should lead other countries. For example, in the 1980s, it is believed that "U.K. must lead Europe" (*Agscene*, 1983 [AG1]) in banning battery cages. Such an appeal to British pride is infrequent; examples of other countries that have progressed chicken welfare further are abundant: "As well as ensuring that the EU retains the ban on battery cages, CIWF is calling for the UK Government to follow Germany's lead and ban 'enriched' cages" (*Farm Animal Voice*, 2003 [FAV4]). Predominantly, the British Government is criticised for allowing cruelty and suffering, in other words, for ignoring chicken welfare issues and for not taking necessary measures to protect chickens. CIWF appreciates steps taken by government representatives on a national and international scale, yet sees them as insufficient:

> In March, Sunderland North MP Bill Etherington (Lab) — with strong support from CIWF — introduced a Bill in the Commons designed to provide the first ever legal protection for the 750 million broilers reared annually in the UK (broilers are the chickens reared for their meat). The health problems of broilers are so severe that if — instead of being slaughtered at six weeks — they were allowed to live on, the majority would die before the age of puberty at eighteen weeks... Bill Etherington tried to put an end to these abuses but — because the government refuses to support it — his Bill is unlikely to become law. (*Agscene*, 1998 [AG11])

As noted previously in Section *3.2.1 Compassion in World Farming*, CIWF sought an improved legal subject status for chickens when campaigning on the EU Broilers Directive 2007, the first set of regulations for farming chickens for meat in Europe. Additionally, in 2003, the charity took the British Government to court for cruel breeding of chickens, building their case on the EU Directive, which prohibits the use of nonhuman animals whose breeding has an adverse impact on their health or welfare. The court ruled against CIWF, but the case gained widespread media coverage and drew attention to restricted feeding of chickens used for breeding:

> We went to Court arguing that this breaches the law which requires animals to be given enough food to keep them in good health and to promote a positive state of well-being. The Judge ruled against us, saying that there is not enough evidence that the chickens are sufficiently hungry to compromise their well-being. This despite the conclusion of the EU's Scientific Committee on Animal Health and Animal Welfare that broiler breeders are "very hungry" and that the severe feed restriction results in "unacceptable welfare problems". (*Farm Animal Voice*, 2004 [FAV5])

With regards to AA, government institutions are identified as culpable agents on fewer accounts. The texts that focus on governmental institutions tend to criticise them for the lack of commitment to animal welfare, similarly to CIWF. The following extract illustrates how AA critiques the government for weak policies and for not following the recommendations of its own advisory body the Farm Animal Welfare Council (FAWC):

> True, the Government has tinkered with existing legislation by introducing one or two minor regulations in the Animal Health and Welfare Act 1984 and by updating the slaughter of poultry (Humane Conditions) regulations. But essentially the FAWC report has been ignored... It is against this background that Animal Aid is organising a week of action between February 23rd and March 1st, pressuring Government to implement the full recommendations of FAWC. (*Outrage*, 1986 [OU3])

The following extract illustrates how AA holds battery farmers culpable for the deaths of chickens and the government for the lack of control. The common argument for animal farming that domesticated animals "give" us their lives in exchange for protection and care (previously also identified in the *Mail* corpus) is rejected. AA disagrees that chickens are cared for and protected by farmers, instead, it is argued that chickens need protection *from* farmers as well as from the government which is indifferent to their suffering:

> The Ministry of Agriculture has decided not to take any action against the New Dawn Group, owners of a battery hen unit in Wiltshire where 76,000 birds died after the failure of the ventilations system... Next time you are faced with the argument that hens in battery cages are protected from the weather and from predators, you should perhaps quote this case, proving that what birds really need is protection form huge companies like New Dawn and the hopeless complacency of the Ministry of Agriculture, who refuse to outlaw the cage system. (*Outrage*, 1988 [OU4])

The campaigners construct themselves and their supporters as the ones speaking on behalf of farmed animals who cannot stand up for themselves. Both CIWF and AA maintain a positive rhetoric when approaching readers as citizens. Their supporters are asked to pressure decision-makers, such as MPs, MEPs and European Commissioners, and are constructed as helpers, bedrocks, watchdogs: "Your support has been the bedrock of all we have achieved so far, but on behalf of more than 400 million laying hens in Europe, please keep supporting our work to achieve the 2012 ban" (*Farm Animal Voice*, 2007 [FAV12]). Both organisations ask their readers to act peacefully, for example, by writing letters to decision makers: "Write to the Ministry of Agriculture... expressing your concern about treatment of broiler breeders" (*Outrage*, 1996 [OU10]).

The positive attitude extends beyond the supporters of the organisations. Europeans are generally presented as caring for chickens: "European citizens care deeply about the welfare of hens and believe strongly that the prohibition on conventional cages must not be postponed" (*Farm Animal Voice*, 2007 [FAV12]). Using the evidence from polls and attitude surveys, the campaigners put chicken welfare on the European political agenda: "Across Europe, public opposition to the cruelty of the battery system is growing. Politicians are becoming increasingly aware that keeping hens in conditions where they cannot spread their wings is no longer acceptable to the citizens they represent" (*Outrage*, 1999 [OU11]). The *fight* for chicken welfare is associated with the values of compassion and fighting for goodness. Below is a representative example of the engaging CIWF approach when mobilising efforts to "defend" chickens against battery cages:

> Our newly-launched Defend the Big Move campaign has already mobilised tens of thousands of supporters to send emails to the UK, Italian, Spanish and Polish governments. This has helped ensure that Poland is currently the only EU member state officially calling for a postponement [of the battery cage ban]. But other countries could still follow suit, so we need all your support — and your family and friends — to ensure that the Big Move really happens — and on time. (*Farm Animal Voice*, 2011 [FAV22])

Overall, combative language is uncommon in the campaigners' corpora, but in instances where war-related metaphors are found, they are soft and are used to evoke social virtues such as heroism and defending the weak. Table 5.10 reveals that the difference in the use of topical lemmas *fight**, *defend** and *battle** and the word *war* is statistically insignificant in the CIWF and AA corpora, yet as the AA corpus is markedly smaller, the word-forms are almost absent from it. This is an interesting finding since military metaphors are known to permeate public discourse (e.g. price wars, gender wars, political battles, war on cancer and war on terror). As Nerlich and colleagues (2002) note, metaphors taken from a well-understood source domain such as war "create a 'common ground' for communication between the media, the public, and policy makers" (p. 93). Since the organisations seek social change and need to motivate the public into action, powerful military metaphors could be expected to be more prevalent in the corpora. The absence of war-like combative language suggests a more diplomatic and nonconfrontational tactic aligned with the nonviolence rhetoric of both organisations.

Table 5.10 Frequency analysis: CIWF and AA

	CIWF corpus		AA corpus		Keyness		
Word or lemma	**AF**	**NF**	**AF**	**NF**	**Over/under-use**	**LL**	**Ratio**
Fight*	30	1.7	5	1.9	-	0.1	0.9 (1.1)
Defend*	23	1.3	1	0.4	+	2.1	3.4
Battle*	9	0.5	1	0.4	+	0.1	1.3
War	3	0.2	1	0.4	-	0.4	0.4 (2.3)
Total word count	**175,613**		**25,975**				

5.7 Chickens as agents

It is striking that CIWF and AA communicate little interest in chickens as individuals beyond intensive farming. The construction of chickens as poorly treated food animals dominates both corpora, with AA providing alternative constructions of an empathic human-chicken relationship proportionally more frequently than CIWF. I identified 11 texts (2%) in the CIWF corpus and 8 texts (13%) in the AA corpus that speak through an emotive and compassionate voice, attribute chickens with agency and invite to empathise and to be interested in them. In these exceptional texts, chickens are constructed as important for themselves and as individuals with interests and personal preferences.

As Still (2015) points out, "In English, sex to some extent goes with personhood... The 'de-sexing' and hence 'de-personalising' of 'it' can be used by bullies" (p. 14). Referring to a human being as "it" would certainly be offensive; equally, the pronoun "it" reduces nonhuman animals to objects and would not be used for valued nonhuman animals such as "pets". In the AA corpus, gender-specific pronouns are used for chickens since the 1990s. In the CIWF corpus, impersonal pronouns for chickens such as "it" are used interchangeably with personal gender pronouns such as "her" until the 2000s. Afterwards, gender-specific pronouns dominate the CIWF corpus. For example, two stories on rescued chickens construct the hen and the cockerel as persons; the stories are written using personal gender pronouns such as "her" and "his" and the proper names "Meg" and "Jim":

> Meg was brought to an animal rescue centre after losing a leg in an accident. She was bandaged up and animal worker Ro Bicen took her home and made space in her kitchen for Meg to recover. Meg gradually got better. Then, one day, she became restless. She started hopping all round the kitchen until she found the cat flap and forced her way outside. She hopped around the yard and found an open rabbit hutch. In she hopped, made a nest and laid an egg. (*Farm Animal Voice*, 2003 [FAV2])

> Jim is a cockerel who was bred for meat and came to us because someone couldn't bring themselves to wring his neck for Christmas. He's been with us for a couple of years and runs around with the other chickens… he came to me for food and, after he'd eaten his tea, he would trot off to my husband Mark each evening for warmth and comfort. He had no fear of either of us, but was quite capable of making choices about the best place to be, according to his needs at any particular time… but until he was fully recovered he would go back to Mark's shoulder and nestle into his neck each evening, cooing and cheeping like a chick. It was as if he needed that emotional input to set him back on track. (*Outrage*, 2008 [OU17])

In the following extract, subjective chicken experiences in the rescue environment are juxtaposed with the experiences and behaviours that chickens are not able to perform under the conditions of intensive farming. The emphasis is placed on naturalness and chicken sentience; a rescued hen is likened to a human recovering from illness. An intimate encounter with hens is contrasted with the "transactional" scientific claims regarding hen welfare in "enriched" cages:

> Apple blossom was in bloom, the grass a fresh green and a group of ex-battery hens, fully feathered now, rested companionably under a tree, basking in spring sunshine. At the far end of the orchard a lone little bird, feathers dull and

> damaged, scraggy body pecked almost naked by her fellow cage mates, painstakingly explored the territory. Like someone emerging from a sick room after a long illness, she moved cautiously. In fact, she was discovering that by putting one foot in front of the other she could, amazingly, walk. Nearby, another hen in a similar state of semi-nakedness was busy taking her first dust bath. Poultry scientists know about the physiology and behavioural patterns of the laying hen. Understanding her is, apparently, another matter altogether. "The enriched cage!" they cry. "That will satisfy the hens, and the welfare lobby!" Enriched cages supply perches, nesting boxes and a few miserable extra square centimetres per bird, but they still spell cruel deprivation. Grass and sunshine, insects and the shelter of trees — a hen's wish list would include all those and more. (*Farm Animal Voice*, 2006 [FAV10])

Similarly, the depictions of chickens enjoying life in sanctuaries are contrasted with miserable existences on intensive farms in the AA corpus. Assigning personality traits and positive emotions such as joy and extensivisation through vivid descriptions help communicate affection and encourage appreciation as chickens are likened to us in their capacity to enjoy life:

> The birds roam around freely, living out their natural lives protected from cruelty. Watching the lucky residents makes you realise what miserable lives the unfortunate birds on intensive farms must lead. At Hen Heaven they spend their days busily scratching in the soil, making nests and having dust baths. They love being out in the fresh air and, like you and me, they particularly enjoy bathing in the sunshine. (*Outrage*, 2000 [OU112])

Although these texts are far-removed from politicising chicken farming or debating the question of what we owe to chickens ethically, they convey the inherent value of chickens. Chickens are valuable for themselves, which tacitly progresses the argument beyond the avoidance of suffering. When discussing three types of American diets, namely "standard" omnivorous (which includes products from intensive farms), conscientious omnivorous (with products from "higher welfare" farms) and vegan, Singer and Mason (2006) have asked "whether it is wrong to kill animals — without suffering — for our food" (p. 246). They conclude giving an example of a free-living bird, pigeon: "the desire to cook a pigeon rather than some beans is not enough to end the pigeon's enjoyment of his or her life" (Singer & Mason, 2006, p. 259). Though Singer and Mason (2006) situate chickens differently to pigeons (due to the fact that farmed chickens depend on us and pigeons are free-living), the recognition of animals' desire to remain alive and capacity to enjoy their lives leads to seeing these animals as ends in themselves rather than means.

To sum up, discursive representations of chickens having charismatic agentive characters encourage appreciation of them and seeing them beyond the conceptual category of "food animal". The construction of a compassionate and mutually joyful human-chicken relationship in rescues serves an antithesis to the exploitation of intensive farms. Nonetheless, these representations are uncommon in the campaigners' corpora. Furthermore, their transformative impact is warded off if the fundamental ethical questions about using chickens for our needs are left undebated. As we have seen, the agentive roles of chickens can be exploited to produce the idea of "happy chickens", "happy meat" and "happy eggs" by the industry. Many children's books, for example, also construct farmed animals as agents in a positive light but simultaneously reinforce their exploitation (Cole & Stewart, 2014). Only a tiny proportion of children's books offers vegan counter-discourses that produce "knowledge of other animals that does not facilitate their objectification and exploitation; rather, it constructs empathic knowledge that facilitates respect and a sense of wonder" (Cole & Stewart, 2014, p. 154).[1]

5.8 Visual representation

While this study revolves around texts, discourses are often multimodal, e.g. language comes together with visuals to convey meaning. Examining the accompanying images thus can enrich discourse analysis; as I discuss in Section 2.1, in *The Pornography of Meat*, Adams (2003) critiques the objectification of women's bodies by examining the images of nonhuman animals. Visual analysis proves helpful when challenging the degrading representations of both women and farmed animals. Likewise, as noted in Section 4.2.5, Glenn (2004) and Cole (2011) operationalise visual methods to analyse the oppression of farmed animals. Glenn (2004) and Cole (2011) examine the ways the advertising images conceal the harsh realities of farmed animals by presenting them as "happy". In like manner, this brief section on visual representations in the campaigners' magazines further demonstrates the value of complementing textual with visual analysis and directs towards an avenue for potential future research. To analyse how "visual texts" communicate power relations, the features of images such as shot size, perspective, camera angle, colour and background can be examined (Kress & van Leeuwen, 2006.) Multimodal CDA scholars David Machin and Andrea Mayr (2012) view visual communication as a means of social construction noting that "elements in images, such as objects and settings, are able to signify discourses in ways that might not be obvious at an initial viewing. We ask which visual features

[1] One of the children's books that Cole and Stewart (2014) analyse is *That's Why We Don't Eat Animals* by Ruby Roth. Roth's book was criticised in the *Mail*'s article "New children's book promoting veganism sparks outrage for graphic images and unhealthy diet message – but how bad is a veggie food plan for kids?", implying that there could only be different degrees of "bad". Despite the article later explaining that a vegan diet can be healthy, it warned that the book "could easily scare a young child into eating vegan" (Cole & Stewart, 2014, p. 157).

and elements are foregrounded and which are backgrounded or excluded" (Machin & Mayer, 2012 p. 31).

Visual representation serves a range of communication purposes in the CIWF and AA corpora. While gritty visuals do not attribute agency to chickens and present them *en masse* rather than individuals, they are effective in highlighting the atrocities involved in farming chickens. In the campaigners' magazines, dry facts as well as vivid detailed descriptions of chicken suffering may be strengthened using pitiful visuals of chickens kept in poor conditions. Hens are shown in extreme confinement behind the bars standing on wire mesh; chickens farmed for their flesh are captured in crowded sheds showing sick and injured birds in filth. Importantly, alongside the texts produced by CIWF that are cold-sounding and dominated by a scientific style of writing, pitiful images are capable of filling in the "gap" for sympathy. For example, an article reviews legislation on chicken farming describing the proposal for the Broilers Directive in detail. Whereas the language is specialist, the accompanying photograph depicts chickens cramped in a large industrial shed adding an emotional, "real-life" meaning to the technicalities of intensive chicken farming:

> The proposal suggests a maximum stocking density of 30 kg/m^2 (around 15 birds), with the option of increasing 38 kg/m^2 if certain environmental conditions are met. Five years ago the European Commission's independent scientific advisers recommended that stocking densities "must be lower for major welfare problems to be largely avoided." They added that "above 30 kg/m^2, even with very good environmental control systems, there is a steep rise in the frequency of serious problems". (*Farm Animal Voice*, 2005 [FAV7])

As CIWF and AA seek to show the public what happens behind the closed doors, "visual honesty" plays a crucial role. Photographs of chickens in crammed cages, windowless sheds or shackled in the production line before the slaughter expose the mechanised industrial environments full of concrete and metal and semantically link farms and slaughterhouses to factory assembly lines. Photographs provide evidence to the messages conveyed and help challenge the optimistic views the consumer might hold on chicken farming. For instance, Figures 5.2 and 5.3 show hens locked behind the bars. The photographs from *Farm Animal Voice* in Figure 5.2 have a neutral angle and the distance between the camera and the hens is shorter, bringing up individual hens closer to the viewer. The top photograph shows hens in battery cages and the bottom photograph depicts hens in "enriched cages". The photograph from *The Uncounted Dead* in Figure 5.3 has a high angle. As chickens are small animals, high-angle shots could be used due to practical reasons. It could also be a rhetorical device to make subjects seem small and vulnerable and evoke an emotional response, strengthening the representation of chickens as victims of abuse. Figures 5.4 and 5.5 problematise the practices of intensive chicken farming for meat as birds are shown in barren and crowded conditions. Figure 5.5 from the AA magazine is particularly graphic as it contains a sick or injured chicken.

Figure 5.2 Hens behind the bar

Source: *Farm Animal Voice* (2015 [FAV30])

Figure 5.3 Caged hens

Source: *The Uncounted Dead* (2014 [UD4])

Figure 5.4 Chickens in an overcrowded shed

Source: *Farm Animal Voice* (2012 [FAV 23])

Figure 5.5 Crippled chickens in a shed

Source: *Outrage* (2008 [OU15])

A change over time in the visual chicken representation is identified in the CIWF magazine; visually the flagship magazine has moved towards a more positive approach, reducing the usage of images exposing cruelty and poor conditions. For convenience, I call aesthetically pleasant close-up headshots of individual chickens or chickens with celebrities "portraits". Artistic portraits of beautiful chickens, baby chicks and celebrities with chickens as well as landscape photographs of chickens ranging in idyllic environments become abundant since the 2000s. In a typical portrait, a chicken is making eye contact with the viewer, which creates an empathic human-chicken relationship. Celebrities help to promote the message; for example, a portrait depicts Spanish actor Antonio Banderas and a chicken sitting comfortably on a luxurious pillow. The bright colours and smiling facial expression of Banderas epitomise a joyful human-chicken interaction and bring chickens into the lives of humans not as mere protein suppliers, but as companions. Idyllic representations of chickens are developed through clean, bright close-up or landscape shots. Colours are bold and fresh. The main colour of the CIWF brand is light green, and the illustrations give an overall impression of *green,* which, as stated in the CIWF Master Brand Toolkit (2015a), should represent nature and life and symbolise calmness, balance, self-respect and wellbeing.

In the CIWF corpus, the pitiful imagery of chickens in intensive farms is frequently contrasted with the images of chickens in more natural environments. Like portraits, photographs of chickens roaming in idyllic environments convey personalities. Whereas chickens are given little agency in texts, visually they can appear curious and lively, enjoying their lives. Chickens are given salience in these photographs — they are presented in the foreground, through a neutral camera angle and in contrasting colours with the background. Colourful aesthetic images showing *happy* free-ranging chickens encourage the viewer to admire their beauty. Yet they support an uncritical attitude towards "higher welfare" farms (See Figure 5.6 and Figure 5.7). Wide-open spaces embed the value of freedom, thereby making a conceptual link with free-range farming. Consequently, the viewer is led to embrace chickens' very limited freedom in these farms, but not the freedom from human exploitation. Figure 5.7 shows chickens ranging in a green environment. The accompanying text and the caption, however, revolve around organic farming and present chickens through food qualities rather than as living beings: "Organic chickens can have 25% less fat than intensively reared chickens" (*Farm Animal Voice*, 2011 [FAV21]).

Figure 5.6 Free-ranging hens

Source: *Farm Animal Voice* (2010 [FAV19])

Figure 5.7 Organic farm

Source: *Farm Animal Voice* (2011 [FAV21])

Figure 5.8 *Agscene/Farm Animal Voice* covers, 1984–2016*

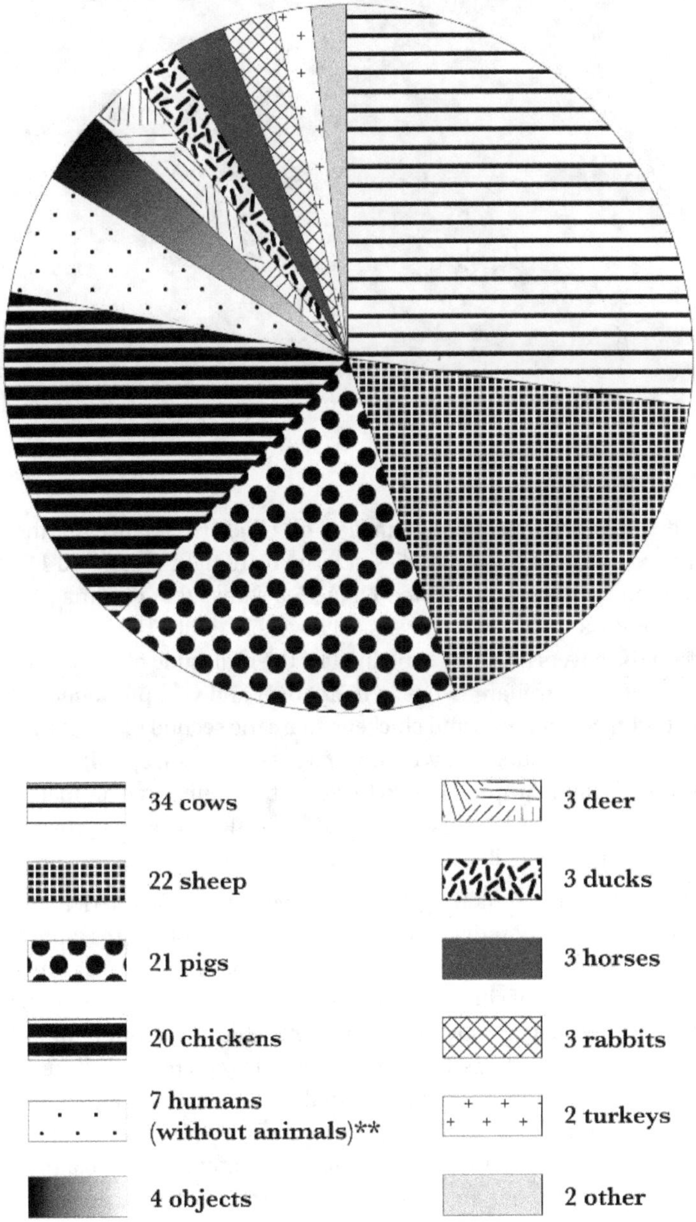

*Some covers contained multiple animal species, so totalling the numbers would give an inflated number of covers analysed.

**Covers that featured humans with farmed animals were accounted to the representation of the nonhuman species.

Figure 5.9 Dead chickens in a bucket

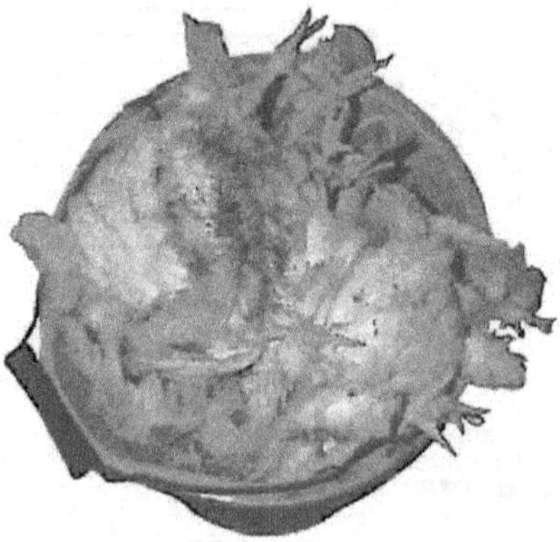

Source: *Outrage* (2008 [OU15])

To understand how frequently images of chickens feature in the CIWF magazine compared to other species of farmed animals, I analysed 112 covers of *Agscene* and *Farm Animal Voice.* Figure 5.8 shows that the images of cows most frequently appear on the covers (34 covers in total). The high occurrence of cows on the covers could be explained by the multitude of issues associated with the species — welfare issues in dairy, beef and veal production and live transportation. Sheep, pigs, and chickens share the second place (22, 21 and 20 covers, respectively) suggesting that welfare issues in sheep, pig and chicken farming are of similar importance to CIWF. Other nonhuman animals, such as ducks and rabbits are less likely to appear on the magazine covers as the industry is relatively small-scale in the UK.

Out of the 20 covers containing chickens, seven feature aesthetically pleasant portrait photographs of individual chickens. One cover features a photograph of Fearnley-Whittingstall with a *happy* chicken. Four magazine covers contain photographs of flocks of chickens in idyllic environments. Three covers feature CIWF mascots, namely Bobby, who represents chickens farmed for flesh, and Hetty, who represents hens farmed for eggs. Three covers feature multiple animal species including chickens; one of the three includes a pitiful image of caged hens. One cover contains a graphic photograph of a caged hen. One cover features a photograph of caged activists campaigning against battery cages. The fact that there are only three covers that contain gritty images in 1986, 1989 and 1992 confirms the shift of CIWF towards a more positive visual representation.

With regards to AA, chickens are placed on *Outrage* covers less frequently, which could be partly explained by the fact that AA campaigns are not restricted to farmed animals. Two covers in 2005 and 2009 contain portraits of chickens and one in 1983 shows activists protesting against battery cages. The number of idyllic and graphic images fluctuates throughout the period, yet no shift towards a positive visual representation is detected. There are two increases in the number of graphic images; in 2008, AA carried out undercover investigations in chicken farms and documented the conditions in photographs. In 2014, *The Uncounted Dead* report, which textually and visually documented chicken deaths during a flood, a transportation accident and due to diseases, was published. As AA generally pays more attention to chicken deaths, accompanying images can be gorier than the ones found in the CIWF magazine. Figure 5.9 is an illustrative example of a photograph showing dead chickens.

Aesthetically pleasant images of chickens found in the AA magazine are similar to the ones in the CIWF magazine. The difference is that AA does not construct certain types of farming positively; photographs that attribute chickens with agency and show chickens in pleasant environments are related to rescue operations and animal sanctuaries rather than free-range farms. For example, a photograph shows rescued chickens with smiling activists. The photograph depicts a compassionate and mutually joyful human-chicken relationship. Chickens are also depicted roaming outdoors in a sanctuary. The caption refers to and personifies the chicken depicted in the centre of the photograph: "Lucky the hen was rescued 20 days after the crash" (*The Uncounted Dead*, 2014 [UD2]).

5.9 Summary and discussion

Overall, the rhetoric deployed by CIWF and AA with regards to chicken farming resemble one another more than expected. Linguistic constructions of chickens as objects and victims continue to be dominant in the campaigners' corpora between 1982 and 2016. The ideological stance of CIWF over the period can be summed up as eliminating *bad* farming and promoting *good* farming. *Bad* farming is intensive, causing chicken suffering and producing *cheap* chicken meat and eggs, whereas *good* farming is less intensive and cares for the subjective wellbeing (physical and mental) of chickens. With regards to AA, the emphasis on vegan lifestyle is increasingly evident since the 1980s.

While thematically the topic of chicken welfare and suffering is present in virtually every text in the CIWF and AA corpora, its subversive potential is difficult to pinpoint. Chickens predominantly appear as victims of cruelty; they are passive, grammatically realised as objects, buried in noun phrases or, if positioned as subjects, chickens rarely do anything other than suffer or die. The representations of chickens as affected participants of material processes which involve abuse, while aimed at inviting compassion and problematising the industry, echo the dominant industry discourse where chickens are merely objects being fed, produced, grown, sold, marketed, debeaked, caught, transported, shackled, slaughtered, etc. Alternative representations of chickens as sensers and doers are uncommon (13% of AA texts and 2% of CIWF texts).

There is an ongoing debate on how people, for example, refugees, rape or violence survivors, should be represented by the media or by NGOs (Schrijvers, 1999; Leisenring, 2006). Should they be shown as victims or empowered as survivors? I suggest that in the case of chickens, both types of framing are needed — chickens as victims to expose the practices of farming and chickens as agents and ends in themselves to increase their status in the eyes of the public. The representations of chickens as objects to whom something cruel is being done can elicit emotions such as pity and could be seen as accurate reflections of intensive farming. Yet constructing chickens as poorly treated food animals does not necessarily provide an alternative vision to exploitative human-chicken relationships. Thus, a discourse where chickens are represented narrowly as passive recipients of cruelty does not sufficiently challenge their objectification. Nor does it inspire appreciation, which is known to play an important role in nonhuman animal protection. In conservation, for example, species of nonhumans that are considered charismatic are more likely to receive attention and support for the protection (Knight, 2008).

While semantically chickens largely remain deprived of agency, visual representation is more diverse. Both campaigners' magazines contain images that expose cruel practices in chicken farming and images that show chickens as *persons* enjoying their lives. CIWF may use pitiful images alongside an "objective-sounding" text to increase empathy and make texts more effective emotionally. Over the period, however, CIWF has shifted towards a more positive, aesthetically appealing visual representation of chickens. The images of *happy* chickens reinstate their agency and are deployed to "sell" the renewed idea of *caring* (pastoral) farming. Compared to CIWF, AA pays more attention to killing and deaths of chickens, and their magazine contains gorier images. Positive images of free-ranging chickens in the AA magazine depict rescued individuals and show a joyful human-chicken relationship where humans are rescuers or companions of chickens rather than consumers.

Returning to language, it is important to emphasise that despite the focus on suffering, the CIWF and AA corpora are characterised by a combination of emotive and knowledgeable tone and an evidence-based approach. Comparably to investigative journalism, the campaigners appeal to the values of honesty and truth when exposing cruelty through their investigations and revealing information on farming practices or product labelling. Littered with fragments of scientific and technical language, facts and figures, both campaigners' magazines develop a knowledge-driven narrative when describing chicken suffering and challenging the "rosy" representations of intensive or "higher welfare" chicken farming.

On the one hand, expert knowledge provides the organisations with credibility and helps balance out emotionally loaded accounts of chickens' realities. On the other hand, the distancing terminology of veterinary science, industry and economics comes at the expense of chicken interests when used uncritically. Scientific and technical registers are not inherently objective, nor constitute a single truth. Multiple partialities, such as the Christian tradition of dominion over animals and an economic interest in the exploitation of farmed animals, affect natural science disciplines as well as technologies. In other words, despite their alleged objectivity, scientific and technical representations of chickens and chicken farming are not unbiased; they are cultural products affected by human interests and values (Kahn, 2001; Marvin, 2001; Birke, 2008). Psychologists Steven Loughnan and others (2014) pinpoint that categorising animals as food refocusses attention on food-relevant characteristics such as taste and reduces the salience of morally relevant characteristics such as sentience, thereby reducing the cognitive dissonance associated with eating animal flesh and at the same time liking animals.[2] The study by animal scientists Emily D. Levine and others (2005) demonstrates that veterinary students' evaluation of pain perception in nonhuman animals is influenced by edible/non-edible categorisation rather than by objective data as the students perceived painful procedures without anaesthesia such as castration less cruel if they were performed on farmed animals compared to companion animals.

CIWF in particular is caught up in simultaneously presenting chickens as sentient beings and victims and as food commodities or value-added products. The charity laments chickens being "caged" and challenges the rhetoric of marketing, such as "farm fresh" or "quality assured", but also embraces industry jargon and celebrates the production and consumption of "higher welfare" products. As CIWF originates from farmers, it is unsurprising that the charity lobbies the industry and maintains industry partnerships to raise baseline standards for chickens and encourage market-led reform. Chicken-centred narratives are exploited to create a "win-win" scenario for chickens, consumers and farmers or suppliers. Chickens are *happy*; their welfare is constructed in a humanist and consumerist way that appeals to economic interests. "Ethical production" is morally elevated, and consumers are rewarded with superior taste and a "clear conscience".

---

2 The meat paradox describes the inconsistency between liking eating meat and simultaneously abhorring cruelty and killing of animals (Loughnan et al., 2010). However, the experimental studies by Loughnan and others (2010) and Bastian and others (2012) are limited to urban Western populations. They do not account for non-Western cultures as well as historical ones. Thus, the theory of meat paradox may hold in certain cultural, social and historical circumstances, but may not apply generally.

From a strategic point of view, the animal welfare message may be harder to communicate not only because it negotiates a view of chickens as sentient beings and commodities, but also because clear lines are difficult to draw on what is or is not "ethical" enough. As observed when analysing the campaigners' magazines and the newspapers, the industry exploits the welfare claims to argue that their practices are chicken-friendly. Inevitably, CIWF is forced to continuously fight over the definition of "humane" and "inhumane" or "good" and "bad" farming. Furthermore, as undercover investigations by the campaigners and newspapers demonstrated, even the certified farms fail to ensure chicken welfare. Singer and Mason (2006) note that even in "humane" farms:

> as long as animals are commodities, raised for sale on a large scale in a competitive market situation, there will be conflicts between their interests and the economic interests of the producer, and the producer will always be under pressure to cut corners and reduce costs. (p. 257)

The argument that the line between "ethical" and "unethical" animal products is vague brings us to the more outright approach to chicken farming identified in the AA corpus. Compared to CIWF, which navigates between problematising intensive farming and normalising "higher welfare" farming, AA considers any type of chicken farming to be cruel. For AA, a vegan lifestyle is integral to the notion of an "ethical" consumer and caring citizen. Although the elements of science, industry and economic registers are present in the AA corpus, chickens are not promoted as food. Objectifying terms and euphemisms are more likely to be challenged to deliver an unambiguous message that chickens are sentient beings. Politically correct terms such as "enslaved chicken", "captive chicken" or "exploited chicken", however, are not used. Instead, AA uses scare quotes to highlight the most of objectifying and value-laden terms and to distance themselves from such a terminology.

Despite AA's stance against all types of chicken farming, the AA corpus is similar to the CIWF corpus in the sense that both are characterised by pragmatism rather than idealism. Strikingly, the *Guardian* and *Mail* opinion pieces are more likely to engage with chicken farming as a moral issue on a philosophical basis. The campaigners' magazines, on the other hand, address the ethics of chicken farming only to a limited extent, predominantly when encouraging "ethical" shopping or political lobbying. CIWF and AA tackle immediate factors and consequences of chicken farming, rather than what I suggest are the root causes of farmed animal exploitation. Although the strong presumption of veganism in the AA corpus suggests an animal rights perspective, an opportunity to reflect on power relations and structural violence towards chickens is repeatedly missed. The discussion of abolition of farming and whether it is morally right for us to use chickens could be rightfully expected in the AA corpus, but these topics remain overshadowed by the suffering and cruelty frames.

The absence of explicit statements on chicken entitlement to the possession of their own lives in the AA corpus could be understood in two ways. The first one is that such ideas are taken as common sense. In other words, AA campaigners might take it for granted without the need to spell out that chickens are entitled to their lives and that chicken farming is fundamentally unjust. Another, and perhaps more likely, interpretation is that the focus is placed on suffering and our treatment of chickens rather than on chickens as ends in themselves. The latter interpretation is supported by the surprising lack of interest in chicken lives outside intensive farming. I suggest that instead of a pragmatic approach, AA could engage more with deontological ethics in order to create authentic subversive discourses. A socio-political and moral analysis of nonhuman animal exploitation could transcend the lifestyle and consumption-focussed rhetoric and offer new openings for change.

In addition, intersectionality in a more-than-human sense could provide the animal rights/welfare agenda with a deeper understanding of dynamics of power, offer opportunities for cooperation and create a wider appeal. Yet an intersectional approach to chicken farming is not developed. For example, no texts in the CIWF and AA corpora link eating meat to the constructions of masculinity. Given meat-eating has long been associated with masculinity (Adams 1990; Birke, 1995; Davis, 1995; Dunayer, 1995; Kappeler, 1995; Kheel, 1995) and advertising of animal-derived products thrives on the constructions of desirable manliness (Rogers, 2008), both AA and CIWF miss out on an opportunity to critically address the patriarchal prerogative for meat. Cultural aspects, such as the conceptual link between meat and affluence or the hyperstimulation of demand for chicken meat and eggs under the conditions of neoliberalism, remain largely overlooked. By comparison, the *Guardian* and to some extent the *Mail* tend to place chicken farming in a wider context, extending the debate to questions relating to ethics, consumer demand and other social, cultural, and environmental issues.

Disappointingly, the negative effect on the environment is insufficiently weaponised against intensive farming. The CIWF and AA corpora lack framing that would tie the harm to chickens to environmental impact and public wellbeing in a biocentric and intersectional way. Considering the ever-growing evidence of animal agriculture as a major contributor to climate crisis, polluter of groundwater, a major cause for deforestation and so on (Steinfeld et al., 2006; UN Environment, 2018), the intersection between chicken welfare and environmentalism could be expected to be more palpable, especially in the AA corpus, since the NGO is also concerned with free-living nonhuman animals. Especially, AA could adopt a biocentric, more-than-human narrative focussing on ecological interdependence. Since current scientific knowledge shows that plant foods are much more sustainable than products from "efficient" chicken farms (World Resources Institute, 2016), a vegan diet is as relevant for sustainability reasons as it is for compassion for nonhuman animals, both farmed and free-living.

Furthermore, since CIWF is more likely to use self-serving motivations such as taste, it could extend the critique of chicken farming to include other human-focussed motives, ranging from environmental degradation (from the perspective of the impact on humans) and hunger to mechanised labour. Some texts in the early issues of *Agscene* take a strong stance against the economic exploitation of developing countries, condemning the chicken industry as greedy and unsustainable. In *Farm Animal Voice*, such a critique is largely absent. I suggest that the impact on less privileged humans such as "animalised" farm and slaughterhouse workers could serve as another compelling argument against intensive chicken farming and help recognise the intersection between the exploitation of nonhumans and humans.

To sum up, discursive representations of chicken farming in the two campaigners' magazines proved to be much more similar than anticipated. Neither CIWF nor AA profoundly redefine chicken use as morally wrong in itself, as would animal rights philosophers Singer or Regan. Both CIWF and AA predominantly focus on chicken suffering as distressing rather than on chickens as ends in themselves — a moral philosophical stance. Both campaigning organisations deploy a humanist rhetoric to promote certain lifestyles. The key difference is that AA promotes a vegan lifestyle, whereas CIWF promotes the consumption of "higher welfare" products. In addition, both organisations are involved in political action and ask their readers to peacefully engage in political lobbying. Their supporters are positively constructed as ethical consumers and as citizens speaking on behalf of chickens.

6.

Conclusions

In this chapter, I consider wider critical reflections and the limitations of this study, return to the overarching research questions and draw conclusions about the discourse around chicken farming in the *Guardian*, *Mirror*, *Telegraph* and *Mail* corpora, as well as in the activist magazines produced by CIWF and AA between 1982 and 2016. In the last section, I go beyond the traditional academic format which calls for further research; in alignment with CAS, the study findings are integrated to draw insights about the present and for the future.

Over the course of writing this book (2014-2020), more literature dealing with the question of nonhuman animals and discourse from a point of view that strives towards liberation became available. I kept moving back and forth between my data and the theory I could obtain at the time, and consequently, have engaged in interdisciplinary research, conversing with critical theory and cultural studies, sociology, media studies and linguistics. A novel multifaceted understanding of the cultural politics of chicken farming has been sought by applying the analytical framework of CDA in combination with CL tools. CL tools have allowed me to work with a large number of texts, preventing accusations of cherry-picking quotations and ensuring breadth, while the qualitative analysis has enabled more in-depth and forensic approach to texts. Ultimately, this mixed qualitative and quantitative method allowed me to draw insights about the entire bodies of texts and then contextualise them.

As noted by CAS scholars Socha and Mitchell (2014), “Each academic area has something to contribute to CAS, and CAS can benefit all areas” (p. 111). My approach to CAS in this book has involved interdisciplinary exploration of the effects of discourse on chickens farmed for their flesh and eggs. CAS has become an essential critical lens through which to examine and contest the exploitation of chickens. Moreover, in the spirit of CAS, this study has emphasised the intersection of chicken exploitation with a range of human and environmental harms fostering a holistic understanding of a larger global, interlocking, system of domination. Thereby, it has demonstrated that CDA is inadequate to its own historic and ethical task if it continues to overlook the multiple points of intersection between human and nonhuman animal oppression.

The limits of my study predominantly concern the timeframe and sources. If the study timeframe had started in the 2000s, analysis of the newspaper readers' comments online would be feasible as it could show the impact on readers. Moreover, internet forums, social media channels, and blogs now play an important role as knowledge and opinion sharing platforms and are worth investigating. Additionally, if the study period proceeded beyond 2016, public perceptions and attitudes towards chicken welfare and food pathways in the light of Brexit would merit a separate study. Nevertheless, this book's engagement with critical perspectives on chicken farming and communication addresses a need of academic research that could inform a variety of users – from CAS, cultural and communication scholars, to journalists, campaigners, and the public. In this respect, the study fulfils its ambition to be of value within and beyond academia; e.g. it demonstrates the relevance of a dual method of CL and CDA to strong effect, while the critique of the campaigners' corpora such as the tendency to rely on "victim" framings could be of immediate practical value to animal welfare and rights organisations, not limited to CIWF and AA and not limited to the UK context.

6.1 Unremarked violence

Domination thrives by masking or rejecting any recognition of the violence and the suffering that it inflicts. It makes exploitation seem natural and any challenge to exploitation not just impossible but inconceivable. (Matsuoka & Sorenson, 2018, p. 1)

The analysis of the *Guardian, Mirror, Telegraph* and *Mail* corpora provides a window into an ideological struggle with regards to the status of commercially farmed chickens in the UK between 1982 and 2016. Analysing newspapers allows us to identify dominant ideas in the public discourse about chicken farming for meat and eggs, understand how these ideas are constructed discursively as well as how (and if) they changed over the course of 34 years. By their sheer repetition, newspapers are co-producing and reproducing an ideology. Ideas that are repeatedly presented in newspapers become a part of legitimate public debate, whereas a continuous exclusion of certain ideas shows the ideological work of newspapers in defining what is unimportant and has little legitimacy.

My findings in the *Guardian, Mirror, Mail* and *Telegraph* corpora demonstrate that Freeman's (2009) conclusion about prevailing speciesism in American print news is valid outside the United States. Across the four British newspapers, 57% of news stories relating to chicken farming omit the animal rights or even welfare perspectives (60% of the *Guardian*, 57% of the *Telegraph*, 57% of the *Mail* and 55% of the *Mirror* news stories). These news items do not follow the guidelines produced by Freeman and Merskin (2016b); chickens are objectified, their sentience is ignored, and the voices of campaigners are not heard. This is an important finding since readers are more likely to encounter chicken farming in the news; the number of news items collected is twice as large as the number of opinion/feature pieces (755 vs 379 items across the four papers). Moreover, in contrast to opinion journalism, which is open about its subjectivity and political involvement, news reporting is more likely to be perceived by writers, editors, and readers as neutral and unbiased.

Across the four newspapers, most news items revolving around agribusiness and public health obscure chicken subjectivities. Violence and exploitation of chickens are visible, but remain largely unremarked, giving the impression that chickens do not have interests at stake. Chickens are routinely abused in farms and slaughterhouses, but the A-IC is sanitised in discourses of *food* production or public health; chicken farming involves "units" and "tonnes" rather than individualised sentient beings. It is also important to note that the broadsheet reporters are more likely to take a detached position than the tabloid reporters. Their factual and *impersonal* voices, however, only ensure *objectivity* as a rhetorical effect rather than a responsibility to account for chickens' interests even though chickens are affected first and foremost.

The public health side effects of the A-IC stretch along and beyond the production of chicken meat and eggs — from *Salmonella* and *Campylobacter* food poisoning to antibiotic-resistant bacteria and the threat of a pandemic. The higher the risk for human wellbeing, the more chickens' experiences are backgrounded in the news. The *Guardian* and *Mail* corpora contain the most stories on public health; warnings about antibiotic-resistant bacteria and zoonotic diseases ran in the *Guardian* and *Mail* news for 34 years, but there is little progress in accounting for chicken interests in these stories. While the link between government policies and news reporting has not been analysed in my study, the status of chickens as objects is reinforced linguistically and in practical terms as health scares result in mass killings of birds rather than welfare reform. During the avian influenza outbreak, the *Guardian, Mirror, Telegraph* and *Mail* news stories have remarkably concentrated on the impact on public health and agribusiness. Although the scale of chickens' deaths defies imagination if considered from the perspective of the loss of life of sentient beings, the language of news reporters sanitises chicken deaths as *economic losses* or *control measures.*

6.2 Inoculation, trivialisation and alibi

When the violence experienced by billions of chickens is not culturally erased in news reporting, it is typically trivialised or minimised. The *Telegraph* news items are particularly characterised by what could be termed "dominance through mentioning" or "inoculation" in the Barthesian sense, i.e. admitting a little bit of evil in an institution so as to conceal its fundamental problems (Barthes, 1991, p. 151). On a sentence level, chicken welfare is mentioned in 43% of the *Telegraph* news stories, which is proportionally slightly higher than in the *Guardian* (40%). Yet the *Telegraph* corpus is considerably smaller, and welfare is introduced vaguely as a marker of the limits of acceptable ideas and a "warden" of the status quo. It appears in a rigidly human-centred discourse which assumes the normality of animal "sacrifice" and dietary indispensability of chicken flesh and eggs.

Furthermore, my findings in the *Telegraph* opinion pieces demonstrate that the significance of chicken suffering is manipulated (diminished or boosted) in a way that is convenient in a situation. In the broadsheet with a high proportion of middle- and upper-class readers, chicken suffering is pitted against food poverty and dismissed as unimportant by comparison. Concern for poverty, however, can be rhetorical, i.e. an alibi for those who identify with the (intensive) chicken farming industry. Furthermore, paradoxically, chicken farming becomes an alibi to blood sports. The *Telegraph* opinion articles on hunting dramatise chicken agony in order to protect the privilege to shoot or hunt other animals, who are presented as suffering less than intensively farmed chickens. In a Barthesian sense, there is a second layer to this "alibi" too; a "myth" of the British caring mentality towards animals is perpetuated.

The *Mirror* and *Mail* corpora also contain a slightly larger proportion of news items that include the welfare perspective than the *Guardian* (45% and 43% against 40%). This difference is explained by the language style and selection of events to cover; for the broadsheets, accidents and cruelty incidents involving chickens are rarely newsworthy. The tabloids, on the other hand, may place chickens centrally in "soft" news and express emotion. Tabloid news may be sensational and "judgemental" but may also show some compassion and empathy towards chicken victims, especially when reporting on deaths. Nonetheless, the occasional focus on deaths, accidents or other brutality in the tabloid corpora does not progress the debate around the ethics of chicken farming nor challenge the A-IC. On the contrary, news stories magnify specific incidents only to render other (structural) instances of chicken suffering as *natural*. The abuse or deaths are problematised precisely because they happen in different places and involve different actors or actions than "normal". The narratives remain depoliticised; the tabloid reporters focus on *how* chickens are treated and *how* they die rather than *why* or *why* it matters.

In Freeman's (2009) American study, humour is not identified as a method to objectify nonhuman animals and reinforce speciesism in the news media. However, in three out of four newspapers analysed in my study, humour has a purpose that goes beyond entertainment and readers' pleasure. As Cole and Stewart (2018) argue in their critical vegan reading of the comedy animation film

Sausage Party, humour is a powerful discursive tactic for deflecting ethical critique. Ridicule may be deployed as a disciplinary instrument for preserving the status quo, thus CAS critique must "engage with the serious implications of comedy that relates to nonhuman animals" (Cole and Stewart, 2018, p. 769). In the tabloids *Mirror* and *Mail*, "soft" news stories emphasise comedy, scandal, and conflict and may present chickens and activists as ridiculous. In *Telegraph* opinion pieces, humour can be used to support the stereotypes of chickens as "foolish" or funny and activists as pathetic or crazy. Constructing chickens or activists as objects of ridicule serves ideological functions; chickens are inferiorised as "naturally" marginal, thereby reinforcing a common-sense assumption that their interests do not matter. It is not possible from my analysis to outline the exact impact on the audience. Nevertheless, it is likely that such light-hearted representations and trivialisation put readers at ease, when otherwise they could be confronted with animal ethics and forced to face their own participation in violence against chickens. My analysis therefore encourages further research to enhance the understanding of the role of humour in nonhuman animal oppression.

6.3 Happy chickens

> Although there are undeniable diminutions of harm that may result from animal welfare measures, the practice of harm-reduction itself can therefore be instrumentalized; such as a "feel-good factor" deriving from consuming signs of "care" for other animals in the purchase of "welfare-friendly" labelled food. (Cole & Stewart, 2014, p. 18)

Overall, over the course of 34 years, all four newspapers continuously support and shape the regime of chickens as protein sources for humans by discourses of entitlement. In the opinion/feature articles, however, the entitlement to chickens' lives is likely to be nuanced through the notion of pastoral *care*. Chicken welfare is noted in 81% of the *Guardian*, 73% of the *Telegraph*, 73% of the *Mail*, and 57% of the *Mirror* opinion/feature articles. Of note, the relatively high number in the *Telegraph* corpus includes stories that mention chicken welfare superficially or even defend intensive farming as providing adequate welfare.

The exact term "higher welfare" first appears in the sources in the 2000s. In 2008, the high-profile welfare campaigns by Oliver and Fearnley-Whittingstall gain momentum in all the newspapers' corpora except the *Telegraph*. In the *Guardian* opinion/feature articles, "higher welfare" farming is predominantly (but not invariably) constructed as an antithesis or solution to intensive chicken farming, which shows intertextuality with the CIWF corpus. In the *Mail* opinion pieces, dominant narratives typically embed the consumption of "higher welfare" (especially artisan, local, organic, free-range) products as a part of a desirable lifestyle and responsible citizenship. In contrast to CIWF, which promotes the consumption positively by encouraging its community of readers, the *Mail* opinion stories are typically negative in tone and sceptical about potentially lazy and penny-pinching consumers. I might reiterate that the *Mail* is a "middle market" daily and just over half of its audience is female. The imagined world of the *Mail* reader reveals itself through the aspiration to an upper-middle-class lifestyle, family values and nostalgia. *Cheap* is used as a moral as well as economic term; chicken lives, farmers' livelihoods, "hidden costs" on the public through health risks and environmental degradation have a moral cost.

By bringing individual responsibility from the margins to the centre of the debate, the *Mail* addresses the silent consent to chicken exploitation given with purchases. It might seem to be a powerful message, but it slips into lament and shaming rather than action, and obscures corporate and government responsibility. For example, the reader is shamed and warned about the danger of *cheap* chicken products using quasi-religious references to sin and punishment which do not necessarily promote action. Furthermore, while scholars have shown that animal rights activists use gendered representations of female sexuality to progress the animal cause (Deckha, 2008; Gaarder, 2011; Glasser, 2011; Wrenn, 2013a), my findings in the *Mail* corpus demonstrate that feminine stereotypes are exploited to defend intensive farming by industry representatives and journalists identifying with the industry. The gendered narratives originate in the *Mail* corpus when blaming housewives for hypocrisy, ignorance and penny-pinching when they do not choose to buy "higher welfare" chicken products. Moreover, in the *Mirror*, *Mail* and *Telegraph* corpora, concerns for chicken welfare can be presented as sentimental and unmanly. Portrayals of Fearnley-Whittingstall, where the chef is under attack for his "tears" over chickens, epitomise the feminisation of campaigners and activists (*Sunday Mirror*, 13/1/2008 [M16]; *The Daily Telegraph*, 30/1/2008 [T17]).

Another point to consider is that the critique of *cheap* is not necessarily bad for the chicken industry, which can adapt to becoming *expensive*. This book has shown that chicken "happiness" in "higher welfare" farms is used as a rhetorical and marketing tool to justify and promote farming and increase the socio-cultural value of chicken flesh and eggs for economic gains. Chicken welfare is instrumentalised in the biological sense of *taste* bringing gustatory pleasure for consumers and in the social sense of *taste* as consumers "buy" their way to a clear conscience and claim a certain social identity. This is not surprising considering that the largest European survey on the attitudes towards animal welfare, conducted in 2015 in the 28 Member States of the EU, revealed that 94% of Europeans consider it important to protect farmed animal welfare (European Commission, 2016). Among the UK respondents, nearly all

(98%) responded that it is important to protect farmed animal welfare (European Commission, 2016, p. 12).

Nevertheless, as argued by the law and philosophy scholar Gary Francione (1996), cooperation with the industry cannot challenge speciesism nor the property status of farmed animals. On the contrary, the notion of chickens as protein providers might become even more ingrained in the long run. Returning to the analogy of human enslavement and amelioration, chickens, similarly to enslaved humans, become the beneficiaries of the system that brings them this supposed "happiness". In her seminal book *The Dreaded Comparison*, Spiegel (1988) puts it in candid words:

> It has long been contended that, for some — and of course, never *us*, but always *them* — life as a slave proves more beneficial than detrimental [italics in original]... Aristotle had used this same approach in his attempt to justify the subjugation and domestication of animals and some humans. For this rationalization to be effective, the victims need to be transformed — in the mind of the captor/master — from oppressed beings to thankful underlings; grateful for being used, appreciated and protected, while fulfilling the needs of their superiors. (p. 66)

Regan (2001) remarks that "it should not be surprising that the loudest, most powerful voices speaking in the name of animal welfare today are those of individuals who have an interest in perpetuating institutionalized utilization of nonhuman animals" (p. 34). As observed in the newspapers' and campaigners' corpora, the farming industry indeed espouses the same welfarist discourse although their interpretation of a "happy chicken" may radically differ from that of activists'. Animal welfare campaigners such as CIWF are thus bound to clash with the industry over the terminology and the actual practices behind the rhetoric of welfare.

6.4 Veganism. Intersection with the environment

We should not forget that it is not essential to consume chicken flesh and eggs at all to survive or to lead healthy lives. Vegans are living examples that chickens do not have to be food. Nevertheless, compared to concerns for chicken welfare, which are acceptable to journalists and embraced (or hijacked) by the representatives of the chicken industry, ethical veganism is nearly invisible in the newspapers. Animal ethics behind veganism have been largely dismissed or, worse, ridiculed in the *Telegraph, Mirror,* and *Mail* corpora. This finding coincides with the finding that AA activists and their vegan agenda receive little coverage. The right-leaning *Telegraph* in particular appears to be unresponsive if not hostile towards veganism. This can be linked back to the demographics of the readership; psychological studies have demonstrated that right-wing supporters are more likely to accept environmental degradation and perceive vegans as a danger to their "way of life" (Hodson & Costello, 2018, p. 194). In other words, vegans might be viewed by right-leaning individuals as presenting "symbolic threats" to the status quo as they undermine the current way of life by rejecting food that is central to it.

The *Guardian* corpus constitutes an exception for its coverage of veganism and sustainability issues. This finding could be linked to the *Guardian* readers being on average well-educated and younger than the readers of the *Mirror, Telegraph,* or *Mail* (as previously demonstrated in Table 3.1). The finding could have also been expected assuming a bond between concerns for the environment, veganism and (even centre-) left politics. Not only is the left traditionally seen as "radical" and "progressive", but also some of the key elements of the contemporary left agenda such as protecting marginalised communities and vulnerable groups overlap with the issue of animal farming; the climate crisis and the appalling labour conditions of low-income slaughterhouse or farm workers are two notable examples. However, the findings are different in the *Mirror* corpus; the left-leaning tabloid, while launching powerful undercover investigations, shies away from veganism and a "green" agenda. Furthermore, the *Mirror* corpus has the largest total proportion of texts (51%) excluding the chicken welfare entirely. These findings may be linked to the *Mirror's* working-class readership and the disappointing finding that the intersections of capitalist exploitation of humans and nonhumans are invisible in the tabloid.

Apart from the *Guardian* corpus, the lack of newspaper articles discussing chicken farming in the light of sustainability is disturbing. Compared to public health risks (338 stories across the four newspapers), the environmental issues associated with industrialised chicken farming receive little coverage (18 stories in total for the period between 1982 and 2016; 16 of them in the *Guardian* corpus). This finding concurs with previous media studies that demonstrated that the grave impact of animal farming on environmental destruction is nearly invisible in the media (Neff et al., 2008; Almiron & Zoppeddu, 2014). Furthermore, it suggests that, as I have argued in Section *1.2.4 Environment,* chicken products may be preconceived as relatively sustainable. This presumption is observed in the newspapers analysed, including the *Guardian*: "In terms of climate pollution, the switch to chicken is a plus as it has a far lighter carbon footprint than beef or dairy farming" (*Guardian*, 14/7/2016 [G52]).

Given the link between environmental degradation and the health of human and nonhuman animals, it had not been anticipated that environmental issues would feature so little in the CIWF and AA corpora. The campaigners' corpora do not reflect the shift in knowledge on the climate crisis and environmental destruction over the past three decades. Landscape degradation, pollution of soil and water, disease, deforestation due to expansion of land to produce chicken feed and greenhouse gas emissions are rarely discussed. This is a striking finding, considering that the ordeal of chickens as well as of the nonhuman world more generally has never been more serious. There are several possible reasons why CIWF does not weaponise environmental destruction in the fight against intensive farming. First, the charity originates from and supports farmers, including "beef" farmers who by comparison should be placed "under fire" for causing greenhouse gas emissions and contributing to the climate crisis. Second, despite covering different types of farming, CIWF may be defined as single-issue group concerned with cruelty in animal farming, which leaves environmentalism as a sideshow.

The scope of interests of AA includes "wildlife", which consequently raises the expectations that environmental destruction and the consequent impact on free-living nonhuman animals will emerge as a key theme in relation to chicken farming. However, these expectations are not met. One explanation could be that AA does not want to send an implicit message, which would suggest that "sustainable" chicken meat and eggs would be acceptable. Anthropocentric campaigns that highlight environmental sustainability may only lead to an *improvement* of the system rather than abolition. Moreover, as reported in the *Mail* and *Guardian* articles on breeding "bald" heat-tolerant chickens for warm countries, the "improvement" may not be chicken-friendly. The depiction of featherless chickens illuminates the point that the intersection between environmental and animal welfare issues is far from straightforward: "The fast-growing, featherless bird may look a little foul, but it was hailed as the environmentally friendly future of chicken farming" (*The Guardian*, 21/5/2002 [G13]).

Nevertheless, the most plausible explanation for the lack of focus on environmental issues linked to chicken farming could lie in the single-issue viewpoint adopted by AA. Like CIWF, AA focusses on animal suffering directly caused by humans rather than the power dynamics between human and nonhuman animals as such. My analysis reveals an anthropocentric environmental perspective: "Put simply, we can feed far more people on a plant-based diet" (*Outrage*, 2014 [OU19]). Little intersection is identified between the AA discourse and radical left politics; the animal rights organisation never situates the exploitation of chickens in the broader context of class society nor addresses the workings of neoliberalism. AA presents (changing) consumption as one of the major tools of social change. However, as findings in the newspapers demonstrate, "ethical" consumption (be it "higher welfare" or vegan) can be perceived as a question of taste and a "middle-class" foodie culture. For instance, Fearnley-Whittingstall is presented by the *Mirror* journalists as "unrelatable" to working-class people (*Daily Mirror*, 7/1/2008 [M15]). I shall add that a vegan diet is also very vulnerable to dismissal as a "luxury" afforded by the middle-classes, for eating vegan may not be necessarily expensive, but can be time-consuming and requires expertise in a (meat) culture where recipes, food outlets and the majority of available food options revolve around animal products.

CAS, however, offers an effective paradigm for animal advocates, who do not wish to be perceived as single-issue thinkers "unwilling to look at the broader implications of animal liberations connection to other liberatory causes" (Socha & Mitchell, 2014, p. 112). As Taylor and Twine (2014) note:

> Just as feminism has had to be attentive to the possibility of, for example, class and "race" privilege within its theory and practice, the same reflexivity, from a CAS perspective, is similarly important within the animal advocacy movement – especially for its coalitionary bridge- building practices with other movements. (p. 5)

The CAS perspective which calls for rethinking of the relationship between humans and "nature" could better acknowledge not only the lives of chickens, but also the lives of free-living nonhuman victims and the inherent value of their habitats (instead of their utility to us). An alliance could be established between those interested in environmentalism and those in animal ethics if activists emphasise that the same ideology, which renders chickens as objects as opposed to sentient beings with any interests or entitlements, is responsible for the collapse of life-sustaining ecosystems. Moreover, animal rights activists could better acknowledge that issues do not exist in isolation and take an intersectional approach to oppression; they could remark on the issues such as the exploitation of (often migrant) workers or, more generally, class conflict in capitalist societies and frame vegan praxis as addressing all nonhuman and human lives ruined by chicken farming.

6.5 Campaigners' pragmatism

> Those who seek to advocate for other animals are constrained by the terms of this instrumentalist discourse and an essential challenge is to critique the ideology and the power relations that are embedded in it. (Matsuoka and Sorenson, 2018, p. 13)

The analysis of the CIWF and AA corpora develops an understanding of the sort of linguistic and discursive challenges animal welfare and animal rights campaigners face when advocating for chickens. Similar to findings by Neo (2015) and Freeman (2014) on activist rhetoric in Singapore and the USA, my analysis of the British campaigners' magazines reveals a struggle in finding authentic ways to address chicken farming. Discourses of AA and CIWF more often than not appear as close points on a continuum; both organisations prioritise conformist and pragmatist approaches, possibly in the hope of designing a widely acceptable message and achieving short-term gains. In the defence of CIWF, I must stress that the campaigners engage readers who likely already have been socialised into the normalcy of consuming chicken products. As for AA, the media representations of animal rights activists as extremists may push the organisation to produce normative arguments and capitalise on sentimentalised human-animal relations. Moreover, the updated official website of the NGO declares an incremental approach towards animal liberation:

> Our ultimate vision is of a world that is free from animal abuse and exploitation… We recognise that this is very much a long-term vision, which will take many decades to achieve. So as well as working towards this, we also take a pragmatic approach, and campaign for measures that will help to reduce animal suffering in the meantime. (Animal Aid, 2019)

My findings in the AA corpus, however, disappointingly suggest that the long-term critical rhetoric and clear communication of the end-goal have been overshadowed by pragmatist efforts "in the meantime" (Animal Aid, 2019). *Pragmatism* is tangible as both AA and CIWF predominantly shape public imagination about chicken farming through the depictions of *suffering*. Both campaigning organisations essentially present chickens as badly treated food animals and produce "knowledgeable" narratives that are backed up by facts and figures from official sources and emotion-eliciting photographic evidence. The key difference is that in the CIWF corpus, the objectification is double-layered; chickens are objectified as passive victims and as commodities, using the language of production as if it was neutral. In the AA corpus, chickens are also predominantly depicted as victims but scare quotes are deployed to address the problematics of commodifying terms.

While exposing suffering undoubtedly has powerful educative effects, it may be insufficient to progress beyond minor welfare reform. If the end-goal of CIWF is to replace intensive farms with "higher welfare" farms, then the reduction message must be much more pronounced, especially considering the continuously growing human population. As for AA, if the end-goal is abolition, then the NGO should wrestle with the "default" speciesist context and challenge the deeply entrenched human/nonhuman binary. The critique of chicken farming could operationalise different dimensions of the A-IC, emphasise their interconnection (i.e. government, industry, science, culture, and media) and closely examine the power dynamics between human and nonhuman animals and relevant socio-cultural aspects. For instance, the intersection between culture and marketing and advertising are explored in the campaigners' corpora but only to a degree. There is a room for a critique of the ways marketing and advertising target children and young people to turn them into hyper consumers of the future, create new habits and continuously reinforce the idea that chickens are products and that animal protein is not only delicious and convenient but *essential* to our diet. In addition, the diversification of chicken products (in the form of wings, breasts, drumsticks, nuggets, chicken popcorn, chicken chips and so on) that plays an important role in making chicken flesh accessible and attractive to wide sectors of the population is unaddressed.

The discourse around chicken farming produced by the campaigners predominantly revolves around "humane" treatment rather than the discussion of our entitlement to use chickens or chickens' entitlement to their own lives. The dearth of socio-structural critique in much of the corpora supports Freeman's (2014) thesis that over and above invoking "compassion" for suffering, the frame of justice for nonhuman animals is critically lacking. Echoing Freeman (2014), justice is a more transformative and ideologically powerful concept than compassion:

> While compassion is a necessary first step or component of justice, as it creates an initial concern and caring for other sentient beings, it is not as fundamental or direct as justice is at implying that these animals have a right to live free of human control. (p. 154)

I shall also stress that the late 20th and 21st centuries are characterised by the abundance of literature on nonhuman animal exploitation; scholars have looked at animal ethics in relation to religion, ritual, culture, patriarchy, psychology, neoliberalism, law and so on. Notable are the explorations of the masculinisation of meat and its symbolic linkage to power and affluence, by scholars such as Adams (1990), who has highlighted the interplay between meat culture and misogyny, and Derrida (1991), who has argued that "carnophallogocentrism" structures Western society. Some of the most prominent works illustrating the "animal turn" include Francione's (1995) account of the property status of animals, Nibert's (2002) ideas on capitalism as the foundation of animal oppression or Regan's (2001) deontological view of animals as ends in themselves. Nevertheless, the campaigners do not make use of such scholarly endeavours. Perhaps it is not the job of campaigners to produce critical analyses but adopting radical perspectives on animal sentience would bring greater disruptive potential; campaigners may have a wider audience than scholars and are the ones who could show the ways how to *practically* use this knowledge and shake the property and food status of chickens.

6.6 The Guardian opinion (best practice)

The period between 1982 and 2016 was initially thought to allow an assessment of how the representations of chicken farming had changed over time, but the lack of pronounced discursive shifts resulted in focussing on the differences between the publications more than the changes over time. Strikingly, the *Guardian* opinion pieces offer most in terms of addressing violence against chickens not only relative to the other newspapers, but also relative to the campaigning magazines. The *Guardian* opinion pieces affirm chicken subjecthood, engage with chicken farming on a philosophical basis, and place it in a broader socio-cultural and environmental context. Moreover, there is an increase in coverage in the end of period. In 2015 and 2016, the *Guardian* corpus demonstrates a shift towards framing chicken farming as having far-reaching consequences on nonhumans, humans, and the planet, which is not identified in the other newspapers, nor the campaigners' corpora. Whether this shift continues after 2016 is an avenue for future studies.

The *Guardian* also stands out from the other newspapers for paying the most attention to national and global politics and governmental institutions and recognising the global intersections between chickens and humans. Deemphasising governmental institutions and international politics is a characteristic of tabloid journalism. However, my findings show that it applies not only to the *Mail* and *Mirror*, but also to the *Telegraph* corpus. The right-leaning broadsheet, apart from stories on Edwina Currie and the *Salmonella* scare and on Labour's anti-hunting campaigns, largely evades debating the governmental responsibilities towards chickens.

The *Telegraph*, *Mail* and *Mirror* corpora, as well as the campaigners' magazines, show interest in *how chickens* are treated as food animals and *how we* treat chickens as food animals. The *Mail* stands out for its long-read pieces that are concerned with *our* morality and interrogate poor treatment of chickens and their commodification. The *Guardian*, however, goes beyond the question of the *poor treatment of chickens* and asks *should chickens be food?* The latter, I suggest, is the key question to raise if the exploitation of chickens is to be dismantled. Here, my findings concur with the sociologist Paula Arcari (2017) who argues that focussing on *how* farmed animals are treated is not enough:

> it is the normative practices and associated elements of which they [nonhuman animals] are a part that need to be made more visible in a way that invites a critical examination of their normative status. In this way, the deeply embedded understanding of non-human animals as food that underpins all practices of meat production and consumption can start to be questioned and unsettled (and ideally de-normalised). (p. 46)

The *Guardian* commissions philosophical pieces and has a long list of prominent columnists who increasingly bring in critical perspectives. In the *Guardian* opinion pieces, authors such as Baggini, Monbiot, Sten or Harari make the normative practices of consuming eggs and chicken flesh visible and challenge their normative status through a critical examination of bias. For example,

Baggini questions the normalcy of intensive chicken farming by pointing out the normalcy of consuming dog flesh in China (*The Guardian*, 23/6/2015 [G39]). Practices of meat and egg production are unsettled based on moral argument. *Animals are people*, declares Sten, — therefore *using* them for food is unethical (*The Guardian*, 6/4/2016 [G49]). What happens to chickens is perceived not only through the lens of compassion but also as a form of *injustice* conceptually comparable to that experienced by other marginalised groups.

6.7 Present and future

The CAS scholar Davis (2011) notes that "the chicken's doom is not to become extinct"; deploying the Procrustean myth to describe the chickens' nemesis, she describes how agricultural systems alter their bodies to suit confinement and slaughter just as Procrustes stretches or cuts the legs of his victims to fit the bed (p. 277). Between 1982 and 2016, probably the biggest milestone achieved by animal advocates with regards to chicken farming was the banning of battery cages in 2012 in the EU. Battery cages have been replaced by so-called "enriched" cages. In 2018, just over half (54%) of British eggs were produced in free-range farms (including estimated 2% organic), whereas 44% were produced in cages and 1% in indoor barn systems (British Egg Information Service, 2018d). Other than that, welfare improvements are minor. As noted in Section *1.2.2 Welfare, legislation and the market*, the UK government keeps postponing the ban on debeaking of hens farmed for eggs. First, the ban was to be introduced in 2011, then in 2016. The practice remains legal to date (as of December 2019). Organic farms do not allow debeaking, but only 2% of all eggs sold in the UK in 2016 were organically produced. With regards to chickens farmed for their flesh, intensive farms that allow "stocking density" up to 39 kg/m^2 dominate the market (Defra, 2018a). Organic systems are still very much a niche market; Defra (2017) informs that chickens raised on organic farms constituted just 1.4% of total chickens farmed for meat in the UK in June 2016 (p. 8).

The recent troubled plan for Britain to leave the EU has produced a new issue — "chlorinated chicken" has become the symbol of the dangers of losing EU standards (Millstone et al., 2019). Chemical rinses that are meant to "wash out" bacterial contamination from chicken flesh have been banned in the EU since 1997; the minimum standards laid in laws make such rinses unnecessary (Millstone et al., 2019). Although laws regulating chicken farming in the EU can rightfully be criticised as insufficient or low welfare, the situation in the USA is in fact worse. The American chicken industry adopts guidelines on a voluntary basis, but no legislation regulates the key practices such as stocking density, access to litter or inspection of birds (ADAS, 2016). If the UK does not keep the EU (or higher) standards after Brexit, the new trade deal between the USA and the UK could allow chemically disinfected chicken meat into the country. The problem here is multifaceted: (a) chlorine-washed flesh can mask severe welfare issues such as overcrowding in chicken farms; (b) it may not be safe and hide poor practices and hygiene breaches in slaughterhouses; (c) British farmers may want to take a step backward and lower their standards if they are to compete with the American produce on price.

Although the environmental crisis may accelerate changes in our diet, chickens seem to escape our compassion; their flesh conveniently replaces "beef" or "pork" and is soon to become the most consumed meat globally. The A-IC is successfully expanding and exploiting the ever-increasing number of chickens. To be precise, 1.05 billion chickens were slaughtered for meat in the UK in 2016 (FAOSTAT, 2018). In 2017, the number has increased to nearly 1.09 billion and in 2018, the number has increased to nearly 1.14 billion (FAOSTAT, 2020). With regards to eggs, in 2016, nearly 12.4 billion eggs were produced in the country; in 2017, the number reached 12.9 billion and in 2018, it surpassed 13.3 billion (FAOSTAT, 2020). The Food and Agriculture Organization of the United Nations (FAO) estimates that the number of chickens slaughtered for meat worldwide has increased from 65.3 billion in 2016 to 66.7 billion in 2017 and reached nearly 68.8 billion in 2018. (FAOSTAT, 2020). In addition, 1.32 trillion eggs were produced worldwide in 2016 (FAOSTAT, 2018). In 2017, the number exceeded 1.34 trillion and in 2018, nearly 1.38 trillion eggs were produced globally (FAOSTAT, 2020).

Borrowing from the *Mail*, "that feathered fool, the chicken" sits low in our moral hierarchy but high as regards our appetite (*Daily Mail*, 11/12/1984 [MA2]). The continuous quest for larger "yields", efficiency and profits is projected to further jeopardise chicken welfare as birds need to grow even more rapidly and convert less feed into more protein (Dawkins, 2012). The expansion and intensification of chicken farming also increase the dangers to global public health, which has yet to recover from the COVID-19 pandemic. As influenza viruses are present in wild bird populations, the threat of a "spillover" event is continuous and global; virologists consider zoonotic influenza as a pandemic-in-waiting (Philippon et al., 2020). Chickens (and pigs) are the perfect "mixing vessels" for recombination of viruses such as influenza and close contact with these animals in farming practices is an important source of human infection (Mostafa et al., 2018). Between 2003 and 2020, WHO (2020a) reported 861 human cases and 455 deaths of the avian influenza virus (H5N1). Furthermore, amid the COVID-19 pandemic in early 2020, two new human infections with avian influenza (H9N2) viruses were reported in China and Senegal (WHO, 2020b).

Zoonotic diseases, of course, are not new. In fact, much of human exposure to infectious disease has been zoonotic.[1] Nevertheless, the COVID-19 pandemic not only reminded us of the potential gravity of the consequences when viruses cross the species barrier, but also put a spotlight on the uncomfortable connections between public health, climate emergency and our destruction of the nonhuman world. The pandemic has shown that the repercussions of our exploitation of the nonhuman world can be catastrophic, and following Latour (2005), challenged human exceptionalism — nonhuman actants (be it viruses, animals, or environmental factors) cannot be removed from the political realm; they demonstrate agency as the driving forces of history.

Nevertheless, the disturbing projections of chicken farming concur with my key finding — despite the ever-growing scientific knowledge on chicken sentience, public health risks and the climate crisis, the discursive representations of chicken farming have not significantly changed in the sources analysed over the course of 34 years. The critically important ethical question of the moral standing of chickens is marginal in the newspapers' corpora, whereas the campaigners' corpora do not break with the values of the past and do not confront the readers with the question of multispecies justice. Further research is needed to analyse whether campaigners are adopting more radical perspectives, whether chicken farming is more frequently situated in the context of ethics, justice and the climate crisis, and whether veganism receives fairer coverage in the newspapers after 2016.

I would like to finish this book with a hopeful note. The popularisation of Meat-Free days, Veganuary and flexitarian, reducetarian or other "conscious" diets in the recent years indicates a degree of "normalisation" of cookery and lifestyles that reduce the amount of animal-derived protein. Furthermore, the number of vegans in the UK has increased from 276,000 (0.46% of the population) in 2016 to 600,000 (1.16%) in 2019, which suggests a growing acceptance of veganism (Vegan Society, 2020). In addition, over the course of writing this book, the *Guardian* has started to change its language. The updated style guidance does not focus on chickens but is a promising sign as it invites a much-needed change in attitudes towards the nonhuman world. The guidance currently recommends the terms "climate crisis" and "global heating" over "climate change" and "global warming" (Carrington, 2019). Furthermore, the *Guardian* editors and reporters are advised to use "fish populations" instead of a commodifying term "fish stocks" and "wildlife" instead of "biodiversity". These, however, are just minor

---

[1] As I discuss elsewhere, "plague crossed from small mammals centuries ago. The Spanish flu pandemic originated in birds. Rabies has terrified civilisations for thousands of years... In the 1920s, when hunters in Africa butchered chimpanzees, HIV was likely transmitted to humans" (Lazutkaite, 2020).

steps. A much bigger effort is required to rewrite the dominant cultural scripts of nonhuman animal exploitation.

To fundamentally challenge the largely unacknowledged violence towards chickens, novel *discourses* are needed; discourses that, where practically possible, would reject the notion of farmed animals as food. Quoting Singer on animal farming, "those who want to kill animals and eat them ought to justify their view. It shouldn't be the other way round" (BBC, 2015). The challenge would also mean framing chicken farming not only through suffering, but also around the principles of justice, as well as acknowledging the multitude of entanglements between chickens, humans, and ecological health. In practice, this would mean that, in the words of CAS scholars Taylor and Fraser (2017):

> the only real call we are left … is for a cessation of meat eating and the promulgation of vegan lifestyles (and by this we mean ideological outlooks, not simply dietary choice). This is no simple solution, as it necessitates a wholesale revision of how we see ourselves, other animals, the earth we live on and the relationships between all three. (p. 196)

References

ABC. (2017a). *The Daily Telegraph.* Retrieved July 26, 2017, from https://www.abc.org.uk/Certificates/48539128.pdf

ABC. (2017b). *The Guardian.* Retrieved July 26, 2017, from https://www.abc.org.uk/Certificates/48538888.pdf

ABC. (2017c). *Daily Mirror.* Retrieved November 26, 2017, from https://www.abc.org.uk/product/576

ABC. (2017d). *Daily Mail.* Retrieved November 26, 2017, from https://www.abc.org.uk/product/2115

Adams, C. J. (1990). *Sexual Politics of Meat: A Feminist-Vegetarian Critical Theory* (20th Edition). Bloomsbury Publishing.

Adams, C. J. (2003). *The Pornography of Meat.* Continuum.

Adams, C. J. (2010). Why feminist-vegan now? *Feminism & Psychology,* 20(3), 302-317.

ADAS. (2016). *Comparison of the Regulatory Framework and Key Practices in the Poultry Meat Supply Chain in the EU and USA.* ADAS UK and The University of Arkansas, from https://www.britishpoultry.org.uk/identity-cms/wp-content/uploads/2018/05/2016-ADAS-EU-US-comparison.pdf

Almiron, N., & Cole, M. (2015). Introduction: The Convergence of Two Critical Approaches. In N. Almiron, M. Cole, & C. P. Freeman (Eds.), *Critical Animal and Media Studies: Communication for Nonhuman Advocacy* (pp. 1–7). Routledge.

Almiron, N. Cole, M., & Freeman, C. P. (2018). Critical animal and media studies: Expanding the understanding of oppression in communication research. *European Journal of Communication,* 33(4), 367–380.

Almiron, N., & Zoppeddu. M. (2014). Eating Meat and Climate Change: The Media Blind Spot: A Study of Spanish and Italian Press Coverage. *Environmental Communication: A Journal of Nature and Culture,* 9(3), 307–325.

Animal Aid. (2016a). *About Animal Aid.* Retrieved July 17, 2016, from http://www.animalaid.org.uk/h/n/ABOUT/

Animal Aid. (2016b). *About Animal Aid Fact Sheet.* Retrieved July 17, 2016, from https://www.animalaid.org.uk/wp-content/uploads/2016/09/About-Animal-Aid-factsheet.pdf

Animal Aid. (2019). *Our Aims.* Retrieved July 17, 2019, from https://www.animalaid.org.uk/about-us/aims-objectives/

Arcari, P. (2017). Perverse visibilities? Foregrounding non-human animals in "ethical" and "sustainable" meat consumption. *The Brock Review,* 13(1), 24–53.

Baker, P. (2010). *Sociolinguistics and Corpus Linguistics* (pp. 57–80). Edinburgh University Press.

Bar-On, Y. M., Phillips, R. & Milo, R. (2018). The biomass distribution on Earth. *Proceedings of the National Academy of Sciences of the United States of America,* 115, 6506–6511.

Barthes, R. (1991). *Mythologies.* The Noonday Press.

Bastian, B., Costello, K., Loughnan, S., & Hodson, G. (2012). When Closing the Human-Animal Divide Expands Moral Concern: The Importance of Framing. *Social Psychological and Personality Science*, 3(4), 421–429.

BBC. (2003). *Tube bans animal welfare poster*. Retrieved November 2, 2017, from http://news.bbc.co.uk/2/hi/uk_news/england/2781149.stm

BBC. (2009). *Bird flu tests continue on farms*. Retrieved November 2, 2017, from http://news.bbc.co.uk/2/hi/uk_news/england/7912529.stm

BBC. (2013). *Bird flu found at Bernard Matthews farm in Suffolk*. Retrieved November 2, 2017, from http://www.bbc.com/news/uk-england-suffolk-22182407

BBC. (2015). *Can we justify killing animals for food?* Retrieved November 2, 2017, from https://www.bbc.com/news/science-environment-34541077

BBC. (2018, February 22). *More KFC outlets reopen as chicken chaos eases*. Retrieved February 22, 2018, from https://www.bbc.com/news/business-43156282

Beck, U. (2010). Climate for Change, or How to Create a Green Modernity? *Theory, Culture & Society*, 27(2–3), 254–266.

Bell, D., & Hollows J. (2011). From River Cottage to Chicken Run: Hugh Fearnley-Whittingstall and the class politics of ethical consumption. *Celebrity Studies*, 2, 178–191.

Bell-Fialkoff, A. (1996). *Ethnic cleansing*. St. Martins Press.

Bennett, C. E., Thomas, R., Williams M., Zalasiewicz, J., Edgeworth, M., Miller, H., Coles, B., Foster, A., Burton E. J., & Marume, U. (2018). The broiler chicken as a signal of a human reconfigured biosphere. *Royal Society Open Science*, 5(12), Article 180325.

Bentham, J. (1789). *The Principles of Morals and Legislation*. Clarendon Press.

Bernard Matthews. (2017). *About us*. Retrieved November 2, 2017, from http://www.bernardmatthews.com/bootiful-story

Best, S. (2007). The Animal Enterprise Terrorism Act: New, Improved, and ACLU Approved. *Journal for Critical Animal Studies*, 5(1), 65–81.

Best, S. (2009). The rise of critical animal studies: putting theory into action and animal liberation into higher education. *Journal for Critical Animal Studies*, 7(1), 9–54.

Bingham, A., & Conboy, M. (2009). The Daily Mirror and the Creation of a Commercial Popular Language. *Journalism Studies*, 10(5), 639–654.

Birke, L. (1995). Exploring the Boundaries: Feminism, Animals, and Science. In C. J. Adams, & J. Donovan (Eds.), *Women and Animals: Feminist Theoretical Explorations* (pp. 55–84). Duke University Press.

Birke, L. (2008). Talking about Horses: Control and Freedom in the World of "Natural Horsemanship." *Society and Animals*, 16 (2), 32–54.

Boykoff, M. T. (2013). Public Enemy No. 1? Understanding Media Representations of Outlier Views on Climate Change. *American Behavioral Scientist*, 57(6), 796–817.

Branum, J. and Charteris-Black, J. (2015). The Edward Snowden affair: A corpus study of the British press. *Discourse & Communication*, 9(2), 199–220.

Breeze, R. (2014). Perspectives on North and South: The 2012 financial crisis in Spain seen through two major British newspapers. *Discourse & Communication*, 8, 241–259.

Briggs, H. (2018, December 12). "Planet of the chickens": How the bird took over the world. *BBC News*. Retrieved June 26, 2019, from https://www.bbc.com/news/science-environment-46506184

British Egg Information Service. (2018a). *Eggs and Salmonella*. Retrieved March 3, 2018, from https://www.egginfo.co.uk/eggs-safety/salmonella

British Egg Information Service. (2018b). *British Lion Eggs*. Retrieved March 3, 2018, from https://www.egginfo.co.uk/british-lion-eggs

British Egg Information Service. (2018c). *Industry data 2004 to 2016*. Retrieved November 15, 2918, from https://www.egginfo.co.uk/sites/default/files/Archive%20industry%20stats%202004%20-%202016.docx

British Egg Information Service. (2018d). *Industry data*. Retrieved March 3, 2018, from https://www.egginfo.co.uk/egg-facts-and-figures/industry-information/data

British Newspaper Archive. (2019). *About the British Newspaper Archive*. Retrieved June 2, 2019, from https://www.britishnewspaperarchive.co.uk/help/about

Budiansky, S. (1992). *The Covenant of the Wild: Why Animals Chose Domestication*. Yale University Press.

Burnley, D. (1992). Lexis and semantics. In N. Blake (Ed.), *The Cambridge History of The English Language Vol II 1066–1476* (pp. 409–499). Cambridge University Press.

Carrington, D. (2019, June 17). Why the Guardian is changing the language it uses about the environment. *The Guardian*. Retrieved August 13, 2019, from https://www.theguardian.com/environment/2019/may/17/why-the-guardian-is-changing-the-language-it-uses-about-the-environment?

Carvalho, A. (2007). Ideological cultures and media discourses on scientific knowledge: re-reading news on climate change. *Public Understanding of Science*, 6, 223–243.

Centers for Disease and Prevention. (2014). *Avian Influenza (Bird Flu) Research. Has CDC done "gain of function" research on highly pathogenic avian influenza A (H5N1) in the past?* Retrieved December 3, 2014, from http://www.cdc.gov/flu/avianflu/research.htm

CIWF, & OneKind. (2012). *Farm assurance schemes & animal welfare: how the standards compare 2012*. Retrieved July 26, 2016, from https://www.compassioninfoodbusiness.com/media/5819111/standards-analysis-report.pdf

CIWF. (2014a). *Factory Farmer exposes ugly truth about your food*. Retrieved May 6, 2018, from https://www.ciwf.org.uk/news/2014/12/factory-farmer-exposes-ugly-truth-about-your-food

CIWF. (2014b). *Welfare issues for egg laying hens*. Retrieved September 14, 2014, from http://www.ciwf.org.uk/farm-animals/chickens/egg-laying-hens/welfare-issues/

CIWF. (2015a). *Compassion in World Farming Master Brand Toolkit*. Retrieved May 13, 2015, from http://ciwf.assetbank-server.com/assetbank-ciwf/assetfile/41914.PDF

CIWF. (2015b). *CIWF annual review 2014-2015.* Retrieved May 6, 2018, from https://www.ciwf.org.uk/media/7426080/ciwf-annual-review-2014-2015.pdf

Cloutier, S., Newberry, R. C., Honda, K., & Alldredge, J. R. (2002). Cannibalistic behaviour spread by social learning. *Animal Behaviour,* 63, 1153–1162.

Cogan, T. A., & Humphrey, T. J. (2003). The rise and fall of Salmonella Enteritidis in the UK. *Journal of Applied Microbiology,* 94(s1), 114–119.

Cole, M. (2011). From "Animal Machines" to "Happy Meat"? Foucault's Ideas of Disciplinary and Pastoral Power Applied to 'Animal-Centred' Welfare Discourse. *Animals,* 1(1), 83–101.

Cole, M. (2015). Getting (Green) Beef: Anti-Vegan Rhetoric and the Legitimizing of Eco-Friendly Oppression. In N. Almiron, M. Cole, & C. P. Freeman (Eds.), *Critical Animal and Media Studies: Communication for Nonhuman Animal Advocacy* (pp. 107–125). Routledge.

Cole, M., & Morgan, K. (2011). Vegaphobia: derogatory discourses of veganism and the reproduction of speciesism in UK national newspapers. *The British journal of sociology,* 62(1), 134–153.

Cole, M., & Stewart, K. (2014). *Our Children and Other Animals: The Cultural Construction of Human-Animal Relations in Childhood.* Routledge.

Cole, M., & Stewart, K. (2018). Speciesism Party: A Vegan Critique of Sausage Party. *ISLE: Interdisciplinary Studies in Literature and Environment,* 24(4), 767–786.

Conboy, M. (2006). *Tabloid Britain: Constructing a community through language.* Routledge.

Conboy, M. (2010). *The Language of Newspapers: Socio-historical Perspectives.* Bloomsbury Publishing.

Cook, G., & Ancarno, C. (2019). "I Do Still Love the Taste": Taste as a Reason for Eating Non-human Animals. *ISLE: Interdisciplinary Studies in Literature and Environment,* 098, 1-25.

Cook, G., & Sealey, A. (2018). The Discursive Representation of Animals. In A. Fill, & H. Penz (Eds.), *The Routledge Handbook of Ecolinguistics.* Routledge.

Coppin, D. (2003). Foucauldian Hog Futures: The Birth of Mega-hog Farms. *The Sociological Quarterly,* 44(4), 597–616.

Crenshaw, K. (1989). Demarginalizing the Intersection of Race and Sex: A Black Feminist Critique of Antidiscrimination Doctrine, Feminist Theory and Antiracist Politics. *University of Chicago Legal Forum,* 14, 538–554.

Croney, C. C., & Reynnells, R. D. (2008). The ethics of semantics: do we clarify or obfuscate reality to influence perceptions of farm animal production? *Poultry science,* 87(2), 387–391.

Croteau, D. (2014). Media and Ideology. In D. Croteu, & W. Hoynes (Eds.), *Media society: industries, images, and audiences* (pp. 152–186). Sage.

Crummy, N. (2007). Brooches and the Cult of Mercury. *Britannia,* 38, 225–230.

Cudworth E. (2008). 'Most farmers prefer blondes': The dynamics of anthroparchy in animals' becoming meat. *Journal for Critical Animal Studies,* 6(1), 32–45.

Cudworth, E. (2011). *Social Lives with Other Animals: Tales of Sex, Death and Love.* Palgrave Macmillan.

Cudworth, E. (2014). Beyond speciesism: intersectionality, critical sociology and the human domination of other animals. In N. Taylor, & R. Twine (Eds.), *The rise of critical animal studies: From the margins to the centre* (pp. 19–35). Routledge.

Davis, K. (1995). Thinking like a chicken: farm animals and the feminine connection. In C. J. Adams, & J. Donovan (Eds.), *Women and Animals: Feminist Theoretical Explorations* (pp. 192–212). Duke University Press.

Davis, K. (1996). *Prisoned Chickens, Poisoned Eggs: An Inside Look at the Modern Poultry Industry.* The Book Publishing Company.

Davis, K. (2011). Procrustean Solutions to Animal Identity and Welfare Problems. In J. Sanbonmatsu (Ed.), *Critical Theory and Animal Liberation.* Rowman & Littlefield.

Davis, K. (2018). The Disengagement of Journalistic Discourse about Nonhuman Animals: An Analysis. In A. K. Matsuoka, & J. Sorenson (Eds.), *Critical Animal Studies: Towards Trans-species Social Justice.* Rowman and Littlefield International.

Dawar, A. (2013, September 19). Chicken study costing £1.9million of taxpayers' funds causes a flap. *The Daily Express,* from https://www.express.co.uk/news/uk/430507/Chicken-study-costing-1-9million-of-taxpayers-funds-causes-a-flap

Dawkins, M. (2012). *Why Animals Matter: Animal Consciousness, Animal Welfare and Human Well-Being.* Oxford University Press.

Dawkins, M., & Layton, R. (2012). Breeding for better welfare: genetic goals for broiler chickens and their parents. *Animal Welfare,* 21(2), 147–155.

Day, K., Gough, B., & McFadden, M. (2004). "Warning! Alcohol Can Seriously Damage Your Feminine Health": A Discourse Analysis of Recent British Newspaper Coverage of Women and Drinking. *Feminist Media Studies,* 4(2), 165–185.

De Castella, T. (2014, October 23). Do people know where their chicken comes from? BBC News Magazine. *BBC News Magazine,* from http://www.bbc.co.uk/news/magazine-29219843

De Jong, I. C., Berg, C., Butterworth, A., & Estevéz, I. (2012). *Scientific report updating the EFSA opinions on the welfare of broilers and broiler breeders.* European Food Safety Authority, Supporting Publications EN-295:116, 1–116.

De Jong, I. C., Van Voorst, S., Ehlhardt, D. A., & Blokhuis, H. J. (2002). Effects of restricted feeding on physiological stress parameters in growing broiler breeders. *British Poultry Science,* 43, 157–168.

De Vries, M., & de Boer, I. J. M. (2010). Comparing environmental impacts for livestock products: A review of life cycle assessments. *Livestock Science,* 128(1–3), 1–11.

Deckha, M. (2008). Disturbing images: PETA and the feminist ethics of animal advocacy. *Ethics and the environment,* 13(2), 35–76.

Deckha, M. (2011). Critical animal studies and animal law. *Animal Law,* 18, 207-236.

Defra. (2005). *A guide to the practical management of feather pecking & cannibalism in free range laying hens.* Retrieved September 13, 2013, from https://www.gov.uk/government/uploads/system/uploads/attachment_data/file/69374/pb10596-feather-pecking-050309.pdf

Defra. (2013). *Chickens for Meat & Breeding (England): Code of Recommendations for the Welfare of Livestock.* Retrieved October 30, 2014, from https://www.gov.uk/government/uploads/system/uploads/attachment_data/file/69372/pb7275 meat-chickens-020717.pdf

Defra. (2014). *United Kingdom Egg Statistics – Quarter 2, 2014.* Retrieved October 30, 2015, from https://www.gov.uk/government/uploads/system/uploads/attachment_data/file/371027/eggs-statsnotice-06nov14.pdf

Defra. (2016). *Farming Statistics Final crop areas, yields, livestock populations and agricultural workforce At June 2016 - United Kingdom.* Retrieved February 19, 2017 from https://assets.publishing.service.gov.uk/government/uploads/system/uploads/attachment_data/file/747210/structure-jun2016prov-UK.pdf

Defra. (2017). *Organic farming statistics 2016.* Retrieved August 18, 2019, from https://assets.publishing.service.gov.uk/government/uploads/system/uploads/attachment_data/file/614552/organics-statsnotice-18may17.pdf

Defra. (2018a). *Code of practice for the welfare of meat chickens and meat breeding chickens.* Retrieved December 17, 2018, from https://assets.publishing.service.gov.uk/government/uploads/system/uploads/attachment_data/file/694013/meat-chicken-code-march2018.pdf

Defra. (2018b). *Family Food 2016/17: Purchases.* Retrieved December 18, 2018, from https://www.gov.uk/government/publications/family-food-201617/purchases

DeMello, M. (2012). *Animals and Society: An Introduction to Human-Animal Studies.* Cambridge University Press.

Derrida, J. (1991). Eating Well, Or the Calculation of the Subject. In E. Cadava, P. Connor, & J. Nancy (Eds.), *Who Comes after the Subject?* Routledge.

Diarrassouba, F., Diarra, M. S., Bach, S., Delaquis, P., Pritchard, J., Topp, E., & Skura, B. J. (2007). Antibiotic Resistance and Virulence Genes in Commensal Escherichia coli and Salmonella Isolates from Commercial Broiler Chicken Farms. *Journal of Food Protection,* 70(6), 1316–1327.

Dierksheide, C. (2008). "The great improvement and civilization of that race": Jefferson and the "Amelioration" of Slavery, ca. 1770–1826. *Early American Studies: An Interdisciplinary Journal,* 6(1), 165–197.

Doig, A. (1989). The Resignation of Edwina Currie: A Word Too Far. *Parliamentary Affairs,* 42(3), 317–329.

Dunayer, J. (1995). Sexist words, Speciesists roots. In C. J. Adams, & J. Donovan (Eds.), *Animals and women: feminist theoretical explorations* (pp. 11–31). Duke University Press.

Dunayer, J. (2001). *Animal equality: language and liberation.* Ryce.

Dunayer, J. (2015). Mixed Messages: Opinion Pieces by Representatives of US Nonhuman-Advocacy Organizations. In N. Almiron, M. Cole, & C. P. Freeman (Eds.), *Critical Animal and Media Studies: Communication for Nonhuman Advocacy* (pp. 91–106). Routledge.

Duncan, I. J. H., Slee, G. S., Seawright, E., & Breward, J. (1989). Behavioural consequences of partial beak amputation (beak trimming) in poultry. *British Poultry Science,* 30(3), 479–488.

EFSA, Scientific Panel on Animal Health and Welfare (AHAW). (2010). Scientific Opinion on the influence of genetic parameters on the welfare and the resistance to stress of commercial broilers. *The EFSA Journal*, 8(7), 1666, 1–82. Retrieved October 30, 2014, from http://www.efsa.europa.eu/en/search/doc/1666.pdf

Elson, H. (2015). Poultry welfare in intensive and extensive production systems. *World's Poultry Science Journal*, 71(3), 449-460.

Esser, F., & Umbricht, A. (2014). The Evolution of Objective and Interpretative Journalism in the Western Press: Comparing Six News Systems since the 1960s. *Journalism & Mass Communication Quarterly*, 91(2), 229–249.

European Centre for Disease Prevention and Control. (2018). Campylobacteriosis. *Annual epidemiological report for 2016*. Retrieved December 25, 2019, from https://www.ecdc.europa.eu/sites/default/files/documents/AER_for_2016-campylobacteriosis.pdf

European Commission (2016). *Special Eurobarometer 442: Attitudes of Europeans towards Animal Welfare*. Retrieved October 22, 2017, from https://ec.europa.eu/commfrontoffice/publicopinion/index.cfm/ResultDoc/download/DocumentKy/71348

Fairclough, N. (2001). *Language and Power*. Second Edition. Longman.

Fairclough, N. (2015). *Language and Power*. Third Edition. Routledge.

Fairclough, N., & Wodak, R. (1997). Critical discourse analysis. In T. van Dijk (Ed.), *Discourse as Social Interaction* (pp. 258–284). Sage.

FAO. (2010). Chicken genetic resources used in smallholder production systems and opportunities for their development, by P. Sørensen. *FAO Smallholder Poultry Production Paper*, 5. Retrieved October 22, 2017, from http://www.fao.org/3/al675e/al675e00.pdf

FAO. (2011). Mapping supply and demand for animal-source foods to 2030, by T.P. Robinson & F. Pozzi. *Animal Production and Health Working Paper*, 2. Retrieved October 22, 2017, from http://www.fao.org/3/i2425e/i2425e00.pdf

FAO. (2014). *Avian Influenza. Questions & Answers. 4. Why does avian influenza subtype H5N1 cause so much concern?* Retrieved October 6, 2014, from http://www.fao.org/avianflu/en/qanda.html

FAOSTAT. (2018). *Food and Agriculture Organization of the United Nations Statistical Databases*. Retrieved December 18, 2018, from http://faostat.fao.org/

FAOSTAT. (2020). *Food and Agriculture Organization of the United Nations Statistical Databases*. Retrieved March 27, 2020, from http://faostat.fao.org/

Feider, M. (2017). *Chickens in the archaeological material culture of Roman Britain, France, and Belgium*. Doctorate Thesis. Bournemouth University.

Ferguson, M. (1998). *Animal advocacy and Englishwomen, 1780–1900: patriots, nation, and empire*. University of Michigan Press.

Food Standards Agency (2015). *Campylobacter survey: cumulative results from the full 12 months (Q1 - Q4)*. Retrieved June 6, 2015, from http://www.food.gov.uk/news-updates/news/2015/14003/campylobacter-survey-results-12months

Foucault, M. (1972). *The Archaeology of Knowledge and the Discourse on Language*. Pantheon Books.

Fowler, R. (1991). *Language in the News*. Routledge.

Fox, N., & Ward, K. (2008) Health, ethics and environment: A qualitative study of vegetarian motivations. *Appetite*, 50 (2-3), 422–429.

Francione, G. L. (1995). *Animals, Property, and the Law.* Temple University Press.

Francione, G. L. (1996). *Rain without Thunder: The Ideology of the Animals Rights Movement.* Temple University Press.

Fraser, A. F., & Broom, D. M. (1990). *Farm Animal Behaviour and Welfare.* Sannders.

Freeman, C. P. (2009). This Little Piggy Went to Press: The American News Media's Construction of Animals in Agriculture. *The Communication Review,* 12(1), 78–103.

Freeman, C. P. (2014). *Framing Farming: Communication Strategies for Animal Rights.* Brill.

Freeman, C. P., & Merskin, D. (2016a). Respectful Representation: An Animal Issues Style Guide for All Media Practitioners. In N. Almiron, M. Cole, & C. P. Freeman (Eds.), *Critical Animal and Media Studies: Communication for Nonhuman Animal Advocacy* (pp. 205–220). Routledge.

Freeman, C. P., & Merskin, D. (2016b). *Guidelines for Journalism.* Retrieved July 26, 2017, from http://www.animalsandmedia.org/main/journalism-guidelines/

Freeman, C. P., Bekoff, M., & Bexell, S. M. (2011). Giving Voice To the "Voiceless." *Journalism Studies,* 12(5), 590–607.

Freire, R., Glatz, P., & Hinch, G. (2008). Self-administration of an analgesic does not alleviate pain in beak-trimmed chickens. *Asian-Australasian Journal of Animal Sciences,* 21, 443–448.

Gaarder, E. (2011). *Women and the animal rights movement.* Rutgers University Press.

Gabrielatos, C. (2018). Keyness Analysis: nature, metrics and techniques. In C. Taylor, & A. Marchi (Eds.), *Corpus Approaches to Discourse: A critical review* (pp. 225–258). Routledge.

Gabrielatos, C., & Baker, P. (2008). Fleeing, sneaking, flooding: A corpus analysis of discursive constructions of refugees and asylum seekers in the UK Press 1996–2005. *Journal of English Linguistics,* 36(1) 5–38.

Gerber, P., Opio, C., & Steinfeld, H. (2007). *Poultry production and the environment – a review.* Animal Production and Health Division, Food and Agriculture Organization of the United Nations. Retrieved October 6, 2014, from http://www.fao.org/ag/againfo/home/events/bangkok2007/docs/part2/2_2.pdf

Glasser, C. (2011). Tied oppressions: an analysis of how sexist imagery reinforces speciesist sentiment. *The Brock review,* 12(1), 51–68.

Glenn, C. B. (2004). Constructing Consumables and Consent: A Critical Analysis of Factory Farm Industry Discourse. *Journal of Communication Inquiry,* 28(1), 63–81.

Glynn, K. (2000). *Tabloid Culture: Trash Taste, Popular Power, and the Transformation of American Television.* Duke University Press.

Godley, A. C., & Williams, B. (2007). The chicken, the factory farm and the supermarket: the emergence of the modern poultry industry in Britain. In W. Belasco, & R. Horowitz (Eds.), *Food Chains: From Farmyard to Shopping Cart* (pp. 47–61). University of Pennsylvania Press.

Goody, J. (1982). *Cooking, Cuisine and Class: A study in Comparative Sociology.* Cambridge University Press.

Gorman, J. (2016, January 18). Chickens weren't always dinner for humans. *The New York Times.* Retrieved February 16, 2017, from https://www.nytimes.com/2016/01/19/science/chickens-werent-always-dinner-for-humans.html

Gorman. (2018, December 11). It Could Be the Age of the Chicken, Geologically. *The New York Times.* Retrieved December 15, 2018, from https://www.nytimes.com/2018/12/11/science/chicken-anthropocene-archaeology.html

Greenhough, B. (2014). More-than-human-geographies. In A. Paasi, N. Castree, R. Lee, S. Radcliffe, R. Kitchin, V. Lawson, & C. W. J. Withers (Eds.), *The Sage Handbook of Progress in Human Geography* (pp. 94–119). Sage.

Gurung, S., White, D., Archer, G., Zhao, D., Farnell, Y., Byrd, J.A., Peebles, E. D., & Farnell, M. (2018). Evaluation of Alternative Euthanasia Methods of Neonatal Chickens. *Animals,* 8(1), 37.

Hall, S. (1975). Introduction. In A. C. H. Smith (Ed.), *Paper Voices: The Popular Press and Social Change, 1935–1965* (pp. 11–24). Chatto & Windus.

Harker, K. S., Lane, C., Gormley, F. J., & Adak, G. K. (2014). National outbreaks of Salmonella infection in the UK. (2000–2011). *Epidemiology and Infection,* 142(3), 601–607.

Harrington, S. (2008). Popular in the twenty-first century: time for a new critical approach? *Journalism: Theory, Practice & Criticism,* 9(3), 266–284.

Hellsten, I., & Nerlich, B. (2010). The bird flu hype: The spread of a disease outbreak through the media and Internet discussion groups. *Journal of Language and Politics,* 9(3), 393–408.

Hester, P.Y., & Shea-Moore, M. (2003). Beak trimming egg-laying strains of chickens. *World's Poultry Science Journal,* 59(4), 458–474.

Hidalgo Tenorio, E. (2011). Critical Discourse Analysis, An overview. *Nordic Journal of English Studies,* 10(1), 183–210.

Hodson, G., & Costello, K. (2018). Psychological implications of undervaluing animals: Dominance-based ideologies and systems of oppression. In A. Matsuoka, & J. Sorenson (Eds.), *Critical animal studies: Towards trans-species social justice* (pp. 184–206). Rowman and Littlefield International.

Horowitz, R. (2006). *Putting Meat on the American Table: Taste, Technology, Transformation* (pp. 103–128). JHU Press.

Humphrey, S., Chaloner, G., Kemmett, K., Davidson, N., Williams, N., Kipar, A., Humphrey, T., & Wigley, P. (2014). Campylobacter jejuni is not merely a commensal in commercial broiler chickens and affects bird welfare. *MBio,* 5(4), e01364–14.

Humphrey, T. (2006). Are happy chickens safer chickens? Poultry welfare and disease susceptibility. *British Poultry Science,* 47(4), 379–391.

iMediaEthics (2014, October 2). *Mail More Interested in Emma Watson's clothes than UN Speech.* Retrieved October 13, 2018, from http://www.imediaethics.org/mail--more-interested-in-emma-watsons-clothes-than-un-speech-commentary/

IPCC. (2019). *History of the IPCC.* Retrieved July 26, 2019, from https://www.ipcc.ch/about/history/

Jasper, J. (1997). *The Art of Moral Protest: Culture, Biography, and Creativity in Social Movements.* University of Chicago Press.

Johansson, S. (2007). *Reading Tabloids: Tabloid Newspapers and Their Readers* (pp. 31–49). Sodertorns Hogskola.

Kahn, M. (2001). The Passive Voice of Science: Language Abuse in the Wildlife Profession. In A. Fill, & P. Mühlhäuser (Eds.), *The Ecolinguistics Reader. Language, Ecology and Environment* (pp. 241–244). Continuum.

Kalechofsky, R. (2003). *Animal Suffering and the Holocaust: The Problem with Comparisons.* Micah Publications.

Kappeler, S. (1995). Speciesism, racism, nationalism … or the power of scientific subjectivity. In C. J. Adams, & J. Donovan (Eds.), *Animals and women: feminist theoretical explorations* (pp. 320–352). Duke University Press.

Khazaal, N., & Almiron, N. (2016). An Angry Cow is Not a Good Eating Experience. *Journalism Studies*, 17(3), 374-391.

Kheel, M. (1995). Licence to kill: an ecofeminist critique of hunters' discourse. In C. J. Adams, & J. Donovan (Eds.), *Animals and women: feminist theoretical explorations* (pp. 85–125). Duke University Press.

Khosravinik, M. (2009). The representation of refugees, asylum seekers and immigrants in British newspapers during the Balkan conflict (1999) and the British general election (2005). *Discourse & Society*, 20(4), 477–498.

Kjaernes, U., Miele, M., & Roex, J. (2007). *Attitudes of Consumers, Retailers and Producers to Farm Animal Welfare.* Welfare Quality Report Series no. 2. Cardiff University.

Knight, A. J. (2008). "Bats, snakes and spiders, Oh my!" How aesthetic and negativistic attitudes, and other concepts predict support for species protection. *Journal of Environmental Psychology*, 28(1), 94–103.

Knowles, T. G., Kestin, S. C., Haslam, S. M., Brown, S. N., Green, L. E., Butterworth, A., Pope, S. J., Pfeiffer, D., & Nicol, C.J. (2008). Leg disorders in broiler chickens: prevalence, risk factors and prevention. *PloS one*, 3(2), 1545.

Kress, G., & van Leeuwen, T. (2006). *Reading images: the grammar of visual design.* Routledge.

Latour, B. (1993). *We have never been modern.* Harvard University Press.

Latour, B. (2005). *Reassembling the Social: An Introduction to Actor- Network-Theory.* Oxford University Press.

Lay, D. C., Fulton, R. M., Hester, P. Y., Karcher, D. M., Kjaer, J. B., Mench, J., Mullens, B., Newberry, R. C., Nicol, C. J., O'Sullivan, N. P., & Porter, R. E. (2011). Hen welfare in different housing systems. *Poultry science*, 90(1), 278–294.

Lazutkaite, E. (2014). *Diners' attitudes towards broiler chicken welfare.* Unpublished MSc thesis. Writtle College, University of Essex.

Lazutkaite, E. (2020, April 7). How did we get here? Covid-19, climate crisis and the sixth mass extinction – opinion. Lithuanian Radio and Television. Retrieved May 29, 2020, from https://www.lrt.lt/en/news-in-english/19/1160498/how-did-we-get-here-covid-19-climate-crisis-and-the-sixth-mass-extinction-opinion

Lee, K., Newell, J., Wolch, J., & Joassart-Marcelli. P. (2015). Cows, climate and the media. In J. Emel, & H. Neo (Eds.), *Political ecologies of meat* (pp. 195–216). Routledge.

Leinonen, I., & Kyriazakis, I. (2016). How can we improve the environmental sustainability of poultry production? *Proceedings of the Nutrition Society*, 75(3), 265–273.

Leisenring, A. (2006). Confronting "victim" discourses: The identity work of battered women. *Symbolic Interaction*, 29, 307–330.

Levine, E. D., Mills, D. S., & Houpt, K. A. (2005). Attitudes of veterinary students at one US college toward factors relating to farm animal welfare. *Journal of Veterinary Medical Education*, 32(4):481–490.

Loughnan, S., Bastian, B., & Haslam, N. (2014). The Psychology of Eating Animals. *Current Directions in Psychological Science*, 23(2), 104–108.

Loughnan, S., Haslam, N., & Bastian, B. (2010). The role of meat consumption in the denial of moral status & mind to meat animals. *Appetite*, 55(1), 156–159.

Luke, B. (2007). *Brutal: manhood and the exploitation of animals.* University of Illinois Press.

Machin, D., & Mayr. A. (2012). *How to do critical discourse analysis: a multimodal introduction.* Sage.

Martin, J. R., & Rose, D. (2003). *Working with discourse: Meaning beyond the clause.* Continuum.

Martison, J. (2017, March 28). Nicola Sturgeon criticises Daily Mail over "Legs-it" front page. *The Guardian.* Retrieved March 29, 2017, from https://www.theguardian.com/media/2017/mar/28/theresa-may-refuses-to-comment-on-daily-mail-legs-it-front-page

Marvin, G. (2001). Cultured Killers: Creating and Representing Foxhounds. *Society and Animals*, 9(3), 273–292.

Matsuoka, A. K., & Sorenson, J. (2018). Introduction. In A. K. Matsuoka, & J. Sorenson (Eds.), *Critical Animal Studies: Towards Trans-species Social Justice.* Rowman and Littlefield International.

McEnery, A., & Hardie, A. (2011). *Corpus Linguistics: Method, Theory and Practice* (pp. 1–24). Cambridge University Press.

Meyer, A. (2010). Too Drunk To Say No. *Feminist Media Studies*, 10(1), 19–34.

Miele, M. (2011). The taste of happiness: free-range chickens. *Environment and Planning A*, 43(9), 2076–2090.

Millstone, E., Lang, T. and Marsden, T. (2019). Food Brexit and Chlorinated Chicken: A Microcosm of Wider Food Problems. *The Political Quarterly*, 90(4), 645-653.

Mintel. (2018). *UK Burger and Chicken Restaurants Market Report.* Mintel Group Ltd.

Mitchell, L. (2006). Animals and the discourse of farming in Southern Africa. *Society and Animals*, 14(1), 39–59.

Mitchell, L. (2012). Nonhumans and the ideology of purpose. *Anthrozoos*, 25(4), 491-502.

Mitchell, L. (2013). Farming: Animals or machines? *Southern African Linguistics and Applied Language Studies*, 31(3), 299–309.

Molloy, C. (2011). *Popular Media and Animals.* Palgrave-MacMillan.

Moran, J. (2005). The strange birth of middle class England. *Political Quarterly*, 76(2), 232–240.

Mosley, M. (2014, August 20). Can eating meat be eco-friendly? *BBC.* Retrieved December 17, 2018, from https://www.bbc.com/news/science-environment-28858289

Mühlhäusler, P. (2003). *Language of Environment - Environment of Language. A Course in Ecolinguistics.* Battlebridge.

Mostafa, A., Abdelwhab, E. M., Mettenleiter, T. C., & Pleschka, S. (2018). Zoonotic Potential of Influenza A Viruses: A Comprehensive Overview. *Viruses,* 10(9), 497.

National Chicken Council. (2016). *U.S. Broiler Performance.* Retrieved August 10, 2017, from http://www.nationalchickencouncil.org/about-the-industry/statistics/u-s-broiler-performance/

Neff, R. A, Chan, I. L., & Smith, K. C. (2008). Yesterday' s Dinner, Today' s Weather, Tomorrow' s News? U.S. Newspaper Coverage of Food System Contributions to Climate Change. *Public Health Nutrition,* 12(87), 1006–1014.

Neo, H. (2015). Battling the head and the heart: constructing knowledgeable narratives of vegetarianism in anti-meat advocacy. In J. Emel, & H. Neo (Eds.), *Political ecologies of meat* (pp. 236–250). Routledge.

Nerlich, B. (2004). War on foot and mouth disease in the UK, 2001: Towards a cultural understanding of agriculture. *Agriculture and Human Values,* 21(1), 15–25.

Nerlich, B. (2007). Media, Metaphors and Modelling: How the UK Newspapers Reported the Epidemiological Modelling Controversy during the 2001 Foot and Mouth Outbreak. *Science, Technology, & Human Values,* 32(4), 432–457.

Nerlich, B. (2011). The role of metaphor scenarios in disease management discourses: Foot and mouth disease and avian influenza: Metaphor, Metonymy and Conceptual Blending. In S. Handl, & H. J. Schmid (Eds.), *Windows to the Mind* (pp. 115–142). De Gruyter Mouton.

Nerlich, B., & Halliday, C. (2007). Avian Flu: The Creation of Expectations in the Interplay between Science and the Media. *Sociology of Health & Illness,* 29(1), 46–65.

Nerlich, B., & Koteyko, N. (2012). Crying wolf? Biosecurity and metacommunication in the context of the 2009 swine flu pandemic. *Health and Place,* 18(4), 710–717.

Nerlich, B., Brown, B., & Wright, N. (2009). The ins and outs of biosecurity: Bird flu in East Anglia and the spatial representation of risk. *Sociologia Ruralis,* 49(4), 344–359.

Nerlich, B., Hamilton, C., & Rowe, V. (2002). Conceptualising Foot and Mouth Disease: The Socio-Cultural Role of Metaphors, Frames and Narratives. *Metaphorik,* 2, 90–108.

Neto, N. A. L., da Silva Mourão, J., & Alves, R. R. N. (2011). It All Begins With the Head: Initiation Rituals and the Symbolic Conceptions of Animals in Candomblé. *Journal of Ethnobiology,* 31(2), 244–261.

Nguyen, H. (2019). *Tongue-Tied: Breaking the Language Barrier to Animal Liberation.* Lantern Books.

Nhung, N. T., Chansiripornchai, N., & Carrique-Mas, J. J. (2017). Antimicrobial Resistance in Bacterial Poultry Pathogens: A Review. *Frontiers in Veterinary Science,* 4(126). Retrieved October 4, 2018, from https://www.frontiersin.org/articles/10.3389/fvets.2017.00126/full

Niamhn, M. (2015, April 1). Better than veggie: Eat chicken to fight climate change. *Food Navigator.* Retrieved January 4, 2019, from https://www.foodnavigator.com/Article/2015/04/02/Better-than-veggie-Eat-chicken-to-fight-climate-change

Nibert, D. (2002). *Animal Rights/Human Rights: Entanglements of Oppression and Liberation.* Rowman and Littlefield.

Nibert, D. (2013). *Animal Oppression and Human Violence. Domesecration, Capitalism, and Global Conflict.* Columbia University Press

Nimmo, R. (2015). Apiculture in the Anthropocene: between posthumanism and critical animal studies. In Human Animal Research Network (HARN) (Eds.), *Animals in the Anthropocene: Critical perspectives on non-human futures* (pp. 177-200). Sydney University Press.

Noske, B. (1989). *Human and Other Animals.* Pluto Press.

Novek J. (2005). Pigs and People: Sociological Perspectives on the Discipline of Nonhuman Animals in Intensive Confinement. *Society and Animals,* 13(3), 221–244.

OECD/FAO. (2016). *Meat. OECD-FAO Agricultural Outlook 2016-2025.* OECD Publishing. Retrieved November 15, 2018, from https://doi.org/10.1787/agr_outlook-2016-en

Ogle, M. (2013). *In Meat We Trust: An Unexpected History of Carnivore America.* Houghton Mifflin Harcourt.

Omond, T. (2012, April 27). Lush's human performance art was about animal cruelty not titillation. *The Guardian.* Retrieved April 14, 2015, from http://www.theguardian.com/commentisfree/2012/apr/27/lush-animal-cruelty-performance-art

Ortner, S. B. (1974). Is female to male as nature is to culture? In M. Z. Rosaldo, & L. Lamphere (Eds.), *Woman, culture, and society* (pp. 67–87). Stanford University Press.

Panelli, R. (2010). More-than-human social geographies: posthuman and other possibilities. *Progress in Human Geography,* 34(1), 79–87.

Perkins, H. F., Parker, M. B., & Walker, M. L. (1964). *Chicken Manure, Its Production, Composition, and Use as a Fertilizer.* Georgia Agricultural Experiment Stations, University of Georgia, College of Agriculture.

Philippon, D. A. M., Wu, P., Cowling, B.J., & Lau, E. H. Y. (2020). Avian Influenza Human Infections at the Human-Animal Interface. *The Journal of Infectious Diseases,* jiaa105.

Piazza, J., Ruby, M.B., Loughnan, S., Luong, M., Kulik, J., Watkins, H. M., & Seigerman, M. (2015). Rationalizing meat consumption: The 4Ns. *Appetite,* 91, 114–128.

Plumwood, V. (1993). *Feminism and the mastery of nature.* Routledge.

Pope, M. K. (1944). *The Anglo-Norman Element in Our Vocabulary: Its Significance for Our Civilization.* Manchester University Press.

Popović, V., & Popović, P. (2014). The Twenty-First Century, the Reign of Tabloid Journalism. *Procedia – Social and Behavioral Sciences.* 163, 12–18.

Potts, A. (2016). *Meat Culture* (Human-animal studies). Brill.

Rayson, P. (2003). *Matrix: A statistical method and software tool for linguistic analysis through corpus comparison.* Doctorate Thesis. Lancaster University.

Rayson, P. (2009). *Significance and Effect Calculator (for comparing 2 corpora)* [excel file]. Retrieved July 4, 2016, from http://ucrel.lancs.ac.uk/people/paul/SigEff.xlsx

Red Tractor Assurance. (2014). *Red Tractor Poultry Scheme – Broilers and Poussin Standards 2014.* Retrieved October 13, 2014, from http://assurance.redtractor.org.uk/contentfiles/Farmers-5616.pdf

Regan, T. (1983). *The Case for Animal Rights.* University of California.

Regan, T. (2001). *Defending Animal Rights.* University of Illinois Press.

Regan, T. (2003). *Animal Rights, Human Wrongs.* Rowman & Littlefield.

Robbins, J. A., Franks, B., Weary, D. M., & von Keyserlingk, M. A. G. (2016). Awareness of ag-gag laws erodes trust in farmers and increases support for animal welfare regulations. *Food Policy,* 61, 121–125.

Roe, E., & Murdoch, J. (2006). UK Market for Animal welfare-friendly Products: Market Structure, Survey of Available Products and Quality Assurance Schemes. *Welfare Quality Reports no. 3.* Cardiff University.

Rogers, R. A. (2008). Beasts, Burgers, and Hummers: Meat and the Crisis of Masculinity in Contemporary Television Advertisements. *Environmental Communication,* 2(3), 281–301.

RSPCA Assured. (2015, June 30). *RSPCA Assured is the new name for Freedom Food.* Retrieved July 26, 2016, from https://www.rspcaassured.org.uk/news/rspca-assured-is-the-new-name-for-freedom-food/

RSPCA. (2005). *The case against cages. Evidence in favour of alternative systems for laying hens.* Retrieved November 3, 2016, from https://www.rspca.org.uk/ImageLocator/LocateAsset?asset=document&assetId=1232712906556&mode=prd

RSPCA. (2006). *Everyone's A Winner: How rearing chickens to higher welfare standards can benefit the chicken, producer, retailer and consumer.* Retrieved September 14, 2013, from http://www.rspca.org.uk/servlet/Satellite?pagename=RSPCA/RSPCARedirect&pg=FarmAnimalsReportsandResources

RSPCA. (2014). *Laying hens – farming (egg production).* Retrieved September 14, 2013, from http://www.rspca.org.uk/adviceandwelfare/farm/layinghens/farming

Salkeld, L. (2013, September 19). A birdbrained idea? Outrage as academics are handed £2m to study how humans interact with chickens. *The Daily Mail.* Retrieved September 23, 2014, from https://www.dailymail.co.uk/sciencetech/article-2425213/Outrage-academics-handed-2m-study-humans-interact-CHICKENS.html

Scarry, E. (1985). *The Body in Pain: The Making and Unmaking of the World.* Oxford University Press.

Schaffer, D. (1995). Shocking Secrets Revealed! The Language of Tabloid Headlines. *ETC: A Review of General Semantics,* 52(1), 27–46.

Schrijvers, J. (1999). Fighters, Victims and Survivors: Constructions of Ethnicity, Gender and Refugeeness among Tamils in Sri Lanka. *Journal of Refugee Studies,* 12(3), 307–333.

Seale, C., Boden, S., Williams, S., Lowe, P., & Steinberg, D. (2007). Media Constructions of Sleep and Sleep Disorders: A Study of UK National Newspapers. *Social Science & Medicine,* 65(3), 418–430.

Shelton, J. A. (2007). Beastly Spectacles in the Ancient Mediterranean World. In L. Kalof (Ed.), *A Cultural History of Animals in Antiquity* (pp. 97–126). Berg.

Shields, S. J., & Raj, A. B. M. (2010). A critical review of electrical water-bath stun systems for poultry slaughter and recent developments in alternative technologies. *Journal of Applied Animal Welfare Science,* 13, 281-299.

Singer, P. (1975). *Animal Liberation: A New Ethics for Our Treatment of Animals.* Avon.

Singer, P. (1990). *Animal Liberation* (2nd edition). New York Review.

Singer, P., & Mason, J. (2006). *The Way We Eat: Why Our Food Choices Matter.* Rodale Books.

Socha, K., & Mitchell, L. (2014). Critical Animal Studies as an Interdisciplinary Field: A Holistic Approach to Confronting Oppression. *Counterpoints,* 448, 110-132.

Soil Association. (2016). *Poultry & eggs.* Retrieved June 26, 2019, from https://www.soilassociation.org/organic-living/why-organic/better-for-animals/poultry-chickens/

Sparks, C. (2000). Introduction. The Panic over Tabloid News. In C. Sparks, & J. Tulloch (Eds.), *Tabloid tales: global debates over media standards* (pp. 1–40). Rowman & Littlefield.

Sparks, C., & Tulloch, J. (2000). *Tabloid tales: global debates over media standards.* Rowman & Littlefield.

Spiegel M. (1988). *The Dreaded Comparison.* New Society Publishers.

Spira, H., & Singer, P. (2006). Ten points for activists. In P. Singer, *In Defense of Animals: The Second Wave* (pp. 214–224). Blackwell Publishing.

Steffensen, S. V., & Fill, A. (2014). Ecolinguistics: the state of the art and future horizons. *Language Sciences,* 41, Part A(0), 6–25.

Steinfeld, H., Gerber, P., Wassenaar, T., Castel, V., Rosales, M., & de Haan, C. (2006). *Livestock's Long Shadow: Environmental Issues and Options.* Food and Agriculture Organization of the United Nations.

Steuter, E., & Wills, D. (2008). *At War with Metaphor: Media, Propaganda, and Racism in the War on Terror.* Rowman & Littlefield Publishers.

Stevenson, P. (2012). *European Union Legislation on the Welfare of Farm animals.* Compassion in World Farming. Retrieved June 26, 2019, from https://www.ciwf.org.uk/media/3818623/eu-law-on-the-welfare-of-farm-animals.pdf

Stewart, K., & Cole, M. (2015). The Creation of a Killer Species: Cultural Rupture in Representations of "Urban Foxes" in UK Newspapers. In N. Almiron, M. Cole, & C. P. Freeman (Eds.), *Critical Animal and Media Studies: Communication for Nonhuman Animal Advocacy* (pp. 124–137). Routledge.

Stibbe, A. (2001). Language, Power and the Social Construction of Animals. *Society and Animals,* 9(2), 145–161.

Stibbe, A. (2003). As Charming as a Pig: The Discursive Construction of the Relationship between Pigs and Humans. *Society and Animals,* 11(4), 375–392.

Stibbe, A. (2012a). *Animals Erased. Discourse, Ecology, and Reconnection with the Natural World.* Wesleyan Press.

Stibbe, A. (2012b). Today we live without them: the erasure of animals and plants in the language of ecosystem assessment. *ECOS,* 33(1), 47–53.

Stibbe, A. (2014). An Ecolinguistic Approach to Critical Discourse Studies. *Critical Discourse Studies*, 11(1), 117–128.

Stibbe, A. (2015). *Ecolinguistics: Language, Ecology and the Stories We Live By.* Routledge.

Stibbe, A. (2018). Positive Discourse Analysis. In A. Fill, & H. Penz (Eds.), *The Routledge Handbook of Ecolinguistics* (pp. 165–178). Routledge.

Still, J. (2015). *Derrida and Other Animals: The Boundaries of the Human.* Edinburgh University Press.

Still, J. (2019). Thoughts from France on the Animal-Human. Borderline: Derrida and Animal Rights Philosophers. In I. Goh (Ed.), *French Thought and Literary Theory in the UK* (pp. 49–65). Routledge.

Stinckens, A., Vereijken, A., Ons, E., Konings, P., Van As, P., Cuppens, H., & Cassiman, J. J. (2015). Art meets science: The Cosmopolitan Chicken Research Project. *Facts, views & vision in ObGyn*, 7(3), 163–172.

Stubbs, M. (1983). *Discourse analysis.* Oxford: Blackwell.

Sykes, N. (2012). A social perspective on the introduction of exotic animals: the case of the chicken. *World Archaeology*, 44(1), 158–169.

Sztybel, D. (2006). Can the Treatment of Animals Be Compared to the Holocaust? *Ethics and the Environment*, 11(1), 97-132.

Taylor, A., & Loopstra, R. (2016). *Too poor to eat? Food insecurity in the UK.* Food Foundation.

Taylor, N. (2016) Suffering is not enough: Media depictions of violence to other animals and social change. In N. Almiron, M. Cole, & C. P. Freeman (Eds.), *Critical Animal and Media Studies: Communication for Nonhuman Animal Advocacy* (pp. 42–55). Routledge.

Taylor, N., & Fraser, H. (2017). Slaughterhouses: The Language of Life, the Discourse of Death. In J. Maher, H. Pierpoint, & P. Beirne (Eds.), *International Handbook on Animal Abuse Studies* (pp. 179–199). Palgrave Macmillan.

Taylor, N., & Twine, R. (2014). Introduction: locating the 'critical' in critical animal studies. In N. Taylor, & R. Twine (Eds.), *The rise of critical animal studies: From the margins to the centre* (pp. 1–17). Routledge.

The Daily Telegraph (2014). *Telegraph style book: AA.* Retrieved July 26, 2014, from https://www.telegraph.co.uk/style-book/a/

The Guardian (2014). *Guardian and Observer style guide: A.* Retrieved July 26, 2014, from https://www.theguardian.com/guardian-observer-style-guide-a

The Happy Eggco. (2017a). *Our happy story.* Retrieved July 26, 2017, from http://thehappyegg.co.uk/happy-hens/hen-welfare-on-our-farms/

The Happy Eggco. (2017b). *Egg facts.* Retrieved October 14, 2017, from http://thehappyegg.co.uk/egg-facts/

The Media Briefing. (2017). *How old are you again? UK newspaper age demographics in 4 charts.* Retrieved October 13, 2018, from https://www.themediabriefing.com/analysis/how-old-are-you-again-uk-newspaper-age-demographics-in-4-charts/

The Publishers Audience Measurement Company. (2018). *Mail monthly all adults.* Retrieved October 4, 2018, from https://pamco.co.uk/pamco-data/latest-results

Tiplady, C. M., Walsh, D. A. B., & Phillips, C. J. C. (2012). Public response to media coverage of animal cruelty. *Journal of Agricultural and Environmental Ethics*, 26(4), 869–885.

Tonsor, G., & Olynk, N. (2011). Impacts of Animal Well-Being and Welfare Media on Meat Demand. *Journal of Agricultural Economics*, 62(1), 59–72.

Twine, R. (2010). Intersectional disgust? Animals and (eco)feminism. *Feminism & Psychology*, 20(3), 397–406.

Twine, R. (2012). Revealing the 'Animal-Industrial Complex' – A Concept & Method for Critical Animal Studies? *Journal for Critical Animal Studies*, 10(1), 12–39.

U.S. Environmental Protection Agency. (2005). *Detecting and mitigating the environmental impact of fecal pathogens originating from confined animal feeding operations: review*. Retrieved November 29, 2014, from http://nepis.epa.gov/Adobe/PDF/P10089B1.pdf

UN Environment. (2018, September 26). *Tackling the world's most urgent problem: meat*. Retrieved May 7, 2019, from https://www.unenvironment.org/news-and-stories/story/tackling-worlds-most-urgent-problem-meat

Uribe, R., & Gunter, B. (2004). The tabloidization of British tabloids. *European Journal of Communication*, 19(3), 387–402.

Valenti, J. (2014, August 4). 'Those women are more oppressed' is a terrible argument against feminism. *The Guardian*. Retrieved November 27, 2017, from https://www.theguardian.com/commentisfree/2014/aug/04/international-women-oppression-feminism

van Dijk, T. A. (1993). Principles of Critical Discourse Analysis. *Discourse & Society*, 4(2), 249–283.

van Dijk, T. A. (2006). Ideology and discourse analysis. *Journal of Political Ideologies*, 11(2), 115–140.

van Dijk, T. A. (2015). Critical discourse analysis. In D. Tannen, H. E. Hamilton, & D. Schiffrin (Eds.), *The Handbook of Discourse Analysis* (2nd edition, pp. 466–485). John Wiley & Sons.

van Leeuwen, T. (2006). Critical Discourse Analysis. In K. Brown (Ed.), *Encyclopedia of Language and Linguistics* (2nd edition, Vol 2, pp. 290–294). Elsevier.

Varner, G. E. J. (1994). In defense of the vegan ideal: Rhetoric and bias in the nutrition literature. *Journal of Agricultural Environmental Ethics*, 7(1), 29–40.

Vecerek, V., Grbalova, S., Voslarova, E., Janackova, B., & Malena, M. (2006). Effects of travel distance and the season of the year on death rates of broilers transported to poultry processing plants. *Poultry Science*, 85(11), 1881–1884.

Vegan Feminista. (2013, January 26). *Sexism in the Animal Rights Movement: LUSH*. Retrieved April 14, 2015, from https://veganfeminista.wordpress.com/2013/01/26/sexism-in-the-animal-rights-movement-lush/

Vegan Society. (2020). *Veganism in the UK*. Retrieved February 3, 2020, from https://www.vegansociety.com/news/media/statistics

Warren, R. (2017, March 9). Don't Bring Saudi Women Into Your (Misguided) Argument Against Feminism. *Teen Vogue*. Retrieved November 27, 2017, from https://www.teenvogue.com/story/argument-against-feminism-saudi-women-rights

WATTAgNet. (2018). *Poultry consumption to surpass beef, pork by 2050.* Retrieved December 17, 2018, from https://www.wattagnet.com/articles/32291-poultry-consumption-to-surpass-beef-pork-by-2050?v=preview

Weitzenbürger, D., Vits, A., Hamman, H., & Distl, O. (2005). Effect of furnished small group housing systems and furnished cages on mortality and causes of death in two layer strains. *British Poultry Science,* 46(5), 553–559.

WHO. (2017, November 7). *Stop using antibiotics in healthy animals to prevent the spread of antibiotic resistance.* Retrieved October 20, 2017, from https://www.who.int/news-room/detail/07-11-2017-stop-using-antibiotics-in-healthy-animals-to-prevent-the-spread-of-antibiotic-resistance

WHO. (2020a, January 20). *Cumulative number of confirmed human cases for avian influenza A(H5N1) reported to WHO, 2003–2020).* Retrieved April 8, 2020, from https://www.who.int/influenza/human_animal_interface/2020_01_20_tableH5N1.pdf?ua=1

WHO. (2020b, February 28). *Influenza at the human-animal interface. Summary and assessment, from 21 January to 28 February 2020.* Retrieved June 18, 2020 from https://www.who.int/influenza/human_animal_interface/Influenza_Summary_IRA_HA_interface_28_02_2020.pdf?ua=1

Windhorst, H. W. (2014). *Global Egg Production Dynamics - Past, Present and Future of a Remarkable Success Story.* International Egg Commission Special Economic Report September 2014. Retrieved January 22, 2020, from https://www.internationalegg.com/wp-content/uploads/2015/08/Economics-Report-StatsReportSept14_web.pdf

Wodak, R., & Meyer, M. (2009). Critical Discourse Analysis: History, Agenda, Theory, and Methodology. In R. Wodak, & M. Meyer (Eds.), *Methods for Critical Discourse Analysis* (pp. 1–33). Sage.

World Resources Institute. (2016). *Protein scorecard.* Retrieved May 7, 2019, from https://www.wri.org/resources/data-visualizations/protein-scorecard

Wrenn, C.L. (2013a). The role of professionalization regarding female exploitation in the Nonhuman Animal rights movement. *Journal of Gender Studies,* 24(2), 113–146.

Wrenn, C.L. (2013b, May 23). LUSH Cosmetics: Kind to Animals, Not to Women. *Feminspire.* Retrieved April 14, 2015, from http://feminspire.com/lush-cosmetics-kind-to-animals-not-to-women/

Yuval-Davis, N. (2006). Intersectionality and Feminist Politics. *European Journal of Women's Studies,* 13(3), 193–209.

Appendix F

Listing of the newspaper texts quoted by source

(Appendices A-E are provided online at https://vernonpress.com/book/1075)

The Guardian

G1. "Poultry: Bird lives but only just — The chicken's lot is not a happy one but neither is that of the turkey" by Colin Spencer, *The Guardian*, 2/12/1989.

G2. "Ranging the fair against the fowl — Colin Spencer contrasts chicken behaviour in the wild with commercial rearing and argues that the more natural the life cycle, the more delicious the flavour" by Colin Spencer, *The Guardian*, 5/5/1990.

G3. "Chicken breeder claims fowl play" by Erlend Clouston, *The Guardian*, 10/5/1990.

G4. "Range of possibilities — New EC regulations demand more accurate labelling of how chickens are reared" by Colin Spencer, *The Guardian*, 6/7/1991.

G5. "The Meat Factory: Progress halves chickens' lifespan — Intensively-reared broilers are now ready for slaughter after 42 days. James Erlichman meets a farmer distressed by the demands of his trade" by James Erlichman, *The Guardian*, 15/10/1991.

G6. "The McFact Factor; Peel the layers of jargon off the burger masters' publicity, says James Erlichman, and the truth isn't quite so clear" by James Erlichman, *The Guardian*, 31/7/1993.

G7. "Pasture to the plate: a vision of the welfare plate; The RSPCA's new Freedom Food labelling scheme aims to raise awareness of animal welfare issues in food production, but will shoppers buy it? Emily Bell reports on a new 'kite mark' for meat" by Emily Bell, *The Guardian*, 10/7/1994.

G8. "Pasture to the plate: a recipe for indigestion; The privations of the war years convinced governments of the need for a diet rich in protein. As a result, British agriculture moved towards intensive farming, a policy Audrey Eyton believes was doubly flawed" by Audrey Eyton, *The Guardian*, 10/7/1994.

G9. "Pasture to the plate: man is the true beast of the field; We stuff our chickens into filthy, overcrowded cages and condemn our cows to a lifetime of unnatural pregnancies, yet we will pay to adopt a whale and protest at the killing of baby seals. Now a fast growing number of us are crying out for change, says Derek Cooper" by Derek Cooper, *The Guardian*, 10/7/1994.

G10. "Veal in its little boxes" (no author cited), *The Guardian*, 13/1/1995.

G11. "Food chains veal meat again" by Joanna Blythman, *The Guardian*, 18/11/1995.

G12. "Feather your nest: Forget Chicken Run: if you're after real star quality in your chooks, you just have to go organic, says Matthew Fort. Recipes by Jeremy Lee" by Matthew Fort; Recipes by Jeremy Lee, *The Guardian*, 15/7/2000.

G13. "Naked ambition: Scientist develops featherless chicken" by Rebecca Allison, *The Guardian*, 21/5/2002.

G14. "The limits of human dominion: Our treatment of animals shows us not at our most civilised or compassionate, but at our most squeamish" by Alison Hills, *The Guardian*, 30/3/2005.

G15. "Ravages of bird flu pluck heart from rural life" by Jonathan Watts, *The Guardian*, 16/5/2005.

G16. "My coop runneth over: Chickens make supreme pets, will thrive in town or country and pay their keep, too. But where to start? Poultry lover Matthew Rice reveals all" by Matthew Rice, *The Guardian*, 8/10/2005.

G17. "Europe on high alert over avian flu: Turkey begins culling as 2,000 birds die at one farm: Romania seals off villages while tests continue" by Luke Harding, *The Guardian*, 10/10/2005.

G18. "Avian flu: As the danger moves closer" (no author cited), *The Guardian*, 11/1/2006.

G19. "Bird flu in UK more likely as H5N1 hits France: Minister warns public and farmers to be vigilant: New restrictions will hit organic producers" by James Meikle, *The Guardian*, 20/2/2006.

G20. "Bird flu: Cases worldwide: Sales fall as the culls begin" by Randeep Ramesh, Barbara McMahon and James Meikle, *The Guardian*, 21/2/2006.

G21. "Goodbye Lenin, Sputnik and Mog: It was the chickens more than anything that rooted Emily Barr and her family to their new life in the French countryside — until bird flu came too close to home" by Emily Barr, *The Guardian*, 15/4/2006.

G22. "Animal pain counts, animal life doesn't" by Julian Baggini, *The Guardian*, 2/5/2006.

G23. "So who's really to blame for bird flu?: According to experts, wild birds are spreading the deadly H5N1 virus that's wiping out poultry worldwide. But are they really to blame? Or is the disease not only a direct result of intensive farming — but actually being spread by the industry? Joanna Blythman reports" by Joanna Blythman, *The Guardian*, 7/6/2006.

G24. "Assault and battery: Mark Cocker on the complex moral journey that our food makes: Jungle Capitalists: A Story of Globalisation, Greed and Revolution by Peter Chapman 220pp, Canongate, £10.99 Planet Chicken: The Shameful Story of the Bird on Your Plate by Hattie Ellis 320pp, Sceptre, £14.99" by Mark Cocker, *The Guardian*, 7/7/2007.

G25. "Last nights TV: From slaughtered piglets to ailing elephants, it was all horror on the animal front last night" by Sam Wollaston, *The Guardian*, 8/1/2008.

G26. "Poultry is not a class issue: The public don't want to be patronised by the sweeping assertion that they can't afford to care" by Hugh Fearnley-Whittingstall, *The Guardian*, 19/1/2008.

G27. "Paying the price for cheap chicken" by Jeremy Blackburn, *The Guardian*, 19/1/2008.

G28. "From battery farm to family pet: The lifespan of an egg-laying battery chicken is 72 weeks, but a rescued 'ex-bat' can live for up to 10 years. Bibi van der Zee meets the activists who rehouse 'spent' birds" by Bibi van der Zee, *The Guardian*, 7/8/2008.

G29. "Free-range cracks egg market as caged sales fall: More hens get chance for open air existence: High-profile campaigns change public attitudes" by Robert Booth, *The Guardian*, 16/5/2009.

G30. "China bird flu scare: 'My family and I don't dare to eat anything these day'" by Nicola Davison, *The Guardian*, 11/4/2013.

G31. "Organic sales slump for first time: Bread, meat and chilled meals hit hardest Sector hopes to reverse downward trend in 2010" by Rebecca Smithers, *The Guardian*, 12/4/2010.

G32. "Why two out of three supermarket chickens could still make us sick: Entrails blocking drains, meat on the floor, water left unchanged. The Guardian investigates industry still plagued by food poisoning bug" by Felicity Lawrence, Andrew Wasley and Radu Ciorniciuc, *The Guardian*, 24/7/2014.

G33. "Smear stories keep Animal Aid in business" by Greg Wood, *The Guardian*, 22/9/2014.

G34. "If you must eat meat, save it for Christmas; From chickens pumped with antibiotics to the environmental devastation caused by production, we need to realise we are not fed with happy farm animals" by George Monbiot, *The Guardian*, 16/12/2014.

G35. "The Billion Dollar Chicken Shop review — behind the scenes at KFC; The fast food company lets in the cameras to the chicken sheds, head office and even the customer loos. But it is left up to viewers to draw their own conclusions" by Sam Wollaston, *The Guardian*, 19/3/2015.

G36. "Faeces, bacteria, toxins: welcome to the chicken farm; Whether it's welfare standards, environmental impact or the emerging threat to human health, we've got to change our insatiable greed for this meat" by George Monbiot, *The Guardian*, 24/5/2015.

G37. "The truth about the poultry industry" by Andrew Large, *The Guardian*, 24/5/2015.

G38. "It's time to wean ourselves off the fairytale version of farming; Children's tales bear no resemblance to the cruelty of most modern farms, yet this image enables us to turn a blind eye to animal welfare and is exploited by the industry for profit — as Kerrygold's recent Guardian advertorial shows" by George Monbiot, *The Guardian*, 29/5/2015.

G39. "Is it OK to eat dogs? Before you sign the petition against the dog meat festival in China, consider that eating man's best friend is a matter of cultural tastes, not moral worth" by Julian Baggini, *The Guardian*, 23/6/2015.

G40. "Will the worst bird flu outbreak in US history finally make us reconsider factory farming chicken? The outbreak has required that farmers resort to fire-extinguisher foam to kill off infected flocks. Can commercial farms protect themselves, or is US chicken farming fundamentally unsustainable?" by Laura Entis, *The Guardian*, 6/8/2015.

G41. "Industrial farming is one of the worst crimes in history; The fate of industrially farmed animals is one of the most pressing ethical questions of our time. Tens of billions of sentient beings, each with complex sensations and emotions, live and die on a production line" by Yuval Noah Harari, *The Guardian*, 25/9/2015.

G42. "How to choose the perfect cut for a great roast; The best parts of an animal to use for a roast dinner will depend on the dish you want to cook, your mood, and budget" by Phil Daoust, *The Guardian*, 21/10/2015.

G43. "Fear, hunger and dirt: Lithuanian migrants on life as chicken catchers; Laurynas Kelpsa and two fellow migrant workers who are suing the 'worst UK gangmaster ever' describe working for UK-based firm DJ Houghton" by Felicity Laurence, *The Guardian*, 11/8/2015.

G44. "UK chicken farming puts workers and food safety at risk; A climate of fear and often appalling conditions grip workers in the UK's chicken abattoirs and processing plants" by Andrew Wasley, *The Guardian*, 22/12/2015.

G45. "Why the egg industry is scrambling to set hens free; Governments, activists and big brands like McDonald's and Nestle are putting increased pressure on egg producers to raise their hens more sustainably" by Marc Gunther, *The Guardian*, 28/12/2015.

G46. "Government planning to repeal animal welfare codes; Poultry industry to oversee chicken-farming standards as ministers move to create industry-led deregulation" by Rowena Mason, *The Guardian*, 26/3/2016.

G47. "We're stuffing ourselves with battery chicken. And it's stuffing the souls of the workers, too; The poultry industry is set to self-regulate, which obviously won't work. We should just eat a bit less chicken — and worry more about the conditions in which it's produced" by Michele Hanson, *The Guardian*, 29/3/2016.

G48. "Factory farming divestment: what you need to know; After the success of campaigns to get investors to divest from fossil fuel companies, factory farming is the next target" by Tom Levitt, *The Guardian*, 5/4/2016.

G49. "Outraged by the new 'free-range' egg definition? Then stop eating eggs; 'Free-range' is a feel-good term that businesses use to make consumers feel kind. In reality, every single egg brand is doing bad things to hens" by Jenna Sten, *The Guardian*, 6/4/2016.

G50. "Ministers abandon plan to scrap farm animal welfare codes; Defra confirms U-turn after outcry over move to repeal legislation and put industry in charge of guidance on chicken farming" by Rowena Mason, *The Guardian*, 7/4/2016.

G51. "The Guardian view on antibiotic resistance: a clear and present danger; The spread of intensive farming in the developing world means were are picking a fight with evolution. This is one we are bound to lose" (editorial), *The Guardian*, 11/4/2016.

G52. "From field to fork: the six stages of wasting food; Americans chuck out two tonnes of food a second — be it at the farm for being 'ugly' or at the table because we're too finicky" by Suzanne Goldenberg *The Guardian*, 14/7/2016.

G53. "I've converted to veganism to reduce my impacts on the living world; Nothing hits the planet as hard as rearing animals. Caring for it means cutting out meat, dairy and eggs" by George Monbiot, *The Guardian*, 9/8/2016.

Daily Mirror & *Sunday Mirror*

M1. "So you think 'free-range' hens spend their days just clucking happily round a field? This is the reality...; Consumer check; Investigation into treatment of free-range hens" by Fiona Wingett and Shiraz Lalani, *Sunday Mirror*, 19/10/1997.

M2. "Is cloning an abuse of nature?" by Larry Moran and Aoife Ni Fhearghail, *Sunday Mirror*, 1/11/1998.

M3. "It's one hen of a storm" (no author cited), *Daily Mirror*, 4/2/1999.

M4. "Dear Michelle: your letters" by Michelle Rower, *Sunday Mirror*, 16/4/2000.

M5. "Bird flu battlers" (no author cited), *Daily Mirror*, 26/1/2004.

M6. "Reader's letter" by Richard Mountford, *Daily Mirror*, 31/7/2005.

M7. "Bird flu: don't get in a flap" by Stephen White, *Daily Mirror*, 19/10/2005.

M8. "Birds killed in flu tests" (no author cited), *Daily Mirror*, 26/11/2005.

M9. "The Great Eggscape; It's no yolk as 7,000 chickens cross the road to go on run after lorry crashes" by Declan Ferry, *Daily Mirror*, 16/12/2005.

M10. "6,000 chickens to be gassed; Fowl slaughter to test bird flu outbreak plans" by Pat Flanaga, *Daily Mirror*, 16/5/2006.

M11. "Shell shock for drivers" by Jenna Sloan, *Daily Mirror*, 6/10/2006.

M12. "Matt fury at fowl play; Irish soccer madness soccer star slams chicken farm plan" by Declan Ferry, *Daily Mirror*, 20/2/2007.

M13. "Barking; This man slaughtered up to 10,000 greyhounds.. Yesterday he was fined just 20p for each one that he killed" by Lucy Thornton, *Daily Mirror*, 17/3/2007.

M14. "Full horror live on a TV show; Exclusive: Jamie's chicken crusade" by Nicola Methven, *Daily Mirror*, 7/1/2008.

M15. "We Love Telly: We Love It! - Henpecked Hero Hugh Hugh's Chicken Run C4, 9pm" by Jane Simon, *Daily Mirror*, 7/1/2008.

M16. "Chicks out of cluck" by Kevin O'Sullivan, *Sunday Mirror*, 13/1/2008.

M17. "Shelley vision: wit of the week" by Jim Shelley, *Daily Mirror*, 22/1/2008.

M18. "They're bettery hens; 600 birds saved from cage hell" by Ron Moore, *Daily Mirror*, 30/6/2008.

M19. "Chicken winner; Exclusive TV Jamie's joy at battery U-turn" by Alun Palmer, *Daily Mirror*, 6/8/2008.

M20. "Nice cardig-hen" (no author cited), *Daily Mirror*, 23/9/2008.

M21. "We are clucked; Farmers are 'not prepared' for EU ban on all battery egg production" by Claire Brennan, *Daily Mirror*, 21/1/2009.

M22. "12,000 chickens roasted; Blaze 'no big deal' insists farmer" by Naomi McElroy, *Daily Mirror*, 25/3/2011.

M23. "We love TV; Pick of the day" by Jane Simon, *Daily Mirror*, 12/6/2012.

M24. "Call the RSPCA... the stag do's become a hen party; Two birds die in boozy lads' prank" by Euan Stretch, *Daily Mirror*, 30/6/2012.

M25. "They're stuffed" by Paul Routledge, *Daily Mirror*, 24/8/2012.

M26. "Crammed together in huge windowless sheds, covered in scabs and too weak to stand.. the unacceptable face of chicken farming in UK; horror of factory farm" by Deirdre O'Brien, *Sunday Mirror*, 23/9/2012.

M27. "185,000 hens destroyed; *Salmonella* bug hits top egg producer" (no author cited), *Daily Mirror*, 9/11/2012.

M28. "The 'good' foods that can be bad for you..; Think you know which foods are healthy? Think again, they could be false friends" by Marina Gask, *Daily Mirror*, 16/4/2013.

M29. "I take in hens who are down on their cluck; Caring Jane has saved 400,000 battery chickens" by Warren Manger, *Daily Mirror*, 28/10/2013.

M30. "Plucky hen's escape plan is fowled up; Runaway" by Martin Fricker, *Daily Mirror*, 24/4/2013.

M31. "Prince's hens killed by fox" (no author cited), *Daily Mirror*, 8/5/2014.

M32. "You think free-range hens live like this... but they are more likely to live like this" by Gethin Chamberlain, *Sunday Mirror*, 27/3/2016.

M33. "Clucky teenager takes on Tesco" (no author cited), *Daily Mirror*, 20/4/2016.

M34. "Shop cracks in eggs fight; City desk" by Graham Hiscott, *Daily Mirror*, 26/6/2016.

The Daily Telegraph

T1. "A fowl's life is not a fair one" by James Gladstone, *The Daily Telegraph*, 16/12/1985.

T2. "400 million eggs to be destroyed in next 4 weeks" by Godfrey Brown, *The Daily Telegraph*, 20/12/1988.

T3. "Whatever Labour says, it can't pretend a ban is moral The Thursday Column" by Boris Johnson, *The Daily Telegraph*, 18/1/2001.

T4. "Crusader at the farm gate Joyce D'Silva's call for more compassionate farming has never resonated more strongly" by Tamasin Day-Lewis, *The Daily Telegraph*, 2/6/2001.

T5. "Today the Commons votes on the future of 'rural man'" by Allan Fowke, *The Daily Telegraph*, 18/3/2002.

T6. "Organic food is no safer than the ordinary cheaper kind Despite the scare tactics of the Green lobby, the public should trust the safety standards of conventional farming, says Oliver Walston" by Oliver Walston, *The Daily Telegraph*, 28/3/2002.

T7. "Make sure it's reared here Thai chicken can masquerade as British, warns Rose Prince" by Rose Prince, *The Daily Telegraph*, 31/1/2004.

T8. "With the publication of his new book, The River Cottage Meat Book, Hugh Fearnley-Whittingstall is on a mission — to educate consumers that it is their moral responsibility to know under what conditions their food is reared and slaughtered. Sam Leith shares an ethical meal with him" by Sam Leith, *The Daily Telegraph*, 1/5/2004.

T9. "I hope Captain Birds Eye isn't telling porkies" by Sam Leith, *The Daily Telegraph*, 26/11/2004.

T10. "Savvy Shopper How to buy good food with peace of mind and a clear conscience. This week: eggs" By Rose Prince, *The Daily Telegraph*, 1/1/2005.

T11. "Claws out for good taste Lewis Jones chews his way through the glut of anecdotes in this foodie's polemic on the food industry" by Lewis Jones, *The Daily Telegraph*, 7/5/2005.

T12. "My year with the animal rights extremists. This week, four activists were jailed for a string of offences, including grave-robbery. David Modell, who has been filming them and their supporters, exposes their extraordinary lifestyle" by Elizabeth Grice, *The Daily Telegraph*, 13/5/2006.

T13. "Worried shoppers may turn to battery produce" by David Derbyshire, *The Daily Telegraph*, 8/4/2006.

T14. "And lo! he looked on his works and he said, 'Bootiful'" by Sam Leith, *The Daily Telegraph*, 5/2/2007.

T15. "Bird flu outbreak threatens overdue price rise and may tip producers over the edge" by Harry Wallop, *The Daily Telegraph*, 6/2/2007.

T16. "A local crop for local people Kate Robinson visits a village on the verge of self-sufficiency" by Kate Robinson, *The Daily Telegraph*, 31/3/2007.

T17. "Reality of cheap food is not for the chicken-hearted" by Jan Moir, *The Daily Telegraph*, 30/1/2008.

T18. "At their peck and call Nicholas Roe on the self-sacrificing work of the birdwoman of Henfield" by Nicholas Roe, *The Daily Telegraph*, 1/3/2008.

T19. "The End of Food: the Coming Crisis in the World Food Industry by Paul Roberts; 390pp, Bloomsbury; Hungry City: How Food Shapes Our Lives; by Carolyn Steel; 383pp Chatto & Windus; There's no such thing as a cheap lunch, either; Paul Levy finds plenty to relish in two accounts of how the modern world struggles to feed itself" by Paul Levy, *The Daily Telegraph*, 26/7/2008.

T20. "When the writer Richard Benson invited the fashion photographer and unashamed urbanite Kevin Foord to take pictures; for a farming project, he risked an embarrassing culture clash; What resulted was an unexpectedly thought-provoking; perspective on British agriculture" by Richard Benson, *The Daily Telegraph*, 11/10/2008.

T21. "Tesco will come clean on labelling of meat" by Harry Wallop, *The Daily Telegraph*, 22/9/2009.

T22. "Ridley Scott loses battle in France over chicken-farming neighbours" by Henry Samuel, *The Daily Telegraph*, 15/12/2009.

T23. "I love my pigs, but I also love roast pork; When it comes to food, we've become a nation of dreadful hypocrites, says Charlie Brooks" by Charlie Brooks, *The Daily Telegraph*, 12/2/2010.

T24. "Facing the truth about food; John-Paul Flintoff meets the author of a book which turned Natalie Portman vegan" by John-Paul Flintoff, *The Daily Telegraph*, 6/3/2010.

T25. "Just my cluck; Cassandra Jardine thought keeping hens at home would be as easy as cracking on egg. If Liz Hurley and Jeremy Clarkson can do it, how hard can it really be?" by Cassandra Jardine, *The Daily Telegraph*, 3/4/2010.

T26. "My name is Clive, and I used to be an organoholic... but I'm all right now; After years of chemical-free eating, Clive Aslet admits that he has given up organic produce in favour of cheaper, local and even (whisper it) intensively reared food" by Clive Aslet, *The Daily Telegraph*, 20/5/2010.

T27. "C'est la folie; There are times when you should look a gift chicken in the beak" by Michael Wright, *The Daily Telegraph*, 28/8/2010.

T28. "Professor Sir Colin Spedding; Scientist who anticipated many of the current trends in farming and became an authority on animal welfare" (no author cited), *The Daily Telegraph*, 22/2/2013.

T29. "Food labels that tell you nothing; Savy supermarket shopper They sound reassuring but some of the claims are empty, says Rosie Murray-West" by Rosie Murray-West, *The Daily Telegraph*, 9/3/2013.

T30. "Widen their circle of friends; When it comes to healthy young minds, a little bit of pet therapy goes a long way, finds Flora Watkins" by Flora Watkins, *The Daily Telegraph*, 14/3/2015.

Daily Mail & Mail on Sunday

MA1. "When beef comes second to video" by Jane Gisland, *Daily Mail*, 9/12/1983.

MA2. "Pecking order" by Dermot Purgavie, *Daily Mail*, 11/12/1984.

MA3. "Time to set the chickens free!" by I. Mullet, *Daily Mail*, 7/12/1988.

MA4. "The unpalatable truth about the food we eat" by Mark Holmes, *Daily Mail*, 18/5/1990.

MA5. "Fowl play" by Robert Haynes, *Daily Mail*, 29/5/1990.

MA6. "A cruel reprieve; Battery cages can stay because free-range hens suffer 'just the same'" (no author cited), *Daily Mail*, 25/7/1997.

MA7. "Free-range chickens and the hypocrisy of being vegetarian; As Marks & Spencer stop selling battery laid eggs" by James Erlichman, *Daily Mail*, 7/10/1997.

MA8. "Tossed into bin bags, the tiniest victims of Hong Kong flu panic. The cull of the chicks" (no author cited), *Daily Mail*, 30/12/1997.

MA9. "Nature's revenge: Our desire for cheap food has led us to accept farming techniques which treat our fellow creatures with utter contempt. But are we now all in danger of paying the ultimate price — being destroyed by a terrible plague which those methods have helped to create?" by Colin Tudge, *Daily Mail*, 28/8/1999.

MA10. "Who's to blame for this food crisis? You are" by Stewart Steven, *Mail on Sunday*, 31/10/1999.

MA11. "Chicks to the slaughter" by Glenda Cooper, *Daily Mail*, 15/3/2000.

MA12. "Cloned chickens on the menu" (no author cited), *Daily Mail*, 16/8/2001.

MA13. "Cockfights, battery farms and now crossbred bald mutants. Why are we so cruel to the poor chicken" by Michael Hanlon, *Daily Mail*, 22/5/2002.

MA14. "Hurrah for red meat!" by Roy Hattersley, *Daily Mail*, 10/7/2003.

MA15. "Chickens boiled alive" by Sean Poulter, *Daily Mail*, 13/8/2003.

MA16. "Piggies have feelings too, you know!" by Val Hennesy, *Daily Mail*, 23/1/2004.

MA17. "Britons are warned as bird flu death toll rises" (no author cited), *Mail on Sunday*, 25/1/2004.

MA18. "Fowl play" by Roderick Gilchrist, *Mail on Sunday*, 22/2/2004.

MA19. "The good life" by Rosie Boycott, *Daily Mail*, 28/3/2005.

MA20. "We all know the horrors of battery farming. Now a devastating report finally reveals just how poisoned our favourite food really is — and the terrifying consequences for our health…" by Michael Hanlon, *Daily Mail*, 16/8/2005.

MA21. "Have you ever tried to inject a chicken? It's no longer a question of if bird flu gets here but when. And we are still ill-prepared" by Richard Hannaford, *Daily Mail*, 14/2/2006.

MA22. "Birds of paradise; Are your lunch guests giving you the bird over your fowl roast? As Tom Parker Bowles reveals, only a happy chicken will do" by Tom Parker Bowles, *Mail on Sunday*, 30/4/2006.

MA23. "Hugh's burger bootcamp" by Bill Mouland, *Daily Mail*, 4/11/2006.

MA24. "Why organic chicken 'isn't as good for you and fails the taste test'" by Fiona Macrae, *Daily Mail*, 4/12/2006.

MA25. "Horrific price of food on the cheap" by Geoffrey Lean, *Daily Mail*, 5/2/2007.

MA26. "Nature's Revenge; Is bird flu the price we're paying for years of cruelty in the pursuit of cheap meat?" By Rosie Boycott, *Daily Mail*, 6/2/2007.

MA27. "Why your organic chicken really is worth all the extra; If you've ever been tempted by 'value' supermarket poultry, think again..." by Hattie Ellis and Ruth Doris, *Daily Mail*, 12/4/2007.

MA28. "What can Kate and Gerry be thinking?" by Allison Pearson, *Daily Mail*, 9/1/2008.

MA29. "Now Thornton joins the war on poison chicken" by Andrea McCullagh, *Daily Mail*, 22/1/2008.

MA30. "The curse of cheap food; Why pay good money to put your child through maths grinds if you're going to feed them 2.99 chicken?" by Tom Doorley, *Daily Mail*, 23/1/2008.

MA31. "Top chicks; As Tesco launches the £1.99 chicken, we road test five very different birds and ask: do you get what you pay for?" by Victoria Moore, *Daily Mail*, 7/2/2008.

MA32. "Tesco is a supermarket, not the guardian of our livers and morals" by Liz Jones, *Mail on Sunday*, 24/2/2008.

MA33. "We fed this crisis; Contaminated feed wasn't the cause of the pork fiasco, says top chef Richard Corrigan... It was our diet of cheap food' by Richard Corrigan, *Daily Mail*, 13/12/2008.

MA34. "The terrible cost of your cheap eggs" by Neil Tweedie, *Daily Mail*, 6/4/2016.

Appendix G
Listing of Compassion in World Farming texts quoted

Agscene

AG1. "Ban batteries in Britain", *Agscene*, 1983 (73), p. 2.

AG2. "Sainsbury's free-range egg", *Agscene*, 1983 (73), p. 3.

AG3. "Focus on broilers", *Agscene*, 1985 (79), p. 4.

AG4. "Priority: chicken or children?", *Agscene*, 1988 (91), p. 13.

AG5. "Poultry Multiply as Harvest Dwindle", *Agscene*, 1989 (95), p. 24,

AG6. "Cage-war intensifies", *Agscene*, 1990 (99), p. 18.

AG7. "The advent of the free-range broiler", *Agscene*, 1990 (99), p. 19.

AG8. "Poultry slaughter less suffering in sight?", *Agscene*, 1991 (105), p. 20.

AG9. "Kidding the Kids — the 'Eggsaggerated' story", *Agscene*, 1992 (107), p.18.

AG10. "Bellamy launches our go free-range roadshow", *Agscene*, 1993 (111), p. 14.

AG11. "Government turns blind eye to broiler misery", *Agscene*, 1998 (129), p. 13.

AG12. "30 years campaigning against battery cages", *Agscene*, 1999, 135, p. 8.

Farm Animal Voice

FAV1. "Major New Threat The "Enriched" Cage!", Farm Animal Voice, 2002 (148), p. 5.

FAV2. "Animal Tales", Farm Animal Voice, 2003 (149), p. 21.

FAV3. "Eye-catching publicity stunt kick-starts broiler campaign in the UK", Farm Animal Voice, 2003 (150), p. 3.

FAV4. "Chris Mullin introduces bill to ban 'enriched cages'", Farm Animal Voice, 2003 (150), p. 6.

FAV5. "Chicken Court Case", Farm Animal Voice, 2004 (153), p. 3.

FAV6. "Chickens without Antibiotics", Farm Animal Voice, 2004 (156), p. 6.

FAV7. "Broilers directive", Farm Animal Voice, 2005 (158), p. 6.

FAV8. "Hide and Seek", Farm Animal Voice, 2005 (160), p. 11.

FAV9. "Global Animal Welfare standards – Keeping up the Pressure", Farm Animal Voice, 2006 (161), p. 7.

FAV10. "Give Them Back The Sunshine!", Farm Animal Voice, 2006 (162), p. 7.

FAV11. "The Facts about Avian Influenza", Farm Animal Voice, 2006 (162), p. 8.

FAV12. "We must win this one!", Farm Animal Voice, 2007 (166), p. 6.

FAV13. "New EU law for chickens – but does it fail the animals?", Farm Animal Voice, 2007 (167), p. 7.

FAV14. "What a Difference a Week makes", Farm Animal Voice, 2008 (169), p. 9.

FAV15. "Chick, chick, chick, chicken…", Farm Animal Voice, 2008 (169), p. 6.

FAV16. "Cracking factory farming", Farm Animal Voice, 2008 (172), p. 20.

FAV17. "Pioneering farming for challenging times", Farm Animal Voice, 2010 (178), p. 17.

FAV18. "The campaigner Philip Lymbery", Farm Animal Voice, 2010 (179), p. 15.

FAV19. "The 2012 barren battery cage ban — a first step towards a world without factory farming?", Farm Animal Voice, 2010 (180), p. 9.

FAV20. "Egg-ceedingly good welfare", Farm Animal Voice, 2011 (181), p. 5.

FAV21. "Are we always what we eat?", Farm Animal Voice, 2011 (181) p. 13.

FAV22. "Defending europe's chickens", Farm Animal Voice, 2011 (183), p. 8.

FAV23. "Promise for chicken country", Farm Animal Voice, 2012 (184), p. 17.

FAV24. "Barren battery cages – illegal in Europe from 2012", 2012 (184), p. 12–13.

FAV25. "It's Time for Honest Food Labels", Farm Animal Voice, 2012 (185), p. 9.

FAV26. "The Power of Food Companies", Farm Animal Voice, 2012 (185), p. 19.

FAV27. "Land of free-range", Farm Animal Voice, 2013 (188), p. 20.

FAV28. "Jamie Oliver Helps Better Chicken Take Flight", Farm Animal Voice, 2014 (191), p. 15.

FAV29. "What a difference a year makes", Farm Animal Voice, 2015 (193), p. 5.

FAV30. "It's time to stop caging hens. Forever", Farm Animal Voice, 2015 (194), p. 8.

Listing of Animal Aid texts quoted

Outrage

OU1. "Chickens", Outrage, 1984 (35), p. 15.

OU2. "Profits from Misery", Outrage, 1985 (41), p. 6.

OU3. "Week of Action against the Poultry Industry", Outrage, 1986 (42), p. 5.

OU4. "No Action on Mass Poultry Deaths", Outrage, 1988 (53), p. 7.

OU5. "Cooking without eggs", Outrage, 1989 (60), p. 10.

OU6. "Case in point. The battery hen", Outrage, 1989 (60), p. 11.

OU7. "Lobby for battery hens", Outrage, 1992 (80), p. 5

OU8. "Battery is best", Outrage, 1992 (81), p. 7.

OU9. "Market Misery at Henley", Outrage, 1994 (91), p. 11.

OU10. "Breeding Hell", Outrage, 1996 (102), p. 13.

OU11. "Beginning of the End for Battery Cages", Outrage, 1999 (115), p. 17.

OU12. "Hen Heaven", Outrage, 2000 (119), p. 11.

OU13. "Death Valley Eggs", Outrage, 2004 (136), p. 7.

OU14. "Close-upon bird flu", Outrage, 2007 (147), p. 16

OU15. "Down on the factory farm", Outrage, 2008 (151), p. 5–6.

OU16. "'Humane' farm scheme under scrutiny", Outrage, 2008 (152), p. 12.

OU17. "From Bad to Worse", Outrage, 2008 (153), p. 11.

OU18. "Animal Aid is different", Outrage, 2011 (165), p. 23.

OU19. "The great vegan challenge 2014", Outrage, 2014 (176), p. 18.

OU20. "The truth about "enriched" hen cages", Outrage, 2015 (180), p. 16.

The Uncounted Dead: Farming's Unofficial Victims

UD1. "Farming's unofficial victims", The Uncounted Dead: Farming's Unofficial Victims, 2014, p. 3.

UD2. "Case study: The M62 crash", The Uncounted Dead: Farming's Unofficial Victims 2014, p. 9–11.

UD3. "The 2013 Lincolnshire Floods", The Uncounted Dead: Farming's Unofficial Victims, 2014, p. 19.

UD4. "Deaths through disease and neglect", The Uncounted Dead: Farming's Unofficial Victims, 2014, p. 34.

Index

A

B

C

J

K

L

M

N

O

P

R

S

T

V

www.ingramcontent.com/pod-product-compliance
Lightning Source LLC
LaVergne TN
LVHW010721210926
848485LV00007B/1412/J
* 9 7 8 1 6 4 8 8 9 0 1 2 3 *